Thomas Jefferson

Thomas Jefferson

A Biography of Spirit and Flesh

Thomas S. Kidd

Yale

UNIVERSITY PRESS

NEW HAVEN AND LONDON

Published with assistance from the Annie Burr Lewis Fund.

Yale University Press books may be purchased in quantity for educational, business, or promotional use. For
information, please e-mail sales.press@yale.edu (U.S. office) or sales@yaleup.co.uk (U.K. office).

Set in Fournier MT type by IDS Infotech Ltd., Chandigarh, India.
Printed in the United States of America.

Library of Congress Control Number: 2021948853
ISBN 978-0-300-25006-0 (hardcover : alk. paper)

A catalogue record for this book is available from the British Library.

This paper meets the requirements of ANSI/NISO Z39.48-992 (Permanence of Paper).

10 9 8 7 6 5 4 3 2 1

I have thought them . . . aristocratical, pompous, clannish, indolent, hospitable, and . . . thoughtless in their expenses.

Thomas Jefferson on elite Virginians, 1785

He does not possess strong nerves: "The spirit is willing, but the flesh is weak."

Maryland senator John Howard on Jefferson, 1798

Contents

Thomas Jefferson

Introduction

This is a biography of a brilliant but troubled person. Thomas Jefferson would seem to need no introduction, yet among the Founding Fathers he is the greatest enigma—and the greatest source of controversy. Jefferson left a massive collection of carefully curated papers, but he seems virtually unknowable as a man. Most of the controversy about him comes back to questions of *character*. How could the author of the Declaration of Independence keep hundreds of human beings in bondage? How could he carry on a long-standing sexual relationship with one of his bondspeople, who was also his dead wife's half sister? His relationship with Sally Hemings produced at least one and perhaps as many as six children. The children who survived to adulthood he acknowledged only by letting them go free, unlike most of the other people he owned.

"Hypocrisy!" Jefferson's critics cry. When you look closer at Jefferson, however, *hypocrisy* doesn't quite penetrate the mystery, doesn't explain Jefferson's troubled genius and vacillating life. For all his blazing intellect and inspired rhetoric, Jefferson held a host of beliefs and inclinations that were unreconciled, and maybe irreconcilable. To be fair, most of us struggle with forms of incoherence and hypocrisy. And it is undoubtedly easier to see these problems with the benefit of historical hindsight. We never know if we would have done better if we had lived the same life as a person in the past. We will never know if we would have outdone Jefferson if placed in his situation.

But Jefferson's inconsistencies often transcended the failure to live up to his stated beliefs, which is the definition of hypocrisy. On issues such as slavery, he held ideas that were difficult to reconcile, even in the context of his time. (A more charitable reading might describe his philosophy as "eclectic.") Many people pointed out the incoherence to him, to little effect. He often failed to connect his theoretical musings to lived reality. We're so used to treating Jefferson as a great thinker—along with Madison, our *founding* thinker—that his unreconciled beliefs can be difficult to discern. Even Joseph J. Ellis, a relatively critical biographer, insisted that Jefferson "knew what he meant and meant what he believed." I am not so sure.[1]

The dissonance between stated belief and practiced reality is perhaps more acute for Jefferson than any other American, ever. That's quite a burden to bear. Yet Jefferson carries it, because of the Declaration of Independence. Jefferson did a great deal to promote the Declaration, listing it first on his epitaph, followed by the Virginia Statute for Establishing Religious Freedom (1786) and the founding of the University of Virginia. By the end of his life Jefferson cultivated his image primarily as the author of the Declaration, and indeed we have come to remember him as the writer of that "American Scripture," in historian Pauline Maier's phrase. But "all men are created equal" is not the definitive word on Jefferson's philosophy, or on his life. That phrase is better understood as a national self-image and lodestar than a code by which Jefferson lived.[2]

His sheer brilliance, political doggedness, inherited resources, and occasional good luck led to history-changing accomplishments, not only the Declaration and the other items listed on his epitaph, but other achievements not included there, such as the Louisiana Purchase. Jefferson could also be mystifyingly impractical, however. By "impractical" I mean that his ideas sometimes failed to manifest themselves in reality, especially on a personal level. Or he stated positions that he did not act upon, at least not in a sustained way. Again, tendencies toward impracticality are common among politicians, perhaps increasingly so in recent decades. America has had innumerable government leaders who have held incoherent positions, though few of them have also been as imaginative as Jefferson. When someone as brilliant and powerful as Jefferson also struggles with incoherence, it can have disastrous consequences. Those consequences meant trouble for many people with less power (meaning virtually everyone around him) around the nation and within his household.

Thomas Jefferson: A Biography of Spirit and Flesh tells Jefferson's story with special attention to the man's dissonant beliefs and actions. This book is a narrative of Jefferson's moral universe more than a traditional biography. It is not a step-by-step account of his political or diplomatic career, although these aspects play a significant role in my account. Readers wanting to know more about politics and diplomacy should consult comprehensive Jefferson biographies by Merrill Peterson, John Boles, and others, or the many excellent books (which I hope are adequately cited in the notes) on Jefferson's presidency, foreign policy, economic views, and other topics.

The vast literature on Jefferson has gone through many stages, some of which started even before Jefferson's death. Great resources for understanding the changing reception of Jefferson are Francis Cogliano's fascinating *Thomas Jefferson: Reputation and Legacy* (2006) and Robert M. S. McDonald's excellent volume *Thomas Jefferson's Lives: Biographers and the Battle for History* (2019). Yet the continental divide in Jefferson studies is still what we might call pre- and post-DNA. Before 1998, Jefferson scholars often treated the allegations about Jefferson's relationship with Sally Hemings as unseemly rumors. Historian Annette Gordon-Reed powerfully analyzed the evidence for that relationship in *Thomas Jefferson and Sally Hemings: An American Controversy* (1997). A year later, the journal *Nature* revealed that a Jefferson male had fathered at least one of Sally Hemings's children. Once the Thomas Jefferson Foundation concluded in 2000 that the evidence for the Hemings-Jefferson relationship was compelling, expert opinion overwhelmingly—though not unanimously— affirmed the relationship, and Jefferson's paternity of her children.[3]

As Cogliano explains, there have been a number of phases in the longer story of scholarship and popular writing about Jefferson. Some phases have been critical of the third president, some not. Following an era of uncritical celebration of Jefferson in the mid-twentieth century, the 1960s saw frequent criticisms of him in the context of broader cultural upheavals and the civil rights movement. Even after the DNA results, some scholars lamented this negative turn as "Jefferson bashing." Many recent scholars, led especially by historian Peter Onuf of the University of Virginia, have moved beyond the celebration/denunciation dichotomy to assess Jefferson as an intellectual, politician, and plantation owner formed by the elite culture of Revolutionary-era Virginia and the transatlantic Enlightenment community. This historicized balance animated Onuf and Gordon-Reed's outstanding *"Most Blessed of the Patriarchs": Thomas Jefferson and the Empire of the Imagination* (2016), a cultural biography of Jefferson's fraught commitments to patriarchy and democracy.

Popular Jefferson biographies since 1998, including Jon Meacham's *Thomas Jefferson: The Art of Power* (2012) and John Boles's *Jefferson: Architect of American Liberty* (2017), have acknowledged the Hemings relationship but have still approached Jefferson in a muted celebratory mode. Boles, a distinguished historian of the American South, sought to reestablish appreciation for Jefferson based on his historic context, not ours. Boles's Jefferson was "the architect of American liberty almost despite himself." He finds Jefferson "the most attractive, most elusive, most complicated, most intellectual, most practical, most idealistic, most flexible, and most quintessentially American Founder of them all."[4]

Jefferson was undoubtedly one of the most intellectual and idealistic of the Founders, a genius of rhetoric and one of the greatest writers in world political history. How attractive or successful he was is debatable. I am deeply appreciative of the abundant fruits of the "historicized" approaches to Jefferson, but this book may still strike a minor chord compared to other scholarly treatments with regard to the third president's character. It is certainly more ambivalent than are the biographies by Meacham or Boles. Yet I too am trying to untangle the thicket of Jefferson's moral, philosophical, and theological commitments in the context of his time, not ours. The resulting picture is hardly one of a secularist hero, or (even less so) of a predecessor of the Christian Right. Instead, as Jefferson put it, he was a sect unto himself. Enigmas abound: Jefferson was a skeptical providentialist, a higher critic of Scripture yet a lifelong reader of biblical texts, and a pioneer of church-state separation who could not have imagined a public sphere stripped of religious symbols and rhetoric.

Deciding what we think about Jefferson has higher political stakes than ever. In the wake of the racial turmoil and violence that rocked American cities in 2020, Jefferson was one of a number of American figures in statue who came under new scrutiny and sometimes literal attacks. But as Boles suggests, if we are to judge historical figures, we should judge them by the standards of their time. I would argue that Jefferson and the major Founders remain valuable and even essential subjects of study, in spite of their manifest flaws. Instead of renaming schools and toppling statues, I propose that we instead ponder perplexing, hard truths about the American founding. Time-bound, self-interested men framed the world's most enduring republic on the bedrock of the slave owner Jefferson's glorious principle that "all men are created equal." These paradoxes warrant sober reflection and further study. We should steer clear of the excesses of either patriotic apologetics or iconoclastic destruction. The Founders, including Jefferson, were hardly pristine saints. But maybe we're not either.

How well does Jefferson stand up according to his own standards? Or those of Revolutionary America? The foremost quandary he faced was slavery. Jefferson regarded slavery as damaging to white southerners, and he knew that holding human beings in bondage (even ones of a race he regarded as inferior) was wrong. Slavery was regressive and immoral in categories derived from the Enlightenment and from Christianity, traditions that he professed to affirm, if after his own fashion. Aside from the fact that he was abjectly dependent upon enslaved people, however, he could never quite reconcile his theoretical antislavery views with his commitment to white male democracy in the fragile southern agricultural empire. Jefferson had count-less opportunities to aid emancipation efforts during his career, but he acted on few of them, often giving little more than a kind word to emancipationists, or a promise to pray for them.[5]

That he repeatedly offered to pray for emancipationists suggests a second source of Jeffersonian dissonance: his religious and ethical beliefs. Portrayals of Jefferson's religious views have ranged from Jefferson as atheist to Jefferson as devout Christian believer. Uncertainties in his thought have facilitated this wide spectrum of religious Jeffersons. Jefferson's beliefs vacillated, especially until his first term as president, when he turned sixty. Then, through the influence of advisors such as the scientist-minister Joseph Priestley, Jefferson resolved his religious doubts by becoming a Unitarian. Unitarians hailed Jesus's moral teachings as the finest ever, but they denied that Jesus was God. Despite his Unitarian settlement, Jefferson never fully worked out the contradictions between his major sources for religious and ethical thought. These sources included Christianity, Epicureanism (the pursuit of tranquility above all), the Enlightenment emphasis on rationalism and universal rights, and the republican values of virtue, limited govern-ment, and political liberty for (white) men. Perhaps the most deeply ingrained of Jefferson's values was the code of gentility and honor he inherited as a Virginia patrician and slave owner. Gentility was more caught than directly taught. From their youth, southern gentlemen like Jefferson imbibed the values of sociability, learning, respect, and personal independence. None of his competing ethical philosophies won out in Jefferson's life, but gentility was arguably the priority to which he most often defaulted.[6]

A third source of dissonance was Jefferson's spending and indebtedness. Much of that spending was in the interest of diplomacy and statecraft; other expenditures adorned his private worlds at Monticello and elsewhere. Yet at the end of his life he staggered into the kind of genteel squalor that only an antebellum slave master could achieve. He failed to get a state lottery to pay off his debts, and his executor sold off hundreds of his bondspeople to pay down a fraction of Jefferson's sprawling obligations. Surely his own pursuit of happiness should have led to more tranquility. But as we shall see, his personal life never quite matched his concepts of republican or Christian virtue, or his early statements against slavery. As historian Edmund Morgan once observed, "If actions are any evidence, [Jefferson] placed a higher value on collecting books and drinking good wine than he did on freeing his slaves." To be sure, Jefferson did make regular donations to charity. Indeed, it is surprising how often he made such donations (often to churches), given his virtually incalculable debts.[7]

In the beginning, the debts came largely from his father-in-law, whose financial obligations he inherited along with lands and enslaved people. Jefferson always touted frugality, and as president he largely manifested it in the national budget, where his first inclination (except in the Louisiana Purchase) was to cut rather than spend. His personal life was different. Though he bemoaned his mounting debt, which by 1819 had become cataclysmic for his family (and at his death, for the people he enslaved), Jefferson could not balance the books. Public service took a major toll, he was never a good farmer, and side ventures like his slave-worked nailery did not generate consistent revenue. Driven by the ironclad expectations of politics and genteel hospitality in a plantation society, Jefferson spent relentlessly and fatefully. He tore down the first Monticello to build a larger, more lavish mansion on the mountaintop. When that house neared completion, he started another mansion on his distant property at Poplar Forest. His inherited obligations, his overspending, and bad harvests had already put his debts beyond his control before the "coup de grace," a big loan he co-signed for Virginia governor Wilson Cary Nicholas, who said he could pay the loan back. Then came the Panic of 1819 and Nicholas's death, upon which Jefferson's financial disaster was complete.

All that remained at the end was for his executors to dispose of Jefferson's bondspeople, far-flung properties, and two dilapidated mansions. The fall of the houses of Jefferson was spectacular, yet tragically predictable. As

Jefferson's hundreds of enslaved men and women waited for news of the master's death in the fiftieth anniversary year of the Declaration, they wondered where they might be sent when the auction began. The consequences of Jefferson's inconsistencies would endure after he passed from a national scene that he, as much as anyone else, had helped to create.

1. "If There Is Such a Thing as a Devil"

The devil was attacking Thomas Jefferson. How else could the lovestruck nineteen-year-old explain the calamities he was enduring? On Christmas Eve of 1762, he had stayed at his sister's house, which had a leaky roof and a rat infestation that ruined a silhouette picture he owned of Rebecca Burwell. Burwell was his first true love, but it was a love unrequited.

In one of his first extant letters, Jefferson shared his woe with a college friend, John Page. It was Christmas, yet the festive day saw him "overwhelmed with more and greater misfortunes than have befallen a descendant of Adam for these thousand years past I am sure; and perhaps, after excepting Job, since the creation of the world." (Jefferson was joking, but kind of not joking.) At least he had not endured the "bodily afflictions" of Job, he conceded. Still, he told Page, "I am now in a house surrounded with enemies, who take counsel together against my soul and when I lay me down to rest they say among themselves 'Come let us destroy him.' I am sure if there is such a thing as a devil in this world, he must have been here last night and have had some hand in contriving what happened to me." That was a telling "if." The urbane student, just finishing studies at the College of William and Mary, was hinting that maybe his misfortune had no malevolent cause. Perhaps the horrific event was just natural and unfortunate. How to account for his exquisitely bad luck, though? Not only did rats chew up his pocketbook, a leak sprung right above his pocket watch, where he kept his prized silhouette! "The Devil came and bored the hole over it on purpose," he insisted. The damp silhouette tore when he tried to pluck it out. It was "the last stroke Satan had in reserve for me," Jefferson wailed, for "he knew I cared not for anything else he could do to me, and was determined to try this last most fatal expedient." Anyway, although the picture of Rebecca was ruined, he had a vital image of her impressed on his consciousness. Jefferson suspected he would "think of her too often . . . for my peace of mind."[1]

At the threshold of adulthood, Thomas Jefferson's mind was brimming with thoughts of Bible characters, satanic torments, and a desirable young lady. Perhaps some of this heady brew was produced by the fluctuating hormones that affect many teenagers. Jefferson's mindset also reflected the milieu in which he came to adulthood. Jefferson is justifiably known for his skepticism about Christianity, but that skepticism emerged only *after* he inherited the pervasively Christian and genteel culture of late colonial Virginia.

Thomas's parents Peter and Jane (Randolph) Jefferson settled in the late 1730s in what became Albemarle County, in Virginia's Piedmont. The hilly Piedmont was at the outer limits of white settlement in Virginia. One evangelical preacher at the time called Albemarle "nearly a frontier country." The Jeffersons had enough resources—partly due to Jane's connection to the wealthy Randolph family—to establish a gentry-style home on this frontier. Albemarle County fueled Thomas's imagination for westward expansion, a dream he would realize most fully in the Louisiana Purchase. Piedmont Virginia did not immerse him in the classically democratic conditions that historians have often associated with the frontier, however. The Jeffersons' frontier was marked by tobacco, slavery, and the power of elite families.[2]

According to family lore, Jefferson's earliest memory was of taking a journey from the Shadwell plantation, where he was born, to Tuckahoe, a Randolph estate about fifty miles to the east. He recalled as a two-year-old being "handed up to a servant [slave] on horseback, by whom he was carried on a pillow for a long distance." A pillow is an apt metaphor for Jefferson's lifelong relationship to bondspeople, as his last request in life was addressed to his enslaved butler Burwell Colbert, asking to adjust him higher on the pillow of his deathbed. Enslaved women and men physically and financially buttressed Jefferson's existence, even as he criticized slavery as an institution.[3]

Thomas Jefferson, Peter and Jane Jefferson's first son, was born at Shadwell on April 13, 1743. Peter and Jane named Shadwell for the London parish where Jane was born and baptized. Thomas was presumably baptized into the Anglican Church, too, though no record of the rite exists. Although parish ministers were supposed to keep such records, it was not unusual for them to be lost, or never kept in the first place.[4]

Shadwell, completed in the 1750s, was a well-appointed but not enormous house by colonial Virginia standards. It stood one and a half stories tall, with four rooms on the ground floor, separated two on each side by a central hallway. The upstairs had two heated bedrooms. The Tuckahoe house, where the Jeffersons spent about six years during Thomas's early childhood, was larger. It was built "in the form of an H and has the appearance of two houses ... each wing has two stories, and four large rooms on a floor." A visitor noted that Tuckahoe was "furnished with four sophas, two on each side, besides chairs, and in the center there is generally a chandelier."[5]

Hospitality was expected of families with homes such as Tuckahoe and Shadwell. Endless dinner parties drained genteel Virginians' finances. Exhibiting generosity to neighbors, visitors, and kin was a reflex born out of social expectation. Peter and Jane equipped Shadwell for hosting, and for the display of consumer products marking their genteel status. Shadwell may have stood on the rural frontier, but inside was a small world of British sociability. The Jeffersons could host up to twenty people for a party. They had formal sets of silverware and plates, much of which was new on the colonial market in the 1740s. They also had pots and cups for serving coffee and tea, both of which surged in popularity among American colonists in the mid-1700s. At £17, a set of tea and coffee pots was the most expensive material item listed in an inventory of Peter Jefferson's estate. Tea was arguably the definitive product of the era. Tea drinking came with a number of associated goods, including sugar, porcelain cups, silver teaspoons, and the Jeffersons' type of "China teapot." (Notably, tea was also the product that would cause the most trouble between the colonists and British authorities in the 1770s.) Conspicuous consumption was woven into colonial Virginia culture. In time Jefferson would fall victim to both its pleasures and its expectations.[6]

Jefferson recalled in his autobiography that his "father's education had been quite neglected, but being of a strong mind, sound judgment and eager after information, he read much and improved himself." Peter was no intellectual, but a "neglected" education among men of means could still be quite impressive by today's standards. We know many of the books Peter owned, despite a fire that burned "almost every book" at Shadwell thirteen years after Peter's death. The mere existence of books in a library doesn't tell much, as books often go unread. A well-stocked library can create an impression as much as a silver tea set. Nevertheless, Peter's home office held typical volumes of biblical and English literature; they represented a kind of intellectual incubator for young Thomas. About half of the volumes Peter Jefferson owned were on history and literature. Some were law books related to Peter's work as a magistrate in Virginia.[7]

Peter owned a Bible with the Book of Common Prayer attached as well as a separate "large prayer book" that he gave to Thomas when he was ten years old. Aside from the King James Bible, the Book of Common Prayer was the most foundational religious text in the English-speaking world. Its resonant phrases shaped rituals of life and death for millions of people. "Dearly beloved, we are gathered . . ." and "Ashes to ashes, dust to dust," are two of the most famous sayings from the Anglican prayer book. Thomas recorded his marriage and the births and deaths of his children in this prayer book. He even noted the time of day—11:45 a.m.—that his wife Martha died in 1782. The rhythms and rhetoric of Anglican Christianity would remain a looming presence in Jefferson's life, even as he became skeptical about key tenets of that faith.

One of the most intriguing items in Peter Jefferson's library was the Anglican tract *The Knowledge and Practice of Christianity Made Easy,* which was framed as a discussion between a Native American and a Christian missionary. This tract, written by Bishop Thomas Wilson, was one of the most widely known publications intended for the conversion of "heathens," including both Native Americans and African Americans. People repeatedly recommended the tract, for example, to Olaudah Equiano, the former slave, Christian convert, and popular antislavery writer. The Anglican Society for the Propagation of the Gospel distributed thousands of copies of the publication in the 1740s, and one of those copies made it into the Jeffersons' library.[8]

If Thomas Jefferson read the tract (family tradition suggested that he had read all the books in Peter's library by the time he was five), it would have exposed him to a standard Anglican view of slavery. To Bishop Wilson, the enslavement of Africans in America was both biblically prophesied and morally tragic. "As to the Negroes," Wilson wrote, "the Descendants of Ham and Canaan, who, according to one of the most ancient prophecies, (Gen. 9:25) are become slaves to Christians." The common but contested theory of Genesis's "curse of Canaan" postulated that Africans were destined to be slaves. But just because slavery was their destiny did not make it morally right, according to Wilson. The only "righteous recompence" for tearing Africans away from their homes and sending them into slavery overseas was to introduce them to Jesus Christ. If white Christians did not make a sincere effort to evangelize bondspeople, Wilson asserted, it would be "difficult to justify the trade of buying, transporting, and selling them as beasts of burden."[9]

Thomas Jefferson had vastly less interest in evangelizing Africans than Wilson did. He did share Wilson's view, in theory, that Anglo-Americans should redeem slavery through gradual amelioration of its brutality and (eventually) emancipating enslaved people. He also held a long-term fascination with missionary work among Native Americans, seeing such efforts as bringing civilizing knowledge to Indians. This fascination helps explain a seemingly incongruous 1803 episode in which Jefferson's administration negotiated a treaty with the Kaskaskia Indians that included a yearly stipend for a Catholic missionary among them. Despite his famous 1802 statement about a "wall of separation between church and state," Jefferson was open to such church-state connections when they served a worthwhile purpose aside from religion, such as education. Jefferson also wanted whites to study and preserve Native Americans' vanishing dialects, and he knew that missionaries were often the greatest non-Indian experts in those languages.[10]

The Bible, Book of Common Prayer, and evangelistic tract in Peter Jefferson's library reflect the deeply Anglican world in which Thomas Jefferson grew up. Scholars have often portrayed Anglican Christianity in the colonial South as nominal. They have seen Anglican Virginians as easy pickings for evangelical insurgents (especially Baptists) who swarmed through the South prior to the American Revolution. Yet colonial Anglicanism could leave a deep imprint on the South's children, including on Thomas Jefferson. The structures of parish life penetrated deep into southern colonial society. Peter and Thomas Jefferson would both serve as vestrymen, the most important lay office in the church. Being on the vestry could reflect social standing as much as piety. Vestrymen were essential to the functioning of the church, however. Elite Virginia planters such as Jefferson, George Washington, and James Madison, Sr., all served as vestrymen.[11]

Vestries were made up of twelve gentlemen who partnered (and sometimes clashed) with the parish minister to do the church's business. Vestries oversaw the church budget and the parson's salary, maintained the church building, and ministered to the poor. George Washington served on the vestries of both Fairfax and Truro Parishes near his Mount Vernon home. He was also chosen as a churchwarden, one of the select vestrymen who did much of the actual work. Jefferson was involved in multiple disputes between vestries and their ministers. These included a 1767 controversy in which the Reverend John Ramsay of St. Anne's Parish, Albemarle County, was charged with getting "drunk with the sacrament wine," among other offenses. Jefferson was speaking from personal experience when he commented later that "an association of men who will not quarrel with one another is a thing which never yet existed, from the greatest confederacy of nations down to a town meeting or a vestry."[12]

Peter Jefferson died at forty-nine in 1757 when Thomas was fourteen. The Anglican parson James Maury, who would soon become Thomas's teacher, received £2 for conducting the funeral at Shadwell. ("Ashes to ashes, dust to dust.") The premature deaths of loved ones buffeted Thomas's life. It was hardly a given, even for members of elite families such as the Jeffersons, to live into old age. Peter left his family a considerable amount of property, including sixty bondspeople. Now Jane would have to manage the properties, the slaves, and her eight living children. The historical record is quiet about the relationship between Thomas and his mother. When he recalled his father's death, Jefferson almost made it sound as if he had been orphaned. "The whole care and direction of myself was thrown on myself entirely, without a relative or friend qualified to advise or guide me," he wrote. Some have suggested that Jefferson and his mother were estranged, or that Jane's control of the family's property generated a "patriarchal rage" revealed in misogynistic entries in Jefferson's commonplace book after his father's death. In any case, Jefferson's relationship with his mother may have been frosty or contentious; it was unlikely to have been mutually supportive.[13]

In 1770, fire destroyed the home at Shadwell, along with many of the family's books and papers. This accounts for a dearth of information about Jefferson's early life, a lacuna that has bedeviled Jefferson biographers. Two years later, Jane inscribed a family Bible with "Jane Jefferson Her Booke— Sept. 6th 1772." Perhaps wanting to replace records lost in the fire, she listed the names, birthdays, and places of birth for all her children on the Bible's blank pages. This was a conventional method of record keeping, and it transformed her Bible into a family heirloom.

As he had Peter's Book of Common Prayer, Thomas inherited his mother's Bible when she died in 1776. He made his own marks in this Bible, such as noting Jane's date of death underneath the line where she had noted her birth date. He also wrote the date that his oldest sister, also called Jane, had died in 1765. Jane was three years older than Thomas, and they seem to have been close. Her death when he was twenty-two was another sorrowful blow. She was apparently pious and a talented singer, and both were reportedly "fond of the solemn music used by the Church of England in the Psalms." The Jefferson family recalled that Thomas himself was partial to psalm singing over nonbiblical hymns, which he regarded as "less suited to the dignity of religious worship." In 1813 Jefferson told John Adams that "the hyperbolic flights of the Psalmist may often be followed with approbation even with rapture; and I have no hesitation in giving him the palm over all the Hymnists of every language." He went on to compare the relative merits of English, Greek, and Latin editions of the Psalter. Whether or not such sentiments suggested a quiet form of biblical piety in Jefferson, they were high praise for the Psalms themselves.[14]

Jefferson's early biographer Henry Stephens Randall, who interviewed members of Jefferson's family, wrote nostalgically about Jane and Thomas's rhapsodies. Jane sang with "the fervor of a deep religious devotion; and many a winter evening, round the family fireside, and many a soft summer twilight, on the wooded banks of the Rivanna [in Albemarle County], heard their voices, accompanied by the notes of his violin, thus ascending together." If anything like these family concerts happened, it paints a different picture of Jefferson than the common one of a hardened rationalist. When Jefferson penned a proposed epitaph for Jane in December 1771, however, there was no hint of their shared Christian connection. Translated from Latin, the epitaph read, "Ah, Joanna, best of girls. Ah, torn away from the bloom of vigorous age. May the earth be light upon you. Farewell, forever and ever." By this time, Thomas was six years past Jane's death, and the epitaph was part of his broader plans for a new gravesite and classical landscape at Monticello. Despite Jefferson's fascination with (pre-Christian) Greek and Roman antiquity, his Latin epitaph for Jane was apparently his only attempt ever at writing classical-style poetry.[15]

Jefferson's childhood was characterized by elite education, genteel refinement, and the stark realities of slavery. As illustrated by his memory of the pillow, enslaved people catered to Jefferson from his earliest days. In the colonial period, Americans were less inclined to portray slavery with

Christian niceties than masters were after the Revolution. Slave masters routinely faced resistance from people in bondage, such as the 1739 Stono Rebellion in South Carolina, four years before Jefferson's birth. Lurid violence against recalcitrant bondspeople was not a matter of plantation secrecy or white vigilantism. Violence was enshrined in the law and in the very landscape of Virginia. In 1705, Virginia made it legal for masters to dismember unruly bondspeople, with escalating severity for each offense. One Virginia village was called Negro Foot, named for a 1733 episode in which a master cut a foot off a runaway slave and posted it on a pike. Another Virginia creek was named Negrohead Run, which gained its moniker under similarly grisly circumstances. When Jefferson was five years old, the sheriff of James Madison's home county (Orange) had an enslaved woman named Eve burned to death because she had allegedly poisoned her master.[16]

Everyday abuse and rigid expectations of deference formed the slave-owning mentality of a boy like Thomas. Jefferson reflected in 1784 on the psychological effects of slavery on everyone from bondspeople to owners, including the master's children. It drew out the tyrannical passions of whites and imposed constant humiliations on enslaved people. He wrote in *Notes on the State of Virginia:*

> The whole commerce between master and slave is a perpetual exer-
> cise of the most boisterous passions, the most unremitting despotism
> on the one part, and degrading submissions on the other. Our chil-
> dren see this, and learn to imitate it; for man is an imitative animal. . . .
> The parent storms, the child looks on, catches the lineaments of
> wrath, puts on the same airs in the circle of smaller slaves, gives a
> loose to his worst of passions, and thus nursed, educated, and daily
> exercised in tyranny, cannot but be stamped by it with odious peculi-
> arities. The man must be a prodigy who can retain his manners and
> morals undepraved by such circumstances.

Such reflections were born out of personal experience. They were also common sentiments in colonial Virginia. Jefferson's fellow Virginian George Mason deplored slavery's effects on American political culture, declaring that "every master of slaves is born a petty tyrant." As we shall see, after the rise of the Cotton Kingdom in the 1790s, some whites began defending slavery as a God-ordained good. The younger Jefferson was typical of many Enlightenment-influenced southerners who admitted that slavery was ethically corrosive. Few masters—and Jefferson was no exception—would pair that sentiment with action for emancipation, however.[17]

Slave owning and classical learning were hallmarks of elite Virginia families. Indeed, slavery was ubiquitous in the classical Greek and Roman worlds that elite Virginians studied. Thomas started his formal education at five years old when he, his siblings, and cousins studied at what he called "the English school," a one-room schoolhouse at Tuckahoe. Jefferson was not enamored with the school. He recalled once slipping out of the schoolhouse, kneeling on the grass, and repeating the Lord's Prayer, hoping to hasten the end of the school day. Maybe this story is true. But there's a suspiciously similar version of it, one in which his dinner was late and he recited the Lord's Prayer in hopes of hastening the meal. Maybe Jefferson was opportunistically prayerful, or maybe some biographers were eager to paint him as a pious youth.[18]

We don't know much about the English school, but it featured lessons in reading, writing, and math, with lots of memorization. After his family came back to Shadwell from Tuckahoe, Thomas went to a school run by the Reverend William Douglas in Goochland County, about forty miles southeast of Shadwell. Douglas deepened young Jefferson's immersion in Anglican learning. Douglas was born in Scotland and studied in Glasgow and Edinburgh. Scholars typically point to James Madison's mentor John Witherspoon, the Presbyterian pastor and Princeton president, when illustrating the Scottish theological influence on the American Founding. Douglas was reared in the same educational environment as Witherspoon, though he became an Anglican clergyman rather than a Presbyterian one. Nevertheless, both Madison and Jefferson had teachers who had studied ethics, church history, and biblical languages in Edinburgh.

Douglas started his career in Virginia as a tutor, but several years before young Jefferson came to study with him, Douglas journeyed to England to receive ordination as an Anglican minister. Since there were no resident bishops in the colonies, prospective clergy had to go to England to complete their ordination. In 1750, Douglas became the rector of St. James Northam Parish in Goochland, where Peter Jefferson served on the vestry.

In addition to teaching, Douglas toiled as a parish minister, keeping meticulous records of life, death, and faith among his parishioners. Over the course of nineteen years, until the outbreak of the American Revolution, Douglas recorded baptizing 2,820 infants. Over the same period, Douglas recorded 767 marriages. These statistics included the baptisms and marriages of African Americans. Ministers like Douglas sought to sanctify slavery by making church rituals available to the enslaved, but parsons did not usually question slavery itself. Douglas's funeral sermons reflected a broad familiarity with the Bible, as he preached from at least ninety-five different biblical texts in his funeral addresses. For a Virginian like Jefferson, ministers were there for virtually every landmark moment in life. The rhetoric of the Bible and the Book of Common Prayer framed those passages, and Jefferson internalized much of their language and meaning. He later used phrases from the Book of Common Prayer to share prayers with friends, such as when he wrote his French correspondent Madame de Staël Holstein after Napoleon's defeat at Waterloo in 1815. Jefferson told her that he prayed God "will be pleased to give [the French] patience under their sufferings, and a happy issue out of all their afflictions." Skeptic though he was, we should not underestimate the formative influence of Jefferson's Anglican upbringing.[19]

As for Rev. Douglas, he was a broad-minded Anglican evangelical, as he made favorable comments about George Whitefield, the greatest English evangelist of the era. But Douglas also admired the "latitudinarian" Archbishop John Tillotson, whom Whitefield had dismissed as knowing "no more about true Christianity than Mahomet." Douglas's broad-mindedness had its limits, though. In 1776, shortly after Jefferson wrote the Declaration of Independence, Douglas noted in his register of deaths that the notorious Scottish philosopher David Hume had "died a meer sceptist." "The Great Infidel" Hume had become internationally reviled for his philosophical arguments against miracles.[20]

Although Jefferson and Hume held similar views about the supernatural, Jefferson was hostile toward Hume, whom he called a "degenerate son of science" and "traitor to his fellow men." Jefferson had admired Hume's *History of England* when he was a law student, but he came to regard the famous work as intellectual "poison," primarily because of the Scot's monarchist sympathies. Despite these qualities, Hume's history became widely read in American editions starting in the 1790s. As was typical of Jefferson, he framed his grievance against Hume as a religious feud, blaming Hume for the "continued advocation of the heresy that, by the English constitution, the powers of the monarch were every thing, and the rights of the people nothing." This "heresy" had won far too many "voluntary converts" by the brilliant felicity of Hume's writing style, and Jefferson himself knew the

David Hume, lithograph by Antoine Maurin, Paris, 1820. (Courtesy New York Public Library)

intellectual "charms" of the Scot's defense of monarchy. Hume might have a proper Enlightenment view of religion, in Jefferson's opinion, but not of English history.[21]

Jefferson's Latin and Greek lessons began in earnest at Douglas's school. Later in life, Jefferson was dismissive about Douglas's teaching, perhaps because Jefferson wished to portray his journey out of a childish religious background to an adulthood informed by the Enlightenment. In his autobiography, Jefferson devoted only half a sentence to Douglas. Calling Douglas's school "the Latin" school, in contrast to his earlier "English" school, he described Douglas as "a clergyman from Scotland" who was "a superficial Latinist, less instructed in Greek, but with the rudiments of those languages he taught me French."[22]

Knowing Latin and Greek was essential for a refined gentleman in eighteenth-century Anglo-America. Thomas was grateful that his father made these languages a priority in his education. In unusually effusive language, Jefferson told his friend Joseph Priestley, the English theologian and scientist, that "to read the Latin & Greek authors in their original is a sublime luxury. . . . I thank on my knees him who directed my early education for having put into my possession this rich source of delight: I would not exchange it for any thing." An 1814 letter made clearer that the "him" due thanks was his father, who made it possible for him to attend Douglas's school. "Were we to consider Classical learning merely as a luxury in literature, I should feel myself more indebted to my father for having procured it to me, than for any other luxury I derive from his bounty," Jefferson wrote. Jefferson depended in more fundamental ways on his father's land and enslaved people than on the classical education Peter gave the boy. Yet Thomas placed enormous value on his early schooling, which began substantially with Rev. Douglas. He would be fascinated his whole adult life with philology (the study of languages), especially of Greek, Latin, and biblical texts.[23]

In an 1819 letter to the Greek scholar John Brazer (a Unitarian minister), Jefferson enthused that he relished Greek and Latin classics as "models of pure taste." Classical languages were essential for more than their literary treasures, however. For Jefferson, Greek in particular unlocked the "virgin purity" of early Christianity. Jefferson asserted that "the divine finds in the Greek language a translation of his primary code"—that is, the Septuagint, or the ancient Greek translation of the Hebrew Bible. Jefferson had an enduring appreciation for the Septuagint, acquiring editions of it including a ten-volume Oxford translation. Jefferson actually thought the Septuagint was of "more importance" to God than the Hebrew Bible, because the Septuagint's translators better understood the Old Testament's kernels of truth than did the Hebrew authors. (This sentiment was not unique to Jefferson. The Dutch Christian humanist Erasmus advanced a similar pro-Septuagint view, for example, because the Septuagint's translators had access to older versions of the Hebrew text. The Orthodox Church has historically regarded the Septuagint as divinely inspired, too.) Jefferson knew little Hebrew and got irritated with John Adams for suggesting it was also a valuable ancient language. Jefferson was even more emphatic with Brazer about the biblical value of Greek for understanding the New Testament and the earliest church fathers, "who lived and wrote before the simple precepts of the founder [Jesus] of this most benign and pure of all systems of morality became frittered into subtleties and mysteries, and hidden under jargons incomprehensible to the human mind." You had to know Greek to purge the impurities of priestly Christianity.[24]

Jefferson also eagerly acquired new English editions of the Bible, an interest that persevered through the storms of his political life. As he waited in December 1800 for the convening of the Electoral College (the indecisive results of which would throw the presidential election into the House of Representatives), Jefferson wrote from Washington to an associate in New York, asking him to buy a newly advertised pocket-sized Bible. "Scatcherd's pocket bible" was bound in Morocco leather and, according to the seller, was four and a half inches long and two and a half inches wide. Jefferson explained that "it is an edition which I have long been wishing to get, to make part of a portable library which the course of my life has rendered convenient." Jefferson traveled so much that it would be handy to have a miniature Bible. This Bible-buying episode fit within his broader patterns of bibliophilia and spending. As we shall see, his expenses on books paled in comparison to his spending on wine and housing materials. Yet it is still striking to see Jefferson making a pocket Bible part of his traveling library, a collection that presumably was not just for show.[25]

Peter Jefferson had launched Thomas into a world of classical and biblical learning. It was likely at Peter's death that Thomas received a copy of Charles Drelincourt's *The Christian's Defense against the Fears of Death*. The book was a gift from Rachael Gavin, the widow of the Reverend Anthony Gavin, Douglas's predecessor in the parish of St. James Northam in Goochland. Thomas's connection with the Gavin family, and with Drelincourt's book, gives deeper insight into Jefferson's religious influences as he adjusted to the loss of his father.[26]

The link to the enigmatic Anthony Gavin put Jefferson in contact with a Protestant hero and anti-Catholic polemicist of international renown. As Jefferson's inscription in the Drelincourt gift book noted, Rev. Gavin was "a Spaniard [and] author of the Master key to Popery." He may have been born in Spain, though Gavin was probably not an ethnic Spaniard. He was reportedly a former Catholic priest who converted to Anglicanism, and who scored a best seller in his sensational anti-Catholic book *A Master-Key to Popery*, first published in Dublin in 1724. The book stayed in print in American and English editions that appeared as late as 1852. The rambling Gavin had arrived in Virginia in 1735, where he pastored until his death in 1750.[27]

It seems that Gavin's wife Rachael remained in the area in 1757; perhaps she attended Peter Jefferson's funeral and gave Thomas the Drelincourt book on death to aid him in his grief. *The Christian's Defense,* a French Reformed classic, had begun appearing in English translations by the 1670s. It was not an entirely comforting book, as it delivered a hair-raising description of the damned in hell to supplement the glories of heaven. *The Christian's Defense* was a standard of eighteenth-century Anglo-American literary culture: Ben Franklin sold copies of the book when he was in the print business. The prolific Rhode Island evangelical writer Sarah Osborn turned to Drelincourt in the midst of grief over her husband's death, taking to heart the French pastor's admonition to imitate Job's submissiveness. "With Job I could say," she wrote, "the Lord gave and the Lord has taken and blessed be the name of the Lord."[28]

Jefferson was likewise drawn to resignation in the face of death. Even in his letter to John Page about the devil's torments, he recalled that "as brother Job says . . . 'Are not my days few? Cease then that I may take comfort a little before I go whence I shall not return, even to the land of darkness and the shadow of death' " (Job 10:20–21). At Peter's funeral, the Reverend James Maury would have used the Book of Common Prayer's liturgy, reminding the family that though they committed Peter's body to the ground, they should hold fast to the "certain hope of the resurrection to eternal life, through our Lord Jesus Christ." Jefferson later recalled to his grandson how he felt adrift after his father's passing. He saw it as a time of moral vulnerability, fearing that he might become just like the "bad company" to which he was regularly exposed in his teen years. His comments about his exclusive dependence on his fourteen-year-old self made it sound, again, as if his mother was absent.[29]

He was not left without male mentors, however. As Jefferson wrote in his autobiography, upon his father's death he "went to the Revd. Mr. Maury, a correct classical scholar, with whom I continued 2 years." Maury had known Peter Jefferson since at least 1748, and Thomas once stood as a baptismal sponsor for Abraham, one of James Maury's sons. Thomas called another of Maury's sons, James, Jr., a "particular friend," and they attended Rev. Maury's school together. In sum, the Jeffersons had a deep, multifaceted friendship with the Maury family, one of a number of significant relationships Thomas had with pastors during his lifetime. These deepened his roots in Virginia Anglicanism.[30]

Like William Douglas, James Maury had to travel to England in order
to receive Anglican ordination. Although James Blair, Virginia's elderly
Anglican commissary (the church's colonial superintendent), had given
Maury a position at the College of William and Mary, his letter of recom-
mendation for Maury's ordination was equivocal. Maury was "ingenious,"
or bright, and had good knowledge of Latin and Greek. But Blair wished that
"his judgment might be better settled in the serious study of the Holy Scriptures" and theology. "His friends have pushed him on too fast," Blair
concluded. Nevertheless, Virginia had open pastorates to fill, so Maury got
ordained and eventually became rector of Fredericksville Parish. There he
also operated his log house school, which was about twelve miles from Shadwell. Jefferson boarded there with the Maurys during the academic year.[31]

In addition to family connections, Maury and Jefferson would come to
share a loathing for the firebrand lawyer and politician Patrick Henry. Maury's
distaste for Henry would develop earlier than Jefferson's did, as a result of the
"Parsons' Cause" of 1763. Maury and other Virginia clergymen were outraged
by the colony's 1758 Two Penny Act, which changed payment to its established ministers from tobacco to cash. (Nothing illustrated the centrality of
tobacco to colonial Virginia more than the fact that it paid its pastors in tobacco
leaf.) The pastors saw the Two Penny Act as a pay cut. Maury led legal protests
against the act, and London's Privy Council took the side of the pastors.
Maury and other parsons sued to recoup their lost pay, and Patrick Henry
represented the vestrymen of Hanover County against the parsons. The irritated Maury called Henry a "little pettyfogging attorney." As was Henry's
wont, he turned the case into a test of royal power. Henry proclaimed that "a
King, by annulling or disallowing laws of this salutary nature [the Two Penny
Act], from being the father of his people, degenerates into a tyrant, and forfeits
all right to his subjects' obedience." Maury thought this claim was ridiculous,
but the pyrotechnics resonated with the jury (a "vulgar herd," Maury reckoned). The jury insulted Maury by awarding him 1 penny in damages. This
triumph set the stage for Henry's 1765 election to the Virginia legislature, the
House of Burgesses. Soon Henry became Virginia's most popular politician.
Jefferson actually met Henry several years before the Parsons' Cause trial, at
Christmas in 1759, when Jefferson was sixteen. (Henry was seven years older
than Jefferson.) Their relationship would survive the early years of the Revolution, but as we shall see, at the end of the war it suffered permanent
estrangement.[32]

As a "correct, classical scholar," Maury reinforced Jefferson's budding love for Greek and Latin and the great texts of English literature. He exposed Jefferson to works including John Milton's epic poem *Paradise Lost*. In Jefferson's commonplace book, in which he periodically recorded literary passages, he copied excerpts from Milton at around the time he was in Maury's school. These included memorable lines from the rebel Satan, who had been kicked out of heaven. One quote was Satan's judgment that it was "better to reign in Hell, than serve in Heaven."[33]

Jefferson was receiving a rich classical education, but he still lived in provincial backcountry Virginia. Around the time he met Patrick Henry, Jefferson began to consider a move at the behest of one of his executors, Peter Randolph. (The executors helped to manage Jefferson's affairs upon his father's death.) Colonel Randolph, a cousin of Jefferson's mother, was part of the extended Randolph clan of colonial Virginia. Randolph and Jefferson's conversation generated the first recorded letter in the Jefferson corpus, the only letter older than the devil's-torments missive two years later. "My schooling falling into discourse," Jefferson wrote, Randolph told him that it would be "to my advantage to go" to the College of William and Mary (established 1693) in Williamsburg, over one hundred miles away, on the other side of Richmond.[34]

The College of William and Mary was founded six years before Williamsburg became Virginia's capital. In the overwhelmingly rural South, Williamsburg was an impressive town, with about a thousand permanent white and black residents. The town ran along Duke of Gloucester Street, anchored by William and Mary at one end, the Capitol Building at the other, and Bruton Parish Church in between. After Harvard, William and Mary was the second-oldest college in Britain's American colonies. Like most colonial colleges, William and Mary was founded partly for training ministers. Its charter explained that the college was opened "to the end that the Church of Virginia may be furnish'd with a Seminary of Ministers of the Gospel." It was never as focused on producing clergy as early Harvard was, but the "orthodox Christian Faith" remained central to the curriculum, which was generally taught by Anglican ministers.[35]

Thomas, on the edge of seventeen, agreed with Peter Randolph that it was "desirous" that he should go to William and Mary. He alluded to the need for a break from constantly hosting people at Shadwell, which distracted him from his studies. Although it seems like a tangential point, escaping the burden of hosting was half of Jefferson's stated justification for going to college. Entertaining guests was an obligation every southern gentleman shared, but even as a sixteen-year-old it greatly added to Jefferson's "expenses in housekeeping." He also saw an educational aim to matriculating at William and Mary, as he could pursue his "studies in the Greek and Latin as well there as here, and likewise learn something of the Mathematics." Williamsburg would also provide political and educational connections that would serve his future ambitions. Jefferson would not be alone there, either. His enslaved valet Jupiter, almost exactly his age, would accompany his master, to dress and shave him and run whatever errands Jefferson required.[36]

Jefferson began at William and Mary in March 1760. He regarded it as providential that his two years at William and Mary overlapped with that of the Scotsman Dr. William Small. This "probably fixed the destinies of my life," Jefferson wrote. Jefferson spoke effusively about Small, who taught most of Jefferson's classes, even though Small was not a clergyman. Small had a "happy talent of communication, correct and gentlemanly manners, and an enlarged and liberal mind." They became personal friends outside the classroom. Small was Jefferson's chief conduit to the Scottish Enlightenment, from which Jefferson and other Americans would derive concepts such as "self-evident truths" rooted in human reason and common sense. Small brought a heavy emphasis on Newtonian science and the laws of motion to the little college. From Small, Jefferson gained his first understanding "of the expansion of science and of the system of things in which we are placed." Jefferson stayed in touch with Small after the science professor moved to England. In a characteristic spasm of generosity, Jefferson sent him three dozen bottles of Madeira wine in 1775. In the letter announcing the gift, Jefferson reported worriedly on "the unhappy news of an action of considerable magnitude between the king's troops and our brethren of Boston." These were the battles of Lexington and Concord, the opening clashes of the Revolution.[37]

Small broadened Jefferson's mind—and his professional network. Through Small, Jefferson met the legal scholar George Wythe, who mentored Jefferson through to his admission to the bar. Jefferson described Wythe decades later as "the best Latin and Greek scholar in the state." He wrote that Wythe's "virtue was of the purest tint; his integrity inflexible, and his justice exact; of warm patriotism, and, devoted as he was to liberty, and the natural and equal rights of men, he might truly be called the Cato of his country."

Wythe also modeled an understated religious devotion that, to Jefferson, represented authentic Christianity. "In his philosophy he was firm, and neither troubling, nor perhaps trusting any one with his religious creed, he left to the world the conclusion that that religion must be good which could produce a life of such exemplary virtue." Although Wythe was a slave owner, he showed more inclination toward curtailing slavery than Jefferson did. Jefferson attributed much of Virginia's antislavery sentiment to Wythe. Young men training to enter public life "sucked in the principles of liberty as it were with their mother's milk" while studying under Wythe, Jefferson wrote. Wythe even tried to overturn the legal basis for slavery in Virginia in an 1806 case in which an enslaved woman sued for her family's freedom. This was one of the last cases the great legal scholar ever heard. Tragically, Wythe was murdered the same year by a disgruntled grandnephew and heir, who slipped arsenic into Wythe's coffee.[38]

For his legal training, Wythe assigned Jefferson Sir Edward Coke's foundational, if laborious, *Institutes of the Laws of England*. Law students all read Coke. Jefferson included Coke among his maladies in the devil's-torments letter of 1762. "I do wish the Devil had old Coke, for I am sure I never was so tired of an old dull scoundrel in my life." He griped with all the gusto of a new law student. "What! are there so few inquietudes tacked to this momentary life of ours that we must need be loading ourselves with a thousand more? . . . But the old-fellows [including Wythe, seventeen years Jefferson's senior] say we must read to gain knowledge; and gain knowledge to make us happy and be admired." Jefferson did learn things from Coke, including the sources of English common law (or the law of precedents, as opposed to laws of legislatures), upon which the English tradition depended.[39]

Jefferson's investigations into the common law prompted one of his most extraordinary writings ever, but one that generates little notice today. This was his essay "Whether Christianity Is Part of the Common Law?" likely written in 1764. This composition was one of the first signs of Jefferson's unconventional religious beliefs, and of his desire to uncouple law from religion. Although the subject was technical, it was not difficult to understand Jefferson's basic argument, which was that "Christianity neither is, nor ever was, a part of the common law." This argument caused a sensation sixty years later, when Jefferson's opinion attracted the attention of traditionalist jurists, most notably Supreme Court justice Joseph Story. Jefferson's thesis was based on the notion that English common law originated with pagan Saxons, who set the law's foundations well before Christianity arrived in England. Jefferson hardly demonstrated that Christianity was not *part* of the common law tradition, given the centuries of precedents that accumulated after Christianity's arrival. Because of Jefferson's unparalleled stature by the 1820s, however, Story and other jurists marshaled evidence to show that English (and therefore American) law was deeply indebted to Christian thought. In today's parlance, this debate was about whether America (or England) was a Christian nation. Jefferson's answer in this case was no.[40]

Almost a year after the devil's-torments letter, the twenty-year-old Jefferson's mind must have been far from the common law as he danced at Williamsburg's Raleigh Tavern with his seventeen-year-old crush, Rebecca Burwell. Swept up in the moment, Thomas tried to talk to her about marriage. "Good God!" he later moaned to John Page. His swirling emotions generated a "strange confusion" of words. The evening ended awkwardly, and another conversation thereafter didn't go better. Jefferson marked his letters to Page as written from "Devilsburg," as some demonic force seemed to foil his romantic schemes. He proposed that he and Page start writing about Burwell in secret code. Burwell and the obsessive Jefferson grew distant, however, and it was not long before she got engaged to someone else. "Well the Lord bless her I say!" Jefferson exclaimed sarcastically.[41]

Jefferson's frustration over Burwell precipitated one of the most puzzling passages in his correspondence: a comment on a Pauline admonition regarding sex and marriage. "Many and great are the comforts of a single state," Jefferson wrote. "For St. Paul only says that it is better to be married than to burn [I Corinthians 7:9]. Now I presume that if that apostle had known that providence would at an after day be so kind to any particular set of people as to furnish them with other means of extinguishing their fire than those of matrimony, he would have earnestly recommended them to their practice." This passage offers many possible interpretations. What "means of extinguishing their fire" did Jefferson have in mind? Masturbation? Prostitutes? If Jefferson was alluding to sex with bondswomen, it would represent an unusual reference to a common practice, one that went largely undiscussed except in a few planters' private diaries. In any case, Jefferson and his friend William Fleming seem to have been engaging in juvenile joking about a man's sexual options in lieu of a wife.[42]

The disappointment with Burwell also coincided with Jefferson's first recorded "violent head ach[e]," a periodic malady that would afflict him his whole life. Jefferson partly coped with relational anger and stress by burying himself in books. His purchases in these years at the office of the *Virginia Gazette* were voluminous and varied. They included a sixteenth-century Greek and Latin dictionary, which Jefferson marked heavily; Hume's *History of England;* and an English translation of the Qur'an, first published in London in 1734, which reflected Jefferson's interest in comparative religion.[43]

He also purchased a copy of the first two volumes of Laurence Sterne's *The Sermons of Mr. Yorick*. Sterne, the Irish-born Anglican minister best known for his popular *Life and Opinions of Tristram Shandy* (1759–67), was one of Jefferson's two or three favorite clerical writers. (George Washington owned the sermons, too.) Perhaps because of Sterne's irreverent reputation, one reviewer denounced the *Sermons* as "the greatest outrage against sense and decency, that has been offered since the first establishment of Christianity." But the sermons mostly offered conventional precepts associated with Anglican Christianity. The most intriguing content in Sterne appeared on page 1 of sermon 1, entitled "Inquiry after Happiness." Sterne opened the sermon with the assertion "The great pursuit of man is after happiness: it is the first and strongest desire of his nature." How did Sterne define the pursuit of true happiness? Warning against the fleshly pleasures of the epicure, Sterne's Parson Yorick prayed, "O God! let us not wander for ever without a guide in this dark region in endless pursuit of our mistaken good, but enlighten our eyes that we sleep not in death—open to them the comforts of thy holy word and religion." We don't know what Jefferson made of Sterne's Christian formula for happiness, but he did include the *Sermons* in recommended library lists. Jefferson even purchased a replacement copy of the sermons in 1815. Sterne's brand of Anglicanism appealed to Jefferson, but he would struggle to make that faith cohere with his commitment to gentility and to Epicurean and Stoic philosophy.[44]

Beginning in 1765, imperial events would sweep Jefferson and his Virginia colleagues into a maelstrom. The Seven Years' War, which ended in 1763, had sent Britain into paralyzing national debt. British legislators and treasury officials concocted tax and tariff programs to recoup some losses. The passage of the Stamp Act in 1765, which placed a tax on most printed goods and legal documents, precipitated major unrest in America. The act's requirement that the colonists pay the tax in silver specie, which was difficult to obtain, was exasperating. By 1764, mutterings against the parliamentary schemes had begun, especially in Massachusetts and Virginia. Virginia leader Richard Henry Lee told a British correspondent in 1764 that he feared some powerful London politicians meant "to oppress North America with the iron hand of power." The same year, Virginia legislators conveyed their emerging anti-tax sentiment in a resolution asserting that the "people are not subject to any taxes but such as are laid on them by their own consent."[45]

Jefferson watched—literally—as Patrick Henry, a new member of the Virginia House of Burgesses, kicked off the imperial crisis by introducing resolutions against the Stamp Act. Henry and Jefferson shared a common devotion to backcountry Virginia, but other similarities were few. Henry was a brash, spellbinding public speaker with little formal education. Jefferson disliked speaking before large groups, tending toward bookishness. Henry wrote at least five resolutions against the Stamp Act, claiming that Parliament should not assert the power to tax the colonists. Doing so had a "manifest tendency to destroy British as well as American freedom." The sixth and seventh resolutions attributed to Henry were even more inflammatory. The twenty-nine-year-old Henry's speech on the Stamp Act was truly astounding, however. Our memory of the speech is shrouded in myth, but a visitor who was there recorded that Henry "said that he had read in former times Tarquin and Julius had their Brutus, Charles had his Cromwell, and he did not doubt but some good American would stand up, in favor of his country." Every classically educated Virginian knew such stories by heart. The suggestion of assassinating King George III was thrilling to some, chilling to others. The Speaker of the House rebuked Henry, saying that he had spoken treason. Henry wisely backed off, apologizing to members for his zeal in defense of his country's liberty.[46]

Jefferson stood at the doorway to the Burgesses' chamber while Henry gave the speech. He could recall it vividly in old age, as if it had just happened. Though Jefferson would come to loathe Patrick Henry, he would nevertheless credit Henry as being the greatest orator he ever heard. Jefferson's Henry was a largely untutored man who inspired awe and wonder by his speaking gifts. Those gifts "were great indeed," Jefferson wrote, "such as I have never heard from any other man. He appeared to me to speak as Homer wrote." Others would call Henry the American Demosthenes, referring to the great Greek orator and foe of tyrants. To founders like Henry and Jefferson, stories and patterns from ancient history and the Bible repeated themselves, revealing the same old threats to liberty. In their mental universe, the Founders followed in the tradition of classical and biblical characters (Cicero, Homer, Job), playing new acts on an American stage. The imperial crisis would form them, like men of old, into defenders of liberty.[47]

2. "I Speak the Sentiments of America"

The imperial crisis with Britain was entering its second, more acute phase. The first had lasted roughly from 1765 to 1770. After the Tea Act and the colonists' brazen dumping of tea into Boston Harbor in 1773, British authorities cracked down with the Coercive ("Intolerable") Acts of 1774. These had closed Boston's port and shut down the duly elected Massachusetts government. What would the other colonists do? Thomas Jefferson wanted Virginians to take an "unequivocal stand" for their Yankee colleagues, but the American colonies had a paltry record of cooperation. How could Virginia's Patriot leaders rouse the people from their "lethargy"? Jefferson thought a day of prayer and fasting might do the trick.[1]

Virginia had not employed such solemn rituals for years. So Jefferson, Patrick Henry, and others searched through English state papers for Puritan proclamations dating to the mid-1600s. "We cooked up a resolution," Jefferson recalled, "for a day of fasting, humiliation, and prayer, to implore heaven to avert from us the evils of civil war."[2]

Edmund Randolph and Jefferson recruited Robert Carter Nicholas, a prominent burgess known for his piety, to introduce the resolution. It passed without opposition. The Burgesses appointed June 1, 1774, for Virginians to pray that the Patriots would be unified, that God would grant the king and Parliament fresh wisdom and moderation, and that God would "remove from the loyal people of America all cause of danger." The Burgesses would visit Bruton Parish Church on that day for a prayer service and a sermon. The solemn occasion had Jefferson's desired effect. It was like a "shock of electricity," Jefferson said. Patriot resistance was rising, and Jefferson and others routinely framed that resistance in the language of faith.[3]

A decade earlier, as Jefferson read law and ruminated on Rebecca Burwell, he also reflected on matters of life and death. Skepticism about Christian views of body and soul had begun to emerge. In summer 1764, he asked a friend's opinion about a strange account that Jefferson had read in a magazine: a man had drowned and stayed underwater for twenty-four hours. When he was recovered from the water, the dead man reportedly resuscitated. The story may seem implausible, but Jefferson accepted it as "undoubted." The medical aspect of the story was not what intrigued him, however. "We are generally taught that the soul leaves the body at the instant of death," Jefferson observed. "But does not this story contradict this opinion? When then does the soul take its departure?" Jefferson believed that the episode undermined the traditional Christian understanding of death. Again, he suggested to the recipient that they take precautions to keep their letters confidential, lest they get circulated and offend "persons of narrow and confined views." In his commonplace book, Jefferson also copied lines from Herodotus on ancient Egyptian beliefs about souls.[4]

This discussion about souls is what Jefferson had in mind when he later told Rev. Isaac Story (the uncle of Supreme Court justice Joseph Story) of Marblehead, Massachusetts, that he had once been interested in speculation about souls. Story had sent Jefferson (then in his first term as president) an exotic theory about the "transmigration" of souls from one person to another. Jefferson told Story that he thought "the laws of nature have withheld from us the means of physical knowledge of the country of spirits and revelation has, for reasons unknown to us, chosen to leave us in the dark." Speculations about such issues were getting him nowhere, and he vowed to treat them as unsolvable puzzles. (He would continue to speculate on the soul-body connection into old age, however.) Jefferson said he had reposed his head "on that pillow of ignorance which a benevolent creator has made so soft for us, knowing how much we should be forced to use it." Echoing a common sentiment among deists, including Ben Franklin, Jefferson averred that all he knew to do was to nourish "the good passions [and control] the bad . . . and to trust for the future to him who has been so good for the past." God had not revealed what happened in the afterlife, Jefferson believed, so he would try to live well in this life and let God sort out his eternal destiny.[5]

Speculation about death was not merely theoretical. Jefferson's early years were punctuated by the untimely passing of family members and friends. His father had died in 1757. Then in October 1765, as the Stamp Act congress was preparing to convene in New York City, his beloved psalm-singing sister Jane passed away. Thomas did not go to the Stamp Act congress. Indeed, no Virginia delegates attended. The assembly represented an important first effort at united colonial strategy against British taxes. Jefferson did take his first trip out of Virginia in 1766, but it was a personal journey. Mortality was still on his mind, as he received inoculation against smallpox while visiting Philadelphia. Smallpox was a great scourge of the era. The inoculation procedure itself could be deadly: the great theologian Jonathan Edwards died from inoculation shortly after becoming president of the College of New Jersey at Princeton in 1758. Jefferson was a supporter of the procedure, however. He even legally represented victims of anti-inoculation riots in Norfolk, Virginia, in 1768 and 1769.[6]

Life was fragile, but Jefferson's ill-fated wooing of Rebecca Burwell had hardly cooled his interest in romantic love. Most of his friends were already married by 1768. With his flourishing law practice and his inherited estate, Jefferson was an appealing candidate for marriage. Instead of pursuing matrimony, however, he attempted to seduce Betsy Walker, the wife of longtime friend John Walker. Jefferson had been a groomsman in their wedding in 1764. In 1768, when John went on a diplomatic mission to Native Americans in New York, Jefferson began visiting the Walkers' home, a short trip from Shadwell. Betsy did not tell her husband about Jefferson's overtures until the 1780s. The accusations of Jefferson's attempted seduction (or attempted rape) of Walker did not become public knowledge until Jefferson became president. Those allegations accompanied those of Jefferson's relationship with Sally Hemings. Jefferson refused to comment directly upon Hemings, but he did concede in 1805 that when he was "young and single I offered love to a handsome lady." He acknowledged the "incorrectness" of doing so. John Walker insisted that Jefferson's sexual overtures toward his wife had continued long after John returned from New York. These included an incident in which Jefferson reportedly "renewed his caresses" and slipped Betsy a note assuring her of the "innocence of promiscuous love." In another episode, Jefferson entered Betsy's bedroom while John was visiting with guests, and found her "undressing or in bed." Jefferson allegedly pressed himself on her, but she repulsed him "with indignation and menaces of alarm" and Jefferson "ran off."[7]

We don't know exactly what transpired between Jefferson and Betsy Walker, beyond his admission of offering "love to a handsome lady." Illicit relationships among the Founders were hardly limited to Jefferson. Ben Franklin admitted visiting prostitutes in London, and trying to seduce a friend's girlfriend there. As a young man, Franklin also became a single father. We do not know the identity of his son William's mother. Franklin engaged in a series of relationships, such as with Paris's Madame Anne-Louise Brillon de Jouy, that were at least flirtatious, if not outright adulterous. George Washington had a much-debated relationship with Sally Fairfax, to whom he professed love after she got married and while Washington was engaged to Martha Dandridge Custis. Alexander Hamilton had an affair with Maria Reynolds, whose husband then blackmailed him to keep the matter private. Hamilton conceded his role in the affair in 1797, once word of the scandal broke.[8]

Jefferson did not face the kind of embarrassment over Walker that Hamilton did over Reynolds. The Walker episode was arguably the most scandalous behavior to which Jefferson ever admitted. John Walker was probably just repeating allegations made by Betsy, including the unwanted visit to her bedroom, when he reported the relationship. Betsy had been trying for years to persuade John Walker to remove Jefferson as an executor of his will, but he did not do so until a few years after she divulged Jefferson's overtures. If these incidents between Jefferson and Betsy Walker occurred, they justify historian Jon Kukla's assessment that the Walker affair "reflected a more predatory sexuality" than what the novice Jefferson demonstrated in his awkward courtship of Rebecca Burwell.[9]

In 1767, Jefferson began initial work at what became Monticello ("little mountain"). Monticello was the greatest creative project of his life, and the most persistent drain on his finances. Jefferson's homes and other building projects reflected his commitment to architecture as a shaper of American political culture. Monticello went through multiple stages over many years. It began with planting trees, cutting lumber, and most remarkably, leveling the top of the little mountain to make space for buildings. Slave workers flattened the crest of the nearly nine-hundred-foot-high hill, without bulldozers or backhoes. The shovel-wielding laborers included two sixteen-year-old girls.[10]

Jefferson's mountaintop home was demanding in myriad ways, such as establishing a reliable water source. Water would always be a problem at

Monticello. Bondspeople had to dig through sixty-five feet of rock before they struck water. But that well was not enough to supply Monticello, so Jefferson paid to install rain-catching cisterns. He often had to have water hauled in. Jefferson was convinced that he could build Monticello without going into debt. In a memorandum from 1769, Jefferson listed furnishings he was buying for the house: "Aeolian harp—refracting telescope 8 Venetian blinds . . . Back gammon tab—Chess board & men . . . Scotch carpet." And this was just the "first" Monticello—he would tear down the house and start over in the 1790s.[11]

What gave Jefferson the idea for such a project? Monticello encapsulated his views of nature and the "sublime." The sublime fascinated eighteenth-century writers, from the conservative British writer Edmund Burke to the German philosopher Immanuel Kant. Sublimity connoted a "scene or feeling of awe or terror, grandeur or elevation, and often of wildness." It's a feeling we might get standing at the edge of the Grand Canyon (though few of us would imagine building a house there). Jefferson's aspiration for Monticello was living in constant mindfulness of the sublime. In Paris in 1786 he wrote to his love interest Maria Cosway, asking her to envision how nature at Monticello had "spread so rich a mantle under the eye? Mountains, forests, rocks, rivers. With what majesty do we there ride above the storms! How sublime to look down into the workhouse of nature, to see her clouds, hail, snow, rain, thunder, all fabricated at our feet!" Jefferson's sublime stirred him to higher planes of moral understanding or feeling. Species of the sublime included Virginia's Natural Bridge ("the most sublime of Nature's works"), reading Greek and Latin authors in the original languages, and Jesus's moral teachings ("the most benevolent & sublime probably that has been ever taught"). Yet there were few precedents for building a home atop a small mountain to take in sublime vistas. Once he locked into the notion, however, expenses became secondary. Construction was barely underway in 1770 when he began living on the mountaintop.[12]

Monticello displayed Jefferson as a learned gentleman and politically connected planter. He was elected to the Virginia House of Burgesses in 1768, when he was twenty-five. Despite his dependence on slaves, Jefferson supported a bill in his first year in the legislature to permit white owners voluntarily to manumit their bondspeople. As he would make clear in *Notes on the State of Virginia* (1785), Jefferson had extremely negative views of blacks as a race, despite his opposition to slavery. He wrote about orangutans' preference for black women over females of their own species. (This alleged attraction was a regularly debated topic in the "scientific" literature on race at the time.) Jefferson also speculated that blacks had possibly been created as a "distinct race" from whites, a theory that undermined the biblical account of Adam and Eve. Jefferson's South Carolina friend David Ramsay commended him for his "indignation at slavery," but thought that the book had "depressed the negroes too low." Other Enlightenment luminaries shared Jefferson's harsh assessment of non-white races, however. David Hume, for example, asserted (in *Essays, Moral and Political,* which Jefferson recommended to correspondents) that all peoples of color were "naturally inferior" to the white race. Non-white peoples had "no ingenious manufac-tures among them, no arts, no sciences," Hume wrote. Jefferson's *Notes* recognized that slavery was bad for Virginia's whites and blacks, however. The manumission bill would pass, but not until 1782. During the Revolu-tionary era, Jefferson and other Virginia politicians were more open to domestic emancipation than they would be in the early 1800s. Still, white resistance to manumission of any sort could be fierce in the 1760s. The manumission bill's promoters were treated with "the grossest indecorum," Jefferson wrote years afterward.[13]

Even at this early age, Jefferson's enlightened ideals and daily practices of slavery clashed. In the same year that Jefferson was co-sponsoring the manumission bill, he placed a runaway slave ad in the *Virginia Gazette.* The ad reveals the gritty realities of life for Jefferson's bondspeople. It concerned an enslaved man named Sandy, who was about a decade older than Jefferson. He described Sandy as short, corpulent, and light-skinned ("a Mulatto"). Sandy was a shoemaker, had carpentry skills, and was "something of a horse jockey." This was not the first time Sandy had given his master trouble. The middle section of the ad deplored the man's character. "He is greatly addicted to drink, and when drunk is insolent and disorderly, in his conversation he swears much, and his behaviour is artful and knavish." Jefferson promised a cash reward for Sandy's return. Jefferson got Sandy back, and sold him less than four years later for £100.[14]

Despite such actions, the years prior to Jefferson's time in Paris saw him take promising steps against slavery. In 1770 he represented (pro bono) a mixed-race indentured servant named Samuel Howell, who had sued to gain his freedom. Howell's case was complex, but Jefferson's argument for Howell's freedom was not. "Under the law of nature," Jefferson insisted, "all men are born free, [and] everyone comes into the world with a right to his own person which includes the liberty of moving and using at his own will. This is what is called personal liberty, and is given him by the author of nature." This statement resonates with the Declaration of Independence, as Jefferson was capable of connecting the themes of equal rights and the plight of unfree people. The court did not agree with Jefferson's reasoning, however, and Howell remained a servant.[15]

It was a good thing that Jefferson had begun construction on Monticello, because Shadwell burned on February 1, 1770. The Shadwell fire erased much evidence of his early life, destroying most of his books and papers. "These are gone," Jefferson told his friend John Page. Paraphrasing Shakespeare's *The Tempest*, he wrote, "Like the baseless fabric of a vision, [they] leave not a trace behind." Jefferson wished that he could relocate closer to Page, but it was not to be. "The gods I fancy were apprehensive that if we were placed together we s[houl]d pull down the moon," he mused.[16]

Thoughts about the "gods" notwithstanding, Jefferson needed to put his life back in order after the fire. One of his first priorities was rebuilding his library. George Wythe sent him a couple of booksellers' catalogues. Jefferson wished to create a library not with his father's titles but with volumes of his own choice. This library would become a key element of the ambience at Monticello. He bought books rapidly. By 1773 he counted more than 1,250 volumes in his collection, or about four times what he had owned at Shadwell. Even the Shadwell library, comparatively modest as it was, probably would have cost a typical day laborer ten years' worth of wages. Now Jefferson was buying on average one new book per day. Mahogany and walnut bookcases added to his book-related expenses.[17]

We can map Jefferson's intellectual world from a list of 148 suggested titles he sent to his friend Robert Skipwith, who had expressed interest in assembling his own library. The titles Jefferson proposed did not exactly reflect the contents of his own library; he suggested some books he never actually acquired. The list does, however, give a taste of Jefferson's ideal literature for a Virginia gentleman.[18]

Books that inculcated virtue were a primary focus. Some have argued that the encouragement of virtue was the premier aim of Jefferson's writing, speaking, and reading. Unlike some Christian observers, however, Jefferson argued that fiction was as valuable for virtue as were sermons and theological treatises. For example, he recommended Shakespeare because "a lively and lasting sense of filial duty is more effectually impressed on the mind of a son or daughter by reading King Lear, than by all the dry volumes of ethics and divinity that ever were written." Moreover, he suggested Lawrence Sterne's popular novel *Tristram Shandy* as well as the Anglican minister's sermons, which Jefferson had purchased earlier. A short section on religion in the list included as much from pre-Christian antiquity, and from skeptical writers such as Lord Boling-broke and David Hume, as it did from Christian writers such as Sterne. Scholars regard Bolingbroke, whom Jefferson quoted at length in his commonplace book, as a key source for Jefferson's heterodox beliefs as a young man. Jefferson also recommended two books by the minister William Sherlock, whom Jefferson regarded as a reasonable Anglican. One of the titles by Sherlock was on God's future judgment of humankind. This might not seem like a topic toward which Jefferson would gravitate. He may have appreciated, however, that Sherlock based his rationale for the future judgment on *both* reason and revelation.[19]

Jefferson conspicuously categorized the Bible under the heading "Ancient History" rather than "Religion." (In a similar list composed a couple years later, however, he included the Bible and Sterne's sermons under "Religion, sectarian.") Under "Ancient History" he also listed Livy and Tacitus. This explains his exhortation to his nephew Peter Carr sixteen years later that he should read the Bible as one "would read Livy or Tacitus." A reader should use the Bible for moral wisdom, he believed, but should not uncritically receive its miraculous claims. This was similar to David Hume's view of miracles, and Jefferson included Hume's *Essays* in his "Religion" category. Despite his loathing for it later, Jefferson also listed Hume's *History of England* under "Modern History." Under "Natural Philosophy," Jefferson recommended titles such as "Franklin on Electricity." Several years later, Jefferson would meet Ben Franklin in the Continental Congress in Philadelphia, where they would collaborate on the Declaration of Independence.[20]

Not only did Jefferson recommend books by Anglican ministers, he remained intimately involved with controversies in the Anglican Church. In the 1771 case of *Godwin v. Lunan*, Jefferson represented the vestrymen of a Virginia parish who were trying to remove their minister, Patrick Lunan, for offenses including drunkenness, wearing "ridiculous apparel unbecoming a priest," and soliciting "negro and other women to fornication and adultery." (The outcome of the case is uncertain.) He could be anticlerical in sentiment, but Jefferson also maintained supportive friendships with Anglican ministers throughout his life. One of them was James Ogilvie, a Scottish immigrant who had traveled to London around the time that Shadwell burned. Ogilvie was a tutor seeking Anglican ordination. Jefferson wrote multiple letters to support Ogilvie's cause, over the opposition of Virginia's Anglican commissary James Horrocks. Horrocks seems to have regarded Ogilvie as insufficiently prepared in Greek. Jefferson thought Horrocks was pompous and incompetent, excoriating his personality as having "no other object in view but to hang out to the world its own importance." In any event, Ogilvie did receive ordination, but in 1778 he was banished from Virginia for loyalty to Britain.[21]

In his correspondence with Ogilvie, Jefferson apprised the minister of his new housing situation—and his romantic prospects. "Since you left us I was unlucky enough to lose the house in which we lived, and in which all its contents were consumed. A very few books, two or three beds &c. were with difficulty saved from the flames. I have lately removed to the mountain from whence this is dated." Although he was living in a one-room brick structure at Monticello, he told Ogilvie that he was hoping to get married soon. He fulfilled that wish on New Year's Day, 1772, when he wed the twenty-three-year-old widow Martha Wayles Skelton. Skelton's husband had died in 1768. Her estate, plus that of her father John Wayles (who would die in 1773), made Martha a financially attractive candidate for marriage.[22]

Martha and Thomas had a genuine fondness for one another, even though romantic connection was not a prerequisite for eighteenth-century marriages. In the Jeffersons' elite circles, marriage was commonly as much about maintaining one's status as it was about love. The Jeffersons' marriage offered both financial and companionate benefits. Jefferson began courting her by late 1770, when he plied her with gifts. He catered to their mutual delight in music, ordering her a German-made clavichord made with the "finest mahogany." (This note appeared in his account books next to the description of the enslaved laborers, including the two sixteen-year-old girls, digging the cellar at Monticello.) Soon after he'd ordered the clavichord, however, he was "charmed" by a pianoforte he had seen, so he canceled the clavichord and asked for the pianoforte instead, with a case of "fine mahogany, solid, not veneered." Jefferson loved mahogany furniture and acquired many such pieces over the decades to come. As historian Jennifer Anderson explains, "Mahogany's smooth, polished surfaces seemed to epitomize the ideal of refinement, then considered an essential aspect of civility." Jefferson and other Virginia gentlemen wished to convey civility and refinement. That desire increased in the 1760s and '70s as London authorities seemed not to concede the colonists' full dignity as British citizens.[23]

We have few textual records of Martha Jefferson's life, as he destroyed their correspondence when she died. She was clearly active in managing the day-to-day affairs of Monticello. One of the only extant manuscripts in her writing is a register from 1777, dominated by the record of animals she had slaughtered by slaves: hogs, geese, cows, and the like. She also contributed to the roster of enslaved laborers the Jeffersons owned. About a year after their wedding, Martha requested that Thomas attend an auction fifty miles away to purchase a "favorite housewoman," Ursula Granger, and her two sons. Thomas was not happy with the purchase because Martha's former brother-in-law Meriwether Skelton, knowing that the Jeffersons wanted to purchase Ursula, deliberately engaged Thomas in a bidding war for her. More than three decades later, Jefferson was still complaining that Skelton had "run me up to £210 an exorbitant price as the woman was old." Nevertheless, Jefferson also bought Ursula's husband "Great George" afterward for £130.[24]

Birth and death hovered over Martha Jefferson's married life. She became pregnant six times, pregnancies that consumed almost half the time of their marriage together. She seems to have gotten pregnant almost immediately after their wedding, as their daughter Martha was born in September 1772. Martha would be the only one of their children to outlive Thomas. Any pregnancy in the eighteenth century could be fatal for the baby and/or the mother. The six pregnancies sapped Martha Jefferson's vitality; she died several months after giving birth to their daughter Lucy in 1782.[25]

Martha's death was devastating to Thomas, but it was not unusual in the mortality-filled world of colonial America. In 1773, Jefferson's close friend, brother-in-law, and former classmate Dabney Carr died suddenly. Carr was not yet thirty years old. Jefferson took personal responsibility for the funeral and for the care of Carr's children, whom Carr had fathered with Jefferson's sister Martha. Jefferson wrote to the Reverend Charles Clay, a traditionalist Anglican minister, to arrange Carr's funeral at Monticello. Jefferson was anxious to schedule the service because he anticipated needing to plan another one soon: his father-in-law, John Wayles, also lay near death. "I would choose the service should begin about half after ten in the morning if agreeable to you," Jefferson told Clay. On Carr's tombstone, Jefferson inscribed: "To his virtue, good sense, learning and friendship / this stone is dedicated by / Thomas Jefferson / who, of all men loved him most."[26]

Jefferson would repeatedly call on Charles Clay to preach and preside at funerals in these years. When the House of Burgesses approved Jefferson and Robert Carter Nicholas's day of fasting and prayer, Jefferson and another burgess from Albemarle County wrote to their constituents, informing them that St. Anne's Parish would observe the prayer day with a service led by Rev. Clay. The people of Albemarle County would join Clay there "devoutly to implore the divine interposition in behalf of an injured and oppressed people; and that the minds of his majesty, his ministers, and parliament, might be inspired with wisdom from above, to avert from us the dangers which threaten our civil rights, and all the evils of civil war."[27]

Jefferson's enthusiasm for Clay, despite Clay's evangelical convictions, was not unique. Jefferson routinely allied with evangelical ministers who shared his political convictions. His enduring friendship with Clay was not based on political expediency alone. Jefferson would become a financial supporter of Clay's new "Calvinistical Reformed" church in Charlottesville in 1777. At a time when Patriot leaders desperately needed the support of the clergy, Clay struck Jefferson as an ardent American partisan. In raising subscriptions to assist Clay's church, Jefferson wrote that by "rejecting the tyrant and tyranny of Britain, [Clay] proved his religion genuine by its harmony with the liberties of mankind, and, conforming his public prayers to the spirit and the injured rights of his country, ever addressed the God of battles for victory to our arms." (The expression "God of battles" was not taken directly from the Bible. The best-known use of it was in Shakespeare's *Henry V.*) Jefferson would assist Clay in bids for public office, too, and they became close neighbors at Jefferson's secondary estate at Poplar Forest.[28]

Jefferson also knew certain evangelical converts personally, including the plantation master Robert Carter III. Carter had embraced deistic principles as a young man, but in 1777–78 he went through a conversion experience, received believer's baptism, and joined a Baptist church. When Jefferson paid a debt to Carter in 1778, Carter took the opportunity to give Jefferson his Christian testimony. "I had imbibed a very destructive notion touching the Religion of revelation that it was of human Institution only," Carter wrote. "I do now disclaim it and do testify that Jesus Christ is the Son of god; that through him mankind can be Saved only; that the old and new testament contain the word of god." Carter later became a Swedenborgian, or a member of the Church of the New Jerusalem. This sect, founded by the Swedish Lutheran scientist and theologian Emanuel Swedenborg, was critical of the traditional Christian idea of the Trinity, and emphasized the obligation of charity. Inspired by Swedenborgian principles, starting in 1791 Carter gradually emancipated his five hundred enslaved people. Again, though we correctly see Jefferson as a skeptic about the Bible and Christian doctrines, he had many meaningful relationships with traditionalist and sectarian Christians.[29]

Martha's father John Wayles passed away in 1773, shortly after the death of Dabney Carr. Wayles's passing was fateful for Jefferson, initiating the inheritance that marrying Martha had promised. Jefferson inherited land, bondspeople, and debt from Wayles. Those were the three factors that came to define Jefferson's economic life. Jefferson estimated that his household wealth doubled because of his share of the Wayles estate. (As the husband, Thomas legally controlled all the family's property.) Yet, like many Virginia gentlemen, John Wayles carried a lot of debt, including £11,000 owed to his largest creditor, compared to the £30,000 estimated value of his estate. Much of that value was not liquid, and it would have required someone with more financial luck and acumen than Jefferson to know how to dispose efficiently of Wayles's debts, which were now his. Jefferson had been worried about fate sweeping "away the whole of my little fortune" even before the Wayles inheritance. Disruptions attending the American Revolution, Jefferson's spending, and the poor productivity of his farms sank Jefferson's finances into ever-deeper disarray. He found it excruciating. "The torment of mind I endure till the moment shall arrive when I shall not owe a shilling on earth is such really as to render life of little value." He wondered if he could ever get free from "the thralldom of Mr. Wayles's debt." His financial standing would only grow worse, despite selling acreage and many enslaved workers over the years.[30]

John Wayles's death also dramatically expanded Jefferson's roster of enslaved people, as he inherited 135 of them. The best-known slaves he received were members of the Hemings family. John Wayles had been in an open sexual relationship with one of them, the mixed-race woman Elizabeth Hemings, following the death of his third wife in 1761. John Wayles and Elizabeth Hemings had six children together. Their last child, Sally, was born in 1773, the year of Wayles's death. Thus, Sally Hemings was the half sister of Martha Jefferson.[31]

After first being separated across Jefferson's properties, Elizabeth and all her children were eventually brought together at Monticello. Thomas would have taken no notice of two-year-old Sally when she moved to Monticello around 1775. She was just one more enslaved child, and Jefferson was already preoccupied with the crisis with Britain. The Coercive Acts of 1774 had put Virginians on notice that the British administration would take severe measures to suppress resistance such as the Boston "Tea Party" in late 1773. The Coercive Acts, instead of forcing the colonists into submission, fueled their boycotts of British goods. The desire for intercolonial cooperation resulted in the First Continental Congress in September 1774 in Philadelphia.

Less famous in 1774 than Patrick Henry or George Washington, Jefferson was not chosen to go to the Congress. The summoning of Congress, however, inspired Jefferson to pen *A Summary View of the Rights of British America,* which he hoped would frame Americans' political prerogatives. Combined with his crafting of the resolution for prayer and fasting, Jefferson's *A Summary View* showed that he wanted to be a leader in Virginia's Patriot movement. He sent copies to Patrick Henry (who characteristically ignored the treatise), and to his relative Peyton Randolph, the Speaker of the House of Burgesses, who circulated it among delegates to a Virginia Patriot convention. *A Summary View* gathered momentum when it was published in Williamsburg, Philadelphia, and in two London editions by the end of 1774. Formerly just a regional planter and politician, Jefferson was suddenly becoming a political and rhetorical figure of Anglo-American renown.[32]

In his powerful tract, Jefferson argued that colonists had unalienable rights as Britons, and as people created by God. The parliamentary measures were violating those rights. He suggested that there was a plot in Britain against American liberty, a theme that would dominate the Declaration two years later. The Coercive Acts were the most extreme evidence of the conspiracy against Americans' freedom. "Scarcely have our minds been able to emerge from the astonishment into which one stroke of parliamentary thunder has involved us," Jefferson exclaimed, "before another more heavy and more alarming is fallen on us. Single acts of tyranny may be ascribed to the accidental opinion of a day; but a series of oppressions, begun at a distinguished period, and pursued unalterably through every change of [government] ministers, too plainly prove a deliberate, systematical plan of reducing us to slavery." To Jefferson, the parliamentary acts were not disconnected errors of judgment. They were all part of a malign British plan to destroy colonists' liberty. This fear of conspiracy was essential to the Patriot mindset. Once people become convinced of a conspiracy, it becomes exceedingly difficult to convince them that there isn't one.[33]

The plot was not just a malign scheme, however, but a "plan of reducing us to slavery." The fear of slavery was ubiquitous in Patriot literature. To the Patriots, a person was either free or a slave. But there was more than one way to be a slave. Being a slave could mean you were a permanently bound agricultural laborer, or it could mean that you were an economic pawn serving a political master. The term *slavery* appeared in dozens of publications in 1774, reflecting both senses of the word's meaning. One of the most florid uses came in a New York broadside warning Patriots that "slavery is clanking her infernal chains, and tyranny stands ready with goads and whips to enforce obedience to her despotic and cruel mandates." Here, slavery was synonymous with living under tyranny.[34]

Jefferson's reference to slavery was a knowing one, however. He understood what it meant to hold human beings in bondage. As historian Edmund Morgan observed, being slave owners made the southern Patriots more sensitive about preserving their own liberty. "Virginians may have had a special appreciation," Morgan wrote, "of the freedom dear to republicans, because they saw every day what life without it could be like." To Jefferson and other slaveholders, some people were better suited to be slaves than others. If all people were created by God, however, the enslavement of any person was still problematic. This dissonance in American slaveholding would grow into a view of slavery as ordained by God, with slaves as a natural part of a godly household. This paternalistic view came to prevail in much of the white South by the time of Jefferson's retirement from politics. Jefferson consistently maintained that history would lead to emancipation, though his practical steps to effect emancipation in the United States became rarer after the mid-1780s.[35]

In *A Summary View,* Jefferson attempted a rhetorical high-wire act, one that would reappear in his draft of the Declaration: blaming the king for chattel slavery in America. Claiming that "the abolition of domestic slavery is the great object of desire in [the] colonies," he based this assertion on an earlier Privy Council ruling against a Virginia trade duty on imported bondspeople. He saw this royal disallowance as evidence of British authorities' tyrannical preference for slavery. If Virginia were ever to abolish slavery, he reasoned, it must first stop importing more enslaved people. The crown had foiled "repeated attempts" at such restrictions, Jefferson wrote, "thus preferring the immediate advantages of a few African corsairs [slave traders] to the lasting interests of the American states, and to the rights of human nature, deeply wounded by this infamous practice."[36]

Jefferson was undoubtedly exaggerating the extent to which Virginia politicians wished to abolish slavery itself. Slave *importations,* on the other hand, had slowed considerably in Maryland and Virginia by the late 1760s. Those colonies had more than enough enslaved workers. The Chesapeake enslaved population had started growing by natural increase by the early 1700s, and importing more bondspeople became less economically desirable. Jefferson's deflecting protests about slavery and the crown allowed white Virginians to build bridges with antislavery northerners, who also resented imperial domination of colonial affairs.[37]

In the conclusion to *A Summary View,* Jefferson directly addressed the king. His Majesty should serve as an impartial arbiter over the empire, according to Jefferson, balancing the power of Parliament with the authority of colonial legislatures such as the House of Burgesses. The king had abandoned that role, however, and had joined the attack on the colonists' rights by continually preferring Parliament's will over the colonists' needs. Jefferson insisted that "kings are the servants, not the proprietors of the people. Open your breast, sire, to liberal and expanded thought. Let not the name of George the third be a blot on the page of history." Jefferson did note that he and his fellow Patriots had no desire for independence. Merely raising the prospect of independence was inflammatory enough, however. Jefferson finished with a reminder of the colonists' common creation by God, a transhistorical basis for equality that no human being could rightly deny. "The God who gave us life gave us liberty at the same time," Jefferson proclaimed. Though Virginia Patriots did not formally endorse *A Summary View,* it was well received across the colonies. George Washington paid in advance for several copies of "Mr. Jefferson's Bill of Rights." John Adams called it a "handsome public paper" that helped Jefferson develop the "reputation of a masterly pen."[38]

In March 1775 Jefferson traveled to St. John's Church in Richmond for the meeting of the second Virginia Convention. The convention immediately faced a choice: to send more petitions for relief to London or to raise a militia and prepare for war. Virginia radicals found their spokesman in Patrick Henry, whose "Liberty or Death" speech called for military preparation. Jefferson, still Henry's ally, also addressed the convention "warmly" about the benefits of summoning the militia. The convention agreed to form a militia, and it put Henry, Jefferson, and George Washington on a committee to equip this force. Circumstances vindicated the preparatory decision, for war broke out in Massachusetts at Lexington and Concord on April 19, 1775. Tensions immediately flared in Virginia, as the royal governor Lord Dunmore removed gunpowder stored at Williamsburg, fearing that the Virginia militia would use it against British forces. Dunmore also began threatening to free enslaved people if the Patriots' insolence continued. Nothing could have been more provocative than the prospect of royal emancipation of Virginia's bondspeople, and Dunmore would later prove his threat was not idle.[39]

The convention also elected delegates to the Second Continental Congress. Once again, Jefferson was not chosen (Peyton Randolph, Washington, and Henry were the top vote-getters), but he was first alternate. As it turned out, Randolph stayed in Virginia as Speaker of the House of Burgesses, so Jefferson went to Philadelphia. He left in mid-June, stopping in Annapolis, Maryland, to buy books. In Philadelphia, almost none of the delegates from outside Virginia knew him personally, but some had already read and admired *A Summary View*. One Rhode Island delegate called him "the famous Mr. Jefferson." Philadelphia introduced Jefferson to a host of brilliant, learned, and opinionated characters, some of whom would have an enduring influence on him. Not least among the new colleagues was John Adams, a Harvard-educated lawyer born eight years before Jefferson.[40]

In Philadelphia, Jefferson also met Pennsylvania delegate John Dickinson, known for his *Letters from a Farmer in Pennsylvania* (1767–68) and its case against British taxation. As the Congress now confronted a war of uncertain duration, Jefferson and Dickinson crafted a document called the *Declaration of the Causes and Necessity of Taking Up Arms*. Dickinson and Jefferson's collaboration was tense, as they were both supremely confident (for good reason) of their respective writing abilities. Dickinson would later adopt a conciliatory approach toward the British, ultimately abstaining from the vote on independence. This probably accounts for Jefferson's (apparently faulty) recollection that his original draft "was too strong for Mr. Dickinson," and that Dickinson produced a more moderate version of the document. Despite their friction, the two were able to produce an acceptable final draft for Congress.[41]

Dickinson heavily amended Jefferson's version of *Declaration of the Causes*, but by comparing the drafts we can discern what Dickinson adopted from Jefferson's original text. Jefferson wrote, "We most solemnly, before God and the World, declare, that, exerting the utmost Energy of those

Powers, which our beneficent Creator hath graciously bestowed upon us, the Arms we have been compelled by our Enemies to assume, we will, in defiance of every Hazard, with unabating Firmness and Perseverance, employ for the preservation of our Liberties." (Here Dickinson added that the colonists were "resolved to die Freemen rather than to live Slaves.") Using Jefferson's language, the *Declaration of the Causes* concluded that "we most devoutly implore his Divine Goodness to protect us happily through this great Conflict." Jefferson was already showing mastery of providential rhetoric in the defense of colonists' rights. Yet he left open the possibility of reconciliation. The Continental Congress adopted the *Declaration of the Causes* on July 6, 1775. Almost exactly a year later, another Jefferson text would countenance no happy outcome of the war, at least for the British.[42]

Jefferson headed for Virginia on August 1, but not before stopping by Robert Bell's store on Third Street in Philadelphia to buy a book. He had obtained a number of items in Philadelphia during his five weeks there. The city's shopping options meant more purchases, and Jefferson kept such meticulous records that we can track many by the date, price, and place purchased. His visit began and ended with book buying at different Philadelphia shops. He bought sangaree (a mix of Madeira wine, sugar, and nutmeg) at the Center House, and a punch at the City Tavern. (Elsewhere in his memorandum book for 1775, Jefferson recorded voluminous purchases of Madeira and Italian wines.) He bought a tomahawk and a sword-chain, which he used to attach his dress sword to his belt. His gifts for Martha presumably included some of the three pounds of chocolate he got. Jefferson was also generous, giving gifts to a fund for the poor, to one for the imprisoned, to the "German church," and to other, unnamed charities.[43]

He must have enjoyed showering Martha with the bounty of Philadelphia's stores. But the sorrows of death remained ubiquitous, and not long after arriving home he had to bury his daughter, a toddler named Jane. She was named after Thomas's beloved sister and for his mother, who would die the following year. The death of young Jane briefly delayed his return to Philadelphia, but he was back in the city by the end of September 1775. Within a month, his mentor Peyton Randolph died in Philadelphia; Jefferson attended the dinner where Randolph suddenly perished from "an apoplexy."[44]

Jefferson was terse about Peyton Randolph's death when he wrote to inform Randolph's brother John (a Loyalist) of his passing. The bulk of the

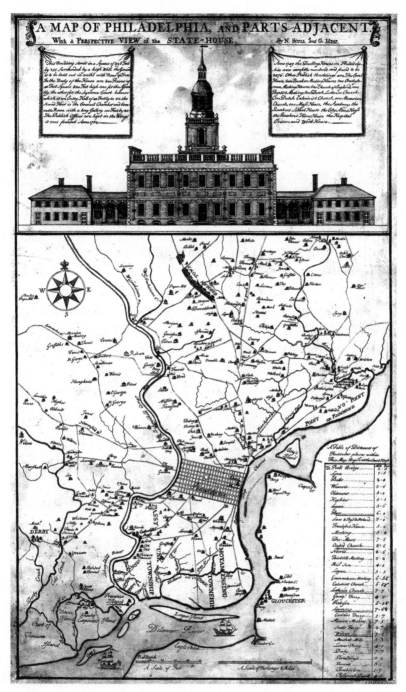

Nicholas Scull and George Heap, *Map of Philadelphia, and Parts Adjacent*, 1752.
(Courtesy Library of Congress)

letter reviewed the early course of the Revolutionary War. The conflict was expanding, even though it would be another seven months before the united colonies would declare independence. Independence was difficult to contemplate or even to discuss. Thomas Paine's sensational *Common Sense* would change that dynamic in January 1776. Still, Jefferson warned Randolph that "after colonies have drawn the sword there is but one step more they can take." Perhaps the British authorities were banking on the colonists not taking that fateful step. Jefferson, for his part, was unwilling to live as a powerless servant under British oppression. "By the god that made me I will cease to exist before I yield to a connection on such terms as the British parliament propose," Jefferson vowed. "In this I think I speak the sentiments of America." References to the creator God were essential in the arguments for liberty made by Jefferson and other American Patriots.[45]

War also drew out Jefferson's providential instincts, his belief that God would intervene on the colonists' behalf. Recalling the famous weather-aided destruction of the Spanish Armada in 1588, he mused that American wind and water might rescue the colonists from "slavery." Upon hearing of the seizure of a British transport and the accidental destruction of a British warship, Jefferson told John Page that "of a certainty the hand of god is upon" the British in judgment. Paraphrasing the great English reformer William Tyndale, he assured Randolph that once the Americans had given the British forces a good "drubbing," the "sceptered tyrant will know we are not mere brutes, to crouch under his hand and kiss the rod with which he deigns to scourge us." Jefferson failed to recall that Tyndale had recommended that Christians should "kiss the rod" and *submit* to a tyrant, in hope that God would give such a ruler a "better heart."[46]

Although he expressed confidence in providence's overruling control of the conflict, Jefferson despaired of seeing any turnaround from King George or his minions. In Virginia, Lord Dunmore took the decisive step when he proclaimed on November 7, 1775, that any "negroes" who took up arms against the Patriots would be freed by the British. This was the nightmare scenario that white Virginians had feared. Jefferson warned "Patty" (Martha) to keep the family's "distance from the alarms of Ld. Dunmore," which thankfully were centered on the Tidewater region, well to the east of Charlottesville. Dunmore's proclamation would have cascading effects. It was of enormous motivational value for Patriots, in both the North and South, who portrayed rebellious bondspeople as tools of the bloodthirsty

British. Jefferson himself would lose dozens of enslaved runaways during the British invasion of Virginia in 1781. In the short term, about eight hundred Virginia bondspeople joined Dunmore's forces before the royal governor abandoned the state in August 1776. John Page advised Jefferson that Williamsburg was rife with fears about a broader "insurrection of the Negros." Jefferson would allude to Dunmore's proclamation as one of the colonists' grievances in the Declaration of Independence.[47]

Jefferson took another arduous journey back to Monticello in late December 1775. His activity is difficult to track until May 1776, when he returned to Philadelphia on the eve of independence. Concerned about the safety of his family, he busied himself in those months at home with mundane affairs. He was ambivalent about leaving Martha, despite his pressing business in Philadelphia. On January 28, he opened a large barrel (a "pipe") of Madeira, vintage 1770, which contained about 110 gallons of wine. In February, a friend in Philadelphia sent him copies of Paine's *Common Sense*. Jefferson expected to return to Philadelphia sooner, but his mother passed away on March 31, 1776. He had Rev. Charles Clay perform the funeral. She was buried at Monticello, just as Dabney Carr had been a few years earlier. His mother's death, and his ambivalence about whether to stay with his family, unleashed a new round of debilitating headaches. These were longer lasting than those he suffered after his failed courtship of Rebecca Burwell. He told Thomas Nelson that the "malady" detained him at Monticello six weeks longer than he had planned.[48]

Jefferson arrived back in Philadelphia in May 1776, just in time to write the most influential document in American history. What if Congress had started debating independence earlier? What if Jefferson's mother had died later, or his malady had detained him longer? Presumably he would not have written the Declaration. This likely would have meant he wouldn't have become president. Jefferson was an ambitious and brilliantly articulate Patriot, as seen in his prayer declaration and the *Summary View of the Rights of British America*. But to become an American icon, he also needed good timing. He got it. In early June, his Virginia colleague Richard Henry Lee moved that the "United Colonies" declare independence.

3. "A Virginian Ought to Appear at the Head of This Business"

Jefferson was thirty-three years old in 1776, not quite a youth but hardly the most venerable member of the Continental Congress. Ben Franklin was more than twice Jefferson's age, but he was incapacitated with sickness. Almost immediately upon arriving back in the city, Jefferson drafted the Declaration of Independence. If Franklin had been in good health, the delegates might have tapped him as the primary draftsman. The other leading contender was John Adams, and Jefferson himself even suggested that Adams write it. Adams recalled years later that he had insisted Jefferson take the lead. Why? Jefferson asked. First, "you are a Virginian," Adams explained, "and a Virginian ought to appear at the head of this business." Virginia was the most populous state, and Massachusetts was notorious for Patriot radicalism. Adams also realized that some saw him as "obnoxious, suspected, and unpopular." But "you are very much otherwise," he told Jefferson. Moreover, Adams confessed, "You can write ten times better than I can." It was settled. Jefferson would pen the document that would become "American Scripture."[1]

No one realized the outsized role that the Declaration would come to play in American civil religion, however. The primary function of the Declaration was to convince Americans in 1776 that independence was justified. Historians have endlessly dissected the sources of the Declaration, but three of its most obvious precedents were Jefferson's *A Summary View of the Rights of British America*, the draft of the preamble to Virginia's new constitution (which he also sketched), and the Virginia Declaration of Rights, recently written by George Mason. Jefferson in 1825 denied that he sought originality. He simply intended the document to express "the American mind" regarding natural rights. The Declaration would reflect the "harmonizing sentiments of the day."[2]

Jefferson then rattled off the names "Aristotle, Cicero, Locke, Sidney, etc." as sources inspiring it. The English political philosopher John Locke was arguably the most formative influence on the Declaration, with his theory of government by consent of the governed. Aristotle and Cicero suggested sources from ancient Greece and Rome. But what about Algernon Sidney? Of this quartet of authors, Sidney is perhaps the least familiar name. Jefferson, John Adams, and other Founders shared a deep admiration for Sidney, the great English republican writer and martyred foe of the Stuart kings from the mid-1600s. Jefferson's copy of Sidney's *Discourses concerning Government,* an Edinburgh edition from 1750, is now held at the Library of Congress.[3]

Along with John Milton, Sidney was one of the chief promoters of "Hebraic republicanism," the idea that ancient Israel was originally a kingless republic led by God alone. Only later did the Israelites faithlessly insist upon setting up a king, as recorded in the book of I Samuel. Thomas Paine reinvigorated Hebraic republican thought in *Common Sense,* which depended on the same reading of I Samuel as Sidney's. "The Hebrew kings were not instituted by God, but given as a punishment of their sin," Sidney concluded in *Discourses concerning Government.* Jefferson was already recommending Locke and Sidney to a correspondent by 1771. Along with Locke's *Second Treatise on Government,* Sidney's *Discourses* was one of the basic political texts Jefferson required at the University of Virginia.[4]

The Calvinist Sidney supplied Jefferson not only with a biblical argument against monarchy but with righteous motivation to reject the king's authority. Everyone knew that independence would require war; war had been going on for fourteen months already. The conflict would not compel the regicide that Parliamentarians had committed against Charles I in the 1640s. This was something that not even the radical Sidney supported. But independence would demand armed revolution against tyranny and "slavery," a cause that Sidney had backed with gusto. As Sidney put it, "Swords were given to men, that none might be slaves, but such as know not how to use them." Sidney might have also been Jefferson's source for the most memorable phrase of the Declaration, as he had written that "nothing can be more evident, than that if many [men] had been created, they had been all equal." Although Jefferson would come to regard himself as a staunch anti-Calvinist, this did not preclude his appropriation of Calvinist sources such as Sidney.[5]

Not all delegates were ready to declare independence in June 1776, so Congress delayed a final vote. In the meantime, members appointed a committee to draft a statement justifying independence. The distinguished group included Jefferson, Adams, Ben Franklin, and Roger Sherman. Sherman, a devout Calvinist from Connecticut, would also play a major role in crafting the Articles of Confederation (the nation's first constitution), and the Constitution of 1787. Sherman was also appointed to a committee to draft what would become the Articles. Sherman's direct contributions to the Declaration seem to have been limited. But his presence on the drafting committee suggests that at least some of the delegates in Philadelphia had a biblicist understanding of the Declaration's invocations of the creator God. Despite his skepticism, Jefferson often had traditionalist Christians like Sherman in his political orbit, sometimes literally sitting next to them in meetings. He needed to be cognizant of their orthodoxy when he spoke in religious terms.[6]

Some scholars insist that the Declaration was "secular" and made no substantial reference to God. Even Pauline Maier's landmark study of the Declaration, *American Scripture* (1997), made the perplexing claim that Congress had to add "two references to God, which were conspicuously missing in Jefferson's draft." In the same sentence, she concedes that God "only" appeared in Jefferson's draft as the "author of nature's laws and the endower of natural rights." In other words, Jefferson's draft already included the celebrated language about "nature's God" and humankind's equal creation by God. Those were significant roles for God, and further examination of the context shows that these concepts were foundational for Jefferson.[7]

The line "all men are created equal, . . . they are endowed by their Creator with certain unalienable Rights" was no new concept, as seen in Sidney's earlier rendering. Jefferson's most immediate precedent for this doctrine, however, was George Mason's Virginia Declaration of Rights. Mason had spoken about the nature of man in the first article of the Declaration of Rights, where he posited that "all men are by nature equally free and independent, and have certain inherent rights." Mason's claim made no explicit mention of the divine. Jefferson reworked the concept, however, to

A Declaration by the Representatives of the UNITED STATES
OF AMERICA, in General Congress assembled.

When in the course of human events it becomes necessary for one people to
dissolve the political bands which have connected them with another, and to
assume among the powers of the earth the separate and equal station to
which the laws of nature & of nature's god entitle them, a decent respect
to the opinions of mankind requires that they should declare the causes
which impel them to the separation.

We hold these truths to be self-evident; that all men are
created equal & independent, that from that equal creation they derive
rights inherent & inalienable, among which are the preservation of
life & liberty, & the pursuit of happiness; that to secure these ends, go-
-vernments are instituted among men, deriving their just powers from
the consent of the governed; that whenever any form of government
shall becomes destructive of these ends, it is the right of the people to alter
or to abolish it, & to institute new government, laying it's foundation on
such principles & organising it's powers in such form, as to them sh. I
seem most likely to effect their safety & happiness. prudence indeed
will dictate that governments long established should not be changed for
light & transient causes: and accordingly all experience hath shewn that
mankind are more disposed to suffer while evils are sufferable, than to
right themselves by abolishing the forms to which they are accustomed. but
when a long train of abuses & usurpations [begun at a distinguished period,
&] pursuing invariably the same object, evinces a design to reduce
them under absolute Despotism, it is their right, it is their duty, to throw off such
[government] & to provide new guards for their future security. such has
been the patient sufferance of these colonies; & such is now the necessity
which constrains them to expunge their former systems of government.
the history of the present king of Great Britain is a history of unremitting injuries and
usurpations, among which, appears no solitary fact to contra-
-dict the uniform tenor of the rest [all of which] have in direct object the
establishment of an absolute tyranny over these states. to prove this, let facts be
submitted to a candid world, for the truth of which we pledge a faith
yet unsullied by falsehood.]

Thomas Jefferson, draft of the Declaration of Independence, 1776. (Courtesy Wikimedia Commons) show God's action in creation and in the conveyance of rights. He originally wrote that from their "equal creation they derive rights inherent & inalienable," which was clearer about the source of liberties than Mason's simple notion that men "have" inherent rights. But Jefferson's original statement about creation also got changed to identify the being who gave people equal rights: "They are endowed by their Creator with certain unalienable Rights, . . . among these are Life, Liberty and the pursuit of Happiness." Jefferson held to this concept of equality by creation throughout his life. Our natural rights derived not from the "Charter of kings or legislators; but under the king of kings," he wrote in 1817, quoting the book of Revelation.[8]

Perhaps the greatest dilemma in Jefferson's thought—maybe the greatest dilemma in American history—is what he meant by "all men." This is not the place to scrutinize every possible interpretation of the phrase, but two points are essential. First, in 1776 Jefferson was referring to all men involved in the controversy between Britain and its colonies. Those men were equal, and they had rights more fundamental than whatever privileges the king and Parliament deigned to grant. Jefferson's "men" were Anglo-American political men, meaning white male property holders. In short, men like Jefferson.

Yet Jefferson and the Congress chose to base equal rights on a broader foundation: humankind's creation by God. This was also a commonplace notion in 1776. In this pre-Darwinian world, even someone as theologically progressive as Jefferson could not imagine that humanity came from some other source besides God. Maybe the creation of humankind did not happen as described in the early chapters of Genesis. But Jefferson and most eighteenth-century Britons and Americans still lived in a world they saw as *created*, and they lived lives they saw as *created*. Equality by creation, because it was so widely assumed, was the most powerful basis on which to argue for equal rights. For observers such as Jefferson, equality by creation did not mean equality of condition or talents. It did mean that all people had basic dignity before God, because all people were created "in God's image," as Genesis put it.

Equality by creation derived from ancient biblical tradition and from countless Christian writers, including Algernon Sidney. From Sidney forward, the concept of God-given equality became a common feature of arguments against tyrannical government. It appeared in Locke's writings during the Glorious Revolution, when Britons replaced King James II with the

Protestant monarchs William and Mary. Evangelical dissenters in America employed equality by creation to argue against oppression by colonial governments during the Great Awakening of the mid-1700s. Equality by creation came naturally to the lips of Patriot leaders. The lawyer James Otis, an early Massachusetts radical, proclaimed in 1762 that "God made all men naturally equal" as he was objecting to royal power in his colony.[9]

Today, we observe the jarring incoherence between equality by creation and the deep inequalities of America in 1776. But it is not just our modern perspective that raises this problem. People at the time, including James Otis, identified the contradiction too. Otis made the argument for equality between the colonists and the people of Great Britain because they were "common children of the same Creator." This circumstantial observation led Otis to make a more fundamental point. To him, all people were "by the law of nature free born," regardless of being "white or black." Otis lambasted those who based chattel slavery on skin pigmentation. You might as easily enslave people because of the length of their hair or the shape of their faces, he said. Owning slaves diminished liberty for all people. "Those who every day barter away other men's liberty, will soon care little for their own," Otis concluded.[10]

Free and enslaved African Americans also contended for humanity's basic freedom, making that case publicly in rare instances when they could do so. The Declaration of Independence gave antislavery advocates a richer vocabulary on which to draw. Some enslaved people petitioned the Massachusetts legislature in 1777, writing in rough script that they had "in Common with all other men a Natural and Unaliable Right to that freedom which the Grat Parent of the Unavers hath Bestowed equalley on all menkind." Likewise, the mixed-race New England pastor Lemuel Haynes, a former indentured servant and soldier, used Jefferson's logic to argue against slavery. Haynes headed his remarkable essay "Liberty Further Extended; or, Free Thoughts on the Illegality of Slave-keeping" (1776) with the pertinent line of the Declaration: "We hold these truths to be self-evident, that all men are created equal."[11]

Jefferson did not disagree with such antislavery sentiments. Recall that Jefferson cited human equality as an argument for freedom for a mixed-race indentured servant in Virginia in 1770. Jefferson addressed slavery's violation of the principles of the Revolution most directly in *Notes on the State of Virginia*. There he bemoaned the effects of slavery, not just on the people enslaved but on white owners. Slave owners' children became trained in despotism through their everyday interactions with bondspeople.

These reflections prompted Jefferson's most memorable statement on slavery. "Can the liberties of a nation be thought secure when we have removed their only firm basis, a conviction in the minds of the people that these liberties are of the gift of God?" Chattel slavery denied the equality principle in the Declaration, he insisted. Ignoring those truths could elicit the wrath of God. "I tremble for my country when I reflect that God is just: that his justice cannot sleep forever," he mused. Jefferson thought this divine judgment would likely entail war between slaves and masters. God would necessarily take the side of bondspeople in such a cataclysm. He hoped that the spirit of emancipation, energized by the Revolution, would bear fruit before a remorseless war engulfed the South. He hoped emancipation would happen "with the consent of the masters, rather than by their extirpation." As he put it to a French correspondent in 1786, he was not sure how the "workings of an overruling providence" would deliver the enslaved people from bondage, but he figured it would come either through the spread of enlightened ideas among owners or by God's "exterminating thunder."[12]

Unlike early abolitionists who advocated against white prejudice and for the integration of blacks into white society, however, Jefferson saw no future for Africans in America. Drawing on principles from the leading French philosopher Montesquieu, Jefferson asserted that colonization of freed slaves outside of the United States must accompany emancipation. Separating the races geographically could prevent the dreaded race war. Jefferson consistently said that he supported emancipation, but only if there was a workable plan to prevent a genocidal conflict. When successive Virginia governors sought Jefferson's assistance for a practical colonization plan during his presidency, Jefferson demurred in most cases. Still, throughout his career, he theoretically supported colonizing the former bondspeople. If sufficient political support and a feasible plan for colonization developed, he said, he would be ready to move on emancipation.[13]

The Declaration charged the king with many violations of colonists' rights and prerogatives. Some charges are plain in their meaning. For instance, Jefferson complained that the British government had imposed "taxes on us without our consent." Other grievances seem more obscure. For example, Jefferson noted that the king had abolished the English legal system in a "neighbouring province" and replaced it with "an arbitrary government," setting the stage for introducing "the same absolute rule into these colonies." This referred to the despised Quebec Act (1774), which allowed the free practice of Roman Catholicism in British-conquered Quebec, and extended the province's boundary south into other colonies' western sections. Most colonists associated Catholic power with political tyranny, so the Quebec Act was one of the most provocative moves ever by the British administration.[14]

Jefferson ended his list of complaints with perhaps the most inflammatory charge of all: the king had "excited domestic insurrections amongst us, and has endeavoured to bring on the inhabitants of our frontiers, the merciless Indian Savages, whose known rule of warfare, is an undistinguished destruction of all ages, sexes and conditions." The meaning of the second point is obvious: the British had allied with "merciless" Native Americans to subdue the colonists. But the meaning of "domestic insurrections" is less clear, at first glance. The final version of this complaint was *meant* to be shrouded, because it concerned slave insurrection. It referenced Lord Dunmore's 1775 offer of freedom to enslaved people in Virginia. Jefferson's "original rough draught" made the point more clearly, as it was included in a lengthy section on slavery that the Congress deleted. The king, Jefferson insisted, was "now exciting those very people to rise in arms among us, and to purchase that liberty of which he has deprived them, by murdering the people upon whom he also obtruded them."[15]

This section on slavery drew upon Jefferson's contention in *A Summary View of the Rights of British America* that Britain had forced slavery on the colonists, and that the administration in London would not allow them to curtail importations of enslaved people. In Jefferson's draft of the Declaration, he insisted that the king's imposition of slavery represented a "cruel war against human nature itself, violating its most sacred rights of life and liberty." Congress deleted this portion, leaving only a remnant of it in the "domestic insurrections" complaint. Why Congress cut the slavery passage was not entirely clear. Jefferson and Adams both recalled that the sensitivity of delegates was part of the explanation. Some from the Lower South did not wish to restrict slavery, while some from the North disliked attention to the seagoing slave trade, in which some northern shippers were implicated. Congress likely did not see Jefferson's argument as especially convincing, either. If slavery represented a cruel war against human nature, why didn't Jefferson or other American leaders free their own enslaved workers?

Jefferson had a ready response: his fears about mass emancipation leading to race war. Members of the Congress surely did not want to broach that topic. It was irrelevant to their purposes, at best.[16]

Congress edited the draft Declaration starting on July 1. Jefferson squirmed as members picked over his wording. Congress would ultimately delete a quarter of the text from the draft. Jefferson would recall these changes as "mutilations" and "depredations." Most were stylistic, and probably resulted in better wording. As Pauline Maier noted, Congress added two references to the divine, with the appeal to the "supreme judge of the world" and members' "firm reliance on the protection of divine Providence." Jefferson's references to the Creator and to equality by creation were of more enduring significance, however. Congress portrayed independence as a cause that God would bless. British critics and American Loyalists would challenge this confidence, pointing to Scripture passages that forbade rebellion.[17]

Jefferson did not employ the Bible directly in the way that Thomas Paine had, although some of Jefferson's phrases echoed Scripture. His charge that the king had "sent hither swarms of officers to harass our people, and eat out their substance" conjured images of the plagues in Egypt from the book of Exodus. It may have recalled language from Job 5:5, which speaks of the foolish man's family "whose harvest the hungry eateth up . . . and the robber swalloweth up their substance."[18]

Regardless of the Declaration's immediate political aims, Jefferson did have an inkling that the document would become enshrined in American civil religion, the blending of national and spiritual zeal. When he gifted his writing desk to his granddaughter Ellen Wayles Randolph Coolidge and her husband Joseph years later, he wrote that "its imaginary value will increase with years, and if [Joseph] lives to my age, or another half century, he may see it carried in the procession of our nation's birth day, as the relics of the saints are in those of the church." The desk may not have become a saint's relic, but it has found a prominent place in the National Museum of American History.[19]

Jefferson was busy in the Congress in summer 1776, but not so busy that he couldn't enjoy some of Philadelphia's pleasures. Almost immediately upon arrival in May 1776 he began buying writing implements and toys, as well as new shoes and stockings for "Bob," or Robert Hemings. Hemings was his fourteen-year-old enslaved valet. He was also Martha Jefferson's half brother and the older brother of Sally Hemings.[20]

Desk on which Jefferson wrote the Declaration of Independence, constructed by Philip Randolph, 1775–76. (Courtesy Smithsonian Institution)

Jefferson also bought personal-care products, including "tooth brushes." Jefferson was fastidious about dental care in an era when even elites (most famously George Washington) lost many of their teeth. Jefferson's efforts apparently paid off, as he reported late in life that he had lost only one tooth "by age, the rest continuing sound." In 1988 excavations, Colonial Williamsburg improbably discovered a bone handle of a tooth-brush inscribed "TH JEFFERSON," assumed to have belonged to him. Tooth-brushes were routinely advertised by the 1770s. A Philadelphia shop (one Jefferson frequented) listed toothbrushes in a June 1776 ad. They were just one among dozens of exotic consumer products, including "Hooper's female pills," "cripple curing oil," and pictures of scenes including "sea fights, land battles, Scripture pieces, flower pieces and a great variety of Japan prints." America in 1776 was already a consumer republic. Jefferson continued to pursue other interests even as July 4 approached. In June, he paid admission to see a monkey on display in the city. (Philadelphia's zoo, the first of its kind in America, was not chartered until 1859.) In early July, he obtained a ther-mometer, soon to be followed by a barometer. These allowed him to keep a weather diary, one he maintained for almost five decades. July 4 was a nice day in the city, at 76 degrees Fahrenheit.[21]

On July 2, after a month's delay, the Congress had approved Richard Henry Lee's resolution "that these United Colonies are, and of right ought to be, free and independent States, that they are absolved from all allegiance to the British Crown." John Adams was exuberant, writing to his wife Abigail that the "Second Day of July 1776, will be the most memorable Epocha, in the History of America.—I am apt to believe that it will be celebrated, by succeeding Generations, as the great anniversary Festival. It ought to be commemorated, as the Day of Deliverance by solemn Acts of Devotion to God Almighty." Procedurally, what happened in Congress on July 2 was more significant than what happened on July 4. But because of the soaring language of the Declaration, Americans came to regard the 4th as the "most memorable Epocha," not July 2.[22]

Jefferson promoted the Declaration, sending drafts and final copies to friends, still grumbling about the changes Congress had made. His college friend John Page encouraged him about the Declaration and the war: "I am highly pleased with your Declaration. God preserve the united States." Citing Ecclesiastes 9:11 and a poem by Joseph Addison, Page assured Jefferson, "We know the Race is not to the swift nor the Battle to the strong. Do you not think an Angel rides in the Whirlwind and directs this Storm?" Jefferson did not disagree with such providential sentiments. Many self-described deists, such as Ben Franklin, believed in God's providence. Sometimes Jefferson wondered if *only* the providence of God was saving the American cause. Jefferson was discouraged by the Patriots' recruiting efforts, especially as compared to those of the British. He told Richard Henry Lee that "our camps recruit slowly, amazing slowly. God knows in what it will end. The finger of providence has as yet saved us by retarding the arrival of Ld. Howe's [redcoat] recruits," who were preparing an invasion of New York City.[23]

Jefferson told Lee that he was "under a sacred obligation to go home" to attend to Martha, who had suffered a miscarriage, but business kept him in Philadelphia for another two months due to the "painful necessity" of establishing the new American government. Some of this business was technical, some symbolic and ceremonial. The symbolic elements were essential, since previous rituals and images associated with the British nation needed replacing. For example, Jefferson sent John Page a new prayer by Congress's chaplain. It was much like the old prayer used to open sessions except it omitted prayers for the monarch.[24]

Congress also tasked Jefferson, Adams, and Franklin with designing an official seal of the United States. Adams proposed an image from Greek mythology: Hercules choosing between virtue and vice. This reflected Adams's conviction that the fate of the new republic hinged on its moral character. Jefferson and Franklin preferred biblical images from Exodus. Jefferson proposed "the Children of Israel in the Wilderness, led by a Cloud by day, and a Pillar of Fire by night." Franklin suggested a more dramatic scene of "Moses lifting up his Wand, and dividing the Red Sea, and Pharaoh, in his Chariot overwhelmed with the Waters." Franklin also proposed a national motto: "Rebellion to Tyrants is Obedience to God." This was a saying that Franklin seems to have coined. Jefferson liked it so much that he adopted it as a personal motto.[25]

The committee ultimately adopted Franklin's image and motto, and reported it to Congress. The seal included on the other side "the Eye of Providence in a radiant Triangle whose Glory extends over the Shield." This image was emblazoned with the motto "E pluribus unum." The busy Congress tabled the report and would take no action on a seal until 1780, when it commissioned a new design. In 1782 it finally approved what remains our national seal today, including the eye of providence. Jefferson's Exodus motif did not survive. This makes it even more conspicuous that Jefferson and Franklin—two of the Founders most influenced by deism—would want to make a Bible scene the national seal. Their proposal suggests the power of the Exodus narrative concerning a beleaguered nation saved from tyranny through God's providence.[26]

By August's end Jefferson prepared to leave Philadelphia. He settled accounts and made purchases of goods difficult to obtain in Virginia. These included "guitar strings" and twelve pairs of shoes, six for himself and six for Martha. He returned to Monticello, but could not avoid politics for long, as the new House of Delegates was meeting in Williamsburg. Jefferson and many of his colleagues felt that state politics were as important as national affairs, if not more so. Jefferson also wanted to put Virginia on solid ground as a newly independent state.[27]

One of the new delegates in Williamsburg was Princeton-educated James Madison. Eight years younger than Jefferson, Madison would become Jefferson's most important ally and a lifelong friend. Jefferson already knew Madison's family. Only months before he had loaned Madison's cousin, the Reverend James Madison, money for books. Rev. Madison and Jefferson had both studied law with George Wythe, but Madison chose to become an Anglican minister instead of a lawyer. Rev. Madison was chaplain to the House of Delegates before becoming president of the College of William and Mary in 1777.[28]

Madison the future president had studied with the Reverend John Witherspoon, the Presbyterian leader of the College of New Jersey at Princeton and arguably the most influential pastor in America. New Jersey elected Witherspoon to the Continental Congress, where he was the only active pastor to sign the Declaration. As a student at Princeton from 1769 to 1772, Madison received a rigorous classical and Christian education. Completing his undergraduate degree in just two years, Madison stayed on for graduate study in law and in biblical Hebrew, supervised by Witherspoon. Madison may have entertained thoughts of entering the ministry like his cousin. In the end, he found his calling in political service and constitution making.[29]

Madison and Jefferson agreed on reforms needed in Virginia, especially disestablishing the Anglican Church. The church in Virginia, as in England, Scotland, and most of the colonies, performed essential social functions such as poor relief, and received tax support and protected status in law. This is what it meant to have an "establishment of religion," as Madison's First Amendment would put it. Madison, Jefferson, and legions of evangelical dissenters, particularly Baptists, wanted the new state government to terminate the Anglican Church's preferred standing. Or at least they wanted non-Anglicans to stop having to give the Church of England tax support.

Jefferson and Madison both knew of Locke and other Enlightenment writers' arguments for religious liberty. Madison cultivated a more visceral commitment to religious freedom as he observed persecution against Virginia dissenters in the 1760s and '70s. Dozens of Baptist preachers were jailed for not complying with the establishment's rules about who could preach and under what circumstances. Shortly after returning to Virginia from New Jersey, Madison wrote a friend about the "diabolical Hell conceived principle of persecution" raging in Virginia. He reported that five or six pastors were in jail in a neighboring county for preaching what amounted to orthodox Christian beliefs. It was not just the civil authorities who perpetrated these outrages. "To their eternal Infamy the Clergy can furnish their Quota of Imps for such business," Madison lamented. "This vexes me the most of any thing whatever." He asked his friend to pray for a revival of "liberty of conscience" in Virginia.[30]

Jefferson heartily agreed with Madison's sentiments. As historian Kevin Gutzman notes, for Jefferson liberty of conscience was "the basis of all other freedom." Jefferson realized that if a state church persecuted evangelicals, it would surely persecute the heterodox as well. As a young man, Jefferson had quietly developed a skeptical streak through the influence of Bolingbroke and other writers. He regarded state churches as emblematic of all that was wrong with institutional Christianity. Christianity would return to its healthy original form only if Americans lanced the boil of the church-state alliance. At Madison's urging, the state had committed itself to the "free exercise" of religion in the June 1776 Virginia Declaration of Rights. Its sixteenth article asserted that "religion, or the duty which we owe to our Creator, and the manner of discharging it, can be directed only by reason and conviction, not by force or violence, and therefore all men are equally entitled to the free exercise of religion, according to the dictates of conscience." This did not quite disestablish the Anglican Church. Some observers (such as Patrick Henry) believed an establishment could coexist with religious freedom. Dissenters, however, barraged the legislature with petitions for disestablishment.[31]

Religion and politics always make for a volatile combination, and the debates over jettisoning the establishment became vicious. Was getting rid of the establishment an attack on Christianity itself? Jefferson recalled that the debates over the dissenters' petitions "brought on the severest contests in which I have ever been engaged." Virginia's process was not exceptional, however, as most other states went through disestablishment debates during the Revolutionary era. Some, including neighboring North Carolina, had an easier time achieving disestablishment than Virginia did. North Carolina's 1776 constitution ended its (light) Anglican establishment and promised that no one would be compelled to attend or financially support a particular church. Virginia did not formalize the voluntary financial support of churches until a decade later.[32]

Jefferson jotted notes for a speech on disestablishment that he likely delivered to the Virginia assembly during late 1776. His sketch gives us an unvarnished view of his argument for religious freedom. He reviewed the long history of persecution of dissenters and apostates in English history. He insisted that the "spirit of the times" was "in favor of the rights of conscience." To the objection that religion would decline if disestablished, Jefferson cited Jesus's words in the Gospel of Matthew 16:18: "Upon this

rock I will build my church; and the gates of hell shall not prevail against it."
This was a key contention, one that Locke also made. If Jesus did not use
coercion to bolster his religion, why should his followers? Jefferson, whose
admiration for Jesus's teachings grew over time, routinely employed Jesus's
example to argue against state-supported religion. He quoted Matthew 16:18
again at the end of his speech, suggesting that supporters of an established
church lacked confidence that Christianity could stand on its own merits.
Christian dissenters agreed with this reasoning. The Reverend John Todd of
the Hanover Presbytery of Virginia commended Jefferson for his Bill for
Establishing Religious Freedom by citing that same passage in Matthew 16.[33]

Jefferson, Madison, and their dissenting allies made substantial but
incomplete progress toward disestablishment in 1776. The legislature
exempted dissenters from taxes supporting the Anglican Church, and they
abolished penalties for failure to attend church. Legislators left open the
possibility of a "general assessment," however. Under a general assessment,
people would pay religious taxes, but they could designate the church to
receive the tax, rather than the funds all going to one denomination. Baptists
still saw the general assessment as "pregnant with various evils destructive to
the rights and privileges of religious society." Jefferson sought to put religious practice on an entirely voluntary basis with his Bill for Establishing
Religious Freedom, which he drafted in 1777. Progress was slow during the
Revolution, however, and Jefferson's bill would not become law, under
Madison's guidance, until 1786.[34]

Reforms concerning slavery were even slower to develop. Some
reforms actually made slavery more punitive. Jefferson helped to make
penalties for lawbreaking bondspeople more severe. White criminals were
set to labor in proportion to their offenses, but Jefferson wanted to expel
enslaved offenders from the country, freeing whites from the "wickedness"
of such slaves. White Virginians failed to approve any plan for statewide
gradual emancipation, and the legislature allowed private manumissions
only starting in 1782. Jefferson was not deeply involved in the manumission
initiative, which gave white masters an option to free their enslaved people.
The fact that the legislature did not yet require expatriation of these freed
slaves suggests that some Virginia whites were more prepared than Jefferson
to accept a growing free black population.[35]

Jefferson reported in Notes on the State of Virginia that a proposed
amendment would also have enacted a program of gradual emancipation, by

which children of slaves would eventually be freed and colonized elsewhere. The fate of that emancipation plan is uncertain. Jefferson did not originally want this gradual emancipation scheme published with the rest of *Notes on the State of Virginia*. Jefferson left the impression in *Notes* that such a plan would be formally introduced in Virginia, but it does not appear that it ever was. In his *Autobiography*, Jefferson explained that the emancipation plan was "kept back" from the official slate of reforms because "the public mind would not yet bear the proposition." Jefferson had claimed in *A Summary View of the Rights of British America* that white Virginians longed to abolish slavery but were kept from doing so by the crown's disallowance. (Virginia did stop the importation of enslaved people in 1778, via a bill that Jefferson may have written.) The cool reception he described toward the proposed emancipation plan seems more plausible than his claims about white Virginians wishing to end slavery. We do not know whether emancipation itself, or the costs and complexities involved with expatriation, generated the most resistance in the "public mind" to Jefferson's tentative proposal.[36]

Still, Jefferson wrote in providential terms in his *Autobiography* about the coming of emancipation. "Nothing is more certainly written in the book of fate than that these people are to be free. Nor is it less certain that the two races, equally free, cannot live in the same government." As Jefferson explained in *Notes*, the prejudices of whites and "ten thousand recollections, by the blacks, of the injuries they have sustained" made their mutual animosity intractable. Seemingly anticipating the 1791 slave uprising in French colonial Saint-Domingue, which ultimately led to Haitian independence in 1804, he predicted that if both races were free, it would "produce convulsions which will probably never end but in the extermination of the one or the other race." Emancipation would bring great peril for masters, if not handled properly.[37]

In May 1777, Martha gave birth to a boy, whom they may have named Thomas. The baby lived only two weeks. Mary ("Polly") Jefferson was likely conceived about five or six months later, and Martha gave birth to her in August 1778. Daughter Martha ("Patsy") and Mary were the only two of Thomas and Martha Jefferson's children to survive into adulthood. Mary, however, would die at the end of Jefferson's first term as president, due to complications during childbirth.[38]

Serving as a legislator afforded Jefferson time for working on home and business matters, including his first house at Monticello. The operation was impressive. In 1778 he commissioned a stonemason to make three columns to grace the house. He credited his onsite brickmaker for "ninety thousand workable bricks made," and agreed to pay him for another one hundred thousand bricks. That August, Jefferson recorded that enslaved bricklayers installed more than fourteen thousand bricks as they built up walls. Jefferson also ordered twelve hundred feet of flooring planks. By late 1778 the "middle building" of the house, containing a parlor and a library for Jefferson's book collection, was roofed. One of Jefferson's friends warned him about the "exorbitant prices" of skilled construction workers during wartime. Jefferson pressed forward, however, hiring British deserters with a reputation for drunkenness as house joiners.[39]

Jefferson also had a canal dug at Shadwell, where his father had constructed a wheat mill that customers paid to use. A flood destroyed the mill a year after the Jefferson home there burned. By 1777, Jefferson began restoring the mill and creating a canal that would make it easier to access via the Rivanna River. Expensive and frequently delayed, the canal was not completed until his second term as president. In 1778, however, he told business associate Isaac Zane that he was "engaged in a great work in the canal way." He inquired whether Zane would be willing to sell him a modern spirit level tool, an improvement over old-fashioned levels, which used a plumb line to ensure that walls were straight. Jefferson told Zane that having the updated level would be convenient, since he was "settled in a country where god almighty has rendered the art of leveling as requisite as in any part of his creation." He really wanted that level, telling Zane to "fix your own price." Zane apparently did not sell it.[40]

Meanwhile, in the first full war year of 1776, America's Continental Army endured one disaster after another. The year concluded, however, with Washington's victories at Trenton, New Jersey, and at Princeton (in 1777). After that, the war in the North descended into stalemate, despite the Americans' brilliant victory at Saratoga, New York, in 1777. In 1778, Ben Franklin and diplomats in Paris secured a much-needed alliance with France, without which America likely would have lost the Revolutionary War. Later that year, the British turned their attention to the South. They imagined they could stir Loyalist resistance in the plantation-rich southern states. The British campaign began with actions in Georgia and South Carolina, but Virginia politicians feared that an attack on their state was inevitable.

Jefferson was elected governor of Virginia in 1779. He replaced Patrick Henry, who was constitutionally limited to three consecutive one-year terms. Jefferson narrowly defeated his college friend John Page. He took a thoroughly republican view of officeholding. "In a virtuous government, and more especially in times like these," he told Richard Henry Lee, "public offices are, what they should be, burdens to those appointed to them which it would be wrong to decline, though foreseen to bring with them intense labor and great private loss." Public office was a short-term responsibility, not a place of profit to be sought and held indefinitely. For some politicians, this kind of republican rhetoric was just talk. Jefferson seems honestly not to have relished the idea of becoming governor, however. He was aware of challenges facing the state, especially the feared invasion, and he had already developed his lifelong concern about the trade-offs between public service and private financial stability. He would have even graver reservations about the office by the time he was finished.[41]

Jefferson had been frustrated by his inability to effect educational reform, so as governor he updated the faculty and curriculum at William and Mary. Limited to just six professorships, Jefferson abolished the college's positions in divinity, in Greek and Latin (which would be covered at earlier stages of education), and in oriental languages. He replaced them with faculty in anatomy and medicine, in law and government, and in modern languages. Dropping the divinity professor, to Jefferson, was a natural result of disestablishing the Anglican Church. Although scholars routinely contend that Jefferson had a secular vision for William and Mary and later for the University of Virginia, "secular" is an imprecise term in this context. Jefferson's broader reform scheme for William and Mary, which was not formally adopted, still envisioned the faculty members teaching religious subjects such as moral philosophy, Hebrew, and ecclesiastical history and law. Plus, Jefferson demonstrated his fascination with Native American languages and culture by proposing that the college appoint a "missionary" to study Indian societies.[42]

Jefferson and the state's leaders were preoccupied with the British Army and Navy in the east, and with Britain's Indian allies in the west. British forces revealed just how vulnerable the state was shortly before Jefferson became governor. In 1779, the British struck Portsmouth on the southeastern coast. They quickly overwhelmed Fort Nelson, a badly undermanned installation guarding the seaport. The British also assaulted Suffolk before withdrawing, uninterested in establishing a permanent foothold in the state yet. Patrick Henry's government delayed for several days before ordering up the state militia. By the time militiamen could get into position, most of the damage was done. All told, the British destroyed or captured 137 ships in Virginia, and millions of pounds worth of goods and supplies. More than five hundred bondspeople (by some estimates as many as fifteen hundred) left on retreating British ships, reminding white owners of their most-feared scenario: slave rebellion.[43]

In these grim years Congress repeatedly asked the states to hold days of public thanksgiving, prayer, and fasting. Many Americans believed that public expressions of religion were better done at the state level than the national, an inclination that culminated in the First Amendment's ban on Congress making laws respecting an establishment of religion. The amendment did not originally limit state expressions of devotion, or even prohibit state establishments of religion. During the Revolution, the national government routinely recommended days of prayer and fasting to the states. Several months after Jefferson became governor, Congress again circulated a request that the states hold a day of prayer and thanksgiving. Jefferson complied, signing and endorsing a proclamation summoning Virginians to meet in churches on the appointed day in 1779. The language of the prayer day proclamation was theologically specific and providential. Congress asked for prayer for the church, the nation, and the war. They enjoined Americans to pray that God "would go forth with our hosts and crown our arms with victory; that he would grant to his church, the plentiful effusions of divine grace, and pour out his holy spirit on all ministers of the gospel; that he would bless and prosper the means of education, and spread the light of Christian knowledge through the remotest corners of the earth . . . that he would graciously be pleased to turn the hearts of our enemies, and to dispense the blessings of peace to contending nations." This kind of congressional proclamation echoed Jefferson's 1774 Virginia resolution for a day of fasting. In 1785, Madison also introduced a Jefferson-framed bill that would have authorized the Virginia governor to declare prayer days, threatening pastors with fines if they did not cooperate. These instances give a fuller context to Jefferson's church-state views than his celebrated "wall of separation" letter (1802) might imply. Jefferson would not declare prayer days as president, believing that this issue was best left to the discretion of states and/or churches. Otherwise, however, Jefferson did little to manifest what today we would call a "strict separationist" approach to church-state relations.[44]

Despite Congress's prayers for peace, a season of chastisement was coming. Jefferson, elected to a second one-year term, echoed the looming dread when he wrote that "we are threatened with a formidable attack from the northward on our Ohio settlements and from the southern Indians on our frontiers convenient to them, our eastern country is exposed to invasion from the British Army in Carolina." Charleston, South Carolina, had fallen to the British, and the British would humiliate American forces at Camden, South Carolina, in August 1780.[45]

The war's horrors had not fully descended on Virginia yet. Some of the thousands of British and Hessian troops who had surrendered at the Battle of Saratoga came to be housed in Albemarle County. Jefferson felt that he and other Virginia gentlemen should show them hospitality, at least to the officers. If they did not, then it might suggest that "humanity was kicked out of doors" in America, he wrote. Soon Jefferson initiated a friendship with several of the German officers, including a chaplain named Kohle. Jefferson took a liking to Pastor Kohle, telling one correspondent, "He is more American than British," presumably meaning American in sentiment. Jefferson loaned books to Kohle and other officers. One of the books he loaned to Kohle was the church father Origen's *Against Celsus*, one of the early church's most important apologetic texts. Wartime conditions hardly precluded continued interest in such classics.[46]

Jefferson sometimes referred to Origen in metaphysical musings, especially when he was arguing that the early church believed in the materiality of "spirit." For Jefferson and many Enlightenment thinkers, there was no realm of the purely spiritual, if "spiritual" meant "immaterial." The human soul and even God himself were material substances. In 1820, Jefferson told his protégé William Short, "I am a Materialist." Jefferson advised John Adams the same year that he did not know when the "heresy of immaterialism, this masked atheism, crept" into the church. "Jesus taught nothing of it. He told us indeed that 'God is a spirit,' but he has not defined what a spirit is, nor said that it is not matter." Citing a Latin translation of Origen, as well as Tertullian and Justin Martyr, Jefferson contended that "the ancient fathers generally, if not universally, held [spirit] to be matter: light and thin indeed, an ethereal gas; but still matter." Jefferson's philosophical discussions transpired in intellectual contexts often framed by church history and biblical studies.[47]

Jefferson's time for leisurely discussion of books and metaphysical theories did diminish as the war pressed on him. The storm finally crashed upon

Virginia a few days after Christmas in 1780. The turncoat American general Benedict Arnold, now working for the British, initiated the long-feared invasion. Delays in intelligence gathering at Richmond, the new state capital, made the situation more dire. Within weeks Jefferson was blaming a "fatal inattention" by commanders for failing to stop Arnold's marauders. By the beginning of 1781, Jefferson called up thousands of state militiamen, but it was too late. Arnold's army roared up the James River. By January 5 they were bombarding Richmond. The state government and militia dissolved into chaos.[48]

Jefferson and most whites in the city fled, with only bondspeople left behind at his Richmond home. Redcoats, bearing a pair of handcuffs in which to take away the governor, charged into the house. They raided Jefferson's ample stores of wine and "Antigua rum," guzzling some and disposing of the rest. They confronted George Granger, one of the enslaved men, demanding to know Jefferson's whereabouts. "He's gone to the mountains," Granger exclaimed. His son, Isaac Granger, recalled that it "seemed like the Day of Judgment was come."[49]

4. "It Is Not in My Power to Do Anything More"

Spring 1781 was the darkest season of Thomas Jefferson's public career, at least until his final year as president. Virginia was in utter disarray, as was his governorship. Members of the state government had fled to Charlottesville when a newly invigorated British Army, led by Lord Charles Cornwallis and cavalry officer Banastre Tarleton, menaced Richmond once again. In April, the Jeffersons lost another infant child, Lucy Elizabeth, who was only four months old. Jefferson dashed back and forth between affairs of state and family. He was worried about Martha, telling a member of the governor's council that "Mrs. Jefferson [is] in a situation in which I would not wish to leave her." Meanwhile, Continental commanders Baron von Steuben and the Marquis de Lafayette, a young French officer, begged Jefferson to bolster Virginia's enlistments and supplies. Jefferson told Lafayette, "It is not in my power to do anything more." The legislature held most of the authority in Virginia. Jefferson was fed up with being governor. He would step down as soon as possible.[1]

Jefferson was convinced that he was not experienced or commanding enough to be a good wartime governor. Struggling to get the legislature to take decisive military action, he pled with George Washington to come home from the North to be the state's savior, but in what precise capacity was not clear. His countrymen always looked to Washington as their protector, Jefferson insisted, and "your appearance among them I say would restore full confidence of salvation, and would render them equal to whatever is not impossible." Jefferson could not rally people the way Washington could. Washington was also the ultimate solution to Jefferson's longing to leave the governorship. "A few days will bring to me that period of relief which the constitution has prepared for those oppressed with the labours of my office, and a long declared resolution of relinquishing it to abler hands has prepared my way for retirement." Jefferson's ideal scenario would not play out, however, as Washington was not able to come to Virginia yet. Still, Jefferson resolved that he would get out of office no matter who succeeded him, or if anyone *could* succeed him in that chaotic moment.[2]

Virginia officials finally assembled in Charlottesville to concoct a plan to counter the British offensive. The legislature gave Jefferson power to call up additional militiamen. Even then, Jefferson's focus was divided between reports of the British Army's movements, news of anti-government uprisings in far western Virginia, and fighting against Native Americans in the Ohio and Illinois territories. Jefferson would soon learn that the British, not Indians, were the most immediate threat to Charlottesville and Monticello. Until that happened, he seemed consumed with confronting relatively distant Indians and cultivating Native American allies where possible. The Continental Army commander Nathanael Greene wondered how Virginia could be so focused on "conquest abroad" when "ruin at home" was certain if Cornwallis was not stopped.[3]

Cornwallis sought to capture the disoriented Virginia leaders, so he sent Tarleton's cavalry to raid Charlottesville in June. Meanwhile, Jefferson's second term as governor was coming to a close. In peacetime, it would have been normal for the state to go a few days without a governor while the legislature chose a successor. Convening a full session of the legislature was going to be challenging, however, even before Tarleton's horde galloped into Charlottesville.[4]

Fifteen years later, Jefferson explained what transpired next, writing about himself in the third person. "His office was now near expiring, the country under invasion by a powerful army, no services but military of any avail, unprepared by his line of life and education for the command of armies, he believed it right not to stand in the way of talents better fitted than his own to the circumstances under which the country was placed. He therefore himself proposed to his friends in the legislature, that Genl. [Thomas] Nelson, who commanded the militia of the state, should be appointed Governor." Such a "union of the civil and military power in the same hands, at this time would greatly facilitate military measures." "Unprepared" for the duties put upon him, Jefferson wanted a military man installed in his place. His first choice was Washington, but the planter and militia commander Thomas Nelson would suffice.[5]

Jefferson explained that "this was the state of things when, his office having expired on the 2d June, and his successor not yet in place, Colo. Tarleton, with his regiment of horse, was detached by Ld. Cornwallis, to surprize him (supposed to be still governor) and the legislature now sitting in Charlottesville." Jefferson's status as governor was not as clear-cut as his legalistic rendering would have it. His term had indeed expired on June 2, but he continued to sign correspondence as governor until June 3. He was eligible for another term, but that was out of the question. It was not clear when he precisely stopped being governor, since the legislature had not chosen a successor, nor could it reasonably have been expected to do as its members fled west. He could have kept functioning as governor until the legislature could meet with a quorum, which is what some asked him to do. Instead, the state went leaderless for about ten days of deepening disarray. In Jefferson's absence, the legislators finally selected an acting governor without taking a proper vote, but only when they could find someone from the governor's council to serve. (The lieutenant governor had also stepped down when the government had relocated to Charlottesville.) When the legislature finally reconvened in Staunton, Virginia, it officially elected Thomas Nelson as governor on June 12. Given the existential threat Virginia was facing, Jefferson had surely put the state in an even worse situation.[6]

Not that Jefferson had no reason to fear for his personal safety after relinquishing his office. Tarleton's men nearly captured him when they entered Charlottesville. The retiring governor was hiding at Monticello. A Patriot scout dashed up the mountain before sunrise on June 4, telling Jefferson he had to leave. Jefferson arranged for his family to depart first, then he rode over to a neighboring mountaintop, one taller than Monticello's summit. There he trained his silver-plated mahogany telescope on the town below. Not seeing any activity, he was about to leave. Then, taking one last look, he spotted Tarleton's soldiers approaching the village.[7]

Jefferson went back to Monticello and shoved papers into his saddle-bags (suspecting the house would be burned). He got on his favorite horse, reportedly one of the swiftest in the state, and took off down the mountain. Tarleton's men arrived at Monticello five minutes later. The rest of Virginia's government was heading west to Staunton. Jefferson set off south, toward his distant property at Poplar Forest. This might have made more sense if he *was* still governor. The last thing the state could afford was to have its sitting governor taken prisoner. Tarleton's forces were already capturing some legislators in town. Jefferson was adamant that he was no longer governor, however. He was just a private citizen, fleeing with his family into the shaded forests south of Charlottesville.[8]

Virginia's remaining leaders were stunned by Tarleton's lightning raid. Jefferson's equally swift departure did not sit well with many. Sure, Jefferson had informed them he would not serve another term, but his handling of the invasion had been lackluster at best. Virginia officials were irritated and wanted to accuse someone for creating their disastrous circumstances. The obvious person to blame was no longer in their midst. Speaker of the House Benjamin Harrison made his feelings known about the state's "distressed condition from the sea to the mountains." Harrison was a religious skeptic like Jefferson, and he could rub people the wrong way. John Adams railed against Harrison while serving with him in the national Congress, writing in his diary that Harrison's "conversation [is] disgusting to every Man of Delicacy or decorum, Obscene, profane, impious, perpetually ridiculing the Bible, calling it the Worst Book in the World." Now Harrison turned his prickly disposition against the fleeing former governor. Harrison wrote an express letter from Staunton to a friend in Philadelphia, explaining that "we have now no Executive in the State. For want of a Senate the governor will act no more, and the remainder of the council will not get together. I hope we shall set these matters right next week."[9]

Richard Henry Lee, who had made the initial motion for independence in the Continental Congress, appealed to George Washington for help ten days after Jefferson's term expired. Virginia was at risk of total collapse. Meanwhile, the governor had "resigned his office." (This was not technically true: his term had expired.) "Thus, we remain without a government at a time when the most wise and most vigorous administration of public affairs can alone save us," Lee wrote. Like Jefferson, Lee hoped that Washington might come back to Virginia to lead the campaign against the British, and perhaps serve as a military ruler while Cornwallis menaced the state. "If relief comes not from you it will probably not come at all," Lee concluded. Rumors swirled that Washington would return to the state as a "dictator." Patrick Henry and other legislators in Staunton did propose that they appoint a dictator, or at least a "governor with enlarged powers." One Virginia

George Washington in 1772, painting by Charles Wilson Peale. (Courtesy Wikimedia Commons)

doctor wrote on June 11 that the state was without a governor, but that the assembly would soon "appoint a dictator at this dangerous crisis, and that General Washington will be dictator." General Washington remained unavailable, however, and cooler heads prevailed in the legislature, which voted against the plan for a dictator. The mere proposal of a wartime strongman illustrated the perplexity that gripped the state's leaders, who only months earlier had shown themselves unwilling to grant Jefferson autonomy to prosecute the war.[10]

Disgusted legislators also received a motion from delegate George Nicholas regarding Jefferson's behavior as governor. Although Nicholas represented Jefferson's Albemarle County, he was an ally of Patrick Henry. Apparently prompted by Henry, Nicholas proposed that the legislature make an inquiry "into the conduct of the Executive of this State for the last twelve months." This inquiry was not directed at Jefferson alone, as the governor's council had not performed well during the invasion, either. The inquiry was likely intended to demonstrate that the governor needed enhanced powers to confront Cornwallis. None of these nuances mattered to Jefferson, however, who took the inquiry as a savage assault on his honor. He would never get over this episode, nor would he forgive Patrick Henry.[11]

Jefferson seethed against George Nicholas, whom he called a "trifling body" who was "below contempt; he was more an object of pity." In a lurid metaphor, Jefferson compared Nicholas to minnows, which "go in and out of the fundament [anus] of a whale." Henry was "the whale himself," however, who was "discoverable enough by the turbulence of the water under which he moved." Herman Melville would not be born for another four decades, but from this moment Patrick Henry became Jefferson's white whale. Three years later, in the midst of James Madison's efforts to reform Virginia's laws, Jefferson told Madison that Henry was determined to oppose every legislative initiative they tried. "What we have to do," Jefferson concluded, "is devoutly to pray for [Henry's] death." Jefferson likely was joking, but he did make the statement in the encrypted code he and Madison used to preserve privacy. Jefferson's loathing for Henry would soften only slightly in the decades after Henry died in 1799.[12]

At isolated Poplar Forest, Jefferson began work on what would become *Notes on the State of Virginia*. The eclectic topics in *Notes* included the disrepair of Virginia's military forces, from its poorly armed militia to its nonexistent navy. This information bolstered Jefferson's explanation for why the state had done so badly during the invasion. Although the ailing Governor Nelson was also absent during much of his first month in office, the war in Virginia improved dramatically by September 1781. Supplies began finally to arrive, and Washington and his French allies focused on Virginia as the site of the decisive showdown of the war. Cornwallis squandered his advantage and hunkered his sickly army down at Yorktown. The British had taken in thousands of Virginia bondspeople, but then began to expel them from York-town due to disease and a lack of supplies. Jefferson lost about twenty-three enslaved people during the war. He grumbled that if the intent had been "to give them freedom [Cornwallis] would have done right, but it was to consign them to inevitable death from the small pox and putrid fever." When Wash-ington's army and French troops laid siege to Yorktown, it signaled the end for Cornwallis's forces. The British commander surrendered on October 17, 1781, heralding the triumph of the Patriots.[13]

With the war coming to a close, Virginia legislators were no longer in the mood for investigating Jefferson. Nevertheless, Jefferson accepted elec-tion to the House of Delegates and worked for the rest of 1781 "with a single object" in mind: clearing his name. The legislature sheepishly exonerated Jefferson from the "rumors" about his conduct. Lest anyone miss the point, the legislators passed a resolution proclaiming "in the strongest manner, to declare the high opinion which they entertain of Mr. Jefferson's ability, recti-tude and integrity, as Chief Magistrate of this Commonwealth." Satisfied, Jefferson resigned from the House, hoping to return to Monticello. In a sentiment he often repeated, Jefferson said he wanted nothing more than to retire to "my farm, my family and books."[14]

Albemarle County voters wanted him to keep serving, but he refused a seat in the House of Delegates in 1782. This was partly because Martha was pregnant again. She gave birth to a girl they named Lucy Elizabeth, the same name they had given the child who died thirteen months earlier. (It was not unusual to give babies the same name as deceased siblings.) Jefferson wrote a letter to his protégé, the future president James Monroe, explaining his desire to stay out of politics. The missive was, as historian Gordon Wood put it, the "most dispirited letter" Jefferson ever wrote. Though fifteen years younger than Jefferson, Monroe was becoming one of his key confidants. Monroe had served as a Continental Army officer and helped Jefferson coor-dinate the efforts of the Continentals and Virginia militia during the war. Now Monroe was studying law under Jefferson.[15]

Jefferson's republican ideals suggested that educated white men needed to set aside self-interest and be willing to serve in public office. He had already done that for more than a decade, however. His republican principles clashed with his Epicurean philosophy. This was an instance of how Jeffer-son's eclectic influences led to an unstable mix in his sense of direction. Jefferson was cognizant of Epicurean philosophy as a young man but gave it increasing attention starting in the early 1800s. "Epicurean" today connotes pleasure seeking. For Jefferson, however, the philosophy of Epicurus, the ancient Greek philosopher, idealized this-worldly tranquility and the avoidance of pain. His Epicurean principles rested uneasily with his republican ones, in that Epicurus advised avoidance of politics as much as possible. Jefferson was certain that the universe reflected a created order, whereas Epicurean philosophy classically posited that it did not. The Virginian also blamed public service for the growing derangement of his finances, having "so totally abandoned all attention to my private affairs as to permit them to run into great disorder and ruin." What did he have to show for all the difficulty entailed in public service? Jefferson narrowly avoided disgrace in the inquiry regarding his behavior as governor. That experience "inflicted a wound on my spirit which will only be cured by the all-healing grave," he confessed to Monroe.[16]

Jefferson's letter was candid, but he likely intended it to circulate among Virginia politicians, including the ones who were irritated by his flight from Charlottesville. Edmund Randolph saw the letter and wrote to James Madison. "The pathos of the composition is really great," Randolph commented, "and the wound, which he received by the late impeachment, is, as he says, to be cured only by the all-healing grave." Jefferson's message to the legislature was that he was hurt, worn out, and broke. It shouldn't ask him to keep giving more.[17]

Jefferson especially wanted a hiatus from public life because of Martha's dire illness. Ever since (the new) Lucy Elizabeth's birth, he confided to Monroe, his wife had been "dangerously ill." Friends of the Jeffersons were worried, and James Monroe, for one, prayed that "it may please heaven to restore our amiable friend [Martha] to health and thereby to you a friend whose loss you would always lament." But it was not to be.[18]

In her last days, the Jeffersons looked for solace to the works of the Anglican minister Laurence Sterne. In a rare instance of the couple's writing, they copied lines from Sterne's popular book *The Life and Opinions of Tristram Shandy*. The passage could not have been more appropriate:

> Time wastes too fast: every letter
> I trace tells me with what rapidity
> life follows my pen. The days and hours
> of it are flying over our heads like

clouds of windy day never to return—
more every thing presses on—and every
time I kiss thy hand to bid adieu, every absence which
follows it, are preludes to that eternal separation
which we are shortly to make!

Martha herself wrote out the lines up to "presses on." Then Thomas took up the pen and finished. The tender sentiments suggest the couple's mutual affection, and explain the deep pain that Jefferson experienced when Martha died on September 6, 1782. Many eighteenth-century marriages were more like business arrangements than affectionate unions, but the Jeffersons' marriage embodied a romantic ideal that Americans would come to prize in later decades. Thomas depended on Martha, and her death was the turning point of his personal life. Her passing sent him nearly into a "state of insensibility," his daughter Patsy recalled. According to recollections of Jefferson's bondspeople, he promised her before she died that he would never remarry.[19]

The "catastrophe" of Martha's tragic death, as Jefferson called it, raises counterfactuals. If she had lived roughly as long as Thomas, would he ever have gone to France? If he had not served in France, would he have become secretary of state and later president? Perhaps Jefferson would have done none of these things, and thus would rank as a lesser-known Founder, along the lines of a John Dickinson, Patrick Henry, or Thomas Paine. At least in 1782, Jefferson was telling friends that he was retired. He aspired to stay at Monticello, make his farms more profitable, and enjoy a life of privacy, books, and family. That dream died when Martha died, and her loss set his public life on a different trajectory. Jefferson wrote to his friend and admirer, the Marquis de Chastellux, that before her passing he had folded himself "in the arms of retirement, and rested all prospects of future happiness on domestic and literary objects. A single event wiped away all my plans and left me a blank which I had not the spirits to fill up."[20]

But he would fill up that blank. He started emerging from his "stupor" of grief a couple months after she died. Congress intuited that Jefferson would be amenable now to a diplomatic appointment in France, where the American delegation was negotiating the end of the Revolutionary War. He had once turned down a similar offer, but now "the state of my mind concurred in recommending the change of scene proposed," he wrote.

Leaving Polly and Lucy behind with relatives, he took Patsy and set out (he believed) to go to Paris at the end of 1782. But the ships they were to take got detained in port. Before they could leave Philadelphia, news arrived of the signing of the Treaty of Paris, bringing a formal conclusion to the Revolutionary War. No longer needed in France, Jefferson returned to Virginia and was promptly elected to Congress. In October 1783 he went back to Philadelphia again. Thoughts of permanent retirement to Monticello had evaporated by a year after Martha's death. As historian Darren Staloff notes, for Jefferson "the prospect of retirement was always more alluring than the reality." The mountaintop enticed him, but so did the pleasures and products of city life. As soon as he got back to Philadelphia, he began buying books from multiple city shops. Soon he borrowed $98 from James Madison. Ten days later he borrowed another $35 from Madison and bought a chessboard. Jefferson would settle his debts to Madison later, partly through acquiring books for him in Paris.[21]

Due to the turbulence of the last months of the war, and threats of mutiny by some Continental soldiers, Congress bounced from Philadelphia to Princeton, New Jersey, and finally to Annapolis, Maryland. Jefferson wanted Patsy, instead of traveling with him, to stay in Philadelphia to continue her studies. Worrying about her as a motherless eleven-year-old, Thomas earnestly gave Patsy advice on learning, morality, and theology. She had heard prophetic theories circulating that a recent earthquake (and maybe the conclusion of the Revolutionary War) might signal that the world would end soon. Thomas wanted to nip such notions in the bud. "Disregard those foolish predictions," he wrote from Annapolis. "The almighty has never made known to any body at what time he created it, nor will he tell any body when he means to put an end to it, if ever he means to do it." Most traditional Christians would have agreed that we cannot know the precise time of the end, but they would have bristled at Jefferson's question of whether Judgment Day would "ever" come at all. "As to preparations for that event," he continued, "the best way is for you to be always prepared for it." Turning moralistic, he told her that she should never do or say anything bad, but should simply obey her conscience. It was how God had designed her. "Our maker has given us all, this faithful internal Monitor, and if you always obey it, you will always be prepared for the end of the world: or for a much more certain event which is death. This must happen to all: it puts an end to the world as to us." If she wanted to be ready for death (or for Judgment Day), she should just never "do a wrong act." Never doing anything wrong was a high standard. Perhaps it is an understandable piece of advice, though, coming from a traveling widower to his nearly teenage daughter.[22]

The peripatetic Congress was not an inspiring venue for Jefferson to act on his revitalized political ambitions. Congress was effectively the only governing unit under the Articles of Confederation (there were no separate executive or judicial branches). Yet the legislature struggled to function. State leaders still did not see the national government as especially important. The Congress could rarely muster the simple majority quorum it needed for routine votes. In order to ratify the Treaty of Paris, it had to round up delegates from nine states, a truly herculean task. By the time it got the requisite number of state delegates together, the Congress had already missed the deadline to approve the treaty, notwithstanding the fact that the Treaty of Paris was arguably the most significant diplomatic achievement ever in American history. It put the new United States on independent footing and set up the enduring boundaries of the eastern half of the nation (with the exception of Florida). Congressmen worked out a technical solution to missing the deadline, but they couldn't even afford a courier to take the signed treaty to Europe. They had to get a French diplomat to pay for it instead. Most irritating to Jefferson, the salary for service in Congress was abysmal, often late coming, and did not cover members' basic travel expenses. He told Madison that the financial situation was "inconceivably mortifying." Due to his experience as general, George Washington was familiar with the difficulties of getting the Congress under the Articles to act swiftly. Jefferson, suffering another bout of debilitating headaches, wrote Washington that he supposed "the crippled state of Congress is not new to you . . . we are wasting our time and labour in vain efforts to do business."[23]

Jefferson did seek to address pressing issues such as the organization of the territories beyond Virginia. Virginia had formally ceded much of this territory to Congress in 1784, and Jefferson worked on a plan for dividing the territory into new states. He was already dreaming of westward expansion to ensure a steady supply of land for white farmers. He also hoped that "diffusing" the slave population in the west, combined with the cessation of importations of enslaved workers, would disperse the threat of slave rebellion and prepare whites for accepting gradual abolition. In *Notes on the State of Virginia* he made the classically republican but theologically ambiguous statement that "those who labour in the earth are the chosen people of God, if ever he had a chosen people, whose breasts he has made his peculiar deposit for substantial and genuine virtue." Historians have generally read this as an endorsement of the virtues of the yeoman farmer class, and Jefferson advocated rejecting vestiges of the feudal system of land tenure in favor of individual landownership as an engine of republican virtue. Jefferson rarely did much to reserve western lands for modest farmers, however. The most powerful farming interests in America after the ordinances of the 1780s generally were slave-owning planters (like Jefferson and his southern political allies), not those who actually "labored in the earth," whether yeoman farmers or enslaved workers.[24]

Jefferson's proposed 1784 land ordinance was a fulfillment of initiatives already begun before he arrived in Congress. Still, it is striking that the ordinance he sponsored would have prohibited slavery in the territories starting in 1800. It was a pioneering initiative, and not a concession that fellow southern delegates appreciated. Only one other southern member backed the idea. When the Ordinance of 1784 came up for a vote, it failed (as Jefferson recalled) due to the absence of one New Jersey delegate. "Thus we see the fate of millions unborn hanging on the tongue of one man, and heaven was silent in that awful moment," Jefferson wrote. The ordinance was arguably the boldest domestic antislavery measure Jefferson ever proposed. His work toward restricting slavery's advancement in America would become exceedingly limited after this moment. This diminution was due to strident opposition from other white southerners, his growing fear of national government power, and the lucrative global trade in short-staple cotton that followed Eli Whitney's 1793 invention of the cotton gin. Congress went on to pass the Northwest Ordinance of 1787, which prohibited slavery in future states north of the Ohio River. Jefferson's ordinance in 1784 had envisioned slavery's prohibition south of the Ohio, too, although not until 1800. By the time the 1787 ordinance passed, Jefferson was well into his diplomatic tenure in Paris. In 1819–20, when Congress began to consider limiting the northern section of the Louisiana Purchase territory to non-slave-owning farmers, the retired Jefferson expressed grave alarm. The time for Jefferson the emancipationist had passed.[25]

In May 1784, Congress again appointed Jefferson to serve as diplomat in France. The appointment ended Jefferson's brief but momentous career as a legislator. Arguably his greatest legislative success (since the Declaration was not really a law) was the Virginia Statute for Establishing Religious Freedom, which Madison shepherded to final passage in 1786 while Jefferson was in Paris. Madison and Patrick Henry had engaged in months of controversy over whether the state should continue to collect taxes to support churches, or whether (as Madison, Jefferson, and evangelical dissenters preferred) the state should stop financially backing any churches at all. This renewed the religious freedom controversy that had erupted at the beginning of the Revolution. The Virginia legislature finally implemented entire religious liberty, to Jefferson's relief, with no forced religious observances or civil disadvantages for one's religious beliefs. Madison kept Jefferson apprised of the fate of the religion bill after Jefferson left for Paris. Jefferson told Madison that he was glad that Henry and the "Episcopalians" had shown their "teeth and fangs" again. He predicted that the controversy would rouse the "dissenters" to fight to end the established church—and so it did. In the meantime, Jefferson advised Madison that they needed to take their opposition against the hated Henry to a higher level, and recommended that they start praying for him to die. Henry did not die quite yet, but he lost this great legal struggle against Madison, Jefferson, and their Baptist allies.[26]

On July 5, 1784, Jefferson, Patsy, and Jefferson's nineteen-year-old enslaved cook James Hemings boarded the *Ceres* in Boston and headed for Europe. Hemings was later described as a "bright mulatto," a light-skinned person still recognizable as having African ancestry. James was part of the extended Hemings clan, which became such an essential part of Jefferson's world once he married Martha. The father of both Martha Jefferson and James Hemings was John Wayles, who fathered the Hemings siblings with Elizabeth Hemings. Jefferson wanted James to learn the art of French cooking. He did not expect to stay long in France, but he relished the idea of having a French-trained chef at Monticello.[27]

Starting in 1785, however, Congress made him the permanent replacement to Benjamin Franklin as minister to France. Staying until the beginning of the French Revolution in 1789, Jefferson worked to secure favorable commercial arrangements for the new American nation. Winning the Revolutionary War did not alter the fact that the United States remained a fledgling, vulnerable country. Franklin and Jefferson both needed to do whatever it took to avoid a potentially fatal rupture between the United States and France. The United States struggled mightily to sustain its booming wartime economy as well as to free itself from restrictive mercantilist regulations that

European nations, especially Britain, had placed on America during the colonial era. Jefferson had enormous confidence in America's vast natural resources to play a commanding role in global trade. The trick was getting the country on a level footing with other nations. Thus he labored feverishly to convince the French to enter trade agreements for American-harvested products including rice, tobacco, and whale oil, a chief source of light on nighttime city streets. The latter issue even led Jefferson to produce a 1788 pamphlet entitled *Observations on the Whale-Fishery*. Jefferson was not able to get all the concessions he wanted from France, but before leaving he secured the Consular Convention of 1788, which regularized diplomatic protocols between the two nations. The treaty went under consideration just as the new U.S. Constitution was going into effect. It became the first treaty ratified by the new Senate under the Constitution, representing a major achievement in Jefferson's diplomatic career.[28]

Paris was a vast and intoxicating metropolis to the Jeffersons and James Hemings. The population of Philadelphia at the beginning of the 1780s was about 32,000, while Paris's was at least 550,000. For James Hemings, the most striking difference from America was that slavery did not exist in France, although French merchants and shippers maintained an active trade in enslaved people and slave-grown crops in its colonies, especially Saint-Domingue (Haiti). Concerned about the growth of the black population, France banned blacks—whatever their status—from entering the country in 1777. James Hemings and his sister Sally, who would come to Paris a couple years after James, were not really supposed to be there, but both were light-skinned and easy to overlook. Jefferson was at least supposed to notify French authorities that they were with him, however. He didn't. French officials did not enforce the rules strictly, especially for foreign dignitaries. As enslaved people, the Hemingses would likely have been able successfully to petition French officials for their freedom, but they did not attempt to do so.[29]

As a diplomat, Jefferson was expected to host many guests, and he was determined that his household, library, and larder would reflect the latest French styles, despite his limited budget. As soon as he arrived in the country, he began buying coffee, liqueurs, nuts, lace ruffles and, of course, books. He spent countless hours at Parisian bookstores, and would eventually send back a collection of titles that occupied 250 feet of shelves at Monticello. Then there was fashion: he immediately spent 167 livres on clothes for Patsy, and almost 100 livres for a sword and sword belt for himself. Jefferson insisted

View of Paris from the Pont Neuf, painting by Nicolas-Jean-Baptiste Raguenet, 1763. (Courtesy Wikimedia Commons)

that Patsy have hand-tailored clothes from head to foot before she could go out in the city. As was the case with his tenure in Congress, his stipend in his new role did not cover his expenses. Toward the end of 1784 he complained to James Monroe that the Jeffersons' household "stile is far below the level, yet it absorbs the whole allowance. . . . I think my expences should be paid in a stile equal to that of those with whom I am classed." Jefferson rented the Hôtel de Langeac for most of his time in Paris, the fanciest house in which he had yet lived. It was considered quite elegant even by Parisian standards. "It suits me in every circumstance but the price," he told Abigail Adams.[30]

Jefferson intended many purchases to ultimately find their way back to Monticello. These included a number of paintings, typically copies of biblical scenes by Old Masters. He engaged in a spate of art buying in February 1785 when he attended an auction and acquired paintings depicting the prodigal son, Saint Peter weeping, and Salome (the daughter of Herodias) bearing the head of John the Baptist. This last scene, based on passages in the Gospels of Matthew and Mark, came to hang in the parlor at Monticello. The great painters of the sixteenth to the eighteenth centuries commonly took biblical stories as their subjects, either by commission or by choice. Those biblical scenes would make up a substantial part of Monticello's notable (if mostly derivative) art collection. Jefferson would later tell American visitors to Europe that European art was "too expensive for the state of wealth among us. It would be useless therefore and preposterous for us to endeavor to make ourselves connoisseurs in those arts." But Jefferson could not resist sampling the art market in Paris, though he was often uncertain whether he was buying copies or the originals.[31]

Jefferson's spending on art, books, clothes, and wine resulted both from his obligations as a public official and from his ideal of private pleasure and tranquility. Living within his means hardly seemed possible, especially when the buying opportunities of urban markets and the requirements of hospitality demanded that he keep on spending. To his horror, Congress reduced the stipends for diplomats instead of increasing them, and he felt that America's diplomatic corps was required to live in near-poverty conditions as compared to those of other nations. Observers confirmed that he was stylistically the "plainest" of the diplomats at the French court (despite his sumptuous quarters at the Hôtel de Langeac). Whoever was to blame, Jefferson's spending habits undermined his Epicurean ideal of a tranquil mind, as indebtedness and perceived lack of provision harried him throughout his adult life.[32]

Jefferson elaborated on financial deprivation in an illuminating letter to Monroe in summer 1785. For his myriad expenses, he said,

> I have already paid twenty eight thousand livres and have still more to pay. For the greatest part of this I have been obliged to anticipate my salary from which however I shall never be able to repay it. I find that by a rigid economy bordering however on *meanness* I can save perhaps five hundred livres a month in the summer at least. The residue goes for expences so much of course and of necessity that I cannot avoid them without abandoning *all respect to my public character*. Yet I will pray you to touch this string which I know to be a tender one with Congress with the utmost delicacy. I had rather be *ruined in my fortune than in their esteem* [italics added].

To gentlemen like Jefferson, there were things more dreaded than debt. Among them were "meanness" and common living, and peers' lack of "esteem" for one's "public character." This is why the Virginia legislature's inquiry into his performance as governor was so painful. His gentlemanly concern for appearances is also why he kept spending even though it was driving him ever further into debt.[33]

Jefferson consistently praised frugality, though that ideal contradicted the way he lived, or the way he felt forced to live. He came to regard financial discipline almost as a form of salvation, if only he could achieve it. He told his old friend and sometime political rival John Page that "would a missionary appear who would make frugality the basis of his religious system, and go thro the land preaching it up as the only road to salvation, I would join his school tho' not generally disposed to seek my religion out[side] of the dictates of my own reason and feelings of my own heart." The simple, thrifty lives modeled by Stoic philosophers and by Jesus of Nazareth attracted him to their teachings. But he certainly felt that he must meet the gentlemanly conventions of diplomatic and public life. This was a major source of personal philosophical dissonance that Jefferson could not resolve.[34]

In France, Jefferson had come to the great wine center of Europe. The wine trade in France was growing during the 1700s, with aged wines becoming especially lucrative. The best Bordeaux wines were fifteen or twenty times more expensive than ordinary non-aged wines that common people drank. Like most diplomats, Jefferson spent vast sums on wine. In mid-August 1784 he paid almost 500 livres/francs for eighteen dozen bottles of Bordeaux. He was surrounded by friends and colleagues who also bought a great deal of wine, including his fellow diplomat Benjamin Franklin, whose Paris cellar contained over a thousand bottles by the late 1770s. Franklin's finances were not nearly as troubled as Jefferson's, however. John Adams also bought hundreds of bottles of French wine. The parsimonious Adams became alarmed about import duties on wine when he was transferred to London, however, so he begged Jefferson to assume responsibility for the bottles he had ordered.[35]

Jefferson wanted not only to meet genteel standards for his Paris household but to find the best educational options for Patsy. He decided to place her in a convent school, the Abbaye Royale de Panthemont, reportedly the most expensive girls' school in the city. At first glance, this was a surprising choice, as Jefferson had inherited the anti-Catholic sentiments common to most Protestants in colonial America. For example, Jefferson called French Catholic colleges "lazy" and "monkish," and he told Abigail Adams that while he loved the French people with all his heart, they needed a "better religion and a better form of government [that is, not monarchy]." Jefferson repeatedly had to answer critics in Virginia who questioned his decision to place Patsy at the convent. He told his friend James Maury, Jr., the son of his old teacher the Reverend James Maury (who had died seventeen years earlier), that Maury's family need not worry about the choice.

"My daughter is indeed in a convent, but in one where there are as many Protestants as Catholics, where not a word is ever said to them on the subject of religion, and where they are as free in the profession and practice of their own religion as they would be in their own country. It is a house of education only." School officials did not expect Protestant students to take part in catechism or the Eucharist (Holy Communion). Jefferson also gravitated toward the convent because the cloistered environment and staff of nuns, he assumed, would give Patsy a wholesome and refined educational experience. To his chagrin, by 1787 Patsy did develop an interest in Catholicism, even expressing a desire to become a nun. This was one of the main reasons Jefferson felt he needed to take her back to Virginia when she reached marrying age.[36]

Jefferson came to realize (as had Franklin) that there were many kinds of Catholics in France, some progressive, some not. During 1787–88, Jefferson began taking trips to a Catholic hermitage and winery at Mont Calvaire, outside Paris. He found the hermitage rejuvenating and a quiet place to get work done. It may have been an inspiration for Jefferson's mansion retreat at Poplar Forest.[37]

Conversely, Jefferson expressed concern about the corrupting manners of Europe, especially for American youths sent abroad. As much as Jefferson enjoyed Paris, his tenure there seems to have secured in him an inflexible preference for America's spiritual and cultural temperament. He told a correspondent in 1785 that many factors recommended that American youths should be educated in America. If a male student came to the Continent, the experience would unfit him for enjoying the salubrious attributes of America. The traveling student would acquire "a fondness for European luxury and dissipation and a contempt for the simplicity of his own country . . . he is led by the strongest of all the human passions into a spirit for female intrigue destructive of his own and others' happiness, or a passion for whores destructive of his health, and in both cases learns to consider fidelity to the marriage bed as an ungentlemanly practice and inconsistent with happiness: he recollects the voluptuary dress and arts of the European women and pities and despises the chaste affections and simplicity of those of his own country . . . he returns to his own country, a foreigner, unacquainted with the practices of domestic economy necessary to preserve him from ruin." It is hard to discern how Jefferson applied such concerns for "domestic economy" to his own life, though there is no reason to think that Jefferson consorted with Paris prostitutes (in contrast to Franklin, who did visit prostitutes in London as a young man). Jefferson would pursue other relational and sexual outlets, however.[38]

The most controversial of those new relationships was with Sally Hemings. Indeed, that relationship may be the most controversial one in American history. The Jefferson-Hemings affair is arguably the central dilemma in Jefferson's moral universe. Their relationship began in a legal sense when Thomas inherited members of the Hemings family as bondspeople. Sally Hemings herself was not of any special interest to Jefferson until she joined his Paris household. Her arrival was prompted by the death of Jefferson's young daughter Lucy, whose birth had led to Martha's death in 1782.[39]

Jefferson learned of little Lucy's death in a blunt, peculiar letter from her attending physician, James Currie. People in the eighteenth century often discussed death, even the deaths of children, in a matter-of-fact way. Jefferson was a genuinely affectionate father to his children by Martha, however, so it must have hit him hard to receive Currie's news. The letter was peculiar in that it relayed news of Lucy's passing after first making rambling comments about Currie's travel plans and the history of balloons. Only then did Currie inform Jefferson of the "demise of poor Miss L. Jefferson, who fell a Martyr to the Complicated evils of teething, Worms and Hooping Cough." Implicitly blaming the Eppes family, with whom Jefferson had left Lucy and her older sister Mary (Polly), Currie claimed he was called too late to do anything for the child. Elizabeth Wayles Eppes, Jefferson's sister-in-law, had also lost a daughter in the whooping cough epidemic. Eppes wrote a much kinder letter to Jefferson a month before Currie's missive, but Jefferson received it four months after Currie's, due to the unpredictability of transatlantic mail delivery. Jefferson's only solace was that Polly had survived. The widowed father had reluctantly left Polly and Lucy in Virginia; now he felt that he must bring Polly to Paris, telling the Eppes family that the thought of Polly "hangs on my mind night and day." He also noted that James Hemings, then laboring in the Paris twilight between slavery and freedom, was "well and salutes all his friends."[40]

Jefferson scrambled to give young Polly fatherly guidance, as he knew it would be some time yet before he could arrange her travel. As a father, Jefferson could be sweet, moralistic, and pushy all at the same time. He scolded her for not writing him, saying that if she knew how much he loved her, she would not neglect him. Jefferson exhorted her to obey the Eppeses and to work hard at her studies. He offered blunt advice on Polly's physical appearance. "Remember too as a constant charge," he wrote, "not to go out without your bonnet because it will make you very ugly and then we should not love you so much. If you will always practise these lessons we shall continue to love you as we do now." To Patsy he wrote, "Nothing is so disgusting to our sex as a want of cleanliness and delicacy in yours." Jefferson's genteel culture assumed that acceptance and love for elite women was contingent upon their physical attributes, skin tone, and style.[41]

Jefferson felt anxious about getting nine-year-old Polly to Paris. He wanted her to travel at the most favorable season, on a reliable, seaworthy ship. He wished the Eppeses to assign some dependable white adult to accompany her, or perhaps a "careful negro woman," assuming that the woman traveled under the "patronage of a gentleman." Polly was understandably hesitant about leaving her Virginia friends and family to make the arduous journey, but Jefferson insisted. Realizing that the little girl's memories of him (and of her mother) had begun to fade, he assured her that "by our care and love of you, we will teach you to love us more than you will do if you stay so far from us." Jefferson would buy her whatever she wished. "When you come here you shall have as many dolls and playthings as you want for yourself" or to send to her Virginia cousins, he promised.[42]

Jefferson's first choice when suggesting a "careful negro woman" was Isabel Hern, a bondswoman he inherited from his father-in-law. Hern was a mother and two decades older than Polly—just the sort of woman he wanted to shepherd his daughter. Hern was recovering from childbirth, however, so the Eppeses decided to send Sally Hemings with Polly. In social terms, as an enslaved teenager and an elite white girl, Sally and Polly were worlds apart. In age and travel experience, however, they were peers. Sally Hemings was fourteen. She might have been eager to reunite with her brother James in Paris, and presumably she had impressed the Eppeses as a responsible person already, despite her youth. The Eppeses told Jefferson that "Isabel or Sally" would join Polly on the Atlantic passage aboard the *Robert,* under the watchful eye of a male patron. Polly's companion turned out to be Sally. If Thomas objected to the plan, he had no opportunity to tell the Eppeses once he got the news. It was a fait accompli.[43]

5. "I Am But a Son of Nature"

Polly Jefferson and Sally Hemings did not arrive in Paris until mid-1787. In the meantime, Jefferson engaged in a month-long flirtation with a married woman named Maria Cosway. Their liaison illustrated his continued longing for female companionship. Cosway was twenty-seven; Jefferson was forty-three. As soon as Jefferson met the "golden-haired Anglo-Saxon," as one contemporary called Cosway, he was smitten. He began canceling appointments to spend as much time with her as possible. Cosway, born to an English family in Florence, Italy, had, like Patsy Jefferson, been educated at a convent. Maria was a devout Catholic; she would later join an Italian convent as a nun for eighteenth months. If anything, her faith seems to have enhanced her exotic aura. In 1781 she married the licentious and wealthy artist Richard Cosway in England, just as the Revolutionary War was ending in Virginia. Jefferson praised her "modesty, beauty, and that softness of disposition which is the ornament of her sex." She seems to have projected a religiously modest but sexually provocative style that Jefferson found irresistible.[1]

This was not the first time Jefferson had wooed a married woman. In contrast to his aggression against Betsy Walker almost twenty years earlier, however, Maria Cosway apparently enjoyed their brief tryst. We do not know the extent to which they were physically involved, but Jefferson and Cosway certainly shared the pleasures of the arts. Maria was a talented musician and painter, and she and Jefferson took in just about every entertainment in Paris during the two weeks after they met. Sometimes her husband (who didn't seem especially concerned about their flirtation) accompanied them. Sometimes thirteen-year-old Patsy did too. Their elysian interlude

Maria Cosway, watercolor over pencil by Richard Cosway,
1785. (Courtesy Wikimedia Commons)

came to a humiliating end in September, however. While Thomas and Maria
strolled in a Paris park, Jefferson took it upon himself to leap over a fence.
His forty-three-year-old legs did not quite manage the feat. He tumbled
hard, breaking or dislocating his right wrist. The injury never healed
correctly, bothering him for the rest of his life.[2]

His aching arm kept him from enjoying the remainder of the Cosways'
time in Paris. Their departure prompted Jefferson to write one of his most
famous letters, the "Head and Heart" dialogue. (He wrote it left-handed, due
to his injured wrist.) Although it is semi-satirical, the romantically charged
letter is one of the most revealing treatises he ever produced. Jefferson
directed the letter to both Richard and Maria so as not to raise questions
about its propriety. He was clearly sorting out his feelings for her, however,
and processing grief, knowing that he and Maria could not continue together

as they had in those magical Paris weeks. He was also articulating tensions within his Epicurean philosophy. His central question: if love's sweetness causes pain in the parting, would it be better not to love at all? (Martha's passing had generated similar reflections, ones of more bitter memory.) It was and is a perennial dramatic problem, akin to Juliet's "sweet sorrow" upon leaving Romeo.[3]

Jefferson's "Head" is the voice of Epicurus, scolding the "incorrigible" Heart for rushing into situations that cause pain. "Do not bite at the bait of pleasure," Head insisted, "till you know there is no hook beneath it." Head declared that "the art of life is the art of avoiding pain." One should prioritize pleasures that no one could steal, such as learning. In reading and study, "we ride serene & sublime above the concerns of this mortal world, contemplating truth & nature, matter & motion, the laws which bind up their existence, & that eternal being who made & bound them up by those laws." For Jefferson and Maria Cosway, studying the world opened the beauty of the created order.[4]

His "Heart," echoing Christian teachings, insisted that people found happiness through love and sociability, not isolated study. Those like Head (and Epicurus) "mistake for happiness the mere absence of pain," Heart declared. Jefferson concluded that the Head preferred cool rationality, but the Heart generated moral action. The Head desired calculated self-interest, while the Heart inspired charitable self-sacrifice. For example, Heart said that if America's Patriot cause had depended on detached calculation alone, it would have gutted the spirit of liberty, and the Patriot leaders would now be "hanging on a gallows as high as Haman's." (Haman was the villain in the biblical book of Esther.) The gifts of life often came with the risk of pain, and Heart thought the risk was worth it. "We have no rose without its thorn," Heart concluded. Jefferson appended to this dialogue an apology to Cosway for its length, imagining that she must be bored from the "ennui of such a sermon." Given her absence and his smarting wrist, Jefferson explained, he was "in a mood for hearing sermons." Although Jefferson and Cosway maintained a correspondence for years, his passion for her cooled. Still, Jefferson had suffered another disappointing romantic relationship. The only satisfying one he ever had was with Martha, and death took her.[5]

The French government was becoming paralyzed by the social and economic strife that would spark the French Revolution. This left the American delegation in Paris without much business to conduct. In early 1787, Jefferson decided to tour France and Italy, going as far as Milan. He visited France's prime wine-growing regions, sampling products and researching vines that might grow in Virginia. Jefferson was enchanted by southern France's climate and landscape. "I am now in the land of corn, wine, oil, and sunshine," he told his secretary William Short. "What more can man ask of heaven? If I should happen to die at Paris I will beg of you to send me here, and have me exposed to the sun. I am sure it will bring me to life again." A resurrection experience might be too much to ask, but a doctor did advise him to try the region's mineral spirits for his wrist. Rambling might have also taken his mind off Maria Cosway.[6]

Jefferson's trip notes were mostly agricultural observations, especially about viticulture. The journey also exposed Jefferson to local Catholic life, confirming his long-standing suspicions about the corruption and ignorance endemic to the religion. In the region of Champagne, Jefferson scoffed at rural Catholics. Although he tended to idealize American farmers, he dismissed French peasants. The French huddled into villages, each centered upon a Catholic church. "Are they thus collected by that dogma of their religion which makes them believe that, to keep the Creator in good humor . . . , they must mumble a mass every day?" he asked. These "illy clothed" people would do better if they lived on their own farms, he thought, independent from the squalid villages and their money-grubbing clergy. Jefferson contemptuously noted the excessive salaries of Catholic bishops in these impoverished regions.[7]

Jefferson was eager to see ancient Roman sites, including the glorious Maison Carrée, the first-century C.E. Roman temple at Nîmes. Jefferson would use this temple as a model for Virginia's capitol in Richmond. He viewed the region's Catholic churches with ambivalence, however. The "celebrated church of the Chartreux" at Pavia he called "the richest thing I ever saw." Jefferson thought that Christian churches, of all institutions, should not be "rich." Thus he was not enthralled with the opulent Catholic cathedral at Milan. He sarcastically called it "a worthy object of philosophical contemplation" because it was "among the rarest instances of the misuse of money." Regarding the Italian churches generally, Jefferson commented that "the same expence would have sufficed to throw the Apennines into the Adriatic and thereby render it terra firma from Leghorn to Constantinople."[8]

While Jefferson returned to Paris, the Constitutional Convention had begun meeting in Philadelphia. Spearheaded by James Madison, the convention proposed a new constitution for America to replace the teetering

James Madison, painting by Charles Wilson Peale, 1783.
(Courtesy Library of Congress)

Articles of Confederation government. Madison regarded that government as horribly inefficient, and felt it was rendered impotent by the unchecked power of the states. Madison and Jefferson both worried about the risks of centralized national government, but Jefferson had more confidence than Madison in the rectitude of state officials and the populace as a whole. Jefferson and Madison, like other southerners, including their inveterate enemy Patrick Henry, were alarmed in 1786 by the Jay-Gardoqui Treaty with Spain. That agreement would have surrendered American navigational rights to the Mississippi River in exchange for preferred commercial status with Spain. This would have been good for the northern states, but detrimental to the South. Though the treaty was not ratified, white southerners feared that a more powerful national government might act more aggressively against their interests. Madison concluded, however, that he could frame a national government in 1787 that would safely balance the competing interests of states, the nation, and the people.[9]

Achieving that balance was difficult in a large country that still possessed little national identity. Southern fears about slavery's future destabilized the convention, too, even though the South was still six years away from the "Cotton Kingdom" birthed by the invention of the cotton gin in 1793. Southern delegates' anxieties kept the convention from doing much about slavery itself, except for allowing the nation to ban the importation of enslaved people after two decades (which it did in Jefferson's second term as president, at his behest). The Constitution seemed evasive about slaves and slavery, choosing to avoid those terms altogether. That evasion did allow delegates to avoid legally endorsing the concept of "property in man," something that Lower South delegates wanted the Constitution to affirm. However, delegates also gave white southerners disproportionate power through the "three-fifths compromise," which counted enslaved people as three-fifths of a person for representation in the House of Representatives and the Electoral College. This decision helped to ensure Virginia's control of the presidency for all but four years from 1789 to 1824, with the election of presidents Washington, Jefferson, Madison, and Monroe.[10]

Madison kept Jefferson apprised of events leading to the Philadelphia Convention. Jefferson, of course, remained detached from the intrigues surrounding the convention, as he had to sometimes wait months to get updates from home. He couldn't make real-time contributions to the proceedings. Jefferson knew that the legacy of the Revolution was at stake, however. He wrote that he had "no fear that the result of our experiment will be that men may be trusted to govern themselves without a master." The failure of that experiment would shake his confidence in creation itself. If the republic collapsed, "I should conclude either that there is no god, or that he is a malevolent being," he wrote. If people could never govern themselves, then why had God created them?[11]

Jefferson was not altogether convinced by Madison's arguments for the Constitution. He worried that it was a step back toward monarchy. Jefferson and Madison also took different views of Shays's Rebellion in Massachusetts in 1786, a key development for the Constitution's supporters. In an uprising of indebted farmers, Daniel Shays's rebels had sought to shut down state courts that were foreclosing on farmers' property. The episode was, among other things, a revolt against high taxes, a grievance that had unified the Patriots a decade earlier. Madison, George Washington, New York's Alexander Hamilton, and other promoters of a new Constitution saw the Massachusetts rebels as "mobbish insurgents" and "restless desperadoes," as Abigail Adams labeled them in a letter to Jefferson.[12]

Jefferson, however, saw the revolt as the people checking the govern-ment's power. He idealized the Shays rebels as the embodiment of American republicanism. Responding to Abigail Adams, Jefferson declared that "the spirit of resistance to government is so valuable on certain occasions, that I wish it to be always kept alive. It will often be exercised when wrong, but better so than not to be exercised at all. I like a little rebellion now and then. It is like a storm in the Atmosphere." A "little" rebellion, in contrast to a massive one, would stabilize relations between people and state. It would remind the government to safeguard the people's liberty. Shays's Rebellion, to Jefferson, was part of a historical cycle by which vigilant people checked the government and preserved liberty for the next generation.[13]

Once Jefferson had a chance to review the proposed Constitution, he became even more emphatic that the convention had exaggerated the threat posed by Shays. He wrote to William Stephens Smith (the Adamses' son-in-law) that Shays did not represent widespread lawlessness. Jefferson whimsi-cally wished that America would experience such a rebellion at least once every twenty years. The convention had created a powerful executive and commander in chief (the president) to control outbreaks of popular resist-ance, in comparison to the Articles of Confederation, which had no execu-tive branch. Jefferson thought the Constitution's executive power represented a dangerous overcorrection. "What country can preserve its liberties if their rulers are not warned from time to time that their people preserve the spirit of resistance? Let them take arms. . . . The tree of liberty must be refreshed from time to time with the blood of patriots and tyrants." Most American politicians have honored the Declaration's principle of revolution in theory, but (understandably) recoiled at any hint of rebellion in actual practice. Jefferson, however, saw an ongoing healthy role for "little" insurrections, even in the fledgling American republic.[14]

Jefferson, echoing Anti-Federalist critics of the Constitution, hoped that its consolidated power would be diminished before final ratification. In particular, he suggested that it should impose term limits on the presidency. "I hope in god this article will be rectified before the new constitution is accepted," he told Smith. It was not to be. Until the Twenty-Second Amend-ment in 1951, the president in theory could be reelected indefinitely. George Washington had set a precedent by retiring after his second term, but Fran-klin Roosevelt's election to four terms showed that under certain circum-stances, a president might serve longer. The Anti-Federalists wanted structural reductions in the government's power, such as a term-limited president, and a Bill of Rights, which the original Constitution did not include. Anti-Federalists would have more success in getting the Bill of Rights adopted than substantially diminishing the national government's prerogatives. The lack of a Bill of Rights also concerned Jefferson, who proposed that the first nine state conventions should ratify the Constitution (lest it be scuttled altogether), but the remaining states should refuse to do so until a "declaration of rights" was added.[15]

Madison skillfully managed the ratification process by promising to get a Bill of Rights adopted *after* ratification (the requisite number of states had ratified by summer 1788). He protected the result of the convention by evading major changes in the government's structure. Jefferson had definite Anti-Federalist leanings, but he largely kept them private, due to his fondness for Madison. In addition, the leading Anti-Federalist in Virginia was Jefferson's nemesis Patrick Henry. Jefferson was determined not to cooperate with Henry, especially if it meant opposing Madison. He communicated his reservations to Madison, however, telling him, "I am not a friend to a very energetic government. It is always oppressive."[16]

Jefferson eventually supported the Constitution with the hope that friendly critics could secure amendments, including a Bill of Rights. He was stung by reports that Anti-Federalists (including Patrick Henry) were claiming that the author of the Declaration of Independence was on their side. Jefferson projected himself as the servant of no faction or party. Jefferson kept his distance from the Federalist supporters of the Constitution, but he professed to be even less sympathetic to the Anti-Federalists. For him, political factionalism paralleled the craving for creeds in religion. Jefferson envisioned himself as an independent thinker with no need for creeds. "I am not a Federalist, because I never submitted the whole system of my opinions to the creed of any party of men whatever in religion, in philosophy, in politics, or in any thing else where I was capable of thinking for myself," Jefferson wrote. "Such an addiction is the last degradation of a free and moral agent. If I could not go to heaven but with a party, I would not go there at all." Yet he had been a part of political factions before (especially the Patriot movement), and he would spearhead one again soon.[17]

Jefferson's ideal of intellectual independence colored the mentoring letters he sent to his teenage nephew Peter Carr. Peter's father Dabney Carr, Jefferson's beloved friend, had died in 1773. Jefferson became a surrogate father to Peter, filling his letters with advice about honor and morality. "Give up money, give up fame, give up science, give the earth itself and all it contains," he told Peter in 1785, "rather than do an immoral act." One of the greatest virtues was a cultivated mind, and Jefferson ordered dozens of books to be sent to Peter from London. He preferred that Carr begin his readings on moral philosophy with the ancient Greeks and Romans, not the Bible. As he had suggested in *Notes on the State of Virginia,* the Bible was a good source of moral precepts, but it was subject to horrible misinterpretations.[18]

As the Constitutional Convention was beginning its final month of meetings, Jefferson wrote to Carr from Paris. This missive contained one of his most revealing commentaries on religion. Carr had enrolled at the College of William and Mary, studying with Jefferson's mentor George Wythe. Jefferson reckoned that Carr was at a transition point into intellectual and moral maturity. Carr concurred. He admired both Wythe and Jefferson, noting that Wythe was "said to be without religion, but to me he appears to possess the most rational part of it, and fulfills that great command, Do unto all men as thou wouldst they should do unto thee." Carr asked for Jefferson's advice on religion and learning. Jefferson excitedly responded, opening with a robust endorsement of the Scottish "commonsense" or "moral sense" view of virtue. Jefferson, following Scottish philosophers such as Francis Hutcheson, believed that all human beings—even African Americans—had a God-given moral sense, separate from one's reasoning capacity. "This sense is as much a part of his nature as the sense of hearing, seeing, feeling; it is the true foundation of morality," he told Carr. Jefferson equated the moral sense and the conscience. "The moral sense, or conscience, is as much a part of man as his leg or arm. It is given to all human beings in a stronger or weaker degree. . . . It may be strengthened by exercise, as may any particular limb of the body." Almost thirty years later, Jefferson, in almost the same language, explained to John Adams that "the moral sense is as much a part of our constitution as that of feeling, seeing, or hearing."[19]

The moral sense, then, was "common" to all humankind, who admired virtuous acts due to a hardwired perception, analogous to taste or sight. The moral sense could be refined through education or through habits of virtue. Jefferson therefore recommended that Carr read "good books" that would bolster his moral sentiments. In particular, he recommended that Carr read the Anglican minister Laurence Sterne, arguably Jefferson's favorite writer. He averred that Sterne's writings formed "the best course of morality that was ever written." (He did not speak of the Bible or even the New Testament in this manner yet, though Jefferson's estimation of Jesus's teachings would grow in the coming years.) Beyond reading, he exhorted Carr to take every opportunity to "be grateful, to be generous, to be charitable, to be humane, to be true, just, firm, orderly, courageous &c. Consider every act of this kind as an exercise which will strengthen your moral faculties." Practicing virtue had a reinforcing effect on the moral sense.[20]

Jefferson's letter then turned to "Religion." He regarded Carr as "mature" enough for this topic now. He enjoined Carr to test all received religious tradition by reason, and to expect that many time-honored beliefs would not survive objective scrutiny. Jefferson had nearly boundless confidence in a rational man's ability to perceive errors in traditional belief. "Read the bible then, as you would read Livy or Tacitus," he instructed. In a mode that became known as "higher criticism" of the Bible, Jefferson recommended that Carr treat the Bible like other ancient texts, holding it to the same standards of rationality and evidence. To Jefferson and other critics, there was no justification for reading the Bible with "extraneous convictions," as theologian Hans Frei put it, which you don't apply to other historical texts. This was especially the case for the Bible's miraculous claims. "For example in the book of Joshua [chapter 10] we are told the sun stood still several hours," Jefferson explained. "Were we to read that fact in Livy or Tacitus we should class it with their showers of blood, speaking of statues, beasts &c." Biblical traditionalists would counter that the Bible's authors were infallible because the Holy Spirit inspired their writings. Jefferson urged Carr to test that claim, too, instead of following believers who accepted divine inspiration. (In unguarded moments, though, even Jefferson affirmed that authors with an "inspired pen" wrote at least some of the Bible.) Carr should remember that there were many "pseudo-evangelists" who also claimed divine authority, but whose teachings were lost and/or rejected by church officials. Finally, he told Carr to evaluate rationally the New Testament's notion that Jesus of Nazareth was "begotten by god, born of a virgin, suspended and reversed the laws of nature at will, and ascended bodily into heaven."[21]

Jefferson's instructions to Carr tended to raise questions, not answer them. His critical approach to Scripture was unmistakable, however. Jefferson urged Carr to follow wherever reason took him, even if it led to atheism. Atheism was a much-discussed belief in Jefferson's time. There were few actual atheists in America or Britain, in the sense of people who professed that God did not exist. There were more atheists in France, however. The question of whether religious belief was required for virtue became a hot philosophical question on the eve of France's revolution. Jefferson figured that having a few atheists around was no problem. Though his political rivals routinely accused him of being an atheist, there is little evidence that Jefferson considered atheism viable. Too much of his thought (such as human equality and the moral sense) depended on a created order. Indeed, historian Richard Samuelson has suggested that Jefferson's "one fundamental belief" was that there was "a logic in Creation that human reason could discern." But Jefferson did not condemn atheism, unlike many of his contemporaries. He did charge traditionalist Christians with encouraging atheism by their irrational beliefs. Thus, in one of the most incendiary passages Jefferson ever penned, he told his nephew that he should not fear open inquiry. "If it ends in a belief that there is no god, you will find incitements to virtue in the comfort and pleasantness you feel in its exercise, and the love of others which it will procure you." Virtuous living had its own rewards, whether a god was watching or not. Jefferson was not troubled by the notion that his nephew could end up an atheist. He just wanted Carr to think for himself.[22]

Regardless of his comfort with atheism, Jefferson still thought virtue got a boost from belief in a superintending God and in an afterlife of heavenly rewards. "If you find reason to believe there is a god, a consciousness that you are acting under his eye, and that he approves you, will be a vast additional incitement. If that there be a future state, the hope of a happy existence in that increases the appetite to deserve it; if that Jesus was also a god, you will be comforted by a belief of his aid and love." Carr was to decide all these matters for himself, not depending on what anyone told him or what he inherited from Virginia's Anglican culture. "Your own reason is the only oracle given you by heaven," Jefferson concluded. Of course, Jefferson assumed that his fatherly advice could also improve Carr's reasoning faculties.[23]

The years prior to Jefferson's departure from France represented an important pivot in his own religious beliefs. Europe had exposed him to more skepticism than he had experienced in America, and it seems to have given him more confidence to express doubts about traditional doctrine. Some of these reservations emerged in *Notes on the State of Virginia,* which he first published anonymously in Paris in 1785. The skepticism in *Notes* came back to haunt him during his presidential candidacies, starting in 1796. *Notes* publicized his doubts about the historicity of Noah's flood and about human-kind originating in a single act of creation. Then in a letter to one of his Virginia neighbors (J.P.P. Derieux) in 1788, Jefferson declined to serve as a godparent because he could not profess "faith in articles, which I had never sense enough to comprehend." In particular, he wrote, the "difficulty of reconciling the ideas of Unity and Trinity, have, from a very early part of my life, excluded me from the office of sponsorship." This is a puzzling state-ment because such reservations should presumably have kept him from serving as a vestryman, too. As early as 1776, Jefferson had questioned the church's belief in the Trinity, but it seems that Jefferson's anti-Trinitarian, or Unitarian, convictions were becoming more concrete by 1788.[24]

Those principles would solidify further through Jefferson's interac-tions with the English Unitarian ministers Richard Price and Joseph Priestley. His active correspondence with Priestley—arguably the most important relationship in Jefferson's spiritual development—would begin in 1800, but his correspondence with Price (whose writings Jefferson had admired for years) started shortly after Jefferson's arrival in Paris. Although the bespec-tacled, wig-wearing Price was twenty years older than Jefferson, he was still a fire-breathing dissenting minister who saw true Christianity as the great engine of human liberation. Price opposed corrupt, state-backed religion, preaching just the sort of morality-based Christianity that Jefferson relished. In 1788, Price's and Jefferson's circles had been stirred into indignation by a recent book by French Protestant and government official Jacques Necker, who argued that religion was essential for morality. Jefferson's secretary William Short told him that Necker had energized a vigorous reaction among those who argued that atheists could be fully moral, too. "I have heard more atheism avowed within these three days than during my whole life before," Short said.[25]

Price wrote to Jefferson in 1788 contending that Necker was not wrong about the value of religion for morality, but that Necker had failed to define true religion. Much of Christianity—both Catholic and Protestant—was grossly immoral and doctrinally aberrant, Price insisted. "Rational and liberal religion" alone linked belief and morality. Traditional worldly forms of faith *separated* morality from religion. "Popery teaches a method of pleasing God without forsaking vice, and of getting to heaven by penances," Price mused. "Mahometans expect a paradise of Sensual pleasures. Pagans worship'd lewd, revengeful and cruel Deities. . . . The religion likewise of many Protestants is little better than a compromise with the Deity for wrong practises by fastings, Sacraments hearing the word &c." Price questioned whether these religions made the world better or worse. Might they actually be more toxic than atheism? Were they perhaps a species of demonism? Price thought that Christians who believed in the blood atonement in Christ's death effectively were demonists. "What is the religion of many persons but a kind of demonism that delights in human Sacrifices?" Price asked. Jefferson agreed. "I concur with you strictly in your opinion of the comparative merits of atheism and demonism," he told Price, "and really see nothing but the latter in the being worshipped by many who think themselves Christians." The Virginian was beginning to believe that while Christianity in its original form was true, most of the "Christian" world had lost sight of Jesus's real teachings. They had been hoodwinked by money-grubbing priests.[26]

Jefferson, looking for theological guides he could trust, found them in Price and Priestley. In mid-1789, Jefferson asked Price if there was "anything good" he could recommend on "Socinian doctrine, leveled to a mind not habituated to abstract reasoning?" "Socinianism" got its name from the Italian jurist Faustus Socinus. Socinians were not only anti-Trinitarian, but they questioned the belief in Christ's blood sacrifice for forgiveness of sins. Price was happy to be asked about Socinian beliefs, and he sent Jefferson a packet of materials, including the tract *Two Schemes of a Trinity Considered*, which he recommended as the best text on Socinian doctrine. This work made an argument, derived from a Unitarian reading of Scripture, that Jesus was a man uniquely favored by God, but not God himself.[27]

A few weeks before Jefferson wrote his letter to Peter Carr, Polly Jefferson came to Paris, accompanied by Sally Hemings. They had first arrived in London, where Abigail Adams looked after them. The ocean journey seems to have traumatized eight-year-old Polly, who had left home to join a father she had not seen in three years. Adams tried to explain the girl's emotional state to Jefferson, but he did not seem to grasp her point. Jefferson let a French assistant fetch Polly in London instead of coming in person. He explained that his recent tour of France and Italy had left him with back-logged work, so he couldn't afford to go. His failure to appear threw Polly into "all her former distresses," Adams informed him.[28]

Whites rarely discussed bondspeople as individual persons, but Abigail Adams (who saw slavery as an "iniquitous scheme") informed Jefferson that

Polly had a "Girl about 15 or 16 with her, the Sister of the Servant you have with you." Sally was actually fourteen. Something about Hemings or her circumstances did not sit well with Adams. Perhaps she thought Sally was too young to be Polly's companion, or perhaps Adams didn't like the idea of a teenage girl living with Jefferson in Paris. In any case, Adams commented on Hemings's alleged immaturity, although she at least allowed that Hemings was "good natured." She also noted, ominously, that Captain Ramsey, their male patron, was "of opinion [that Hemings] will be of so little Service that he had better carry her back with him." Exposing Sally to additional weeks of travel on a ship, likely as the only female onboard, would have put her in a dangerous situation. Adams left it up to Jefferson to decide what to do about Hemings. Jefferson wanted Hemings to continue as Polly's servant and companion, so she came to Paris. Sally's twenty-two-year-old brother James was undoubtedly delighted to show her the city. James was about to become the head chef in Jefferson's household, having learned French cooking.[29]

The changing nature of Jefferson's connection with Sally Hemings is difficult to track. According to their son Madison Hemings, Sally became Thomas's "concubine" sometime after her arrival in Paris. This is not the place to review the great controversy over their sexual relationship and children that culminated in the 1998 article in the journal *Nature*. That article confirmed that "an individual carrying the male Jefferson Y chromosome fathered Eston Hemings (born 1808), the last known child born to Sally Hemings." This revelation was enough to convince most Jefferson scholars, and the Thomas Jefferson Foundation at Monticello, that Jefferson and Hemings did have a sexual relationship that produced at least one and probably more children.[30]

Jefferson maintained strict silence about the Hemings relationship, but a few tantalizing comments suggest how he might have thought about it. One comment is in Jefferson's exuberant description of a painting of the biblical patriarch Abraham, his wife Sarah, and their servant Hagar that he saw on a trip to Germany in 1788. We might partially explain his gushing reaction to the painting by the fact that it appeared in a letter to Maria Cosway. Jefferson's feelings for her had cooled, but he could still wax poetic to Cosway about art and literature. He told Cosway that he "wished for" her while he was in Düsseldorf, as he viewed the gallery of the elector Johann Wilhelm von der Pfalz. The work that "affected" him most was Adriaen van der Werff's painting of Sarah presenting Hagar to Abraham. (In Genesis 16, the childless Sarah told

Abraham, "Go in unto my maid; it may be that I may obtain children by her.") Few others have regarded the painting as especially distinguished, but Jefferson told Cosway that he found it "delicious." Nude or near-nude females were not unusual in European art, but van der Werff's erotic painting accentuated Hagar's desirable figure and chaste demeanor as well as Abraham's chiseled classical physique. Jefferson exclaimed that he "would have agreed to have been Abraham though the consequence would have been that I should have been dead five or six thousand years." It is impossible to definitively interpret the comment, or to determine if he had Cosway, Hemings, both, or neither in mind as a prospective Hagar to his Abraham. Jefferson explained that he was voicing his intuitive reaction to the scene: "I am but a son of nature, loving what I see and feel, without being able to give a reason, nor caring much whether there be one." At the time he was either just beginning his relationship with Sally Hemings or soon would, making the envious comments about the painting potentially more suggestive.[31]

Jefferson also styled himself a "patriarch," especially when describing retirement at Monticello. In 1795, after he had stepped down from Washington's cabinet, he said that he lived on the mountaintop like an "antediluvian patriarch among my children and grandchildren, and tilling my soil." Similarly, in a 1793 letter, he envisioned himself living among his growing family "as blessed as the most blessed of the patriarchs." He did not address concubinage in these letters, but others in social and intellectual circles similar to Jefferson's occasionally spoke in those terms. For example, James Boswell, the great biographer of Samuel Johnson and a serial philanderer, wondered about the moral permissibility of "concubinage" since the patriarchs practiced it. Many figures of the Anglo-American Enlightenment admired a type of patriarchy, and Jefferson certainly believed in the existence of a "natural aristocracy" whose members were best suited to govern a republic. Whatever Jefferson's writings contributed to American democracy, his mountaintop idyll also had him living like an Old Testament pater familias.[32]

What was the precise nature of Hemings and Jefferson's bond? Did one or both of them "love" the other? We have almost no direct evidence about their relationship, much less about their feelings. Thus we must resist any temptation to characterize their connection as if it were happening today, in the context of modern American mores regarding sex, race, and slavery. It seems plausible to assume, however, that Jefferson wished to have an available sexual partner, one whose existence was almost purely private and domestic, and whose movements he strictly controlled. He could not marry or publicly recognize Hemings because of her race and legal status. Yet he knew that concubinage was practiced by patriarchs of ancient Israel, Rome, and Greece. The practice of taking an enslaved woman as a "substitute for a wife" was widely known in Jefferson's southern social class, though most would have publicly disparaged the practice. He likely figured sex with Hemings would help maintain his vigor. His beloved Martha was gone; he would never remarry. Given these realities, private recourse to the young and accessible Hemings would have been an appealing arrangement for him.[33]

Like most southern planters, Jefferson felt he had paternal responsibility for members of his household. He accordingly paid for Hemings to be inoculated against smallpox. It was an expensive operation, at 240 livres, done by one of Paris's elite doctors. This fee was, for example, ten times more than Jefferson paid for a hat for himself the same month. In the broader context, it was not that unusual an expense for him: Jefferson routinely made single wine orders that cost far more than the inoculation did. Strikingly, he also paid wages to Sally Hemings in France, albeit irregularly. (Jefferson also paid James Hemings.) These payments would have been quite unusual for a master-slave relationship in America. Jefferson and Hemings both knew, however, that she really couldn't be treated as a slave in France. Her pay, which was better than average for a live-in servant in the city, was one of the most notable accommodations Jefferson made to their French setting.[34]

In April 1789, the first violent episodes of the French Revolution transpired, with dozens of Parisians dying in fights between workers and police. That same month, almost two years after her arrival, Jefferson engaged in a conspicuous burst of clothes buying for Hemings, spending 168 livres in just ten days. This undoubtedly was so Sally could accompany Patsy socially. Jefferson had already begun spending a lot more on Patsy's clothes a year earlier. One wonders whether the sixteen-year-old Hemings accompanied Jefferson on the shopping trips for her clothes, or whether he just authorized the purchases without consulting her. All we see is the occasional terse entry in his memorandum book: "clothes for Sally." In any case, personal attention to an enslaved person's clothes was unusual.[35]

Soon the Jefferson household would leave Paris for good. Jefferson had been growing anxious about the city's turmoil. In mid-1788 he had written that "the confusion here at present is really distressing. Society is spoilt by it. Instead of that gaiety and insouciance which has distinguished it heretofore, all is filled with political debates into which both sexes enter with equal eagerness." Jefferson disliked women who "wrinkle their foreheads with politics," so he found their nonstop political talk repulsive. The politicized ladies of Paris made him long for America. American women "value domestic happiness above all other," he told his friend Anne Willing Bingham, the wife of one of Philadelphia's richest men. The Americans' focus on the home compared favorably to the French women's scramble for public intrigues, he averred. Jefferson preferred American women; the two groups were a "comparison of Amazons and Angels." He may have been teasing Bingham, who was known for her intellectual and political engagement. She would receive none of his musings about domesticity. French women, Bingham wrote Jefferson, "have obtained that Rank and Consideration in society, which the Sex are intitled to, and which they in vain contend for in other Countries. We are therefore bound in Gratitude to admire and revere them, for asserting our Privileges." Jefferson was sanguine about political reform in France, but he repeatedly expressed concern about the way France's crisis drew women into politics. Jefferson's theoretical zeal for representative democracy was nearly boundless, but his democracy was, in practice, for white men only.[36]

Jefferson's nostalgia for America grew out of his unsettledness in France. He wanted to go back to America, but he thought he was just taking a leave of absence. He did not predict the violence into which France would soon descend. Jefferson was always mindful of the mounting disarray of his finances, even though he assured Elizabeth Wayles Eppes that "he who feedeth the sparrow must feed us also." Jefferson was afraid that the change of constitutions in America might jeopardize his reimbursements as minister to France. In 1788 he anxiously told New York's John Jay, the secretary of foreign affairs, that he had no "ambition for splendor. My furniture, carriage, apparel are all plain. Yet they have cost me more than a year's salary." Jefferson was sure that the Hôtel de Langeac met only the minimum decency required of a respectable diplomat. Some observers might have balked at the "chariot" he bought at the end of 1788 for nearly 1,000 livres, or the 400 livres he had just spent on gold and silver watches the same week he sent the letter to Jay. Then there was the alcohol he purchased, via his French "wine man," Etienne Parent. Jefferson was in regular contact with Parent during his last three years in Paris, telling him in January 1789 that he should procure the best wine available. "I rely on you always for the quality," he confided to Parent, "and let the price be what it has to be, always however considering quality more than price." Parent happily complied. Enough wine would be left over for Jefferson to bring 363 bottles back to America. More was to come when he shut down his Paris household for good, and he began ordering even more French wine as soon as he became secretary of state.[37]

Jefferson's public responsibilities and spending habits help interpret one of his most-discussed letters from France, a September 1789 missive in which he told James Madison that "the earth belongs in usufruct to the living." (The term "in usufruct" was from English common law. It meant, roughly, "in trust.") This was arguably the most radical political letter that Jefferson ever wrote. It stood in stark contrast to conservative sentiments such as those held by the British statesman Edmund Burke. The next year, in his *Reflections on the Revolution in France* (1790), Burke warned against rash social transformations because society represented a "partnership not only between those who are living, but between those who are living, those who are dead, and those who are to be born." Jefferson countered that the dead exercised too much influence already. The living should act in their best interest, no matter how sharply it departed from precedent.[38]

Jefferson's "self-evident" proposition was that " 'that the earth belongs in usufruct to the living': that the dead have neither powers nor rights over it." Jefferson made various applications of this concept over the decades. As framed in 1789, however, Jefferson's primary point was about *debt*. As a good republican, he hated debt, but he also felt increasingly paralyzed in his personal finances. He inherited the foundation of that "thraldom" of debt from his father-in-law. Jefferson benefited from the Wayles inheritance in land and bondspeople (including Sally Hemings), the value of which considerably exceeded the cost of the original debt he took on. Still, Jefferson suggested to Madison that inherited debt was rooted in the irresponsibility of ancestors, which made such liabilities illegitimate and possibly void. He proposed an example: say King Louis XV (who died in 1774 and was known for lavish spending) borrowed massive sums, with the intention "that we may eat, drink, and be merry in our day" (a phrase from the King James Bible). The deal stipulated that he would pay no interest until after nineteen years—one generation, in Jefferson's calculation. After that, a crippling interest rate would kick in. "The money is lent on these conditions, is divided among the living, eaten, drank, and squandered. Would the present generation be obliged to apply the produce of the earth and of their labour to replace their dissipations? Not at all," Jefferson concluded. Lawmakers in France and America should consider ways not only to avoid public debt but to stop imposing debt obligations on future generations, he suggested.[39]

Not coincidentally, Jefferson's creditors were getting impatient with his failure to pay them back. If Jefferson had been a common farmer, he probably would have gotten into legal trouble for his financial arrears. He had always hoped that his salary as minister to France, plus revenue from his Virginia farms, would allow him to make up ground. He only got farther behind, however, due to management errors in farms and accounts, and his chronic inability to implement financial restraint. By 1789, he needed to return to Virginia to deal with his personal affairs. Jefferson longed to keep advising French revolutionary leaders, especially his revolutionary ally the Marquis de Lafayette, whose political cohort strategized at Jefferson's house. Jefferson and Lafayette had become friends when Lafayette had played a key role in the Continental Army's decisive fight in Virginia in 1781. But Jefferson could see that Paris was becoming dangerous, especially for French elites, some of whom fell victim to murders and beheadings. Jefferson nervously joked to Maria Cosway that "the cutting off heads is become so much á la mode, that one is apt to feel of a morning whether their own is on their shoulders." Yet he remained sanguine about France's struggle, counting himself fortunate to have witnessed two revolutions in just fourteen years.[40]

One delicate matter needed to be resolved, however: Sally Hemings was pregnant. According to her son's account, she was reluctant to return to Virginia, knowing that she could stay in France as a free woman. Madison Hemings went so far as to say she "refused to return with [Jefferson]." This seems a bit unlikely for an enslaved teenager, but with James's help she may have realized that she would never have a chance at freedom again like she had in Paris. To get her to go back, Madison Hemings said, Jefferson "promised her extraordinary privileges, and made a solemn pledge that her children should be freed at the age of twenty-one years." Hemings, "implicitly" relying on his word, accompanied Jefferson to Virginia. She reportedly gave birth soon after their return, but the child did not live.[41]

In October 1789, Jefferson, his daughters, and James and Sally Hemings set sail from the port of Le Havre. He made a few last-minute purchases before leaving, including a dog he identified as a "chienne bergere," or a Briard sheepdog. He left most of the furnishings at the Hôtel de Langeac, assuming that he would return. When it became clear that he would not go back to France, Jefferson arranged for William Short to cancel his lease and to pack the rest of the house for shipment. The result was eighty-six crates, including furniture, kitchen, and table items. These included foodstuffs he likely could not get in America, such as olive oil and macaroni, as well as another 680 bottles of wine.[42]

6. "None of Us, No Not One, Is Perfect"

Soon after Jefferson returned to Virginia, President Washington asked him to become secretary of state. Jefferson was ambivalent about the offer. He could have gone back as minister to France. Jefferson's hankering for private tranquility told him that direct engagement in national politics meant more pain and frustration. Yet Jefferson admired Washington, and he worried that saying no would marginalize him politically. He could never stomach being sidelined, despite his idealization of retirement. Friends like James Madison encouraged him to accept Washington's invitation. The English dissenting pastor Richard Price saw Jefferson's promotion to the cabinet as part of the providential progress of liberty. Over his long life, Price mused, he had witnessed "the human species improved, religious intolerance almost extinguished, the eyes of the lower ranks of men opened to see their rights; and nations panting for liberty that seemed to have lost the Idea of it. Wishing that you may be long continued to contribute towards this growing improvement of the world."[1]

Jefferson agreed with Price's sentiments about liberty, and about his own role in its epic story. In a sense, liberty had become Jefferson's religion. Responding to an appeal from Virginians for him to return to public service, he accepted his responsibility in sermonic terms. He had served the "holy cause of freedom" during the Revolution, as had his fellow Virginians. "Heaven has rewarded us with a happy issue from our struggles. It rests now with ourselves alone to enjoy in peace and concord the blessings of self-government, so long denied to mankind. . . . Let us then, my dear friends, forever bow down to the general reason of the society. . . . Wherever I may be stationed, by the will of my country, it will be my delight to see, in the general tide of happiness, that yours too flows on." The progress of happiness and liberty was inexorable, he told his supporters. "That it may flow thro' all times, gathering strength as it goes, and spreading the happy influence of reason and liberty over the face of the earth, is my fervent prayer to heaven." As he later noted, the progress of liberty and the decline of tyranny proved that "there is a god in heaven." The spread of liberty was in that god's hands. Jefferson told Washington that he would serve in the administration; the freedom tide would keep rolling on.[2]

His move to New York (the seat of the national government) and cabinet office set the stage for Jefferson's rivalry with Alexander Hamilton. Hamilton is more famous now than ever due to the phenomenal success of Lin-Manuel Miranda's *Hamilton: An American Musical* (2015). Hamilton started life in obscurity, however, as a child of unmarried parents on Nevis, in the British West Indies. Patrons including a Presbyterian pastor arranged for Hamilton to go to King's College (now Columbia University) in New York City. During the Revolutionary War, Hamilton served as aide-de-camp to General Washington, leading a heroic charge against British dugouts during the siege of Yorktown in 1781. Hamilton also married into the prominent Schuyler family of New York, making him a major figure in the state's politics. After participating in the Constitutional Convention, Hamilton, with James Madison and John Jay, penned *The Federalist*. These essays sought to persuade New Yorkers to ratify the federal Constitution.

Hamilton and Madison's collaboration on *The Federalist* masked deep differences between them. The split between Hamilton and the Virginians would emerge when Jefferson joined the administration. As Virginians, Jefferson and Washington had known each other since before the Revolution started. But Washington and Hamilton had served together as brothers in arms, and their bond proved more durable. Hamilton would soon replace Patrick Henry as Jefferson's most despised political enemy. Everyone entering the Washington administration assumed that government by consensus was preferable to factionalism, however. For a time, Jefferson and Hamilton sought to compromise.

Hamilton crafted a national economic policy that he believed would make America friendly to business and financially sound. Jefferson hardly opposed economic flourishing, but he worried about the threats of centralized power, indebtedness, and special-interest politics he saw in Hamilton's scheme. Hamilton's plan included having the federal government assume responsibility for state debts, pass new tariffs and excise taxes, and create a Bank of the United States. Assuming state debts was divisive because some states, including Virginia, had already settled obligations incurred during the Revolution. Why should they assist states such as Massachusetts and South Carolina, which had not? Madison regarded this disparity as "wrong radically & morally & politically wrong," as he wrote in 1790. In their concern for Virginia's welfare, Madison and Jefferson reflected the state-centered mentality that characterized much of American politics (not just in the South) through the Civil War and beyond.[3]

The House of Representatives—with Madison leading the opposition—narrowly defeated Hamilton's debt assumption plan in April 1790. Hamilton was shaken, thinking his scheme might be doomed. He still believed he might be able to persuade Madison and Jefferson to compromise, however. According to Jefferson's account, he and Hamilton met one day outside George Washington's house in New York, and Hamilton broached the assumption of state debts. In Jefferson's recollection, Hamilton was in a bad way. "His look was sombre, haggard, and dejected beyond description," Jefferson recalled. "Even his dress uncouth and neglected." Hamilton thought the American union was at risk if they could not settle the problem of state debt, with New Englanders feeling particularly aggrieved by the national government's inaction. Threats of secession already loomed before the American constitutional experiment had really started. Jefferson would soon stoke the fires of states' rights sentiment in the controversy over the Alien and Sedition Acts. As of 1790, however, Hamilton was most worried about the loyalty of New Englanders.[4]

Jefferson proposed that he, Madison, and Hamilton should broker a solution. This led to the so-called Dinner Table Bargain. After Jefferson and Hamilton's meeting at Washington's house, Madison and Jefferson had a meal with Hamilton and agreed on the state debt plan, in exchange for placing the new national capital on the Potomac River. The Constitution had provided for the creation of a new capital, but did not stipulate where it would be located. Jefferson and Madison assumed that having easy access to a centrally located capital would be politically advantageous for southerners, and that it would bring financial benefits to its neighboring state(s). Washington's location has not always been advantageous for the broader South, but it certainly has been an economic boon to Virginia's and Maryland's D.C. suburbs.

Virginia's congressmen were still not thrilled about the debt assumption deal. One representative told Jefferson that the idea of flipping his vote on the issue of state debts gave him a "revulsion of stomach almost convulsive." But the congressman did flip, along with several other Virginia and Maryland representatives. Getting the national capital was ultimately worth it. Hamilton would not cooperate much with Jefferson and Madison after this point, and Jefferson's loathing for Hamilton had begun to stew. For the moment, however, they had their deal.[5]

In the midst of the debt assumption negotiations, Jefferson wrote a revealing letter to his daughter Martha (Patsy). Upon the family's return from France, she had gotten engaged to her third cousin (and a Jefferson protégé) Thomas Randolph. The complex connections between the Jefferson and Randolph families were of long standing. Jefferson was happy about the romantic match, even though Martha was just seventeen. That was young to get married, even by Revolutionary America's standards. He gave her advice about marriage and family, including tips about relating to her in-laws. Paraphrasing the Psalms and Romans chapter 3, Jefferson told her, "None of us, no not one, is perfect." (The Bible actually said no one "doeth good.") "Were we to love none who had imperfections this world would be a desert for our love. All we can do is to make the best of our friends: love and cherish what is good in them, and keep out of the way of what is bad," he wrote. Jefferson was sympathetic toward Enlightenment theories of human perfectibility, advanced by writers such as the Marquis de Condorcet and Richard Price. But he also realized (from experience and from the biblical tradition) that most people— and most political deals—were imperfect. Jefferson did not always apply his fatherly advice in his dealings with political rivals. Like many politicians, he tended to focus on the bad qualities in enemies more than the good.[6]

State debt was only one part of Hamilton's ambitious program. The Constitution had neither authorized nor prohibited a Bank of the United States, so Hamilton's intent to create one precipitated the first great national debate about constitutional interpretation. Madison and Jefferson argued that the Constitution fundamentally limited the national government. If the Constitution did not mention a bank, then no bank was permitted. The Tenth Amendment reserved all nondelegated powers to the states or to the people. Hamilton argued that Congress had power to create agencies that performed essential functions, such as the receipt of tax payments. Jefferson, reflecting

Anti-Federalist concerns about national power, wrote that permitting the bank would grant the national government a "boundless field of power, no longer susceptible of any definition." The bank represented a slippery slope of tyranny. Jefferson also considered banks and their inflated paper currency as get-rich-quick schemes. He wrote years later that "legerdemain tricks upon paper" could never "produce as solid wealth as hard labor in the earth." Nothing could "redeem man from the original sentence of his maker that 'in the sweat of his brow shall he eat his bread,' " he concluded, citing Genesis 3:19. (He never reconciled this ideal, of course, with his use of slave labor.) Virtually all southern congressmen opposed the bank, yet it passed in Congress. Washington signed it into law.[7]

Jefferson saw the split with Hamilton as part of a transatlantic struggle between the (pro-French) forces of liberty and the (pro-British) "anglomen" represented by Hamilton, Parliament's Edmund Burke, and Vice President John Adams. Jefferson penned letters to rouse support for his "republican" faction against the quasi-monarchists. Jefferson took to speaking of the "heresies" of his political opponents. (Meanwhile, Jefferson kept ordering books such as the anti-Christian text *Histoire critique de Jesus Christ*, which historian Jonathan Israel has called "extremely seditious.") To Jefferson, the religion of the Revolution was republican liberty. Deviating from that faith, or going back to old monarchical ways, entailed heresy. The history of heresy was an interest of Jefferson's, dating to his early efforts to establish religious liberty in Virginia. Following John Locke, he defined a heretic as "an impugner of fundamentals." By the 1790s, he reflexively spoke of political rivalries using the rhetoric of orthodoxy and heresy. Madison used that type of language, too, but not as much as Jefferson did.[8]

Hamilton also spoke of creeds and faithfulness as he told others about his frustrations with Jefferson and Madison. In mid-1792 Hamilton wrote a long letter to "unbosom" himself to Virginia politician Edward Carrington. He assumed that he and Carrington shared the same "political creed," one not held by his enemies. Hamilton thought that Jefferson's tenure in Paris had radicalized the secretary of state. "He drank deeply of the French Philosophy, in Religion, in Science, in politics," Hamilton told Carrington. "He came from France in the moment of a fermentation which he had a share in exciting." Hamilton assessed Jefferson as "a man of profound ambition & violent passions." A man familiar with "profound ambition" himself, Hamilton recognized the trait in Jefferson. Hamilton's ambition was not complicated by a hankering for Epicurean repose, however. By mid-1792, Washington became distressed by the "internal dissensions" in his administration, which were "tearing at our vitals." He wanted Hamilton and Jefferson to muffle their disagreements. But it was not to be.[9]

One charge of heresy by Jefferson caused estrangement with his onetime ally John Adams. Jefferson had received a copy of Thomas Paine's *The Rights of Man*, a rejoinder to Edmund Burke's *Reflections on the Revolution in France*. Burke's prescient warning about the French Revolution has become one of the most influential conservative arguments ever against precipitous social change. Paine, who electrified colonists with *Common Sense* in 1776, defended the French Revolution as a natural complement to American independence. Jefferson loved Paine's response to Burke, and he told Paine's Philadelphia publisher that he was pleased that something was "to be publicly said against the political heresies which have sprung up among us." This was a reference to Adams's *Discourses on Davila*, which criticized the French Revolution and recommended respect for traditional institutions. Without Jefferson's permission, the publisher used the "political heresies" quote as an endorsement for his edition of *The Rights of Man*. Jefferson was appalled, telling Madison that he "certainly never meant to step into a public newspaper with that in my mouth."[10]

The printer's "indiscretion," as Jefferson called it, set off a flurry of letters among Washington, Jefferson, Madison, and Adams, explaining what happened and what Jefferson meant by "heresies." Vice President Adams denied being a monarchist, but the correspondence trailed off without resolution. Despite the fracas, Jefferson kept using inflammatory rhetoric in a letter to Paine months after the initial controversy broke. Jefferson told Paine that he thanked God that Americans appeared to be "firm in their republicanism, notwithstanding the contrary hopes and assertions of a sect here, high in names, but small in numbers." The monarchist faction sought to convert people "to the doctrine of king, lords, and commons." Those hopes were checked by *The Rights of Man*, which confirmed the people's "good old faith." To many Jeffersonians (and to some Federalists), this was a contest of rival religions.[11]

Adams became increasingly disgusted with what he saw as Jefferson's fractiousness and lavish lifestyle. After the 1792 election, John told Abigail that he was "astonished at the blind Spirit of Party which has Seized on the whole soul of this Jefferson: There is not a Jacobin in France more devoted to Faction. He is however Selling off his Furniture and his Horses: He has been I believe a greater fool than I have, and run farther into Debt by his French Dinners and Splendid Living." Adams reckoned that Jefferson's anti-British animus resulted from the thousands of pounds he owed to British lenders. If someone would just pay those debts off, Adams believed, Jefferson's rational faculties might revive.[12]

The feuds within Washington's administration played out among elite men alone. Jefferson's vision of American democracy centered on a political nation of white men. Yet in his capacity as secretary of state, he also encountered the diplomatic concerns of certain people of color. The most jarring of such episodes was the Haitian Revolution, which broke out in 1791.

Inspired by the ideals of the French Revolution, the rebellion on Saint-Domingue (Haiti) was the most successful slave uprising ever in the Americas. The Caribbean islands were generally more profitable for European powers than were the Atlantic seaboard colonies. The French colony at Saint-Domingue was the wealthiest of them all, with bumper crops of sugar and coffee. As in other Caribbean plantation colonies, its working conditions were brutal for the enslaved laborers, who typically did not survive long on the sugarcane farms. The 1791 slave uprising plunged Saint-Domingue into a complex civil war, with crosscutting alliances involving free and enslaved blacks, poor whites, and plantation masters. Out of the chaos arose Toussaint Louverture, a former bondsman and devout Catholic, who became the colony's leader until French forces defeated him in 1802. Louverture died in a French prison in 1803, but Napoleon Bonaparte decided to cut his losses in Saint-Domingue. The colony, assuming the indigenous name Haiti, gained its independence from France in 1804.[13]

Jefferson was a great proponent of liberty and of the French Revolution. The news from black-dominated Saint-Domingue terrified him, however, as plantation masters fled from their own enslaved people. "Never was so deep a tragedy presented to the feelings of man," he told James Monroe. Saint-Domingue was the sort of cataclysm that Jefferson feared might happen in America. He forecast that "a total expulsion of the whites sooner or later [will] take place" in the West Indies. "It is high time we should foresee the bloody scenes which our children certainly, and possibly ourselves (South of Potomac) have to wade through, and try to avert them." As secretary of state in 1793, he forwarded rumors that mulattos from Saint-Domingue had entered South

Toussaint Louverture, about 1795, illustration by Sir Harry Hamilton
Johnson, 1910. (Courtesy New York Public Library)

Carolina to "excite an insurrection among the negroes." Jefferson still thought
the best way to avert race war was to enact gradual emancipation and to remove
freed blacks via colonization. Such plans were increasingly impractical,
however. In 1793 Eli Whitney invented the cotton gin, a device that would
make slavery's westward expansion a certainty. With the gin's efficiency, cotton
cultivation became massively profitable in the South's interior. Still, Jefferson
urged American planters to avoid the fate of Saint-Domingue. "If something
is not done, and soon done," he told William and Mary professor St. George
Tucker, "we shall be the murderers of our own children."[14]

In public discussions, Jefferson tended to see enslaved people only in the abstract. He rarely confronted the personalities or intellectual capacities of African Americans as individuals. Of course, he did have everyday dealings with individual slaves, including Sally and James Hemings, the latter of whom went with Jefferson to New York and Philadelphia during his tenure as secretary of state. Nonetheless, those relationships did not seem to do much to challenge Jefferson's views about African Americans' capacities. He assumed that people of African descent were passionate but unable to develop complex thoughts. "Never yet could I find that a black had uttered a thought above the level of plain narration," he wrote in *Notes on the State of Virginia*. They could not produce decent poetry, that most sophisticated of the literary arts. "Their love is ardent, but it kindles the sense only, not the imagination." Jefferson singled out Phillis Wheatley, the first published African American woman and celebrated evangelical author. "Religion indeed has produced a Phyllis Whately [*sic*]; but it could not produce a poet," he sneered. He could not concede that she had written the poems attributed to her, even though he considered them worthless. They were "below the dignity of criticism." Jefferson seems to have particularly despised the piety of evangelical women, white or black. He scoffed at their "night meetings, and praying-parties, where attended by their priests, and sometimes a hen-pecked husband, they pour forth the effusions of their love to Jesus in terms as amatory and carnal as their modesty would [not] permit them to use to a more earthly lover." Jefferson was contemptuous of both evangelical devotion and African American intellect. When blended in someone such as Wheatley, they were a deplorable combination.[15]

Jefferson never had to face Wheatley as an individual. Though her poetry brought her remarkable notoriety, and even earned her a personal audience with George Washington, she died in poverty and obscurity in 1784. Jefferson encountered a different type of challenge from the free black scientist Benjamin Banneker of Maryland. Banneker wrote an extraordinary letter to Jefferson in 1791, the year the Saint-Domingue revolution broke out. Though Banneker toiled in relative anonymity on a Maryland farm, the autodidact had interests in science and technology that paralleled Jefferson's. He had also briefly worked for Jefferson's State Department to survey land for the new District of Columbia earlier in 1791. In his letter, Banneker appealed to Jefferson's sense of noblesse oblige and asked him to work against race prejudice.[16]

Banneker had gotten the impression that Jefferson was more flexible on racial issues than other white southerners. His reason for this impression is unclear, since Jefferson's best-known comments about race were in *Notes on the State of Virginia* (American edition 1788), with its revolting comparison of blacks to orangutans and its dismissal of Phillis Wheatley's poetry. Nevertheless, Banneker sought to persuade Jefferson via commonsense moralism, the Bible, and the Declaration's concept of equality by creation. Echoing Acts 17:26 (God "hath made of one blood all nations of men"), Banneker wrote that "one universal Father hath given being to us all, and that he hath not only made us all of one flesh, but that he hath also without partiality afforded us all the Same Sensations, and endued us all with the same faculties, and that however variable we may be in Society or religion, however diversifyed in Situation or colour, we are all of the Same Family, and Stand in the Same relation to him." Banneker assumed that Jefferson understood that one of the chief "obligations of Christianity" was assisting the oppressed. He pointedly reminded Jefferson that even the secretary of state had received his freedom "from the immediate hand of that Being, from whom proceedeth every good and perfect gift" (James 1:17). This graciousness was especially obvious in the manner that God had miraculously delivered the Patriots from British tyranny, Banneker said.[17]

Having established Jefferson's purported views on race and slavery, Banneker sprung a trap, charging Jefferson with hypocrisy. How awful, Banneker mused, that Jefferson would believe in equality by creation but "should at the Same time counteract his mercies, in detaining by fraud and violence so numerous a part of my brethren under groaning captivity and cruel oppression." Banneker did not presume to tell Jefferson how emancipation might be accomplished, but simply suggested that members of the master class should wean themselves "from these narrow prejudices which you have imbibed with respect to them, and as Job proposed to his friends, 'Put your Souls in their Souls stead' " (Job 16:4).[18]

Given Jefferson's stated belief in blacks' inferiority, Banneker's mere existence as an accomplished scientist threw his contradictory views into sharp relief. To Jefferson's credit, he responded personally to Banneker's letter. Because their correspondence was private, Banneker's charges were not too embarrassing. Jefferson could afford to be magnanimous yet evasive. Their exchange was published two years later, however, causing Jefferson some trouble among southern Federalists in the 1796 presidential election. His enemies cited Jefferson's accommodating reply as evidence of the "delusive and visionary principles" about slavery he had imbibed in France. Jefferson professed eagerness to see more proofs of black talent and intellectual capability that he saw in Banneker. (Jefferson wrote the same day to the Marquis de Condorcet and commended Banneker's genius, but implied Banneker was an outlier among blacks.) He also reasserted his desire to see African Americans emancipated and educated "as fast as the imbecility of their present existence, and other circumstances which cannot be neglected, will admit." Those "other circumstances" were always the problem. How could you achieve freedom without risking Saint-Domingue's bloody scenes? As for his ownership of enslaved people, Jefferson ignored Banneker's charges of inconsistency. Still, this personal exchange with a black man seemed inappropriate to some more absolutist southern politicians, who criticized the secretary of state for "fraternizing with negroes." The conflicted Jefferson did not forget Banneker's boldness, however, writing contemptuously eighteen years later (three years after Banneker's death) that Banneker must have had help in composing his almanac, and that his letter revealed that the black scientist had "a mind of very common stature indeed."[19]

Jefferson nurtured different fears about Native Americans than about blacks. His vision of America becoming an "empire of liberty" assumed the seizure of Indian lands and the assimilation or expulsion of Native American tribes. This assumption made Jefferson interested in Native American languages, with the hope of preserving some before they became extinct. Taking cues from his French correspondent the Comte de Volney, Jefferson contemplated the origins of Native American dialects. He believed that they had Asiatic parallels. As *Notes on the State of Virginia* explained, collecting Indian vocabularies before the tribes vanished would supply the "best evidence of the derivation of this part of the human race." Unlike some of his correspondents, Jefferson theorized that America's Indian civilizations were actually older than Asian ones, giving America a claim on civilizational primacy. He also wanted to debunk the widespread Christian theory that Indians were descended from the "lost tribes" of ancient Israel, ones that had disappeared after the Assyrian conquest of Israel described in the Hebrew Bible. The interest in the Indians' origins accounted for Jefferson's interactions with missionaries to Native Americans, including Jonathan Edwards, Jr., son of the revered evangelical pastor-theologian of Northampton, Massachusetts.[20]

James Madison sent Jefferson a copy of Edwards's *Observations on the Language of the Muhhekaneew Indians*. Unlike Jefferson, Edwards subscribed to the "lost tribes" theory. Thus, Edwards's book identified ostensible similarities between Mohegan and Hebrew dialects. Madison spoke admiringly of Edwards, saying that his "observations deserve the more attention as they are made by a man of known learning and character, and may aid researches into the primitive structure of language." Jefferson was glad to receive the Edwards pamphlet, telling Madison that he endeavored to "collect all the vocabularies I can of the American Indians, as of those of Asia, persuaded that if they ever had a common parentage it will appear in their language." This sentiment was the inspiration behind Jefferson's "Indian Vocabulary Project," which lasted from 1791 to 1809. A careless thief wrecked this collection while plundering Jefferson's baggage during his move back to Monticello from Washington in 1809. Jefferson retained his interest in Indian languages and missionary work, however. In 1814 he sent the American Philosophical Society (APS) a copy of Eleazer Williams's *Good News to the Iroquois Nation: A Tract, on Man's Primitive Rectitude, His Fall, and His Recovery through Jesus Christ* (1813), an evangelistic work composed in a "specimen" of Iroquois language. Jefferson did not like the missionary agenda behind the tract. He thought that religion should be the last component of Indian education. Starting with theological tracts "is beginning at the wrong end for the improvement of their faculties and conditions," he told APS members. Partly due to his skepticism about the lost tribes theory, Jefferson believed that it would prove difficult to communicate theology to Indians in their elementary dialects. He did not think their native languages could serve as "vehicles for ideas of the fall of man, his redemption, the triune composition of the god head, and other mystical doctrines, considered by most Christians of the present date as essential elements of faith." It would be better for missionaries to focus on moral precepts rather than doctrine anyway.[21]

In 1798, Jefferson could no longer find his copy of Edwards's pamphlet on the Mohegan language, so he asked Rev. William Linn of New York (who would become one of Jefferson's greatest enemies) if he had an extra copy. Linn noted Jefferson's disagreements with the linguistic theories of missionary writers, including Edwards. Linn was not committed to the lost tribes thesis, either, as he reported to Jefferson that he had heard of a Moravian minister who worked both among the Delaware Indians and among people in Asia's Caucasus mountains, and found their languages were nearly identical (thus bolstering their Asiatic connections). In retrospect, all these theories were based on flawed assumptions about the age and historical development of Native American societies. Even before the thief scattered his Indian vocabulary papers, Jefferson had despaired of finding the ur-language(s) of the American tribes. As he told Linn, "My object being the true fact, I do not permit myself to form as yet a decisive opinion." Theological guesses about the Indians' biblical roots would not help him ascertain those facts, he believed.[22]

Even as Jefferson collected information on Indian languages, his feud with Hamilton and the "anglomen" became more bitter. Jefferson kept defending the French Revolution as it descended into the murderous Reign of Terror, with its mass executions of aristocrats. Jefferson held a romantic view of (white-led) rebellion, and he could be insensitive about the deaths involved. He knew some of the executed French aristocrats personally, but he saw their demise as a price of progress. He told his protégé William Short, who was becoming troubled about events in France, that "the liberty of the whole earth" depended on what happened there. "Was ever such a prize won with so little innocent blood?" he asked Short. "Rather than it should have failed, I would have seen half the earth desolated. Were there but an Adam and an Eve left in every country, and left free, it would be better than as it now is." To Jefferson, the Age of Revolutions represented a new moment of creation. But he might have more appropriately cited the desolation of Noah's flood as a biblical parallel. The earth had become wicked with the spirit of monarchy and priestcraft, Jefferson believed. The god of liberty intended to make a fresh start, even if it meant pouring deadly wrath on humankind. Less than three weeks after Jefferson wrote to Short, French revolutionaries guillotined King Louis XVI. Then the French Republic declared war on Britain, precipitating an international conflict that would consume much of Jefferson's political life for the next decade and a half.[23]

The new war between France and Britain raised the question of whether the Franco-American alliance of 1778 required the United States to come to France's aid. Washington and Hamilton did not believe it did, since the French Republic had replaced the monarchy with which America had signed the original treaty. Thus Washington issued a Neutrality Proclamation in 1793, declaring that the United States would not get involved in the war. Hamilton defended the Neutrality Proclamation in his "Pacificus" essays. Jefferson and Madison believed the Neutrality Proclamation was bad policy and an unconstitutional intrusion on congressional prerogatives. Jefferson wrote to Madison in the summer of 1793, exasperated that no one had publicly countered Hamilton. "For god's sake, my dear Sir, take up your pen, select the most striking heresies, and cut him to pieces in the face of the public." Again, for Jefferson, this was a matter of heresy versus orthodoxy.[24]

Jefferson's agitation was also attributable to the disastrous 1793 tour of "Citizen" Edmond-Charles Genêt, the French envoy to the United States. Jefferson originally liked the charming Genêt, but Genêt's professions of friendship toward America masked an insidious desire to mobilize U.S. support at any cost. Genêt lost most of his remaining support when, over Jefferson's protests, Genêt ordered that a captured English ship that had operated out of Philadelphia be converted into a French privateering vessel. Genêt insisted that Americans allow the French to use their ports as bases to harass English ships. If American authorities did not permit this, Genêt threatened to go straight to the American people for assistance. Jefferson thought Genêt was a fool: "hotheaded, all imagination, no judgment, passionate, disrespectful & even indecent," he told Madison. As secretary of state, Jefferson finally issued a formal request for France to recall Genêt.[25]

Despite Jefferson's turn against Genêt, the secretary of state kept hearing allegations that he was a Francophilic radical himself. One of the most evocative critiques of Jefferson was *A Peep into the Antifederal Club,* a drawing created in the midst of Genêt's machinations. The drawing was a parody of the Democratic Society of Pennsylvania, one of a network of pro-Jefferson, pro-French clubs appearing around the nation in 1793. *A Peep* depicted the chaotic society presided over by Jefferson, playing on popular fears of the French and of racial leveling. *A Peep* framed the conflict between Federalists and Jefferson's Democratic-Republicans as a clash between competing religions. Jefferson's religion, to this Federalist artist, was egalitarian and demonic. The image listed the seven-point "Creed of the Democratic Club," including the precepts "The people are All and we are the People" and "Liberty is the power of doing any thing we like." In the lower left-hand corner of the drawing, a reclining black devil muses, "I never knew an Institution Equal to this since the Creation. What a Pleasure it is to see ones work thrive so well." On the opposite side, an African American man, "Citizen Mungo," calls the club a "fine ting" and asserts that it will be "our time nex."[26]

Jefferson found the incessant conflict with Hamilton and the Federalists stressful. The fracas contradicted his ideal of apolitical tranquility. He said

A Peep into the Antifederal Club, etching, New York, 1793. (Courtesy Library Company of Philadelphia)

he longed to go home. Madison pled with him to remain in the administration, but Jefferson felt that he had served long enough. He was exhausted with the "eternal contest against a host who are systematically undermining the public liberty and prosperity . . . cut off from my family and friends, my affairs abandoned to chaos and derangement." Jefferson always imagined that retirement would enable him to address the "derangement" of his finances. In the meantime, he told Madison, he was tired of "giving every thing I love, in exchange for every thing I hate."[27]

Not all retirements were the same to Jefferson, however. For example, he heard in 1793 from his correspondent Angelica Schuyler Church that his old flame Maria Cosway had entered an Italian convent. His correspondence with Cosway had lapsed for a few years, and he was perplexed by the news. Cosway had always been a committed Catholic, but joining a convent seemed outlandish to Jefferson. "I knew that, to much goodness of heart, she joined enthusiasm and religion: but I thought that very enthusiasm would have prevented her from shutting up her adoration of the god of the Universe within the walls of a cloyster; that she would rather have sought the mountain-top." Jefferson seems to have imagined Cosway (and possibly Angelica

Church) coming to live with him under some circumstances at Monticello, but it was not to be. Determined to leave the administration, he told Church that he was liberated from political strife and planned to "sink into the bosom of my family, my farm and my books. I have my house to build, my fields to farm, and to watch for the happiness of those who labor for mine." This was an unusually direct mention of his enslaved people, making clear that he regarded them as part of his extended family. If he could gather that family to himself at tranquil Monticello, "I shall imagine myself as blessed as the most blessed of the patriarchs." Maybe he could live like one of the kindly fathers of ancient Israel. The next year, however, he called his enslaved people "animals" who required regular feeding as his other livestock did.[28]

Jefferson's desire to return to Monticello and his sprawling family was no doubt sincere, but it was also a stylized republican gesture of surrendering power to retire to one's farm. Washington had made this move to great effect with his resignation from the Continental Army in 1783. Now Jefferson chose to retreat to Monticello rather than keep fighting with Hamilton. Hamilton and John Adams thought it was a strategic feint that would better position Jefferson to become president. Adams, who had become somewhat obsessed with Jefferson, wrote an extended (and confidential) analysis to his son John Quincy Adams immediately upon Jefferson's resignation. Adams cited reasons for Jefferson's move, including "1. Mr Jefferson has a habit as well as a disposition to expensive Living, and as his Salary was not Adequate to his Luxury, he could not Subdue his Pride and Vanity as I have done, and proportion his Style of Life to his Revenue. 2. Mr Jefferson is in debt as I have heard to an amount of Seven thousand Pounds before the War, so that I Suppose he cannot afford to Spend his private income in the Public service." Adams thought that ambition was the root motive, however. "Jefferson thinks he shall by this step get a Reputation of a humble, modest, meek Man, wholly without ambition or Vanity. He may even have deceived himself into this Belief. But if a Prospect opens, The World will see . . . his soul is poisoned with Ambition." A couple days later, John wrote to Abigail that "Jefferson went off yesterday, and a good riddance." Adams was almost tempted to hope that Jefferson would be elected vice president in the 1796 election, "for there if he could do no good, he could do no harm." This hope would come true, but from Adams's perspective, it turned out that Jefferson could do enormous harm as vice president.[29]

7. "The Little Spice of Ambition"

Jefferson wanted to retire from politics because he had a "house to build." More specifically, he had a house to demolish and *re*build, for he was dissatisfied with the first Monticello. It was too small for his extended family and for hosting the visitors he constantly invited over. Monticello had always been a work in progress, but the second Monticello became a never-ending operation with incessant delays and unexpected expenses. Of course, the house was on a rural mountain, and Jefferson was absent for much of the construction. These factors made the delays and expenses worse.[1]

Some building materials, such as glass and mahogany window sashes, had to be shipped from Philadelphia. Jefferson worked with suppliers including a sash maker named Daniel Trump. Trump explained to Jefferson that "Saint-Domingue mahogany" was rare, accounting for the sashes' high prices. Jefferson's classical ideals led to more fiascoes. The Doric columns had to be reinstalled twice because they were crooked. It was years into Jefferson's presidency before the columns were correctly installed. Still, friends like Maria Cosway (who had left her convent) commended his retirement as an opportunity for otherworldliness: "How glad am I to hear your detachment from the bustling world, what is this world? Happy, very happy those who Make it a good passage to a better One, to an everlasting life." His detachment from the bustling world would not last long, however.[2]

Jefferson's frenetic project-starting accorded uneasily with his Epicurean and ethical Christian ideals. Monticello didn't foster peace, frugality, or simplicity. Perhaps he figured that if he could get his home and farms finished, he could rest in tranquility. Jefferson also began shifting his farms away from tobacco to grain crops and produce. Enslaved laborers planted hundreds of peach trees for fruit, firewood, and landscaping. Monticello was always something of a showpiece property. The farms around Poplar Forest, to the southwest, remained dependent on tobacco throughout Jefferson's lifetime. He saw tobacco as a cash engine, even if it often disappointed him.[3]

It would take time to replenish the Monticello soils exhausted by tobacco, so Jefferson opened a nail factory to bolster revenues. (Doing this also sat uneasily with his idealization of yeoman agriculture, though Jefferson generally approved of household-level manufacturing.) He tasked a dozen enslaved boys, ages ten to sixteen, to work the nailery. They hammered out nails all day long in the smoky workshop, earning Jefferson a daily profit of 60 cents. Taking inspiration from moral reformers in Philadelphia, Jefferson gave the nailery the character of both a school and a prison. Jefferson tried to increase productivity through a system of rewards rather than violence (except in "extremities"). He was pleased with the results; by 1795 the nailery was profitable enough to support his family's expenses. However, that profit margin did not last when Jefferson left Monticello to become vice president.[4]

His return to Monticello put Jefferson back in regular contact with Sally Hemings. She gave birth to a girl, Harriet, in October 1795. Harriet would live for only two years. Jefferson reluctantly granted Sally's brother James his freedom in 1796. James's tenure as Jefferson's cook had familiarized him with the free world beyond Monticello. He could have plausibly claimed his freedom in either Paris or Philadelphia, so Jefferson struck an agreement with James to let him leave as soon as he trained a replacement, which turned out to be James's brother Peter. Although James briefly returned to Monticello as a paid cook in the summer of 1801, he soon went back to Baltimore, where he had been working for some time. Not long after he left, the Hemingses got word that James had committed suicide. Rumors attributed his "tragical end" to excessive drinking. Jefferson's life was intertwined with those of the Hemingses in a fabric of intimacy, coercion, and tragedy.[5]

Jefferson enjoyed the brief return to Monticello, his imagined agrarian refuge. Monitoring national politics, however, he worried about anti-agrarian policies under Hamilton and Washington. In 1794, anger over an excise tax on whiskey (part of Hamilton's financial program) boiled over in western Pennsylvania. Whiskey was one of the most reliable sources of income for wheat growers, so some farmers began to menace tax collectors with tar and feathering. Hamilton seized the opportunity to project national power: the treasury secretary personally led a mammoth twelve-thousand-man army to suppress the rebels. The Whiskey Rebellion collapsed upon the army's arrival. Jefferson and his supporters regarded the show of force as symptomatic of autocracy. The Washington administration was suppressing resistance to its policies. True, some of the whiskey rebels had contacted British and Spanish diplomats about seceding from the United States and allying with a European nation. Jefferson told Madison, however, that this was just talk. "To consult on a question does not amount to a determination of that question in the affirmative, still less to the acting." Jefferson regarded the excise tax as "infernal" and unconstitutional anyway. If the tax dismembered the union, he feared it would set Americans "all afloat to choose which part of it we will adhere to." Secession was already seen as an option for disgruntled Americans six decades before the Civil War.[6]

Jefferson and Hamilton also clashed over the Jay Treaty in 1795. John Jay had negotiated a commercial agreement with Britain following Washington's Neutrality Proclamation of 1793. Critics regarded the Jay Treaty as a fiasco, giving England preferential trade status in exchange for paltry concessions. One exasperated Republican fumed, "Damn John Jay!" and "Damn everyone that won't damn John Jay!!" Jay and his supporters regarded their critics as Francophile "Jacobins" who admired the worst excesses of the French Revolution. The Jay Treaty became the most divisive issue in a decade of unprecedented political vitriol. The treaty fueled more speculation about the secession of southern states. Jefferson's Republicans had taken control of the House of Representatives, but treaties required only the approval of the Senate. The Jay Treaty passed. "A bolder party-stroke was never struck," Jefferson lamented.[7]

The Jay Treaty got Jefferson thinking about a Republican successor to President Washington. His first choice was Madison. Craving tranquility, he persuaded himself that it would be better to remain retired. He also described his health in mid-1795 as "entirely broken down." Jefferson noted his continuing desire to put his "affairs in a clear state"—meaning to pay off his debts. "The delights I feel in the society of my family, and the agricultural pursuits in which I am so eagerly engaged" precluded a return to office, he said. "The little spice of ambition, which I had in my younger days, has long since evaporated." The question of higher office was "forever closed."[8]

But it was not closed. Not that Jefferson was being dishonest. The year 1796 witnessed the first contested presidential election, pitting Jefferson against Adams. Candidates were not yet expected to "campaign" for office, and Jefferson was mostly uninvolved in orchestrating his candidacy. Madison was the prime mover, lining up Republican supporters to back Jefferson in the Electoral College. Madison convinced Jefferson to accept the presidency, if elected. By fall 1796, Jefferson was telling supporters that he did not have "the arrogance to say I would refuse the honorable office you mention to me; but I can say with truth that I had rather be thought worthy of it than to be appointed to it." This was polite deflection. The conflicted Jefferson had become intrigued by the thought of being president.[9]

The contested election was nasty. One of the most commonly employed attacks on Jefferson in 1796 and 1800 was that Jefferson was an atheist. Federalist backers of Adams proclaimed that Jefferson's tenure in Paris had infected him with radical skepticism. One Connecticut Federalist wrote that "We are not Frenchmen, thank God that made us . . . and until the Atheistical Philosophy of a certain great Virginian shall become the fashion (which God of his mercy forbid) we never shall be." Writing in Philadelphia's *Gazette of the United States,* "Phocion" (the South Carolina Federalist William Loughton Smith) excoriated Jefferson for his friendship with the anti-Christian infidel Thomas Paine. Should Jefferson become president, Phocion assured readers that Paine would join the administration and the two would "philosophize against the Christian religion."[10]

Jefferson's own writings supplied evidence to Phocion that the Virginian was a dangerous heretic. Phocion cited Jefferson's controversial defense of religious freedom in *Notes on the State of Virginia,* where Jefferson averred that "it does me no injury for my neighbor to say there are twenty gods, or no god. It neither picks my pocket nor breaks my leg." Phocion was indignant. "What? Do I receive no injury, as a member of society, if I am surrounded with atheists . . . on whom there are none of those religious and sacred ties, which restrain mankind from the perpetration of crimes, and without which ties civil society would soon degenerate into a wretched state of barbarism?" Phocion exclaimed, "Good God! Is this the man the patriots have cast their eyes on as successor to the virtuous Washington?" Even though many sectarian evangelicals (especially Baptists) loved Jefferson's Statute for Establishing Religious Freedom, Phocion saw irreligion in it instead. He suspected Jefferson of having ulterior motives in promoting the law, namely, protecting himself from persecution and saving himself from having to attend church. "Who ever saw [Jefferson] in a place of worship?" Phocion demanded. Other Federalists reminded voters of Jefferson's last days as Virginia governor, when he abandoned his office "at the moment of an invasion." Jefferson reconsidered his enlightened view of human nature because of the election. "I do not recollect in all the Animal kingdom," he told Madison, "a single species but man which is eternally and systematically engaged in the destruction of its own species."[11]

In the end, Adams narrowly won. Under the original electoral system, Jefferson became vice president as the second-place finisher. (The Twelfth Amendment, ratified in 1804, created separate ballots for president and vice president.) Votes largely split along regional lines, with Jefferson dominating the South and Adams winning most of the North. Prior to the Electoral College vote, Jefferson told a South Carolina ally that he half hoped that Adams would win. Serving as president would deal a terrible blow to his Epicurean longings. "I had retired after five and twenty years of constant occupation in public affairs and total abandonment of my own. I retired much poorer than when I entered the public service, and desired nothing but rest and oblivion. My name however was again brought forward, without concert or expectation on my part," he wrote. "On my salvation I declare it," he swore, using an odd phrase for him. "Salvation," as used in Jefferson's writings, normally referred to political or military matters, but here he seemingly used its traditional spiritual meaning. "I protest before my god that I shall, from the bottom of my heart, rejoice at escaping. I know well that no man will ever bring out of that office the reputation which carries him into it. The honeymoon would be as short in that case as in any other, and its moments of extasy would be ransomed by years of torment and hatred." It would be better to run, out of respect for one's supporters, and then lose and remain retired. In any event, Jefferson got the consolation prize: the vice presidency.[12]

The election of 1796, though heated, did no additional harm to Jefferson's relationship with Adams. The two remained on speaking terms, and Jefferson figured that Adams was preferable as president to the despicable Hamilton. Adams swiped at Jefferson in his inaugural address, however, when he assured the nation that he carried "veneration for the religion of a people who profess and call themselves Christians, and a fixed resolution to consider a decent respect for Christianity" into the president's office. Jefferson did not seem to take offense at that comment. Rage over the Jay Treaty and a burgeoning maritime conflict with France would soon threaten Jefferson's fragile friendship with Adams, though, and with former president Washington.[13]

Given his earlier "endorsement" of Thomas Paine, Jefferson must have realized by the mid-1790s that *anything* he put in writing could be used against him. Yet it took the leaking of a disastrous 1796 letter he wrote to Italian correspondent Philip Mazzei to teach Jefferson this lesson for good. He told Mazzei that America's republican love of liberty had been replaced by bitter factionalism, which he blamed on the "Anglican, monarchical and aristocratical party." Jefferson thought the pro-British faction had little popular support, representing only a small number of "men who prefer the calm of despotism to the boisterous sea of liberty." Jefferson again defaulted to heresy and orthodoxy to describe the rivals' differences. "It would give you a fever were I to name to you the apostates who have gone over to these heresies." Among the apostates were "men who were Samsons in the field and Solomons in the council, but who have had their heads shorn by the harlot England." Jefferson had read and copied excerpts from John Milton's *Samson Agonistes* as a teenager, and Samson's betrayal by Delilah was one of the most memorable stories in the Hebrew Bible. Whomever else Jefferson might have had in mind, these allusions clearly referred to Washington.[14]

Mazzei incautiously showed the letter to correspondents. Somehow the "Samsons in the field" missive made its way into a Paris newspaper in January 1797. The New York Federalist editor Noah Webster obtained the French translation of the letter and ran it (translated back to English) in *Minerva* in May 1797. As we might say today, Jefferson had "lost control of the narrative." Washington had endured public criticism during his second term in office, but for Jefferson to accuse Washington of corruption and cowardice was unpardonable in many quarters. It gave Jefferson's opponents ammunition for the rest of his political career. To cite just one example, the anti-Jefferson caricature "The Providential Detection" (1797) showed Jefferson dropping a copy of the letter to Mazzei while he prepares to burn the Constitution on an altar to "Gallic Despotism." The all-seeing eye of providence exposes what Jefferson is doing.[15]

Being vice president was not enormously demanding, and Jefferson shuttled between Philadelphia and Monticello for much of 1797. One of those visits home began on July 11, and almost nine months later, Sally

Hemings gave birth to a boy, William Beverly, whom they called Beverly. Beverly would be Jefferson and Hemings's first child to live to adulthood. Financial duress continued to plague Jefferson, as he told a similarly indebted friend that he could not loan him money because "I have not at this moment more than 50 dollars in the world at my command." Jefferson continued attributing his dire financial situation to the demands of public service.[16]

Jefferson's finances made it even harder for him to act upon his oft-stated desire for a gradual emancipation plan for slaves. Such an initiative presumably would have required him to free his bondspeople, too, but he could barely finance his debts as it was. By contrast, George Washington went out of his way to emancipate his enslaved people (upon his wife's death), despite Washington's own struggles with debt. Yet Jefferson could never set schemes for emancipation aside completely, due to correspondents who kept reminding him about the moral necessity of freedom. One of these was his protégé William Short, who was still in Paris. Short presumably did not know about the recent birth of Beverly Hemings, nor the identity of Beverly's father. This lack of knowledge made Short's 1798 letter more extraordinary, because Short saw racial mixing as a path for the amelioration of slavery and eventual freedom for enslaved people. Jefferson had opposed the sexual mixing of whites and blacks in *Notes on the State of Virginia*, arguing that emancipation must include the physical removal of the freed people "beyond reach of mixture" in order to avoid the "staining" of white blood. Short likewise knew that some of the "most enlightened & virtuous minds" (such as Jefferson) had registered concerns about "mixture of the two colors."[17]

Short took a different approach, suggesting that the sexual mixing of whites and blacks could produce lovely people. He cited the example of a dark-skinned white woman whom they knew, but Short was talking about mixed-race people like the light-skinned Sally Hemings, too. In any case, Short thought that racial mixing could alleviate the anti-black prejudice that bolstered slavery. If Virginians did not emancipate, Short insisted, they remained subject to charges of hypocrisy. Overly cautious whites shared blame for the enormity of the slave trade. "How many good Christians are there, who consider themselves the beloved of Christ & the invariable followers of his gospel," Short wrote, "who with all his precepts in their mind go to Africa, wrest the mother from the infant—the husband from the wife—chain them to the whip & lash, they & their posterity forever."

Despite Short's prodding, Jefferson simply would not respond. Jefferson found it easier to admit to Short that he had been quietly borrowing cash from one of Short's accounts to pay bills than to address racial mixing. He said he intended to pay Short back as soon as possible. He would keep his word about his debt to Short, but only a decade and a half later, when he sold his library to the federal government.[18]

The intense partisanship briefly subsided at the beginning of Adams's presidency. But the publication of Jefferson's "Samsons in the field" letter and deteriorating relations with the French renewed partisan rancor to levels that would have few parallels prior to the nation's secession winter of 1860–61. One of the most damaging episodes with the French was the "XYZ Affair," in which American envoys faced demands for a massive $250,000 bribe. When word broke about the boorish behavior of the French officials, code-named X, Y, and Z, Adams recommended to Congress that the nation begin preparing for war. He expected clashes between French privateers and American merchant vessels. Jefferson regarded Adams's message and the seemingly inexorable march to war as "almost insane." Madison saw the war preparation message as evidence of the "violent passions and heretical politics" that governed the president's decisions. By early 1798, Jefferson thought everyone could see that the nation was breaking into two sects. One of the sects was "called Federalists, sometimes Aristocrats or Monocrats and sometimes Tories, after the corresponding sect in the English government, of exactly the same definition: the latter are styled Republicans, Whigs, Jacobins, Anarchists, [and] Disorganisers." American politics descended into malevolent hysteria, and Philadelphia boiled with street violence and rumors of roving arsonists. A Federalist newspaper warned the City of Brotherly Love to watch out for incendiary Francophile Republicans: "When your blood runs down the gutters, don't say you were not forewarned."[19]

Political instability and threats of war often stoke hostility toward immigrants. Federalists exploited the feverish mood to pass the Alien and Sedition Acts, some of the most reactionary laws in American history. In 1798, Congress passed a set of anti-immigrant (anti-"alien") laws designed to monitor suspected foreign enemies. A new Naturalization Act also extended the time before an immigrant could become a citizen from five years to fourteen. Federalists assumed immigrants, if eligible to vote, were likely to back Jefferson's Republicans. Jefferson believed that the Alien Acts

were designed to deport pro-Jefferson foreigners. Among the most prominent of these foreigners was the English Unitarian minister and scientist
Joseph Priestley, who had moved to America in 1794. Jefferson intuited that
the Comte de Volney, a French philosopher and Jefferson correspondent,
was the Federalists' chief target. Volney did flee the country when the Adams
administration accused him of being a spy for the French. Priestley and
Volney were both significant influences on Jefferson's religious ideas,
although the two quarreled with each other over Volney's alleged atheism.
Priestley would ultimately turn Jefferson away from Volney's radical skepticism. In the meantime, Jefferson helped to translate Volney's scandalous *Les
ruines* (1791), which posited that people invented gods in order to answer
difficult philosophical questions. Jefferson recommended to protégés both
Volney's *Les ruines* and Priestley's sprawling two-volume *History of the
Corruptions of Christianity*.[20]

Even more ominous than the Alien Acts was the Sedition Act, which
threatened fines or prison for anyone convicted of "false, scandalous and
malicious writing or writings against the government of the United States,"
or who sought to bring the government "into contempt or disrepute; or to
excite against them . . . the hatred of the good people of the United States."
To a modern audience, this law appears to be a blatant violation of the free
speech and free press guarantees of the First Amendment, ratified seven
years before the Sedition Act. Free speech, however, has never been an
unlimited right. Before the 1960s, American jurists commonly assumed that
speech had special limitations during war or military crises. Congress passed
laws during World War I that were similar to the Sedition Act, and the
Supreme Court upheld them.[21]

Nevertheless, the Sedition Act was harsh, and Federalist judges meant
to enforce it. Republican editors and a Republican congressman ran afoul of
the measure. Congressman Matthew Lyon was sentenced to four months in
prison and a $1,000 fine for violating it. Undeterred, Lyon ran a successful
reelection campaign from his jail cell in Vermont. Federalists also prosecuted
and jailed the Virginia journalist James Callender for breaking the sedition
law. Callender was one of the most complicated figures in Jefferson's life. He
went from being one of Jefferson's most avid supporters to the person who
first published the allegations that Jefferson was in a sexual relationship with
Sally Hemings. A Federalist newspaper called Callender the "scum of party
filth," and historian Annette Gordon-Reed characterizes him as "a despicable

individual ruled by venom and racism." In his 1800 pro-Jefferson pamphlet *The Prospect before Us*, Callender railed against Adams's "malignant passions," claiming that Adams intended to "calumniate and destroy every man who differs from his opinions." Callender's lawyers defended him on the basis of the distinction between political opinions, which were constitutionally protected, and libelous false statements, which were not. The Federalist judge in Callender's case refused to recognize such a distinction. After Jefferson became president and Callender got out of jail, the Jefferson administration rebuffed Callender's requests to get a plum political appointment. Callender's frustration eventually led him to publicize the charges about Jefferson and Hemings.[22]

The Federalists' tactics were extraordinarily aggressive. Perhaps the best thing to do, Republicans thought, was to let the Federalists overreach. They might accordingly lose seats in the 1798 elections, and perhaps lose the presidency in 1800. As of the summer of 1798, just before the Sedition Act was passed, Jefferson was still subdued in his reaction to the Federalist-Republican fracas. His gloomy ally John Taylor of Caroline (Caroline County, Virginia) suggested that southerners should contemplate secession. Jefferson cautioned Taylor that factionalism was just built into the nature of humankind. Echoing Madison in *The Federalist*, Jefferson wrote that any association of men, whether large or small, was bound to fall into bickering factions. If he had to choose a regional opponent, it would be New Englanders, because their prospects for growth were naturally capped. He compared New Englanders to Jews. "They are circumscribed within such narrow limits, & their population so full, that their numbers will ever be the minority, and they are marked, like the Jews, with such a peculiarity of character, as to constitute from that circumstance the natural division of our parties." Here Jefferson was alluding to the anti-Semitic stereotype of the "Wandering Jew," a people whose peculiar characteristics meant that they never were fully at home, and could never (overtly) dominate a national community.[23]

The future did not belong to New England, Jefferson figured. Republicans should simply bide their time. In one of his most evocative phrases, Jefferson promised that they would soon see "the reign of witches pass over [and] their spells dissolve." Again he employed language of faith and orthodoxy, as he was hopeful of "the people recovering their true sight [and] restor[ing] their government to its true principles." Jefferson cautioned Taylor that no one could anticipate the effects of secession. "If the game

runs sometimes against us at home, we must have patience, till luck turns."
In a postscript he asked Taylor not to publicize his letters. "A single sentence
got hold of by the Porcupines will suffice to abuse & persecute me in their
papers for months," he wrote. "Porcupine" was a reference to William
Cobbett's viciously critical *Porcupine's Gazette* in Philadelphia, which began
publishing in 1797.[24]

Once the Sedition Act actually passed, it prompted Jefferson to do
more than bide his time. He drafted the Kentucky Resolutions, in which he
argued that states could nullify unconstitutional federal laws. (Madison
wrote similar resolutions on behalf of Virginia.) Jefferson was chiefly
concerned to keep Congress and the states within their proper bounds, and
to keep Federalists from running roughshod over the nation. Jefferson's
views were employed later in South Carolina's nullification crisis of the
1820s and '30s and in the secession crisis of 1860–61. In the nullification
controversy, South Carolinians cited Jefferson in their attempt to forbid the
collection of the federal government's "Tariff of Abominations." Jefferson
lived to see neither that crisis nor the Civil War, and we should not overstate
his states' rights radicalism. He had discouraged the secessionist sentiment
of John Taylor of Caroline, a true states' rights militant. Nevertheless,
Jefferson's loathing for the Alien and Sedition Acts led him to articulate a
hard-edged "compact theory" of the union, one that recalled Anti-Federalist
fears from a decade earlier.[25]

In the draft of the Kentucky Resolutions, Jefferson explained that
states were not "united on the principle of unlimited submission to their
general government." Alluding to the Tenth Amendment, he noted that the
states reserved a "residuary mass of right to their own self-government"
beyond the enumerated powers they had granted to the national government. Whenever the national government assumed "undelegated powers,"
he concluded, "its acts are unauthoritative, void, & of no force." Jefferson
did not clarify what it meant that the Sedition Act was "void & of no force,"
but he did assert that "where powers are assumed which have not been delegated, a nullification of the act is the rightful remedy." Jefferson's allies in
Kentucky adopted the resolutions (without revealing Jefferson's authorship)
as a formal protest against the Alien and Sedition Acts. They deleted the
section on nullification, however. The next year, Kentuckians protested the
Alien and Sedition Acts again, but this time they used Jefferson's resolution
on nullification. They conceded that they would "bow to the laws of the

Union," however, deferring any practical effort to nullify. Thus, it was left to South Carolina in 1832 to determine precisely what state nullification of a federal law might entail. Kentucky did adopt Jefferson's most menacing rhetoric in 1798, in the claim that continued federal intrusion on state power "may tend to drive these states into revolution and blood." The southern states were unprepared to take up Jefferson's nullification banner, although Georgia and Tennessee both adopted resolutions condemning the Alien and Sedition Acts as well. Other southerners condemned the Kentucky Resolutions as irresponsible sectionalism, however.[26]

The more controversy Jefferson endured, the more he mused on philosophical matters. Jefferson believed if the nation adhered to its first principles, the details of policy would take care of themselves. This accounts for Jefferson's "profession of political faith"—a platform for the upcoming presidential election—which he offered to Massachusetts Republican Elbridge Gerry in 1799. He thought the United States needed to return to tenets including "an inviolable preservation of our present federal constitution, according to the true sense in which it was adopted by the states." Moreover, he confessed, "I am for freedom of religion, & against all maneuvers to bring about a legal ascendancy of one sect over another: for freedom of the press, & against all violations of the constitution to silence by force & not by reason the complaints or criticisms, just or unjust, of our citizens." Finally, he maintained that society should shrug off the burdens of tradition and superstition. Jefferson refused to "go backwards instead of forwards to look for improvement, [or] to believe that government, religion, morality & every other science were in the highest perfection in ages of the darkest ignorance." Federalists opposed these first principles, he believed, but Jefferson was certain the "great body of our fellow citizens" embraced them, and would realign the national government with his ideals in 1800.[27]

Jefferson still upheld the power of education to form young white men's minds according to such republican precepts. He spent a great deal of time as vice president advising one such man, William Munford, on the best sources for learning. He had done the same with other protégés such as his nephew Peter Carr. Munford asked for book recommendations, and Jefferson responded to him at length not long after the adoption of the Kentucky Resolutions. The Anglican faith of the vice president's upbringing seemed relatively distant in this compilation, with no Bible and no works by the Anglican

Laurence Sterne, though such sources would reappear on book lists he compiled later. This list did include many of Jefferson's other standard recommendations, such as Locke's and Hume's works, Madison and Hamilton's *The Federalist*, and books by the French philosophes Voltaire and Condorcet.[28]

Munford, who turned out to be a scoundrel, had the temerity to ask Jefferson (the vice president, mind you) to acquire some of the books for him. Remarkably, Jefferson complied with his request—never one to turn down opportunities to go to bookshops. By early 1799 he had found several titles for Munford, including Condorcet's *The Progress of the Human Mind*. This volume had been published in English translation by Benjamin Franklin Bache. Bache was the grandson of Benjamin Franklin, one of the most outspoken Republican newspapermen, and a target of the Sedition Act.[29]

In a 1799 letter to Munford, Jefferson showed how much he agreed with Condorcet's much-discussed theory of human perfectibility. That theory stood in stark contrast to the significant (though hardly universal) Calvinist strain within Anglican thought. Jefferson told his protégé that he was "among those who think well of the human character generally. I consider man as formed for society, and endowed by nature with those dispositions which fit him for society. I believe also, with Condorcet . . . that his mind is perfectible to a degree of which we cannot as yet form any conception." Jefferson did not consistently maintain this cheerful optimism, and routinely took more negative views of humanity's proclivity toward faction. But the letter to Munford was an occasion for idealism. Jefferson regarded as "cowardly the idea that the human mind is incapable of further advances. This is precisely the doctrine which the present despots of the earth are inculcating, & their friends here re-echoing; & applying especially to religion & politics." The friends of despots were the Federalists and Adams; that is, the authors of the Alien and Sedition Acts. "As long as we may think as we will, & speak as we think," he assured Munford, "the condition of man will proceed in improvement."[30]

Jefferson would be hard-pressed to preserve optimism as the 1800 election approached. The political calculus in Virginia changed dramatically in 1799 with the deaths, six months apart, of Jefferson's nemesis Patrick Henry and George Washington. President Washington was the last emblem of a founding politics of consensus. Washington and Jefferson never reconciled following the publication of Jefferson's "Samsons in the field" letter.

Jefferson later professed to have felt, upon hearing the news of the first president's passing, that "verily a great man hath fallen this day in Israel" (II Samuel 3:38). As for Henry, the Federalist-turned-Republican Tench Coxe of Pennsylvania told Jefferson that his death was "a very important event: Since it has pleased God to dispense it." Antipathy toward Jefferson and toward the French had turned Henry into a Federalist in the 1790s. In his final months, Henry had warned against the consequences of the Kentucky Resolutions, though he also opposed the Alien and Sedition Acts as unwarranted assertions of national power. Jefferson was muted about the death of Henry in 1799. Years later, in characteristic language, Jefferson was still complaining about the late Henry's "apostasy" from republican principles.[31]

As illustrated by his bookstore trips for William Munford, Jefferson's personal life retained moments of genteel leisure. One of the most consequential elections in American history loomed, but Jefferson still had time to discuss making Parmesan cheese with his friend Charles Clay, the former pastor of the Calvinistical Reformed Church in Charlottesville. "I shall be glad to have the pleasure of trying a bit with you some of these days on the spot where made," Jefferson wrote to Clay in 1799.[32]

Time for science and theology remained, too. Jefferson began a significant four-year correspondence with Unitarian minister and scientist Joseph Priestley in early 1800. Priestley, a decade older than Jefferson, was one of the first scientists to isolate oxygen as an element. He was an embodiment of Jefferson's maturing religious and intellectual ideals, and his chief conduit into Unitarianism. Enlisting in the Jeffersonian cause, Priestley had criticized the Adams administration and the Alien and Sedition Acts. This earned Priestley contempt from Federalist editors. "You have sinned against church and king and can therefore never be forgiven," Jefferson wrote sarcastically to the minister. Jefferson noted that John Ward Fenno of the *Gazette of the United States* (Philadelphia) had taken up the "Anglican" side of the Federalists' critique. This referred to columns like one from 1799, simply titled "PRIESTLEY," in which the *Gazette* called Priestley a "Sectarian of a peculiar religious creed" with few adherents in America (Jefferson, of course, was one of those few). The *Gazette* said that Priestley had stigmatized "with the odious charge of idolatry, every sect and denomination of Christians, who do not with him believe in the non-entity of the Holy Ghost, and that our Lord and Saviour, Jesus Christ, is a private person." To Jefferson, this critique of Priestley's rational theology exemplified the hidebound Christianity he rejected.[33]

Joseph Priestley, portrait by Gilbert Stewart, 1889, based on an engraving by W. Hall. (Courtesy Library of Congress)

Conversations with pastors including Clay, Priestley, and others remained a steady feature of Jefferson's life. By comparison, Ben Franklin's explicit interest in religion faded a bit after his diplomatic career began in the 1750s. Franklin engaged in deeper theological conversations as a young man than Jefferson ever did, and Franklin had a more thorough knowledge of the English Bible than any of the major Founders. Jefferson's biblicism extended further into the ancient languages (especially Greek and Latin) than Franklin's. Franklin knew Priestley much longer than Jefferson did, but Priestley had a deeper impact on Jefferson's thinking. It would have been understandable if Jefferson's engagement with theological topics had waned once he became secretary of state, too. But it didn't. Undoubtedly this sustained interest in theology, and relationships with pastors and theologians, reflected Jefferson's close linkage of politics, liberty, and religion. His political enemies also tended to be his religious enemies.[34]

Jefferson's correspondence with Priestley began at the outset of the most eventful fifteen months of Jefferson's political life. All Epicurean considerations of Jefferson leaving behind the "bustling world" were forgotten. Presidential candidates maintained a muted approach, but the election of 1800 promised a decisive showdown between Republicans and Federalists. Partisanship was on full display, and in 1800 John Adams took a trip through Pennsylvania and Maryland that looked suspiciously like a campaign tour, arguably the first one ever in American history. The 1800 election would also enshrine the role of partisan newspapers in America. The Federalist drumbeat against Jefferson was clamorous. The attacks on Jefferson were riding on a massive proliferation of news that took place in the early national period. A search for "Jefferson" in the standard digital collection of historic American newspapers yields sixteen times as many hits in the year 1800 than in 1796.[35]

Even more than in 1796, the 1800 partisan hubbub focused on Jefferson's religion, or lack thereof. The most glaring instance of religion-baiting in the 1800 election was the *Gazette of the United States'* "Grand Question," which ran repeatedly during fall 1800. That question was, "Shall I continue in allegiance to GOD—AND A RELIGIOUS PRESIDENT; or impiously declare for JEFFERSON—AND NO GOD!!!" The latter phrase was an allusion to Jefferson's statement in *Notes on the State of Virginia* that "it does me no injury for my neighbor to say there are twenty gods, or no god." That quote was frequently cited by his critics in 1800, in addition to Jefferson's comments on religion, the races, and geology in *Notes,* Jefferson's support of the French Revolution, and his friendship with Thomas Paine.[36]

The Reverend William Linn spoke for many of Jefferson's adversaries with the pamphlet *Serious Considerations on the Election of a President.* Linn and Jefferson had earlier exchanged information about Native American linguistics. Now the Dutch Reformed pastor became one of the vice president's most vociferous opponents. "My objection to his being promoted to the Presidency," Linn explained, "is founded singly upon his disbelief of the

Holy Scriptures; or, in other words, his rejection of the Christian Religion and open profession of Deism." Scholars often refer to Jefferson as a "deist," but Jefferson rarely discussed deism, and when he did so he was usually referring to others, not himself. Linn equated Jefferson's apparent doubts about biblical authority with deism, however, pointing to Jefferson's evident skepticism in *Notes on the State of Virginia*, including his implication that Africans were created as a separate race from whites. To Linn, this denied the Genesis account of Adam and Eve. Linn also cited the "twenty gods, or no god" passage. Jefferson said that one's beliefs made no difference in one's capacity for public life. Linn disagreed. "Let my neighbor once persuade himself that there is no God, and he will soon pick my pocket, and break not only my leg but my neck." Unbelief, to Linn, fed chaos and criminality. A man who would profess such heresies was not fit to be the president of a "Christian nation," Linn insisted. Federalists were alarmed by the prospect of such a person becoming president. Hamilton, for one, pled with John Jay to consider emergency measures in the New York legislature to help stop "an Atheist in Religion and a Fanatic in politics" from becoming president.[37]

Jefferson's supporters countered the charges of skepticism and atheism. New York's DeWitt Clinton, writing as "Grotius," insisted that there were instead "the strongest reasons to believe" that Jefferson was a "real christian" and a "believer." Clinton made a valiant effort to construe Jefferson's statements as ones that a mainstream Christian could make. He chastised Linn for torturing "some speculative notions of Mr. Jefferson on philosophy, into a disbelief of christianity." Federalists were not impressed by such defenses, however. "That Mr. Jefferson is a CHRISTIAN is now for the first time rung in our ears," observed the *Newport Mercury*. The writer urged New Englanders not to be fooled. "The lucubrations of Mr. Jefferson are now before me, and I think he discloses his cloven foot in every page. Find out what Hume and Voltaire were, and then you will see what this mighty Virginian is." As evidence of the vice president's "wanton malignity," the columnist cited the "twenty gods, or no god" passage.[38]

An overwhelming majority of white Americans in 1800 would have identified as Christians. Sectarian evangelicals—especially in the South and on the western frontier—supported Jefferson in large numbers, due to Jefferson's sterling record on religious liberty. It is not entirely accurate, however, to say that "revival country was also Jefferson country," as historian Forrest McDonald once surmised. But that was basically true everywhere outside of the Northeast. The nation began to enter the era of the Second Great Awakening just as Jefferson became president. Some of his evangelical supporters connected the two events. They said that full religious liberty made true revival more likely. Federalists, by contrast, contended that the nation needed a devout believer as president, implying that John Adams was one and Jefferson was not. Republicans put more emphasis on Jefferson's policies regarding religion, rather than issues of personal faith. Both parties catered to certain kinds of Christian voters in the 1800 election, but Republicans erected a bigger religious tent. Their movement encompassed evangelicals and skeptics alike, mainly because of Jefferson's and Madison's commitment to religious freedom. They also appealed to white southerners generally, whose votes counted more because of the three-fifths clause's bonus. Jefferson was grateful for the support of evangelical pastors. He told a Baptist correspondent in 1800 that he had begun to question his former opposition to clergy serving in public office. Perhaps he was thinking of examples such as Charles Clay, whom Jefferson sometimes assisted politically. The Virginia constitution prohibited clergy in public office as part of disestablishment. Jefferson was always suspicious of "priestcraft," but this hardly meant that he had no pastors as friends and allies.[39]

Jefferson himself stayed quiet about his alleged atheism and deism, despite pleas by supporters who asked him to affirm Christian faith publicly. One of the starkest differences between politics in 1800 and today is not the relative nastiness of campaigns, but the candidates' ability to *avoid* speaking about contentious issues. (Jefferson also avoided addressing his relationship with Sally Hemings, which would become a minor issue in the 1804 election.) In any case, Jefferson chose not to address his faith directly, letting defenders cast him as an acceptable alternative for devout voters. Jefferson told James Monroe that "as to the calumny of atheism, I am so broken to calumnies of every kind . . . that I entirely disregard it." He supposed that if he addressed the allegations, it would only fuel the Federalists' fire. He figured that the electorate could judge him by his three decades of public service.[40]

Stung by Federalists' attacks, however, Jefferson became keen to present himself as a rationalist Christian, not a deist. Priestley's influence had helped to convince him that there was a reasonable type of Christianity that he could take seriously. Jefferson found similar encouragement from the Philadelphia physician and Patriot leader Benjamin Rush. Jefferson was so candid with Rush about his religious views that he nearly panicked when

Rush died, fearing that Rush's family might expose their letters to the public. Rush had grown up in an evangelical Presbyterian family. He retained those influences, but as an adult, Rush's Christian beliefs became virtually synonymous with republicanism. Rush told Jefferson that he saw Christianity as the "strong ground of Republicanism. . . . It is only necessary for Republicanism to ally itself to the christian Religion, to overturn all the corrupted political and religious institutions in the World." Rush wanted to confirm that Jefferson shared his certainty about Christianity's compatibility with republicanism, and he cited notable examples (such as Scotland's Lord Kames) of intellectuals who allegedly transitioned from skepticism to Christian faith in their mature years.[41]

Like Rush, Jefferson became convinced that *true* Christianity (as opposed to priestcraft) enhanced liberty and republican virtue. This stance was sincere but also politically calculated. Adherence to "true" Christianity allowed Jefferson to refute the Federalists' allegations about his radical skepticism. Rush's queries about Jefferson's beliefs elicited an illuminating response just months before the 1800 election. Jefferson assured Rush that he had a view of Christianity "which ought to displease neither the rational Christian or Deist; & would reconcile many to a character they have too hastily rejected." The only doubters Jefferson figured he could not convince were the "*genus irritable vatum*" ("irritable tribe of poets/prophets," a phrase taken from Horace) who craved a national established church. He could not be reconciled to that tribe, because he had "sworn upon the altar of god eternal hostility against every form of tyranny over the mind of man." The quote would come to encircle his statue at the Jefferson Memorial in Washington, D.C.[42]

Federalists were badly divided in 1800, with some Hamiltonians disliking John Adams almost as much as they disliked Jefferson. Adams *did* detest Hamilton more than Jefferson, repeatedly calling Hamilton a "bastard." Hamilton likewise hated Adams, coming out publicly against his reelection. The intra-Federalist feud did not guarantee a Jefferson victory, however, because Aaron Burr became an unexpected Republican contender for the presidency too. Burr had helped to orchestrate an impressive state victory for New York Republicans in May 1800, which boded well for Jefferson's prospects outside the South. Many Republicans understood Burr to be the vice presidential choice. Party leaders, however, inexplicably failed to arrange for

Jefferson Memorial. (Courtesy Wikimedia Commons)

at least one Republican elector to vote for Jefferson for president, and not Burr. When the electoral votes were counted, Jefferson and Burr were tied. Thus the election careened into the House of Representatives.[43]

The Electoral College tie led to one of the gravest political crises in American history. A Virginia uprising of enslaved people, led by the black-smith Gabriel in summer 1800, also fueled the year's edgy mood. Some Federalists blamed Gabriel's revolt on Jefferson's radical democratic views, or on reckless egalitarian preaching by his Baptist supporters. "If anything will correct and bring to repentance old hardened sinners in Jacobinism, it must be an insurrection of their slaves," a column reprinted in Federalist newspapers mused. For his part, Jefferson was relatively lenient toward the slave rebels, recommending that those who had not yet been executed should be deported instead. This leniency may have been rooted in Jefferson's earlier statements that slave rebellion, while intolerable, was an understand-able act by a people enslaved and oppressed. In any event, by fall 1800 America's cities were rife with rumors of civil war, secession, and assassination attempts on Jefferson.[44]

Meanwhile, Republicans controlled more House of Representatives delegations, but they did not possess a clear majority. The Federalists could

Mad Tom in a Rage, etching, 1801. Historians are not certain whether the human depicted in this Federalist cartoon is Thomas Paine or Thomas Jefferson—the devil might represent Jefferson. (Courtesy Metropolitan Museum of Art)

not win the election outright, but they could bog it down by refusing to give Jefferson a majority in the House. Aaron Burr complicated matters by letting it be known that he was willing to serve as president should he emerge as the consensus candidate. Some Federalists planned to make Burr president, hoping he might prove more pliable than Jefferson. Hamilton, whose list of political enemies was virtually endless, hated Burr even more than he hated Jefferson. Even though Jefferson was a "contemptible hypocrite," Hamilton said, he was still preferable to Burr. (Burr would eventually kill Hamilton in a duel.) At least the Republicans would take all the blame for a Jefferson presidency. The Federalists would bear responsibility for a Burr win, Hamilton warned.[45]

Burr didn't actively seek the Federalists' support, however. After an excruciating series of inconclusive votes, in February 1801 some Federalists in the House finally capitulated. They withdrew their votes, allowing Republicans to elect Jefferson on the thirty-sixth ballot. Adams and the Federalists, to their credit, accepted the result, averting a constitutional crisis. Years later, Jefferson called this election the "revolution of 1800." It "was as real a revolution in the principles of our government as that of '76," he observed. In the immediate aftermath of the election, he exclaimed to Priestley, "What an effort, my dear Sir, of bigotry in Politics & Religion have we gone through. The barbarians really flattered themselves they should even be able to bring back the times of Vandalism, when ignorance put everything into the hands of power & priestcraft." To his Massachusetts ally Elbridge Gerry, Jefferson exulted that New England Federalists had failed in their attempt to take America "back to the times when we burnt witches." Contrary to the book of Ecclesiastes, Jefferson told Priestley, "we can no longer say there is nothing new under the sun. For this whole chapter in the history of man is new." The false priests, heretics, and witch-burners had lost; true believers had taken charge of the republic once more.[46]

8. "Diamonds in a Dunghill"

During the bruising 1800 presidential campaign, Jefferson asked himself "whether my country is the better for my having lived at all?" The publication of a semi-accurate campaign profile of Jefferson had precipitated the question. The vice president jotted thoughts about how he might narrate his political autobiography. Some notable successes jumped to mind, though he wasn't sure if his role was essential in any of them. One accomplishment that he highlighted was the passage of Virginia's Statute for Establishing Religious Freedom. That piece of legislation was pure Jefferson, and when it passed in 1786 (via Madison's adroit politicking), it put Virginia in the vanguard of religious liberty. There was much left for Jefferson to do, however, and much damage to undo from the Federalist "reign of witches." Jefferson's self-doubt also pointed to an unsettledness in him that would fuel new explorations of faith. This season of spiritual wrestling unfolded as he struggled with the weight of being president.[1]

Federalists saw a new reign of witches rising too, in Jefferson and his ostensible crew of Francophile radicals. A month before he secured the election, Jefferson attended Sunday service in the Capitol Building, where a sermon was delivered by Episcopal chaplain Thomas Claggett, the bishop of Maryland. Although church attendance was not unusual for him, Jefferson undoubtedly regretted coming to this service in particular. Claggett launched an anti-French screed, hardly attempting to mask his intended target. Representative Roger Griswold, a Connecticut Federalist, recorded that Claggett raged against the "visionary plans of the French Philosophers." Jefferson, according to

Griswold, "took every word to himself, and thought the Bishop was delivering a Philippic upon his theories." The vice president "blushed like a young girl of fifteen, and . . . no doubt wished the Bishop and his Prophecies at the devil."[2]

In public statements, Jefferson was almost always magnanimous, and he hated being singled out in person by critics. Throughout most of American history, magnanimity has oiled the machinery of formal politics. Effective presidents make humble and unifying public comments, even if vitriol and animosity swirl just below the surface. Jefferson's skills as a wordsmith, and his republican ideal of public service, served him well in this capacity. When the House formally declared him the president-elect, Jefferson graciously replied (echoing Philippians 4:8) that "whatsoever of understanding, whatsoever of diligence, whatsoever of justice, or of affectionate concern for the happiness of man, it has pleased providence to place within the compass of my faculties, shall be called forth for the discharge of the duties confided to me." His talk of providence was heartfelt. Who but the flintiest skeptic could have won the presidency and not interpreted it as a sign of God's unfolding purposes? Some supporters saw more specific significance in his election. The Swedenborgian church of Baltimore exulted that "the Heavenly Doctrines of the 'New Church' [the Swedenborgians] confirm us in the belief, that, 'God rides on the Whirlwind, and directs the storm'!— and encourage us to anticipate, with indescribable sensations, an approaching period . . . when Reason and Religion shall fully unite their sacred & all powerful influence.' " A rationalist millennium seemed at hand.[3]

Jefferson's generous statements culminated in his first inaugural address, delivered before a packed Senate chamber. The speech marked the first transfer of power between parties under the new Constitution. Jefferson heralded the moment with one of the finest orations in presidential history, surpassed only by Abraham Lincoln's second inaugural address. Jefferson pled for American unity, asserting, "We are all Republicans, we are all Federalists." But Federalist critics were dismayed when Jefferson interpreted the feuding of the previous decade as another episode of fighting over political religion. "Having banished from our land that religious intolerance under which mankind so long bled and suffered," Jefferson said, "we have yet gained little if we countenance a political intolerance, as despotic, as wicked, and capable of as bitter and bloody persecutions." Federalist aggressions such as the Sedition Act sprang from the same spirit that led Catholics and Protestants to torture and murder each other, he believed.[4]

Echoing Madison in *The Federalist,* Jefferson insisted that although human nature would present a perennial threat, the American system remained "the world's best hope." Where was the pristinely moral man who could serve as a benevolent autocrat? "Have we found angels in the forms of kings . . . ? Let history answer this question," Jefferson mused. America had special resources that would ensure the republic's survival, however. These included geographic separation from the old European world and plenty of room to grow "to the thousandth and thousandth generation." (Here he quietly assumed the expropriation of Native Americans' lands.)[5]

Jefferson also cast America's Christian commitment as a basis of republican strength and national cohesion. He was prompted to do this by the accusations that he was hostile to Christianity. Benjamin Rush had also convinced him that true Christianity was the perfect religion for a republic. In the inaugural, Jefferson noted that Americans were "enlightened by a benign religion, professed indeed and practised in various forms, yet all of them inculcating honesty, truth, temperance, gratitude and the love of man, acknowledging and adoring an overruling providence, which by all its dispensations proves that it delights in the happiness of man here, and his greater happiness hereafter." The pursuit of happiness, rightly practiced, would elicit the blessings of providence. Enlightened Christianity, far from a source of strife, represented a centripetal moral force. If America had a "creed" of political faith, he said, it was based on the principles of the Bill of Rights: freedom of religion, freedom of the press, and impartial justice. In closing, Jefferson prayed, "May that infinite power, which rules the destinies of the universe, lead our councils to what is best, and give them a favorable issue for [the people's] peace and prosperity." Echoing the Declaration's invocation of rights granted by the Creator God, Jefferson's first inaugural address envisioned an American civil religion based on enlightened Christian virtue and on God's providential guidance.[6]

As presidents, Washington and Adams took on regal bearings. By contrast, Jefferson's administration combined the image of republican modesty with massive expenditures on hospitality. In one episode, a flummoxed English diplomat encountered Jefferson at his residence "not merely in an undress, but actually standing in slippers down at the heels, and both pantaloons, coat, and under-clothes indicative of utter slovenliness." Jefferson assiduously eliminated trappings that smacked of monarchy.[7]

Amid its relative informality, Jefferson's presidency was dogged by the unending expenses that had already trapped him as a Virginia gentleman and diplomat. "However he may neglect his person," noted one observer, Jefferson "takes good care of his table. No man in America keeps a better." Margaret Bayard Smith, the wife of a Jeffersonian editor in Washington, observed that his household combined "republican simplicity" with "Epicurean delicacy." At ease in small-group settings, he dined with other politicians or diplomats virtually every night, the only exceptions being occasions when Jefferson hosted large parties that he called "campaigns." Especially when Congress was in session, these functions were planned for maximum political influence. He hosted dinners in a French manner, including a choice selection of wines. Benjamin Latrobe, architect of the U.S. Capitol, was dazzled by a visit to the President's House in 1802, noting that the "dinner was excellent, cooked rather in the French style (larded venison), the dessert was profuse and extremely elegant. . . . Wine in great variety, from sherry to champagne, and a few decanters of rare Spanish wine." The evening's conversation, led by James Madison, was equally rich. Topics included architecture, science, and the writings of Joseph Priestley. Louisa Catherine Adams, spouse of John Quincy Adams, was struck by Jefferson's "French servants in livery, a French butler, a French cuisine, and a buffet full of choice wines." Jefferson was paid well, with an annual salary of $25,000, but the president had to cover household expenses himself, including the staff's pay.[8]

The Washington, D.C., home's most visible servants were French. Enslaved people mostly labored in the background. The Hemings family, including Sally, were generally left at Monticello, although she and other Hemingses likely visited Jefferson in Washington periodically. Jefferson hired and then purchased an enslaved man named John Freeman, who was effectively a body servant. Freeman commonly traveled from Monticello with Jefferson and his daughters. Jefferson also brought a series of three enslaved female teenagers to the President's House, primarily so they could train as cooks. Free workers, both white and black, did menial duties at the house too, including cleaning and nursing. They also tended the presidential flock of sheep, which by the end of his second term totaled forty animals.[9]

Jefferson's expenses were astronomical, but he viewed them as nonnegotiable. In some years, paying his staff took more than 15 percent of his $25,000 salary; expenses on wine alone sometimes consumed more than 20 percent of it. He imported most of the wines from France, Spain, Portugal, or Italy, though he occasionally served American-grown vintages as well. The most comprehensive list of Jefferson's wines in Washington was appended to his memorandum book for 1803. His "Wines Provided at Washington" is a significant document in the history of American wine consumption. Line after line, year after year, the list records Jefferson's purchases of thousands of bottles and dozens of "pipes," at about 110 gallons per pipe. The bulk of the drink expenses in his early presidency went for pipes of Portuguese Madeira wine, which was virtually the American "national beverage" after the Revolution.[10]

Jefferson laboriously acquired, recorded, and consumed the European wines he and his guests liked best. For example, he procured half the personal stock of champagne owned by a Spanish diplomat, then began working with the man he had appointed as the American commercial agent in Paris to obtain supplies directly. In one ledger entry for 1804 Jefferson gave a minutely detailed record of how the champagne was being drunk. "There remain on hand 40 bottles of the 247 of Champagne. . . . The consumption then has been 207 bottles, which on 651 persons dined is a bottle to 3 1/7 persons. Hence the annual stock necessary may be calculated at 415 bottles a year or say 500." Jefferson was ostensibly calculating exactly how much champagne he needed in the future—then he upped his anticipated order by 20 percent more bottles, just to be safe. That ledger entry emblemizes his fiscal disarray. Jefferson kept precise records, but he never seemed to confront his disastrous financial situation realistically. Political decorum as president afforded little consideration of belt-tightening.[11]

Jefferson also commissioned improvements to the President's House and its environs. Since the Adamses had only lived there a few months before Jefferson became president, the house remained a rustic work in progress. Enslaved and free workers tore down many of the shacks and construction-related buildings on the property, though on-site projects remained visible through the end of his second term. Jefferson wished to get rid of the outhouse on the lawn, but he had to wait until 1803 for the installation of indoor water closets. Decorators turned the "oval room" on the first floor (the modern Blue Room of the White House) into a drawing room, with four mahogany sofas and twenty-four gilded Louis XVI chairs upholstered in blue silk. Jefferson had bells installed in the residence so he could summon servants instantly and discreetly.[12]

Once the electoral storm had passed, Jefferson got down to the business of governing. Depredations on American shipping by the so-called Barbary

A View of the President's House, engraving by William Strickland, 1814: a depiction of the president's residence as it appeared six years after Jefferson's tenure there. (Courtesy Library of Congress)

pirates of North Africa presented an immediate crisis. North African corsairs were among the longest-standing threats to American vessels, dating to the colonial era. The fact that the corsairs were Muslims exacerbated concern over this seemingly ineradicable threat. In the 1790s, the Washington and Adams administrations had secured costly peace deals with Algiers, Tripoli, and Tunis, which required payoffs for hostages and tributes to North African leaders. All told, the treaties cost an enormous $1.25 million, or more than 20 percent of the entire federal budget. Jefferson had needed to deal with the Barbary pirates since his tenure in Paris. He developed a conviction that Americans required enough naval power to act decisively against the North Africans. The national government should not allow them to threaten America's seagoing merchants, who sent fish, timber, and agricultural products to ports in the Mediterranean world.[13]

In 1801, the tentative peace with Tripoli was crumbling. Tripoli's pasha Yusuf Karamanli directed corsairs to resume attacks on American ships. Pasha Yusuf, twenty-three years younger than Jefferson, had seized power in Tripoli in 1795. Jefferson decided to make an example of Tripoli, and in 1801 the American schooner *Enterpriȝe* defeated the corsair *Tripoli* in battle. Delighted, Jefferson conveyed thanks to the commander of the *Enterpriȝe*. "Too long, for the honour of nations," Jefferson wrote, "have those barbarians been suffered to trample on the sacred faith of treaties, on the rights & laws of human nature." "Barbarians" came from the same root word as "Barbary," a Greek term (*barbaros*) roughly meaning "foreigner."[14]

The Jefferson administration struggled to resolve tensions with Tripoli, however, and in 1803, Tripolitan forces captured the U.S.S. *Philadelphia* and its crew of 307 sailors. The loss was mitigated in early 1804 when U.S. commander Stephen Decatur led a successful expedition to destroy the *Philadelphia* to keep Tripolitans from using it. The conflict with Tripoli renewed long-standing fears about Muslim predations, and the possibility of American Christians converting to Islam. "From a Midshipman," a letter written from a Tripoli prison, related that several of the *Philadelphia*'s crew had already "turned traitors to their country, by embracing the Mahometan religion and taking up arms against their country." Jefferson, determined not to compromise, sent most of the rest of the American navy to the Mediterranean, and allowed American hostages to languish in captivity for a year rather than pay for their release. After the American defeat of Derne (east of Tripoli), Yusuf Karamanli signed a treaty with the United States. The captives were freed after the United States paid a small ransom. Jefferson had inherited a messy situation with the Barbary corsairs, and North Africa would become a major problem again during James Madison's second term as president. Yet Jefferson's naval war against Tripoli became one of the most successful examples of his executive forcefulness.[15]

In December 1801, in accord with constitutional requirement, Jefferson gave his first annual message to Congress (in the twentieth century this became known as the State of the Union address). He "gave" it literally, sending written copies to Congress via his secretary Meriwether Lewis. Jefferson, always a better writer than public speaker, regarded oral delivery of the message as pompous and quasi-monarchical. Much of the address was filled with assurances that Jefferson would control government expenses. Jefferson also used the speech to confirm that the administration would offer due reverence to God. Observing a global trend toward peace, Jefferson declared that "whilst we devoutly return thanks to the beneficent being who has been pleased to breathe into [European nations] the spirit of conciliation and forgiveness, we are bound, with peculiar gratitude, to be thankful to him

Decatur Boarding the Tripolitan Gunboat, oil painting by Dennis Malone Carter, 1841. (Courtesy Naval History and Heritage Command, Washington, DC, (NH 44647-KN).

that our own peace has been preserved through so perilous a season." God was the author of peace among the nations. There is no reason to think that Jefferson was insincere in crediting providence for the relative peace the United States enjoyed, except for the conflict with North Africa. Jefferson's language also undercut Federalists' charges that his presidency would unleash Jacobin atheistic rule.[16]

Among Jefferson's most important allies in undermining charges of his irreligion were sectarian Christians. Anglicans and Congregationalists, especially in northern states, tended to accept connections between church and state, connections that originated in colonial-era establishments of religion. Many sectarian groups, including Baptists and smaller movements such as the Sandemanians, revered Jefferson because of his defense of religious freedom for all. Their congratulations to Jefferson showed that not all American Christians viewed him as a threat. For example, the Delaware Baptist Association sent an admiring address to Jefferson, declaring, "With emotions of Gratitude to the Almighty Ruler of the Universe, who manageth the affairs of the Terrestrial Globe ... we lift up our hearts, and render the

Tribute of Thankfulness to him who hath indulged us with worshiping according to the sacred Scriptures and the dictates of our Consciences." A delighted Jefferson wrote back to the Baptists, joining them "in rendering the tribute of thankfulness to the Almighty ruler, who, in the order of his providence, hath willed that the human mind shall be free." He thanked them for prayers on his behalf "to that being whose counsels are the best guide, & his favor the best protection under all our difficulties."[17]

The Danbury Baptists of Connecticut engaged in similar dialogue with Jefferson. Their plea for help, however, precipitated one of the most legally momentous exchanges of his career. New England Baptists represented a reliable pocket of support for Jefferson in an overwhelmingly Federalist region. Massachusetts and Connecticut maintained established churches after the adoption of the First Amendment to the Constitution, which restricted Congress alone from making any "law respecting an establishment of religion, or prohibiting the free exercise thereof." It was only in the mid-twentieth century that judges "incorporated" the First Amendment into the Fourteenth Amendment, applying it to states. The Danbury Baptists, representing congregations in western Connecticut and eastern New York, rejoiced in Jefferson's election. They wondered, too, if he had any means of challenging Connecticut's official Congregationalist establishment.[18]

The Baptists commiserated with Jefferson for the Federalists' attacks on him as a closet atheist. No wonder that the agents of Christian establishment "should reproach their chief Magistrate, as an enemy of religion Law & good order because he will not, dares not assume the prerogative of Jehovah and make Laws to govern the Kingdom of Christ." They knew that as president, Jefferson could not meddle with the laws of a state. They hoped that his example and sentiments for religious liberty, however, might influence the states until every species of spiritual tyranny disappeared from America. In conclusion, they assured Jefferson that they believed "that America's God has raised you up to fill the chair of State out of that good will which he bears to the Millions which you preside over. . . . And may the Lord preserve you safe from every evil and bring you at last to his Heavenly Kingdom through Jesus Christ our Glorious Mediator."[19]

The Danbury Baptist missive did more than show that Jefferson enjoyed support from some devout Christians. It also afforded him a possible opportunity to explain his disinclination to proclaim days of fasting and prayer. Washington and Adams had issued such proclamations. The New England states had held such prayer days at the outset of Jefferson's presidency, too, and his allies suggested that Jefferson might blunt criticism by at least "taking some favorable Opportunity to deny the Authority of the Executive to direct such religious exercises." Some urged Jefferson to announce a national prayer day, even if he needed to employ "decorous language" to make clear he was not *ordering* people to pray. Jefferson remained convinced that he should never expect credit from the Federalist clergy on any religious issue. There was no persuading them that he was not anti-Christian, whatever he did about prayer days. Comparing the Federalist clergy to Jesus's Jewish foes (and implicitly comparing himself to Jesus), Jefferson wrote, "They crucified their Saviour who preached that their kingdom was not of this world, and all who practice on that precept must expect the extreme of their wrath."[20]

Jefferson reckoned that days of prayer and fasting were better left to the states' discretion. As president, he was often meticulously principled about the division of powers under the federated Constitutional system. The Constitution clearly left religious matters to the states, not to the national government. He made this distinction clear in a letter to Presbyterian pastor Samuel Miller in 1808, in the midst of a desperate crisis over Jefferson's embargo on American exports. Jefferson knew that the New England states were proceeding as usual with days of prayer and fasting. However, "No power to prescribe any religious exercise, or to assume authority in religious discipline, has been delegated to the [national] government," Jefferson wrote. "It must then rest with the states, as far as it can be in any human authority." He didn't especially want the government sponsoring religious ceremonies, anyway, even though Jefferson had crafted and endorsed prayer proclamations as a Virginia officeholder in the 1770s and '80s.[21]

Jefferson drafted a response to the Danbury Baptists in hopes of "sowing useful truths & principles" about church-state relations. He told Attorney General Levi Lincoln that the letter furnished an opportunity "of saying why I do not proclaim fastings & thanksgivings, as my predecessors did." The Baptists had not requested that he explain this issue, but he figured this was a good chance to do so. In his original draft, Jefferson characterized proclamations of prayer days as "practiced indeed by the Executive of another nation as the legal head of its church." This was a reference to the king of England, which made this statement (had the sentence remained) an attack on executives who did declare days of prayer. He might as well have publicly labeled Presidents Washington and Adams as monarchists. Given that the New England states had just recently held official prayer days, and given the touchiness about criticizing the deceased Washington, Levi Lincoln advised him to tone down the letter. Even Republicans in New England respected the annual days of prayer, Lincoln reminded the president. Lincoln suggested that he make the language "guarded" so that no one would construe it as an attack on his predecessors or the New England states.[22]

In the end, Jefferson was convinced by Lincoln's warning, and he abandoned the discussion of prayer days altogether. It was too volatile a topic. Silence might serve him better than forcing the issue. Just the fact that Jefferson was having a mutually "affectionate" exchange with devout New Englanders spoke volumes. He considered the final letter less offensive than the first draft. Ironically, the toned-down final missive became the most debated letter in the history of American church-state relations.[23]

The president told the Danbury Baptists that he believed, like them, "that religion is a matter which lies solely between Man & his God, that he owes account to none other for his faith or his worship, [and] that the legitimate powers of government reach actions only, & not opinions." He commended the First Amendment, "that act of the whole American people which declared that their legislature should 'make no law respecting an establishment of religion, or prohibiting the free exercise thereof,' thus building a wall of separation between Church & State." To Jefferson, this meant that the nation could have no established church. He hoped that the same principle would eventually extend to Connecticut and all the states. "I shall see with sincere satisfaction the progress of those sentiments which tend to restore to man all his natural rights." Progress in natural rights would include the disestablishment of the state churches, a transition that Virginia had enacted in 1786. But the states alone decided about disestablishment. The Constitution did not empower the national government to force church-state separation upon the states. He concluded by reiterating his appreciation for the Baptists' support, saying that he reciprocated their "kind prayers for the protection & blessing of the common father and creator of man."[24]

We don't know where he got the phrase "wall of separation," but Jefferson was not inventing a new concept. Something like that phrase had regularly appeared in writings of Protestant reformers such as Martin Luther. When "wall of separation" appeared in print prior to 1802, however, it was often referring to the description in Ephesians 2:14 of a "wall of partition" separating Jews and Gentiles. Roger Williams, the founder of Rhode

Island and pioneer of religious liberty, had once written of a "wall of separation between the garden of the church and the wilderness of the world." A
wall separating the holy church and the profane world is not the wall
Jefferson was referencing, however. There's little evidence that Jefferson
had read Williams. Historian Daniel Dreisbach, the top expert on the wall
metaphor, has shown that if Jefferson had a direct source for the wall quote,
it likely was the Scottish educator and writer James Burgh. Jefferson and
friends of his, including Joseph Priestley, read and admired Burgh. In the
mid-1760s, Burgh had written of the need to erect "an impenetrable wall of
separation between things sacred and civil" to avoid corrupting the churches.
That wall was similar to the one Jefferson posited in 1802. Jefferson might
have read that passage in Burgh, and may have remembered it when
addressing the Danbury Baptists. In any case, whatever the states might do
with regard to religion, the First Amendment prohibited the nation from
sponsoring an established church. Jefferson certainly had no intention of
acting like the head of a national denomination.[25]

Jefferson's reply to the Danbury Baptists garnered little notice in 1802.
For the time being, his chance for "sowing useful truths & principles" was
largely lost. A few newspapers in New England printed the reply, but not
even the Danbury Baptists seem to have circulated it themselves. After 1802,
the reply was confined to occasional appearances in collections of Jefferson's
writings. The landmark case of *Reynolds v. United States* (1879), concerning
the criminalization of Mormon polygamy, turned the Danbury Baptist letter
into a fixture of church-state jurisprudence. The Supreme Court's opinion in
Reynolds cited the letter to the Danbury Baptists as "almost . . . an authoritative declaration of the scope and effect" of the First Amendment's establishment clause. (This despite the fact that Jefferson did not participate in the
deliberations about the First Amendment.) Not only has the phrase "wall of
separation" appeared in many church-state cases since 1879, but it has
become the most common—and disputed—metaphor for church-state relations in the United States. It has come up repeatedly in controversies ranging
from town council prayers to Ten Commandments monuments. Whatever
Jefferson would think about those controversies, he would be pleased that his
"useful truths & principles" have not been forgotten.[26]

First there was Jefferson's reply to the Baptists. Then came the mammoth
cheese. January 1802 represented an opportunity for him to regain control of

the narrative on religion, and a big block of cheese played a major role in the effort. The cheese was four feet wide and weighed twelve hundred pounds. It was crafted by the Baptist "Ladies" of Cheshire, Massachusetts, who made it, a Republican newspaper noted, "as a mark of the exalted esteem they had of [Jefferson] as a man of virtue, benevolence, and a real sincere friend to all Christian denominations." Written on the rind was "Rebellion to Tyrants is Obedience to God."[27]

The cheese's escort from Cheshire to Washington was the Baptist preacher John Leland, one of the era's most influential evangelical leaders and a Jeffersonian zealot. Leland was eleven years younger than Jefferson and a native of Massachusetts. He had experienced conversion and had become a Baptist in the early 1770s. Thereafter, he began preaching and relocated to Virginia, where he served Baptist churches and the cause of religious liberty. In Virginia he became an ally of Madison and Jefferson. Madison and Leland reportedly met in 1788, when Leland urged Madison to support a religious liberty amendment to the Constitution. (The original Constitution in 1787 did not include a Bill of Rights.) Leland agreed to back ratification of the Constitution if Madison would promote the amendment in the First Congress. When Leland returned to New England in 1791, he directed his political energies against the established churches of Connecticut and Massachusetts while pastoring in Cheshire.[28]

Critics lambasted the "MAMMOTH CHEESE," while newspapers punned incessantly about all things mammoth and cheese. This moniker was an allusion to Jefferson's fascination with mastodon bones recently discovered in New York, and his assumption that wooly mammoths still lived in the American interior. One Federalist watched as Jefferson's supporters paraded with the cheese in a "ludicrous procession, in honor of a cheesen God." The cheese proceeded down the Hudson River to New York, then by sea to Baltimore, and finally to Washington, where it arrived at the end of 1801. Jefferson himself used the "mammoth cheese" phraseology when he noted its arrival, saying it was "an ebullition of the passion of republicanism in a state where it has been under heavy persecution." The widely reprinted address of the delegation from Cheshire echoed the Danbury Baptists' belief that "the Supreme Ruler of the Universe . . . has raised up a Jefferson at this critical day, to defend Republicanism." Jefferson responded with gratitude to the Cheshire Baptists the same day he sent the Danbury Baptist letter. Perhaps hoping not to overlap themes, Jefferson's response to the Cheshire address focused on agrarian ideals, hailing the cheese as a "mark of esteem from freeborn farmers."[29]

We would know less about that religious liberty weekend in Washington were it not for a letter by a hostile Federalist representative, Manasseh Cutler. The congressman reported that Leland delivered a sermon before Jefferson and members of Congress on January 3, 1802. On New Year's Day Cutler had reluctantly visited the President's House, where the staff treated members of Congress with "cake and wine" and allowed them to view the mammoth cheese. The Yale-educated Cutler, who was also a Congregationalist minister, thought that the "cheesemonger" Leland's sermon two days later was a travesty. Leland, a "poor, ignorant, illiterate, clownish preacher," spoke on Matthew 12:42: "Behold, a greater [one] than Solomon is here." To Cutler, the oration was a "farrago, bawled with stunning voice, horrid tone, frightful grimaces, and extravagant gestures." No "decent auditory" had ever heard anything like it, Cutler scoffed. Cutler and other Federalist critics may have reviled Leland, the cheese, and Jefferson's unwashed Baptist supporters, but public pageantry of this sort was key to political mobilization in the early national era. Until the cheese became too maggot-ridden to save, Jefferson made a viewing of it a standard experience for visitors. He even had a special frame built to hold the cheese together as it aged.[30]

Jefferson's presidency hardly dulled the nation's partisan rancor, despite his magnanimous statements and constant dinner parties. Every step he took elicited a chorus of derision from the Federalist press. At the end of John Adams's presidency, Federalists had put their final imprint on the government, particularly in the form of last-minute judicial appointees. Jefferson and the Republicans rolled back those measures, including abolishing some judgeships and refusing to deliver judicial appointments. Several Federalist officials alleged that James Madison, as secretary of state, had illegally declined to deliver their commissions as justices of the peace. One of these officials, William Marbury, lent his name to the landmark 1803 decision *Marbury v. Madison*. In that case, Jefferson's cousin and adversary John Marshall, the chief justice of the Supreme Court, avoided a showdown with the Jefferson administration over the Marbury commission, a showdown that Marshall would have lost. But the decision deftly allowed Marshall to establish the court's power to review the constitutionality of laws (judicial review), a prerogative that has become central to the modern Supreme Court's authority.[31]

Alarming controversies were emerging within Republican ranks, too. The union between Jefferson and Vice President Aaron Burr represented no more than a political marriage of convenience. Jefferson never regained trust in Burr after the electoral intrigues of 1800. Alexander Hamilton, hating both Burr and Jefferson, reported with delight in mid-1802 that there was "a most serious schism between the chief and his heir apparent; a schism absolutely incurable, because founded in the breasts of both in the rivalship of an insatiable and unprincipled ambition." Jefferson made clear that he did not want Burr to continue as vice president, and Burr futilely sought to get elected as governor of New York. After a reported insult against Burr by Hamilton in 1804, the two engaged in a duel, in which Burr fatally wounded Hamilton. Burr managed to serve the rest of his term as vice president. Charges related to his killing of Hamilton were state-based matters, ones that he evaded. Burr's role in Jefferson's Republican Party was over, however. Yet Jefferson's ordeal with Burr was only beginning, as Burr's quixotic intrigues in the Southwest led to him being tried for treason in 1807.[32]

Jefferson grew weary of incessant Federalist attacks, too. One might assume that the great foe of the Sedition Act might have always defended a free press. Jefferson had more tolerance for the free press than did John Adams, but he nevertheless maintained that states could prosecute writers and editors for seditious libel, broadly construed. We may also recall that Jefferson's argument in the Kentucky Resolutions focused more on the limits of national government power than it did press freedom per se.[33]

Jefferson's patience with a free press was tested when his aggrieved former ally James Callender went public with allegations about the president's relationship with Sally Hemings. In 1802, in the *Richmond Recorder*, Callender wrote that it was well known that "the man, *whom it delighteth the people to honour,* keeps, and for many years past has kept, as his concubine, one of his own slaves. Her name is SALLY. . . . The African Venus is said to officiate, as housekeeper at Monticello." (The "delighteth the people to honour" quote was a reference to the villain Haman in the book of Esther 6:6–11.) As we have seen, Callender was a desperate, drunken race-baiter who resented Jefferson for not making him postmaster of Richmond. He also loathed Jefferson for his relationship with Hemings, whom he reviled as a "slut as common as the pavement." Yet his report was a blockbuster, and it correctly reported the existence of the relationship, even if it apparently erred in some factual details.[34]

Federalist outlets picked up the report regarding Hemings, issuing lurid satires about Jefferson's affair. One of these outlets was the *Port Folio* of Philadelphia, which also excoriated Jefferson for the mammoth cheese, for his friendship with the anti-Christian skeptic Thomas Paine, and for fostering licentious democracy in general. ("Democracy" in the early 1800s still had negative connotations, especially among Federalists.) In 1803, the *Port Folio*'s editor Joseph Dennie published an anti-Jefferson rant against democracy that earned Dennie state prosecution for libel. Dennie wrote that "democracy is scarcely tolerable at any period of national history. . . . It is on its trial here, and the issue will be civil war, desolation, and anarchy." In an earlier letter Jefferson wished to be kept "entirely confidential," the president had suggested that the governor of Pennsylvania should prosecute the most obnoxious Federalist editors. "The press ought to be restored to its credibility if possible," Jefferson wrote. "The restraints provided by the laws of the states are sufficient for this if applied: and I have therefore long thought that a few prosecutions of the most eminent offenders would have a wholesome effect." Although Dennie would eventually be found not guilty, his case dragged on for years. It had a chilling effect on the *Port Folio*'s criticisms of Jefferson.[35]

In the midst of the partisan maelstrom, one of Jefferson's top priorities was geographic expansion west in the interests of America's "empire of liberty." White settlement in Ohio, Kentucky, and Tennessee was growing at a breakneck pace, a pace surpassed only by the phenomenal growth of Protestant churches (especially Baptist and Methodist congregations) during the Second Great Awakening. Despite his skepticism about evangelical piety, Jefferson assumed that the spread of Christianity would stabilize the frontier.

This assumption helps explain President Jefferson's support for a treaty with the Kaskaskia Indians that provided federal financial assistance to the Catholic Church. The treaty stipulated that since the "greater part of the said tribe have been baptised and received into the Catholic church to which they are much attached, the United States will give annually for seven years one hundred dollars towards the support of a priest of that religion. . . . And the United States will further give the sum of three hundred dollars to assist the said tribe in the erection of a church." The United States already owed this money to the Kaskaskias due to a land cession the Indians had made. It is still notable, however, that payments to the church were coming from the government with Jefferson's blessing. Madison, realizing that this arrangement could appear to violate the First Amendment, advised Jefferson not to discuss the details of the treaty in his 1803 annual message to Congress, lest they suggest "a principle, not according with the exemption of Religion from Civil power."[36]

A desire to secure American navigation rights to the Mississippi River and the port of New Orleans prompted Jefferson to send his protégé James Monroe to Paris in 1803. Jefferson did not realize that the stage was being set for the Louisiana Purchase, the greatest triumph of his presidency. France's Napoleon Bonaparte despaired of trying to manage the French empire in North America and the Caribbean, partly due to the French military's ongoing failures in Saint-Domingue. This fabulously lucrative sugar-growing island had been the crown jewel of France's colonies. As we have seen, enslaved people in Saint-Domingue initiated a successful insurrection against French rule in 1791. As Jefferson was on the cusp of winning the American presidency, Napoleon began crafting a plan to reassert French control of Saint-Domingue and to reimpose slavery there. Napoleon got Spain to return the Louisiana Territory to France in exchange for French concessions in continental Europe. At the end of 1801, Napoleon sent tens of thousands of soldiers to Saint-Domingue. Jefferson was concerned about the reassertion of French sovereignty in both Saint-Domingue and Louisiana. Jefferson and other Americans were especially sensitive about the control of New Orleans. The president wrote that the Gulf of Mexico port was the one place in the world that "the possessor of which becomes our natural and habitual enemy," because of its centrality to American trade and agriculture. He worried that if the French campaign against Saint-Domingue was successful, Napoleon might transfer troops to secure New Orleans, too.[37]

The French campaign in Saint-Domingue ended in a disastrous quagmire, due to formidable resistance by black rebels and epidemic yellow fever among the French. Revolutionary leader Jean-Jacques Dessalines declared Saint-Domingue officially independent from France on January 1, 1804, and renamed the country Haiti. Deciding to cut his losses, Napoleon made a clean break from all of France's North American possessions. In April 1803, he offered to sell not just New Orleans but the vast Louisiana Territory to the United States for $15 million. American diplomats had an opportunity to double the size of the nation, adding much of the land between the Mississippi River and the Rocky Mountains.[38]

Although the price for Louisiana was substantial, and Jefferson doubted whether the Constitution permitted such a purchase, the value of the deal and the allure of western lands overcame his misgivings. An already-planned surveying expedition by Meriwether Lewis and William Clark took on additional urgency in 1803 when news arrived of the diplomatic coup. Newspapers fortuitously carried the announcement of the purchase on the Fourth of July. Federalist criticism of the Louisiana Purchase was muted, as Federalists generally approved of the treaty's goals, if not the costs or method of acquisition. Even some critics of Jefferson acknowledged that the unexpected opportunity was another of the "kind interpositions of an over-ruling Providence . . . by which we have more than once been saved from the consequences of our errors and perverseness." Still, some Federalists put their opposition to the treaty in familiar spiritual terms. Josiah Dwight of Massachusetts, one of the venerable Dwight clan of New England Federalists, explained that Jefferson had the American people "as completely blinded as were the Sodomites who would have defiled the men of God [Genesis 19]—A thick film is upon their eyes which it would seem nothing short of miraculous power can remove—When their City shall be on fire they will see the error of their ways—but it will be too late for them to repent." Most politicians would not repent about the Louisiana treaty, however, which overwhelmingly passed in the Senate in October 1803.[39]

The months before and after the Louisiana Purchase witnessed the most decisive season of religious reflection in Thomas Jefferson's life. He had regularly thought about religious and ethical matters since his time at William and Mary. He had never formed a definite theological position, however. His eclectic strains of Epicurean, republican, and Christian thought had not crystallized into a personal creed. The reasons 1803–4 became so decisive for Jefferson in this regard are unclear. Why does anyone go through a spiritual or intellectual transformation at the specific time that they do? Many experience their most decisive changes in early adulthood, as was the case for Jefferson's fellow skeptic Ben Franklin. Jefferson's moment of religious commitment came much later in life. By 1804, the sixty-one-year-old concluded that Jesus's ethical teachings were the "most benevolent & sublime" ever known to humankind. They were superior to all others. This was the basis upon which Jefferson concluded he was a Christian—or a Christian rationally understood.[40]

Jefferson had gone through seasons of severe stress before, most obviously in the death of his wife, and the political crises of the 1790s. The furor of the 1790s had abated little in Jefferson's first term. If anything, criticisms against him in 1800 became more bitter, and more focused on his alleged atheism. In 1802, Thomas Paine returned to America after a lengthy tenure in Europe, giving Federalist newspapers fresh opportunity to associate Jefferson with the most notorious anti-Christian writer among the Founders. Jefferson must have also been horrified by Callender's public revelation of his relationship with Sally Hemings. Jefferson would never address those charges directly. They may have made him anxious, however, to present himself as a supporter of Christian morality in the eyes of friends—and in those of his daughters, Martha and Mary.[41]

Jefferson's wide reading in religion and relationships with Benjamin Rush and Joseph Priestley gave him essential resources to craft a rationalist, ethics-focused version of Christianity. As we have seen, by 1800 Rush had planted the notion in Jefferson's mind that true Christianity was uniquely suited to republicanism. Then in 1803 Jefferson read Priestley's Unitarian tract *Socrates and Jesus Compared*. It provided an explanation for why Jesus's ethics possessed "infinite superiority," as Priestley put it, to ancient pagan philosophy. Priestley believed that Jesus's preternatural teaching authority originated in divine revelation. Those claims did not interest Jefferson so much as the superiority of Jesus's teachings themselves. As Priestley noted, Jesus's universal mandate to love represented a "purer and more sublime morality respecting God and man than any heathen could have a just idea of." Jefferson, wanting to read everything Priestley had written on religion, asked his Philadelphia book buyer to obtain copies of the rest of Priestley's works.[42]

Meanwhile, the president wrote Priestley that in light of *Socrates and Jesus Compared* and his conversations with Rush, he had begun to outline his own "view of the Christian system." Jefferson proposed to evaluate ancient pagan philosophers such as Epicurus and the "ethics of the Jews," showing their strengths and deficiencies. This would allow him to project Jesus as the preeminent ethical teacher, who inculcated the "principles of a pure deism, and juster notions of the attributes of god, to reform their moral doctrines to the standard of reason, justice, & philanthropy." ("Deism" here meant religion in its simplest form, especially belief in one god.) Jefferson told another correspondent that "Jesus embraced, with charity & philanthropy, our neighbors, our countrymen, & the whole family of mankind." Unlike Priestley, Jefferson "would purposely omit the question of his divinity & even of his inspiration." Jefferson noted that the biblical records of Jesus's life were imperfect and incomplete because they were recalled by flawed men long after they had heard him teach. "Yet such are the fragments remaining as to shew a master workman," the president surmised. The Gospels still captured the moral brilliance of Jesus's teaching.[43]

Jefferson remained unwilling to publicize these crystallizing opinions. He kept reminding correspondents to keep his letters private. "I never will," he wrote, "by any word or act, bow to the shrine of intolerance, or admit a right of enquiry into the religious opinions of others." Yet during the extraordinary month of April 1803, he was sufficiently motivated to write "Syllabus of an Estimate of the Merit of the Doctrines of Jesus, Compared with Those of Others." He showed the "Syllabus" to Benjamin Rush and others whose opinion he valued. Reminding Rush of the "delightful" personal conversations they had in the late 1790s about Christianity, he assured the doctor that the views expressed in the "Syllabus" were "very different from that Anti-Christian system, imputed to me by those who know nothing of my opinions."[44]

Jefferson then offered the most succinct statement of faith he ever made. "I am a Christian, in the only sense in which he wished any one to be; sincerely attached to his doctrines, in preference to all others; ascribing to himself every human excellence, & believing he never claimed any other." Jefferson saw himself as a rationalist and ethical Christian. Opposing the "corruptions of Christianity" imposed by the priests of Jesus, he embraced "the genuine precepts of Jesus himself." Jefferson told Rush that when he read *Socrates and Jesus Compared* on a short vacation at Monticello, it afforded him an opportunity to gather his views put forth in the "Syllabus." Again, he asked Rush to keep the "Syllabus" private, hoping that it would not be "exposed to the malignant perversions of those who make every word from me a text for new misrepresentations & calumnies." Jefferson wanted confidants to know that he had become a naturalistic Christian, but he did not want this change reported in newspapers.[45]

Jefferson sent the "Syllabus" to Priestley, Rush, his daughters, and others. It began by considering the greatest ancient philosophers, including Socrates, Epicurus, and Seneca. He admitted that he still regarded their teachings on the passions and tranquility as "really great." But they focused too much on the interior life. "In developing our duties to others, they were short and defective . . . still less have they inculcated peace, charity, & love to our fellow men, or embraced, with benevolence, the whole family of mankind." Jews advanced a true idea of one god, but their ideas about that god were "degrading and injurious." Jesus entered this milieu as a great reformer. Jesus operated under manifest disadvantages, including his Jewish context, his lack of education, and the fact that he passed on his teachings to "the most unlettered, & ignorant of men." (One of Jefferson's correspondents suggested that he moderate his characterization of the Gospel writers and call them "men of but little literary information.")[46]

Jefferson saw Jesus's ethical code as "the most perfect and sublime that has ever been taught." The records we have of those teachings, he emphasized, are "defective" and underdeveloped. Jesus had only three years to develop his philosophy before his tragic death. He did not record his teachings personally, and "fragments only of what he did deliver have come to us, mutilated, misstated, & often unintelligible." The Gospel accounts, Jefferson wrote, "have been still more disfigured by the corruptions of schismatising followers" who altered the simple purity of Jesus's philosophy for other ends. (Jefferson later exclaimed that money-grubbing priests had "adulterated" Jesus's teachings "by artificial constructions, into a mere contrivance to filch wealth & power to themselves." Those corrupters were the "real Anti-Christ," he wrote.) Jefferson explained that the "question of his being a member of the god-head, or in direct communication with it, claimed for him by some of his followers, and denied by others, is foreign to the present view." He knew that he and Priestley did not agree about Jesus's divine mission, and Jefferson told Priestley as much when he sent him the "Syllabus." Jefferson's interest in Jesus was merely ethical. It was in Jesus's "universal philanthropy . . . to all mankind" that he found the "peculiar superiority of the system of Jesus over all others." He did concede that a "future state" was essential to Jesus's teachings, as a chief incentive to moral behavior. He had hoped that Priestley would do more to assess Jesus's teachings in their ancient context, and to produce an edited version of the Gospels with only Jesus's authentic precepts included. But Priestley died in February 1804, depriving Jefferson of his most influential religious interlocutor.[47]

Jefferson's fascination with Jesus also led him to produce the first version of what's called the Jefferson Bible. He reckoned that he could mine the Gospels for the real teachings of Jesus. Biblical scholars have fought many wars since Jefferson's time regarding the reliability of the Gospels, but Jefferson was confident that distinguishing Jesus's true words in the New Testament was like picking out "diamonds in a dunghill." Sometime during

February and March 1804, he cut and pasted his compilation of the Gospels (only in English) onto blank sheets and had them bound into a volume. He recalled later that he did the work in "one or two evenings only, while I lived at Washington, overwhelmed with other business."[48]

The text of the first Jefferson Bible, unfortunately, is lost, but we do know its title: "The Philosophy of Jesus of Nazareth . . . Being an Abridgement of the New Testament for the Use of the Indians." Given his interest in Indian missions, languages, and education, Jefferson might have hoped that the volume would introduce some Native Americans to authentic, rationalist Christianity. Some scholars, however, have posited that "Indians" was code for his Federalist enemies. In any case, he told John Adams later that he made "The Philosophy of Jesus" for his "own use," and that he regarded the forty-six-page volume as a distillation of Jesus's "pure and unsophisticated doctrines, such as were professed & acted on by the unlettered apostles, the Apostolic fathers, and the Christians of the 1st century." It was an attempt at recovering and clarifying true Christian teaching.[49]

Years later, Jefferson still told correspondents about the "wee little book" he had pasted together in 1804. "It is a paradigma of his doctrines, made by cutting the texts out of the book, and arranging them on the pages of a blank book . . . a more beautiful or precious morsel of ethics I have never seen." He presented "The Philosophy of Jesus" as "proof that I am a real Christian, that is to say, a disciple of the doctrines of Jesus, very different from the Platonists, who call me infidel." This "morsel of ethics," along with the "Syllabus," encapsulated Jefferson's beliefs. With the Gospel compilation complete, his religious pilgrimage had arrived at its destination. In retirement, he would flesh out his beliefs with correspondents including John Adams, who became his most engaging conversation partner on religion after Rush and Priestley. Aided by this small epistolary community, Jefferson had settled upon an intellectually satisfying version of Christianity.[50]

9. "Strange Inconsistant Man"

The year 1804 saw Jefferson's greatest triumph in politics: his resounding reelection as president. But the year was also clouded with grief. Deaths magnified his sense of advancing age as he entered his sixth decade of life. Joseph Priestley died in February 1804, but he and Jefferson were always closer intellectually than they were personally. A severer blow came in April, when his daughter Mary (Polly) died of complications from childbirth. He told his oldest friend John Page that "others may lose of their abundance; but, I, of my want, have lost, even the half of all I had. My evening prospects now hang on the slender thread of a single life"—the life of Martha (Patsy), his remaining child.[1]

A Christian framework helped him to interpret death—that of Mary and his own. "Every step shortens the distance we have to go," he reminded Page. "The end of our journey is in sight, the bed wherein we are to rest, and to rise in the midst of the friends we have lost." Citing I Thessalonians 4, Jefferson noted, " 'We sorrow not then as others who have no hope'; but look forward to the day which 'joins us to the great majority.' But whatever is to be our destiny, wisdom, as well as duty, dictates that we should acquiesce in the will of him whose it is to give and to take away [Job 1:21], and be contented in the enjoyment of those who are still permitted to be with us." But Jefferson could not unhesitatingly embrace hope of a reunion with Mary or with his long-deceased wife. Even amid the pain of losing Mary, Jefferson could not say for sure if death was the end of existence, or if there was a future with lost loved ones. He resonated with an argument advanced by the French scientist and theologian Blaise Pascal in *Pensées* (1670), a book Jefferson had recently acquired. Pascal believed that it was prudent to accept

Martha Jefferson Randolph, painting by Thomas Sully,
ca. 1820–30. (Courtesy Library of Congress)

the deaths of relatives as God's will, and to hope for reunion in heaven. If
the afterlife did not exist, death would just end one's consciousness. There
was little lost in hoping for an afterlife, and much to gain if it was true.[2]

As the 1804 election approached, the Federalists were in deep trouble.
Jefferson was popular, and not just in his traditional areas of strength. Most
observers recognized that negotiating the Louisiana Purchase without war
against France was a brilliant success. Federalists tried to renew fears about
Jefferson as an anti-Christian zealot, but Jefferson had not given them much
evidence of such fanaticism during his first term. He attended religious services regularly, and his speeches and letters were full of providential language.
Federalists still scrambled to find hints of the president's infidelity. One
account noted that Jefferson seemed to do all his traveling on the Sabbath,
which struck some devout Americans as heedlessly provocative. The president's defenders not only highlighted his respect for religion, but emphasized the fact that his first term had coincided with the outbreak of the Second
Great Awakening. Far from a reign of godlessness, Jefferson's protection of

religious freedom had led to massive increases in evangelical Christian adherents, they contended. Republicans now mocked the president's Christian Federalist critics. "No language is too foul, no epithet too severe for the *virtuous* feds to attach to the President," wrote the *Republican Spy* of Springfield, Massachusetts. "Will the good sense of the people be much longer imposed upon by such factious scribblers?"[3]

Allegations about Jefferson's relationship with Sally Hemings faded somewhat after the drowning death of James Callender in 1803. The election of 1804, however, was the presumed occasion for a stunning print, *The Philosophic Cock*, by the cartoonist James Akin. Jefferson is depicted as a rooster, Sally Hemings as a hen. Akin put a human face on Hemings, but there is no reason to think the image is what she actually looked like. *Cock* in the early 1800s meant a rooster, but it was also slang for a penis. The controversy over Hemings sparked again in 1805 when a Virginian published a letter in a Boston newspaper giving more details about the relationship, which the letter characterized as "unquestionably true." Another Massachusetts newspaper article in 1805 recapitulated standard charges against Jefferson, including that he had "taken to his bosom a sable damsel." (This piece generated yet more controversy when Jeffersonian legislators tried to revoke the editor's publishing contract with the state.) In 1806, a Connecticut court charged a minister with seditious libel for allegedly saying that Jefferson had taken from his enslaved people "a wench as his whore." Jefferson still did not address the Hemings allegations. In his second inaugural address, however, he did comment that the "artillery of the Press has been levelled against us, charged with whatsoever its licentiousness could devise or dare."[4]

The 1804 election was almost as easy for Jefferson as 1800 had been difficult. There would never be another debacle quite like 1800, in any case, since the Twelfth Amendment created separate ballots for president and vice president. Parties no longer had to worry about securing an elector to withhold one vote for the vice presidential candidate. Riding the wave of Jefferson's popularity, the Republicans in 1804 triumphed in both the Electoral College and Congress. Only Delaware and Connecticut went for the Federalist candidate, Charles Cotesworth Pinckney. Even Massachusetts, the onetime stronghold of Federalist politics, voted for Jefferson, which delighted the president. He compared the results in Massachusetts to the return of the prodigal son in the Gospel of Luke. "This is truly the case," he wrote, "wherein we may say 'this our brother was dead, and is alive again: and was lost, and is found.' "[5]

Philosophic Cock, engraving by James Akin, ca. 1804. (Courtesy American Antiquarian Society)

In his second inaugural address, Jefferson struck a confident balance between the free exercise of religion and God's providential rule over the nation. Addressing prayer days, a topic he had dropped from the 1802 Danbury Baptist letter, Jefferson explained that he had "undertaken, on no occasion, to prescribe the religious exercises suited to [the nation]: but have left them, as the constitution found them, under the direction & discipline of the state or church authorities." Not wanting to leave the matter there, however, Jefferson advanced one of his most aggressively providential interpretations of American history. Recalling his proposal for the national seal in 1776, Jefferson compared America's relationship to God to that of Israel. He proclaimed that "I shall need too the favour of that being in whose hands we are: who led our fathers, as Israel of old, from their native land; and planted them in a country flowing with all the necessaries & comforts of life; who has covered our infancy with his providence, & our riper years with his wisdom & power." The president asked Americans to pray that God would grant wisdom to him and all their leaders.[6]

For all his skepticism and ambivalence toward traditional religion, Jefferson's second inaugural address confirmed his willingness, even eagerness, to employ providential rhetoric as a statesman. It is difficult to ascertain to what extent Jefferson's talk of providence reflected political posturing and how much was personal conviction. He spoke of his sense of providence to the Marquis de Lafayette in 1811, when the retired Jefferson felt free to be candid about his religious sentiments. Watching the horrors of the Napoleonic Wars unfold in Europe, he assured Lafayette that "if there be a god, & he is just, his day will come. He will never abandon the whole race of man to be eaten up by the leviathans and Mammoths of a day." On one hand, Jefferson seemed certain that God would not permit the cruel empires of Europe to extinguish liberty. On the other, it sounded agnostic to question whether there was a God, or whether God was just. Such talk reminds us of Jefferson's letter to Peter Carr in 1787 when he exhorted his nephew to "question with boldness even the existence of a god." But even more traditional Christians frequently used the wording "if there be a god," more a turn of phrase than an assertion of agnosticism. Jefferson's mentor Joseph Priestley, for example, wrote that "if there be a God, a providence, and a future state, which are the objects of religion, it must be of the greatest consequence to men to be apprized of them." Used this way, the phrase was a reminder that we should focus on God's providential care, and not doubt it. After Napoleon's defeat and exile, Jefferson wrote that the development "proves that we have a god in heaven, that he is just, and not careless of what passes in this world." On balance, it seems probable that Jefferson was a committed providentialist.[7]

Two-term American presidents generally do worse in their second term than in the first. But few presidents have enjoyed more good fortune in their first term, and less in the second, than Thomas Jefferson did. After the election, the Republicans began to splinter. Jefferson's cousin and onetime ally, Virginia congressman John Randolph of Roanoke, became one of his most effective and bitter rivals. Complaining about the expansion of national power under Jefferson, Randolph struck themes that recalled the Anti-Federalists' critiques of the Constitution. In response to attacks by fellow Republicans, Jefferson mused that he "had always expected that when the republicans should have put down all things under their feet [paraphrasing I Corinthians 15:27 and similar passages], they would schismatise among themselves."[8]

John Randolph of Roanoke, oil painting by John Wesley Jarvis, 1811.
(Courtesy Smithsonian Institute)

Randolph assumed the role of Virginia nemesis that Patrick Henry had once played in Jefferson's life. Even more flamboyant and aggravating than Henry, Randolph regularly wore a riding outfit in Congress, complete with boots, spurs, and a whip. His hunting dogs accompanied him to the floor. A medical condition seems to have kept Randolph in a prepubescent state throughout adulthood, and he spoke in a high-pitched tone that grated on rivals' nerves. Randolph was a master of the political insult and, according to one observer, a "flowing gargoyle of vituperation." He took to calling Jefferson the "prince of projectors" and "St. Thomas of Cantingbury."[9]

Randolph frowned at the Jefferson administration's efforts to settle a corrupt land deal for the Yazoo territory in Georgia. Additionally, as chairman of the House Ways and Means Committee, Randolph refused to cooperate with the administration's efforts to purchase Florida for $2 million. Randolph's strident opposition to Jefferson, and to James Madison as secretary of state, made him persona non grata in establishment Republican circles. Jefferson saw Randolph as a cocky, puritanical pest. Randolph turned to biblical language to frame what was happening inside Republican ranks: "I am tired of setting up idols for the mere honor of being sacrificed upon their altars. . . . 'Tis time for Republicans and Republicanism to make a stand against Patriots (or rather wolves in sheep's clothing) who are secretly acted upon and supported by the federal party." Randolph referred to his faction as "Quids" as he publicly repudiated the Republican Party in 1806. This term derived from *tertium quid*, or a "third something," but the abrasive Randolph would never lead a third party to rival the Republicans and Federalists. He would just prove a constant annoyance to Jefferson.[10]

As 1806 wore on, Jefferson fell into deeper personal turmoil. He still grieved over Mary's death. His old mentor George Wythe died in May, allegedly from poisoning by a troubled grandnephew. Jefferson was distraught, writing that "such an instance of depravity has been hitherto known to us only in the fables of the poets." Bizarre reports began to emerge about Aaron Burr's secessionist machinations in the west as well. In 1805–6, Burr traveled down the Ohio and Mississippi Rivers, apparently gauging how much support he might raise if western states or territories broke away from the United States and/or Spain. Writing to his pastor friend Charles Clay, Jefferson called Burr's plan the most extraordinary enterprise "since the days of Don Quixote." Burr was eventually betrayed by a co-conspirator, but acquitted at his treason trial. It was never clear what the former vice president had really plotted to do in the western territories.[11]

Jefferson's financial trouble kept festering. Monticello and Pantops, his family's nine-hundred-acre plantation near Shadwell, remained active construction zones. Jefferson was always frustrated by his inability to afford all his purchases. Writing from Monticello, he told his widowed son-in-law John Wayles Eppes that he wished to improve the property at Pantops, but he had "gotten so into arrears at Washington, as to render it necessary for me not only to avoid new engagements, but to suspend every expence which is not indispensable: otherwise I shall leave that place with burthens contracted there, which if they should fall on my private fortune, will doom me to a comfortless old age." A "comfortless old age" was a real prospect. At the least he faced an old age in which he would have to live on a "fixed income," as we might say today. Jefferson cut back on expenses for wine and discretionary household items during his second term. Paying down debt seemed unattainable, however. Jefferson's stress mounted; his old headaches returned.[12]

The year 1807 saw the United States and Britain veer toward war, especially after a clash between a British warship and the U.S.S. *Chesapeake* near Norfolk, Virginia, resulted in the deaths of three American sailors. The feverish moment passed as the nation had perforce to wait for the British to explain and/or apologize for the *Chesapeake* disaster. It was not until the late 1850s that telegraphs improved the speed of transatlantic communication, and the diplomatic machinery in England moved slowly. Critics implied that Jefferson's personal immorality contributed, via God's judgment, to the crisis with Britain. "If half the vices, and immoralities are true, which are reported of our President," one anonymous correspondent wrote to Jefferson, "then may we not in a great measure impute the present gloomy situation of our country to him?"[13]

Jefferson knew that the British Navy was a far more menacing force—especially in American waters—than the Barbary corsairs ever could be. America was surging in commercial power, but its military remained small. French privateers were also threatening American ships, so England was not the only rival about which he needed to worry. Jefferson soon ordered all armed British vessels to leave the U.S. coast. But he ultimately pursued a policy of economic coercion rather than military force to get the British to stop their depredations. This led Jefferson to propose a trade embargo. The United States would stop most commercial ships from exiting its ports until Britain removed its restrictions on American shipping. A supportive Congress passed the embargo by large majorities.[14]

The spirit of the embargo was pragmatic. The United States was not in a good position to fight a naval war against Britain. Why choose war before trying economic leverage first? However admirable its intent, though, the embargo wrought economic carnage. The policy caused far more damage in the United States than in Britain. In one year, the value of American exports dropped from $108 million to $22 million. Hate mail stacked up on the president's desk. William Penn, a descendant of Pennsylvania's founder, called Jefferson a "strange inconsistant man! always at variance with Thyself." Quoting II Samuel, Penn exclaimed, "How are the mighty fallen!" All another anonymous correspondent said to Jefferson was "You are the damdest fool that God put life into. God dam you." James Madison had been one of the embargo's leading defenders, but even he realized it had backfired. When Madison was inaugurated as Jefferson's successor in 1809, Congress repealed the embargo. They replaced it with a more focused Non-Intercourse Act, which banned trade just with Britain and France. The animosity between the United States and Britain lingered, leading finally to the War of 1812 at the end of Madison's first term.[15]

Correspondents from across the country—including Republicans—pled with Jefferson to declare a day of fasting and prayer during the embargo crisis. He wouldn't do it. One anonymous writer from South Carolina commended him for his commitment to religious liberty, but insisted that "in Times of general Calamity, when the judgments of a sin avenging God, are hovering over our guilty Land;—it is to you, Sir, that [the people] must unitedly look, for calling them together to deprecate the Divine Vengeance." The exasperated writer wondered if America was "doom'd to slumber in security, on the verge of perdition,—thro' the infidelity of her chief pilot!" His failure to call a fast had "long been observed and deplored, by many thousands of your religious fellow citizens." As Jefferson had already explained to his supporter the New York Presbyterian pastor and theologian Samuel Miller, he believed that if anyone was going to declare such solemn days, it should be state governors, or churches and denominations themselves. Miller, who would become one of the first professors at Princeton Seminary (founded in 1812), turned into a vociferous critic of Jefferson, in part because of Jefferson's unwillingness to call for days of national solemnity. Miller wrote later that he had originally thought Jefferson "was an infidel; but I supposed that was an honest, truly republican, patriotic infidel. But now I think that he was a selfish, insidious, and hollow-hearted infidel." While some traditional Christians, especially Baptists, remained steadfast Jefferson supporters, Jefferson's unwillingness to declare prayer days tested the resolve of other devout Americans, who thought that the president's convictions regarding religious freedom and the First Amendment had led him to behave foolishly in a time of national crisis.[16]

Jefferson's presidency sputtered to an end in 1809. The embargo overshadowed his final year in office. Among the only comforts of 1808 was that Madison would succeed him. He kept accumulating more personal debt as president, even in the last weeks of his term. He could never reconcile the genteel demands of office and home with his longing for financial independence. As he was leaving Washington, he got Madison to co-sign a new loan for him, drawn ironically from Hamilton's brainchild, the Bank of the United States. Jefferson sent a sheepish letter to Madison about the loan, saying that he received it "willingly altho' painfully, notwithstanding a fixed determination to take care that at the termination of my duties at Washington my pecuniary matters should at least be square." They would not be square, however. Leaving office, he regaled the citizens of Albemarle County with a republican ode to laying down the "distressing burthen of power" and returning to his farm and family. He would entrust his reputation to the citizens of Charlottesville. Quoting I Samuel 12, he asked, "Whose ox have I taken, or whom have I defrauded? Whom have I oppressed, or of whose hand have I received a bribe to blind mine eyes therewith?"[17]

Back at Monticello, Sally Hemings had another baby, Eston. He had been born a year earlier, just after Jefferson turned sixty-five. Eston was the focus of the 1998 DNA study that proved a Jefferson male had been his father. Jefferson was at Monticello when Eston was conceived, during the late summer and early fall of 1807, and was also there when Eston was born, in May 1808. Sally Hemings had also given birth to a son, Madison, in 1805. Assuming Thomas Jefferson was the father of both Madison and Eston, it means that he and Hemings continued their sexual relationship after James Callender's published revelations in 1802, and throughout the media's mockery of her during the rest of his presidency. Even after he retired, enemies taunted him about Hemings. One mock Federalist toast in summer 1809 punned that while Jefferson was "not famed in War, he has achieved much honour by way of a Sally." Jefferson must have wearied of such barbs, though he was careful not to acknowledge them directly. Once during his second term, he did clip a mock "Federalist Dictionary" out of a Republican newspaper. Among the satirical definitions in the dictionary were "GOSPEL PREACHING— Calling Mr. Jefferson, in the pulpit, an infidel, a debauchee and a liar," and "HOLINESS—Moll Carey's songs, negro letters, [and] *black Sal* stories."[18]

Their continuing relationship would suggest Sally Hemings's importance to Jefferson, though we should be careful not to speculate about the precise nature of their connection. Their relationship proceeded in the coercive context of enslavement, where harsh deprivation and punishments were ever-present possibilities. Their persistence after its public exposure also reminds us that while the media environment of Jefferson's presidency could be nasty, it was also more shielding of politicians than today's environment sometimes is. There were no paparazzi waiting outside Monticello to snap pictures of the president or Sally Hemings. Reporters did not badger him with questions about her.[19]

Certain observers did comment upon Hemings's presence at Monticello, however. One was Elijah Fletcher, a Vermont-born Federalist educator who visited Monticello in 1811. Fletcher was pleased to meet the former president, who was always a generous host, regardless of a visitor's politics. An enslaved waiter handed out glasses of liquor and wine to Fletcher's party, and Jefferson showed Fletcher his library. But Jefferson's warm welcome could not overcome Fletcher's revulsion for the man, or for his domestic arrangements. "I learnt he was but little esteemed by his neighbors," Fletcher wrote. "Republicans as well as federalists in his own County dislike him and tell many anecdotes much to his disgrace—I confess I never had a very exalted opinion of his moral conduct—but from the information I gained of his neighbors, who must best know him—I have a much poorer one." Fletcher assured his father that "the story of black Sal is no farce—That he cohabits with her and has a number of children by her is a sacred truth—and the worst of it is, he keeps the same children slaves." For the Vermonter, the horror of this scenario was somewhat mitigated by the fact that it was not unusual in the South. Fletcher saw the Jefferson-Hemings relationship as "an unnatural crime which is very common in these parts . . . such proceedings are so common that they cease here to be disgraceful." Yet, although Fletcher originally found the brutality of slavery revolting, after living a couple years in Virginia he came to terms with it, and became a slave owner by marriage.[20]

Jefferson was, as always, silent about what retirement meant for his relationship with Sally Hemings, or for his children by her. He was clear about his post-presidency Epicurean ambitions, however. He would leave political strife behind and fulfill long-deferred dreams of reading, farming, and playing with his grandchildren. On Christmas Day 1808, while waiting for Madison to take office in a few months, he wrote his longtime friend Charles Thomson about Thomson's translation of the Septuagint into English, the first of its kind. Almost exactly eight years earlier, as he waited for the Electoral College to convene, Jefferson had contacted a correspondent about acquiring a copy of "Scatcherd's pocket bible." Now, at the opposite end of his presidency, he told Thomson how much he looked forward to studying the Septuagint. "I have dipped into it at the few moments of leisure which my vocations permit, and I perceive that I shall use it with great satisfaction on my return home. I propose there, among my first employments, to give to the Septuagint an attentive perusal." Quoting Galatians 6:9, Jefferson commended the seventy-nine-year-old Thomson for not being "wearied with well-doing."[21]

Jefferson was not prepared to read everything that came across his desk in retirement, however. His frequent correspondent, the Philadelphia tobacco dealer Thomas Leiper, sent him a copy of the English Unitarian minister Joseph Towers's *Illustrations of Prophecy* (1796). Leiper, Jefferson's onetime landlord in Philadelphia, assured Jefferson that the book would inform him what "God in his Providence intends to do with the Ten Kings and the Ten Kingdoms of Europe. . . . No man in my opinion can read the Book without believing the truths therein." Jefferson politely told Leiper that he had no interest in prophecy or dogmatic Christian theology. "As to myself, my religious reading has long been confined to the moral branch of religion, which is the same in all religions; while in that branch which consists of dogmas, all differ, all have a different set. The former instructs us how to live well and worthily in society; the latter are made to interest our minds in the support of the teachers who inculcate them." Even though Towers believed that the Bible predicted a "Revolution in France . . . the Overthrow of the Papal Power, and of Ecclesiastical Tyranny, the Downfall of Civil Despotism," and even though this book was a favorite of Joseph Priestley, Jefferson did not see biblical prophecy as an intellectually valid topic. John Adams agreed with Jefferson's assessment, regarding Towers's "two ponderous volumes" as "irrational."[22]

Leiper would not let the subject go, writing to Jefferson four years later, "From your Answer to me on your receipt of Towers illustration of Prophecy it appeared to me the Book was in no great estimation with you. . . . Do read the Book for certain I am after you have read it you would not be at a Loss to know how the thing would wind up." Leiper was convinced that the books of Daniel and Revelation predicted the political developments of recent decades in Europe. Jefferson responded quickly, trying to put the topic to rest. "If we differ in our opinions about Towers and his 4 beasts and 10 kingdoms, we differ as friends," Jefferson assured Leiper.[23]

Jefferson often received religious advice from correspondents. Friends such as Leiper felt that Jefferson would profit eternally from greater devotion to God and personal application of the Bible. One anonymous correspondent who seems to have been a guest at Monticello wrote letters to

Jefferson under the pen name "Goodwill." Right after he retired as president, Goodwill implored him to reflect upon the Bible, faith, and death. "Respected friend, you must be sensible, that your continuance on earth will not be long. . . . O that we may take hold of Christ by faith & rest entirely on him for our salvation." Goodwill told him several years later that he was praying that Jefferson would "shortly embrace & openly espouse the Christian Religion." No response from Jefferson to Goodwill survives.[24]

Jefferson was more inclined to dialogue with supporters who asked for his views on spiritual matters, instead of telling him theirs. This inclination produced a remarkable exchange with his Kentucky ally James Fishback, who in 1809 was a Presbyterian but by 1816 had become a Baptist. Fishback authored a pamphlet defending biblical revelation by "philosophical demonstration," and shared it with Jefferson. The president suggested that he had no time for metaphysical speculation, and figured that it was better for him to remain silent on such topics. Yet Jefferson was retired from the rough-and-tumble of politics, so he summarized his religious views for Fishback. The final version of his letter was more succinct than the draft was, however. In the draft, Jefferson argued that "every religion" agreed on the most important moral prohibitions, such as those against murder and theft. On doctrinal questions, they did not agree. Even among Christians, "we all agree in the obligation of the moral precepts of Jesus: but we schismatize & lose ourselves in subtleties about his nature, his conception maculate or immaculate, whether he was a god or not a god," and other theological and liturgical debates. "It is on questions of this, & still less importance, that such oceans of human blood have been spilt," Jefferson lamented. Though he did not chastise Fishback, he thought arguments in favor of authoritative biblical revelation were a waste of time. Yet Jefferson was more dogmatic in his Unitarian convictions than figures such as Ben Franklin, for example. Partly this had to do with Franklin's jovial personality, compared to Jefferson's penchant for brooding. But if Franklin's Christianity was virtually doctrineless, Jefferson's increasingly tended toward dogmatic Unitarianism, of his own variety.[25]

Jefferson was at his rhetorical best when speaking about the meaning of the American experiment. His retirement gave him many opportunities to reflect on America's destiny, as many people, towns, and associations thanked him for his service to the nation. To the citizens of Washington, D.C., Jefferson wrote that America's republican responsibilities were inspiring and fearsome. "Trusted with the destinies of this solitary republic of the world, the only monument of human rights, & the sole depository of the sacred fire of freedom & self-government from hence it is to be lighted up in other regions, of the earth, if other regions of the earth shall ever become susceptible of its benign influence. . . . To what compromises of opinion & inclination, to maintain harmony & union among ourselves, & to preserve from all danger this hallowed ark of human hope & happiness." In a republican sense, Jefferson's America was akin to the Israelites' ark of the covenant.[26]

Jefferson never could bask in the pleasures of musing on republican theory, however. Grubby realities of his daily life kept tugging at his attention. Never was that the case more than when he moved out of the President's House and returned to Monticello. Transporting his personal property back to Monticello proved exasperating. One of his trunks got stolen on the way back to Charlottesville, apparently while it was on a ship docked in Richmond. The trunk contained a telescope, a dynamometer, and an experimental plow Jefferson had just received from France. Most painfully, the trunk held records Jefferson had compiled on Native American languages. The disappointed pilferer apparently pitched these papers into the James River. Jefferson wrote that "some leaves floated ashore & were found in the mud; but these were very few, & so defaced by the mud & water that no general use can ever be made of them." The rest of the collection was lost.[27]

The accused thief, a slave named Ned, probably did not know that Jefferson was the owner of the trunk. If he had, he might have had second thoughts about taking it. Petty theft was an everyday occurrence on the wharfs of Richmond. Jefferson was incensed about the episode, however, especially when he learned that the culprit was an enslaved man with a criminal record. Jefferson hoped that Ned would be executed. Execution for this crime would have been outlandishly harsh, even for the time. Ned did not get off easily, though. Instead of being hanged, Ned was whipped, and his hand was branded by burning.[28]

The transition from Washington to Monticello prompted Jefferson to make more purchases. Figuring it was easier to get new furnishings for Monticello before he left Washington, he bought eighteen dessert spoons and a silver pudding dish, as well as a coverlet of crimson silk. Jefferson also bolstered his library holdings with various Unitarian writings, including a Unitarian New Testament. He frantically tried to settle accounts, including payments to a Genoese wine dealer. As he tried to balance his books, he caught glimpses of how dire his financial situation was. Jefferson and his advisors tried to shift his debts out of Washington to Virginia sources, including a private loan of $8,000 he secured from Frances Peyton Tabb of Amelia County.[29]

Jefferson wrote to his son-in-law Thomas Mann Randolph in 1809 about his financial straits. "Nobody was ever more determined than I was to leave this place [Washington] clear of debt. But trusting to estimates made by my head and confident that I had the thing quite within my power, I omitted till too late the taking an accurate view of my calls for money. The consequence is that I shall fall short 8. or 10,000 [dollars]." This estimate accounted for the loan from Tabb. He also got his old Revolutionary ally Thaddeus Kościuszko, a Polish leader living in Paris, to assume control of a $4,500 loan he owed to the Bank of the United States, with Kościuszko asking only that Jefferson pay the interest. Jefferson contemplated selling some of his far-flung properties. He did dispose of a chariot for $500 before he left, in addition to selling items to the incoming president. Madison bought items from him including a horse, one hundred bottles of Madeira, and the remaining six years of servitude due from the hired-out enslaved man John Freeman, who worked in the President's House.[30]

Shortly after returning to Monticello, Jefferson realized that he was in an even worse position to pay off his loans, including the one to Frances Tabb. In a letter to his relative and business manager George Jefferson, he wrote that bad tobacco harvests and low prices meant that he could expect his profits to "make a much less impression on my note to Mrs. Tabb than I had hoped." Frances Tabb proved not to be a gracious lender, for she called promptly for payment of her loan in 1810. Jefferson asked a bank in Richmond to assume responsibility for the debt.[31]

He also wrote to Jonathan Shoemaker, whose family was renting a gristmill at Shadwell. Shoemaker owed Jefferson money, but the gristmill operation was struggling, partly due to flood damage in 1807. Now Jefferson was receiving ominous reports about the poor flour Shoemaker was producing at the mill. Jefferson's daughter Martha was furious, knowing that her father desperately needed reliable revenue. As he prepared to return to Monticello, she wrote, "I can bear any thing but the idea of seeing you harassed in your old age by debts or deprived of those comforts which long habit has rendered necessary to you." She railed against the Shoemakers as no-accounts who might deprive Jefferson of retirement comforts. The man actually running the mill, she warned, "is not a man of business, his bargains are ruinous to himself and more over he has not one Spark of honesty." She urged Jefferson to reclaim the mill from the Shoemakers. Jefferson explained to Shoemaker "how sorely" he was pressed, and said that it was a "sincere affliction to me to be so importunate with you on the subject of my rents." He simply had to have Shoemaker pay him. Shoemaker's remittances trickled in during 1809 and 1810, but they were not nearly enough to cover what Jefferson needed. By the end of 1812, Martha's husband Thomas Mann Randolph had taken over the mill from the Shoemakers. Jefferson despaired of ever getting paid what the Shoemakers owed him. Jefferson's rickety finances were an acute problem, but characteristic of broader patterns in the region. Much of Virginia's economy rested on an unstable mountain of unpaid debts.[32]

Slave and free construction workers were putting the final touches on the "Second Monticello" when Jefferson returned to his eleven-thousand-square-foot mansion. Honoré Julien, Jefferson's French chef at the President's House, came to Monticello to finish setting up the kitchen and to train the enslaved cooks Edith Fossett and Fanny Hern. Monticello's furnishings reflected the fruit of Jefferson's travels, and his interests in science and natural history. There were animal bones and antlers, Native American artifacts, and paintings of favorite historical figures and biblical scenes. The first eleven entries in Jefferson's "Catalogue of Paintings" were images from the Bible or early church history. As we have seen, Jefferson acquired a number of these paintings (often copies of Old Masters' works) while in Europe. One large painting hanging in the parlor was a copy of Guido Reni's 1630s depiction of Salome bearing the head of John the Baptist. Jefferson owned copies of six of Reni's works, most of them depicting biblical images.[33]

Below the painting of Salome was a rendering of Christ's descent from the cross. This was a common image in medieval and early modern European art, and the motif appeared multiple times in Jefferson's Monticello collection. The small painting in the Monticello parlor—kept at eye level for easier viewing—was unusual in that it was an original, one attributed to the Flemish artist Frans Floris, who was active in Antwerp in the mid-1500s. As Jefferson described it in his catalogue, the painting had "a group of 5 figures. The body of Jesus is reclined on the ground, the head & shoulders supported in the lap of his mother."[34]

In the entrance hall, next to a painting of Saint Jerome and near an engraving of John Trumbull's depiction of the signers of the Declaration of

Independence, was a copy of Jan Gossaert's *Jesus in the Praetorium* (1527). Jefferson was under the impression that this was an original, too. In his entry for the painting, Jefferson wrote that Jesus was "stripped of the purple, as yet naked & with the crown of thorns on his head. He is sitting a whole length figure of about 4 feet. The persons present seem to be one of his revilers, one of his followers, & the superintendent of the execution. The subject from Mark 15:16–20." There is no reason to assume that Jefferson attached devotional significance to these paintings. Yet it is striking to think of the visual environment at Monticello, where biblical images—especially pictures of Jesus—surrounded the former president.[35]

The furniture at Monticello was similarly reflective of Jefferson's travels, tastes, and fascination with functionality. He had acquired much of the existing furniture in Paris a quarter of a century earlier, and some of that furniture was worn out. Jefferson, realizing that he simply had to cut costs, commissioned much of the new furniture to be built at the on-site joinery (woodworking shop) near Monticello's nail factory. Both white and enslaved carpenters worked at the joinery. Some of the most distinctive wood furniture at Monticello was constructed there, including a couple of Jefferson's "dumbwaiters," or tables with multiple tiers of shelves for serving dinners, and his revolving bookstand. Arguably his most talented carpenter was John Hemings, the half brother of Sally. Jefferson regarded Hemings's work highly. When they were young, Jefferson had his enslaved children Beverly, Madison, and Eston work on the Poplar Forest house with John so that they would learn a marketable trade. One of John Hemings's masterpieces was a writing desk for Jefferson's granddaughter, Ellen Randolph Coolidge, but tragically, the desk was lost during sea transport. Jefferson's response to his granddaughter when the desk was lost suggested his personal relationship with Hemings. "John Hemings was the first who brought me the news . . . he was au desespoir! That beautiful writing desk he had taken so much pains to make for you! Every thing else seemed as nothing in his eye, and that loss was every thing. Virgil could not have been more afflicted had his Aeneid fallen a prey to the flames." Jefferson granted John Hemings his freedom in his will. As we shall see, he also freed Sally Hemings's children Madison and Eston, having let Beverly and Harriet Hemings run away several years earlier, perhaps as a way to fulfill part of his promise to Sally that he would free any children they had together. He did not, however, free Sally Hemings herself, as doing so would have required a conspicuous petition to the state legislature asking that she be allowed to remain in the state after her emancipation.[36]

Jefferson held grudges with a ferocity unsurpassed among the Founders. But John Adams could definitely nurse a grievance, too. They had many unresolved issues left over from the bruising "Revolution of 1800." Retirement opened up new possibilities, however, and fueled their nostalgia for their surviving Revolutionary brothers. (Washington and Franklin were both gone. So was the much-hated Hamilton. Madison and Jefferson, of course, had remained allies throughout the era.) Jefferson and Adams still needed a third person to broker reconciliation, and that person appeared in their mutual friend Benjamin Rush. Rush urged Jefferson to consider resuming his correspondence with Adams. Jefferson also heard something heartening from the Virginians John and Edward Coles regarding a visit they made to Adams's Massachusetts home. Adams told them, "I always loved Jefferson, and still love him." Jefferson was touched by this sentiment, and advised Rush that "this is enough for me. I only needed this knowledge to revive towards him all the affections of the most cordial moments of our lives." Soon their correspondence resumed, and it would produce one of the intellectually richest dialogues in American history. Jefferson was not able to put all his troubles behind him; anxiety over debt and other troubles continued to ravage his household. But the letters he and Adams exchanged afforded both men great pleasure as the glories of 1776 faded into hazy memories.[37]

10. "Coup de Grace"

When John Adams and Thomas Jefferson started corresponding again, one of the first topics they discussed was prophecy. "Although you and I are weary of Politicks; you may be Surprised to find me making a Transition to Such a Subject as Prophecies," Adams told him. It was 1812, a year of turmoil as the United States faced a new war with Britain. Prophetic writings proliferated in Britain and America in the post-Revolutionary era, and interest in the end-times surged in 1811–12 due to a series of earthquakes, fires, unusual astronomical phenomena, and war. Among the most popular works was Joseph Towers's *Illustrations of Prophecy,* which Thomas Leiper had earlier urged a reluctant Jefferson to read. Adams also knew of Towers's "ponderous volumes," which Towers had written "to prove that The French Revolution was the Commencement of the Millennium," Adams noted.[1]

An incredulous Adams sketched a comparative view of prophets across races and religions. Virginia had recently seen the publication of prophetic volumes by Nimrod Hughes and Christopher McPherson, whom Adams believed were both "mulattoes." (Hughes was actually white; McPherson was a person of mixed race.) Adams wondered if "two Such Mulattoes might raise the Devil among the Negroes in that Vicinity: for though they are evidently cracked, they are not much more irrational than Dr. Towers." Prophets might be entirely deluded, but that did not necessarily make them bad writers. Even the revered Joseph Priestley had believed in prophecy, Adams reminded Jefferson.[2]

Comparative religion has always been a favorite topic for critics of traditional Christian belief. Christianity's credibility depended on its unique truth claims. If it was just one of many religions, whose prophets all made revelatory assertions, Christianity might become more an object of study than a source of divine knowledge. Thus, Adams opened his long list of contemporary prophets with the supposed mulatto prophets of Virginia, and ended by citing the "Prophet of the Wabash." This was the Shawnee visionary Tenskwatawa, the brother of Tecumseh. Tenskwatawa, some-times called simply the Prophet, had received a series of visions beginning in 1805. His teachings made him one of the most influential Indian leaders in the Ohio and Indiana regions. In 1811, Tenskwatawa's base at Prophetstown, Indiana, was destroyed by American forces under future president William Henry Harrison. Adams thought that Tenskwatawa's example demonstrated that white devotees of prophecy were as superstitious as Indians. He concluded that "whenever any great Turmoil happens in the World, [it] has produced fresh Prophets." Their verifiable prognostications were invariably refuted by the passage of time.[3]

Adams thought Jefferson might know more about the Virginia prophets, or about Tenskwatawa, since the Prophet had risen to prominence during Jefferson's administration. Jefferson said that he had never heard of Nimrod Hughes, but he had known Christopher McPherson for decades. The literate McPherson had received freedom from slavery in 1792. In 1799 McPherson received a shattering vision in which Jesus removed his heart, took it to heaven, washed it, and gave it back to McPherson. The experience confirmed his prophetic vocation. Despite McPherson's zeal, he managed to secure government secretarial jobs in both Philadelphia and Richmond. In these capacities, Jefferson came to know and like McPherson, even though he regarded him as "crazy, foggy, his head always in the clouds." Jefferson gave him occasional errands and legal assistance out of pity for McPherson's vulnerable situation. Jefferson whimsically reminded Adams, however, of Jeremiah 29's injunction that "every man that is mad, and maketh himself a prophet, thou shouldest put him in prison, and in the stocks." Adams was shocked by that obscure reference, since he assumed he knew the text of the Bible better than Jefferson did. But Jefferson had not cited chapter and verse, so Adams had to pull out his concordance to find out where it was located in the Bible.[4]

Jefferson was more contemptuous than pitying toward Tenskwatawa. This was because Tenskwatawa and Tecumseh sought an alliance with the British to counteract U.S. power in the Great Lakes region. Jefferson regarded the Prophet as a charlatan and "rogue." The Prophet "was a visionary," Jefferson concluded, "enveloped in the clouds of [Indian] antiquities, and vainly endeavoring to lead back his brethren to the fancied beatitudes of their golden age." Especially after the Louisiana Purchase, that golden age was not coming back. Jefferson was fascinated with Indian culture and languages, but mostly for scholarly purposes. Actual Native Americans, to Jefferson, needed to accept white Americans' expansion into the west. Jefferson saw Indian resistance, bolstered by this reckless prophet, as an instance where religious fervor turned from pathetic to dangerous.[5]

Jefferson had haltingly confronted his crippling debts as he approached retirement. Yet as the house at Monticello was being finished, he started building another expensive mansion at Poplar Forest. Construction began in 1806, and by 1809 a "somewhat habitable" house was in place. It would take another sixteen years for Jefferson's workers to finish Poplar Forest. He hoped that somehow Poplar Forest would become the final retreat for his extended family, and a refuge from bustling Monticello. As we have seen, Jefferson's Epicurean ideal focused on tranquility, an aspiration that he emphasized more than ever in retirement. He told Adams and many other correspondents that ease of body and peace of mind were now his "summmum bonum." Jefferson apparently assumed he must spend whatever it took to create a domestic idyll. As usual, he purchased imported furniture, ceramics, and crystal for the new house. Ellen Randolph Coolidge captured the Jeffersonian tension between consumerism and simplicity when she wrote that Poplar Forest had a "very tasty air; there was nothing common or second-rate about any part of the establishment, though there was no appearance of expense." By 1810 Jefferson called Poplar Forest "the most valuable of my possessions." Whether by "most valuable" he referred to the house itself, the surrounding farmland, or the symbolic importance of his idyll is not clear.[6]

Although Monticello was more monumental, Poplar Forest was in its way a more difficult undertaking. Although some architectural historians regard Poplar Forest as an "original and lucid masterpiece," impractical design and a lack of personal oversight meant that the secluded mansion suffered from innumerable problems. These included poor brickwork, misaligned windows, leaning Tuscan columns, and a chronically leaky roof. Poor chimney design probably contributed to a catastrophic fire at the house in 1845, two decades after Jefferson's death. The materials for the house were

Poplar Forest. (Courtesy Wikimedia Commons)

a mishmash of imported items from Europe, New York, Philadelphia, and woodwork from the Monticello joinery. Wherever the materials came from, teamsters had to take them on an arduous trip by water, and then overland. Poplar Forest, near Lynchburg, was even more rural and isolated than Monticello was. Much of the carrying and building work was conducted by enslaved people.[7]

One of the bondspeople who worked at Poplar Forest was James Hubbard. Hubbard had a long record of disappointing Jefferson. As a boy he worked in Jefferson's nailery, where Jefferson regarded Hubbard as inefficient. His performance apparently improved, however, and Hubbard stayed on at the nailery after many other boys left for the fields. In 1805, Hubbard made his first runaway attempt. He was arrested in Fairfax, Virginia, and forcibly returned to Monticello. Hubbard spent the next half decade splitting time between Monticello and Poplar Forest. Sometime around New Year's 1811, Hubbard again left Monticello without permission, this time heading west, disappearing into the rugged, foggy hills. Before Hubbard was tracked down, Jefferson cut his losses and sold Hubbard (in absentia) to a carpenter named Reuben Perry. This was standard practice: Jefferson wanted slaves who ran away or showed other signs of "delinquency" banished from his properties. Jefferson kept up the search for Hubbard, however. If Hubbard was captured and delivered to Perry, Jefferson would receive more money. More than a year after Hubbard stole himself from Monticello, he was discovered hiding in Lexington, Virginia, and he ran off again. A bounty hunter finally captured Hubbard and brought him back to Monticello in chains. Jefferson assured Hubbard's new master that he had Hubbard "severely flogged in the presence of his old companions, and committed to jail" before turning the runaway over. Jefferson advised Perry to sell Hubbard out of state, for he had proven himself incorrigible.[8]

The story of Hubbard's flight, capture, and flogging was a microcosm of Jefferson's dealings with unruly bondspeople. On the macro level, one of his most momentous acts with regard to slavery was the Louisiana Purchase. That acquisition fueled the expansion of America's "empire for liberty" for white planters—and slavery for African Americans. Even legislators who wanted to hold the total enslaved population in check advanced the "diffusionist" argument that the Louisiana Territory presented an opportunity to ship surplus slaves west and lessen the chances of slave rebellion. Jefferson could not have known that the question of slavery in Kansas (part of the Louisiana Purchase) would turn that territory into "Bleeding Kansas" and move the nation to the threshold of civil war by the mid-1850s. Conversely, Jefferson promoted and signed a bill that banned the importation of new enslaved people into the United States as of January 1, 1808, as permitted by the Constitution. Jefferson declared in his 1806 annual message to Congress that the slave import business was a trade that "the morality, the reputation, and the best interests of our country, have long been eager to proscribe." The ban on new imports of enslaved workers bolstered the domestic slave trade. Since the enslaved population was growing by natural increase, the ban generated little opposition among planters. Jefferson always professed he would curtail slavery when white political opinion would allow for it. Indeed, the import ban was the most decisive direct step he ever took against the trade in slaves as a national institution.[9]

Correspondents kept asking him to do more to curtail slavery, though. On Christmas Day of 1810 (around the time that James Hubbard ran away), John Lynch, the Quaker founder of Lynchburg, Virginia, wrote to Jefferson, enclosing a note from the Philadelphia Quaker antislavery activist Anne Mifflin. Quakers wanted Jefferson to use his influence with European governments and the Madison administration to promote a colony for freed slaves outside the United States. Creating a refuge for freed people would osten-sibly make emancipation more feasible. Jefferson had expressed support for such plans in the past, and Lynch reminded Jefferson that since "it must be a Gradual work the sooner it is set on foot the better."[10]

Jefferson replied with characteristic support for colonization. But he raised many reservations about its practicality, and about his own role in promoting the colony. There had been discussions about colonization after Gabriel's Rebellion in Virginia in 1800, Jefferson recalled, but those bore little fruit. Now that he was out of government, he was even less optimistic about any contributions he could make. "I am but a private individual, & could only use endeavors with private individuals," he wrote (despite the fact that he maintained routine contact with the president of the United States). "Nothing is more to be wished than that the U.S. would themselves undertake to make such an establishment on the coast of Africa. Exclusive of motives of humanity, the commercial advantages to be derived from it might repay all its expenses." Were Americans, including whites and freed slaves, ready for such a massive undertaking? Jefferson thought not. "The national mind is not yet prepared. It may perhaps be doubted whether many [freed slaves] would voluntarily consent to such an exchange of situation, and very certain that few of those advanced to a certain age in habits of slavery would be capable of self-government." Having basically declared the project unworkable, Jefferson concluded with half-hearted encouragement: "This should not however discourage the experiment." Jefferson was likely correct about the widespread reluctance concerning an actual colonization project, and he was not willing to spend much political capital to boost the scheme.[11]

Jefferson received a more pointed challenge from Edward Coles, James Madison's private secretary. Coles had been one of the key figures in resus-citating Jefferson's friendship with John Adams. As a young man Coles had developed radical antislavery convictions under the teaching of Bishop James Madison, the president's cousin. For Jefferson, it was one thing to receive requests about slavery from people like John Lynch and Anne Mifflin, or the letters on race prejudice he got from the black scientist Benjamin Banneker in the 1790s. The fact that Coles was well connected in Virginia politics made his 1814 missive to Jefferson about slavery more pressing. Coles himself worried that he was being "presumptuous" for bringing up the issue. Nevertheless, he urged Jefferson to champion gradual emancipation. If the "revered Fathers" of the Revolution set the pace, it would make all the difference. Coles pled with Jefferson to "put into complete practice" the principles of the Declaration.[12]

Jefferson's response to Coles was similar to his reply to Lynch: positive in the abstract, discouraging in practice. Jefferson again reviewed previous efforts to effect gradual emancipation. He had hoped that the "younger generation" would achieve freedom for slaves, but found Coles to be a "solitary" voice clamoring for change. Still hoping that emancipation was inevitable, Jefferson confessed that he could not see how it would transpire. "The hour of emancipation is advancing in the march of time. It will come; and whether brought on by the generous energy of our own minds, or by the bloody process of St Domingo, excited and conducted by the power of our present enemy [Britain]," he did not know. Freeing all enslaved people at once would be reckless. People who had been slaves from birth were largely incapable of liberty, he figured. Prematurely freed slaves were "pests in society." Worst of all, free blacks' "amalgamation with the other colour produces a degradation to which no lover of his country, no lover of excellence in the human character can innocently consent." Given Jefferson's children with Sally Hemings, this is one of the most jarring statements in the Jefferson corpus. But it was not a unique one. Six months before his death, Jefferson reminded William Short of his "great aversion" to the race mixing that he feared would follow emancipation, if freedom were not accompanied by mass colonization of the former bondspeople outside the United States.[13]

Jefferson effectively told Coles that he would not act on gradual emancipation. Perhaps the former president anticipated that if he indicated openness, Coles might press him for specifics. Citing his advancing age, Jefferson told Coles, "This enterprise is for the young. . . . It shall have all my prayers, and these are the only weapons of an old man." Whether Jefferson actually prayed for emancipation we do not know. But he urged Coles to stay in Virginia and fight for the cause. Coles was contemplating leaving to get his freed slaves out of the state (as was legally required upon emancipation) and establishing them as farmers in the Midwest. Coles should remain in Virginia and "become the Missionary of this doctrine truly Christian," Jefferson wrote. Citing a phrase from the New Testament, Jefferson exhorted him not to be "wearied in well doing." Seeking emancipation was a noble Christian calling, but not one that Jefferson felt he could pursue at his age.[14]

The dissatisfied Coles replied to Jefferson respectfully but forcefully. Jefferson's prayers were welcome but hardly sufficient. Jefferson and the other surviving leaders of the Revolution *must* lead on emancipation. "They are the only persons who have it in their power effectually to arouse and enlighten the public sentiment," Coles insisted. He cited the long-dead Ben Franklin, who "was as actively and as usefully employed on as arduous duties after he had past your age as he had ever been at any period of his life." Coles and Jefferson likely both knew that even Franklin had owned slaves for much of his life, but he lent his name to the antislavery cause in old age, to great symbolic effect. Coles and Jefferson's correspondence on the subject halted after this letter. Coles, however, did move to Illinois in 1819 and freed his enslaved people.[15]

A number of antislavery zealots had gotten the impression, not least from his "energetic and forcible expressions" in *Notes on the State of Virginia*, that Jefferson was open to acting against slavery. Pleas for help kept coming to the retired president from people who knew him (like Coles), or people who admired him from afar, like the Baptist minister David Barrow. In 1798 Barrow had moved from Virginia to Kentucky, which he hoped would be a more congenial environment for farming without enslaved workers. In 1808 Barrow helped to organize the Kentucky Abolition Society. Barrow, a thoroughgoing Jeffersonian Baptist, had long appreciated Jefferson's commitment to religious liberty. But did Jefferson's Christian and republican principles not also extend to slavery? In 1815 he asked that Jefferson "drop me some Hints, that your Knowledge, Feelings & Observations on the Subjects of Slavery & emancipation may dictate, which may be helpful to us."[16]

To his credit, Jefferson also replied to Barrow. As with Coles and Lynch, his answer to Barrow assumed that slavery would fade away, but it was unclear what practical actions could be taken against slave owning, beyond what he had said long ago in *Notes*. Jefferson appealed to providence as the key to freedom's progress. "We are not in a world ungoverned by the laws and the power of a superior agent," he told Barrow. "Our efforts are in his hand, and directed by it; and he will give them their effect in his own time." It would take longest in the South to eradicate the "disease," Jefferson believed, because there slavery was "incorporated with the whole system." Still, he said that he prayed that providence would hasten the march toward abolition. Jefferson's antislavery correspondents hoped he would do more than that, but they were usually disappointed.[17]

Adams and Jefferson mostly avoided the subject of slavery, implicitly agreeing to disagree. Energized by their friendly letters, Adams didn't want to force Jefferson to address such an unpleasant subject. Adams cheerily fired off one missive after another to Jefferson, chattering about political and theological topics. Jefferson did not seem to mind the frequent letters, but he was not prepared to answer each query. Reflections on Joseph Priestley's work and legacy took up much of their correspondence in 1813. Jefferson appreciatively told Adams that "if thinking men would have the courage to think for themselves, and to speak what they think, it would be found they do not differ in religious opinions, as much as is supposed. I remember to have heard Dr. Priestley say that if all England would candidly examine themselves, & confess, they would find that Unitarianism was really the religion of all." Jefferson could not conceive that intelligent people actually believed in the Trinity. (Adams agreed, telling Jefferson that even if they had been with Moses on Mount Sinai and "there told that one was three and three, one," they still could not have believed it.) Jefferson assumed that most Christians affirmed the Trinity out of unthinking traditionalism, or as a concession to social pressure.[18]

Moved by their shared fondness for Priestley, Jefferson cautiously sent Adams a copy of his "Syllabus of an Estimate of the Merit of the Doctrines of Jesus." Scarred by decades of unauthorized disclosures, he insisted that Adams keep the document private. The "Syllabus," the comparative religious sketch Jefferson had written a decade earlier, appeared during the remarkable months of 1803 when Jefferson decided, under the influence of Priestley and Benjamin Rush, that he believed in the superiority of Christian ethics. Not that Jefferson was entirely in accord with Rush's and Priestley's views. They were both more comfortable than Jefferson with the idea that Jesus was divine. Jefferson also told Adams that he wished Priestley had compared the morality of the Old Testament with that of the New, as "no two things were ever more unlike." Jefferson figured that Priestley was limited in what he could do, both by his advancing age and by the knowledge that even Unitarians had their "Cannibal priests" who would have torn Priestley apart if he strayed from Unitarian orthodoxy. Nevertheless, Jefferson said that he rested on Priestley's writings and other key texts as "the basis of my own faith."[19]

Other correspondents urged him to consider a more traditional commitment to Christ. This was the approach of the Delaware Quaker and anti-slavery advocate William Canby. Canby had known Jefferson since the time of his presidency, and Jefferson wrote a candid reply to Canby's entreaty, one that would be reprinted (without permission) in newspapers throughout the nation by 1814 and for years afterward. Some newspapers headed the letter with the title "The Sage of Monticello." Jefferson assured Canby that "he who steadily observes those moral precepts in which all religions concur, will never be questioned, at the gates of heaven." Doctrines such as the Trinity, which divided sects and denominations, were irrelevant to one's acceptance there. Yet Jefferson continued to affirm that of all the world's moral codes, the teachings of Jesus were the best. As for doctrinal disputes, he said, "I am too old to go into enquiries & changes as to the unessential." He did not wish to debate such matters with people like Canby, who might contradict him theologically. John Adams, in this sense, was a safer interlocutor.[20]

Jefferson was optimistic that Americans would embrace freedom of thought, especially in religion. That freedom would inexorably lead people to rationalist, ethics-centered Christianity. Troubling episodes of religious enthusiasm and censorship still worried Jefferson, however. Jefferson knew that Virginia and the nation were in the throes of the Second Great Awakening, which would make evangelical faith pervasive in the United States by the Civil War. Sometimes he also encountered blatant episodes of the kind of intolerance he had hoped the Virginia Statute for Establishing Religious Freedom and the First Amendment would abolish. One of those episodes came when Philadelphia's Nicolas Dufief, a French-language teacher and one of Jefferson's book suppliers, was investigated for selling Jefferson the ostensibly blasphemous book *Sur la création du monde* by Regnault de Bécourt. (Julian Boyd, longtime editor of *The Papers of Thomas Jefferson*, characterized Bécourt's work as an "infantile attack on the system of philosophy of Sir Isaac Newton.") Philadelphia authorities saw something menacing in its content, and charged Dufief with selling subversive literature. Jefferson successfully pled for Dufief's exoneration, but he was incensed by the attempt at censorship.[21]

Jefferson wrote to Dufief, raging about freedom of thought. Is this America? he asked. "Is this then our freedom of religion? And are we to have a Censor whose imprimatur shall say what books may be sold, and what we may buy? And who is thus to dogmatize religious opinions for our citizens?" Jefferson had merely glanced at the contents of Bécourt's book and was not impressed. Did Isaac Newton need the government to protect his legacy from a feeble attack such as this? "Still less," he fumed, did "the holy author of our religion" need government to shield people from works critical of traditional faith? "Holy author of our religion" was a phrase the Statute for Establishing Religious Freedom had used as well. The term helped Jefferson depict religious coercion as a violation of divine prerogative.[22]

Jefferson was far more impressed with Thomas Law's *Second Thoughts on Instinctive Impulses* than he was with Bécourt's work. In retirement, Jefferson eagerly plowed through new works on ethics, science, and other topics. In 1814 he read Law under the leaky roof at Poplar Forest. Law was a former British East India Company official who had moved to New York in 1794. Jefferson had known Law since before he was president. In 1811, Jefferson had written to Law about their common passion for reading, and the "bibliomany" that had driven Jefferson's spending on his library. Now he wrote effusively to Law about his new tract on moral sensibility.[23]

Second Thoughts on Instinctive Impulses contained, he told Law, "exactly my own creed on the foundation of morality in man." His letter to Law was probably his most direct commentary on moral philosophy, a widely debated topic throughout the Revolutionary era. Arguably the key question in the debate was, does a person need God to be good? Jefferson thought not. "Some have made the love of god the foundation of morality," he told Law. "If we did a good act merely from the love of god, and a belief that it is pleasing to him, whence arises the morality of the Atheist? It is idle to say as some do, that no such being exists." He insisted that atheists could be moral. Jefferson cited several French philosophes, including Diderot and Condorcet, as examples of virtuous atheists.[24]

Jefferson pointed to the parable of the Good Samaritan as an example of a person who responded to others' suffering with feeling and action. People with a functioning moral sense took pleasure in doing good. Why did such acts make us happy? "Nature hath implanted in our breasts a love of others," he told Law, "a sense of duty to them, a moral instinct in short, which prompts us irresistibly to feel and to succour their distresses." By nature, Jefferson meant the creator's natural order, which was both good and social. "The creator would indeed have been a bungling artist," he concluded, "had he intended man for a social animal, without planting in him social dispositions." God did not need to transform one's heart for a person to be truly moral, as Calvinists and evangelicals taught. The creator had given all people the inborn moral sense. The moral sense might be faulty or undeveloped in some people, but it was still universal to human nature.[25]

For Jefferson, however, the distinctions between morality, tranquility, and gentility were unclear. He periodically advised others about moral behavior, even developing versions of his own "decalogue" of aphorisms, the so-called Canons of Conduct. Some of these sayings were not original to Jefferson, but they reveal Jefferson's code for living, or at least his code for people younger than himself. He told Charles Clay in 1817 that he was recommending his ten virtuous habits to Clay's son Paul, at Clay's request, but only with due deference to the "Decalogue of first authority" (the Ten Commandments). Jefferson's sayings included Epicurean proverbs, which aimed to avoid unnecessary pain and conflict. The first two commandments were financial ones, however, including the first injunction: "Never spend money before you have it." Ironically, this has become one of Jefferson's most-quoted phrases, appearing in countless self-help books, guides to personal finance, and social media posts.[26]

One wishes that Jefferson, like Ben Franklin, had tracked his own compliance with the moral mandates to which he referred. (Franklin famously monitored his practice of thirteen key virtues in his "Art of Virtue.") There is indeed evidence of some tracking Jefferson did in his memorandum books of obligations to be charitable, hospitable, and to take care of one's family. His records are replete with donations to churches and charities. Mostly, however, he found the moral sense philosophy satisfying as theory. It offered a way to have a universal "standard of reason, justice, and philanthropy," as he put it to Joseph Priestley, without sectarian conflict. That widely applicable standard was shared by the major religions, but it came ultimately from the creator God. The moral sense did not derive from institutional religion or from the (whole) Bible. Jesus's teachings, Priestley had convinced him, were the best articulation of that moral standard. In that sense, Christianity deserved universal assent.[27]

In Jefferson's 1811 letter to Thomas Law in which he admitted his "bibliomany," he conceded that he owned more books than he could possibly read. Monticello and Poplar Forest's libraries were overflowing. His advancing age made it obvious that he was never going to read many of these texts. Jefferson thought of donating his books to a new university he hoped to establish in central Virginia. As of the mid-1810s, however, that university remained a dream. The British, meanwhile, had burned Congress's library in 1814 in their depredations against Washington, D.C., during the War of 1812. The destruction of the congressional collection, plus Jefferson's financial straits, prompted him to sell his books to Congress.[28]

Jefferson's personal library was considerably bigger than the one Congress possessed before the fire. He wrote with pride about fifty years of "sparing no pains, opportunity or expense to make" the library. He recalled the many afternoons he had spent in Paris scouring the bookstores for new volumes, and the standing orders he kept in other European capitals should the dealers come across a book he desired. The resulting collection could probably never be replicated. He generously allowed Congress to fix its own price and schedule of payments, and he noted that eighteen or twenty wagon-loads could deliver the books to Washington as soon as Congress was ready.[29]

Although the deal would be a good one for him and for Congress, his library offer did not escape the notice of Federalist critics. They were in the last stages of their long-running rivalry with Jefferson's Republicans. While Jefferson regarded the War of 1812 as "providential," Anglophile Federalists were incensed by the conflict, lambasting it as "Mr. Madison's War." Federalists would meet at the Hartford Convention in Connecticut in 1814 to protest the conflict, issuing objections that would damage the Federalists' national reputation when the war ended. Jefferson reveled in the Hartford debacle, interpreting the episode in typical religious categories. "Like bawds, religion becomes to [the Federalists] a refuge from the despair of their loathsome vices," Jefferson wrote. "They seek in it only an oblivion of the disgrace with which they have loaded themselves, in their political ravings, and of their mortification at the ridiculous issue of their Hartford convention." Hartford signaled the beginning of the end for the Federalist Party, and for the first American party system. Jefferson's Virginia ally James Monroe trounced his Federalist opponent in the 1816 election, and by 1820 Federalists could no longer field a presidential candidate.[30]

Some Federalists lampooned the idea of Congress acquiring Jefferson's library, which they assumed was full of atheistic French titles. In a satirical Federalist piece authored by "Johannes Vonderpuff" of Missouri, Vonderpuff offered to sell Jefferson his library. The author claimed to be almost eighty, and to have no children "*to whom my estate can descend*" (an allusion to Jefferson's enslaved children). Vonderpuff promised that the library had "entire sets of the works of all the atheistical writers in every age." He also had "forty different editions of the Bible, thirty nine of which are in the Arabic, and one in the Hebrew idiom; they are as good as when they came from the hands of the book binder." Despite considerable opposition in Congress, a slight majority voted to purchase the library. The official record counted just under sixty-five hundred volumes in the Monticello library (well under the number Jefferson estimated in 1811) and priced them at $23,950 total. Liquidating the library was helpful, as it allowed Jefferson to pay off many debts, including more than $10,000 to his longtime friend William Short.[31]

Jefferson's financial prospects also improved in 1815 when he turned over management of his plantations to his grandson Jeff Randolph. Randolph, a tall, strapping man in his mid-twenties, was a more effective manager than Jefferson. Randolph was also a more ruthless master, willing to whip an enslaved worker personally when he believed circumstances warranted. Monticello's wheat production under Randolph ballooned to three times the output under Jefferson's watch. Still, being a local farmer is a tenuous business, even under the savviest management. Jefferson and Randolph repeatedly lost harvests to pests, drought, and flooding rains, and they struggled to compete with more fertile farms coming into use farther west. Jefferson was always reluctant to sell land and enslaved people, as he understood they were his "capital." He was concerned especially that overseers not damage the health of bondswomen, or require them to neglect their children. The enslaved women's most valuable roles, to Jefferson, were as "breeding" mothers. "I consider a woman who brings a child every two years as more profitable than the best man of the farm," he observed. "What she produces is an addition to [my] capital, while his labors disappear in mere consumption." Jefferson saw results to bolster this belief, as about one hundred enslaved children were born on Jefferson's properties between 1810 and 1822, compared to only about thirty slaves lost to death, sale, or running away.[32]

Jefferson's memorandum books also suggested he was really trying to control his spending and settle his debts. Partly because he was no longer living in a city, his purchases of luxury items slowed. He continued to spend on building repairs, hospitality, wine, and books, however. He told his Tuscany-based wine dealer in 1816 that he considered "light and high flavored wines a necessary of life with me." He also sought to purchase remnants of Joseph Priestley's library when it went on sale the same year. His requested titles included a copy of the Lord's Prayer in one hundred languages.[33]

Although Jefferson's financial situation brightened briefly in the mid-1810s, he engaged in some dubious schemes to cover his obligations. One was when he sold properties in Richmond owned by Philip Mazzei, his Italian friend and recipient of the notorious 1796 "Samsons in the field" letter.

Mazzei had entrusted his Virginia lots to Jefferson when he moved back to Italy, and in 1813 Jefferson sold them for more than $6,000, a sizeable increase over the original price. Saying that it was impractical to send Mazzei the money during the war, Jefferson loaned himself the $6,000 with interest. When Mazzei found out about the sale, he asked that Jefferson send him the money right away. Jefferson did not. Mazzei died in 1816 with the principal and interest on the "loan" yet unpaid.[34]

Jefferson would not have died with his financial affairs in such horrible arrears were it not for what he called his "coup de grace": his co-signing a $20,000 loan for Wilson Cary Nicholas in 1818, just before the Panic of 1819 crippled the American economy. Nicholas, part of Jefferson's vast web of familial and Republican connections, had recently served as Virginia governor. In that position, Nicholas appointed Jefferson, Madison, and James Monroe to the inaugural Board of Visitors for the incipient University of Virginia. Nicholas had helped Jefferson secure loans in the past, and now it was Jefferson's time to return the favor. Nicholas was confident that his real estate holdings could cover the loan. But disruptions in the banking, real estate, and cotton sectors devastated the economy, and Nicholas proved unable to pay. Then Nicholas died in 1820, leaving Jefferson responsible for the $20,000. Fittingly, Nicholas was buried at Monticello, as his loan would loom as a ghostly presence over the remainder of Jefferson's life.

Co-signing Nicholas's loan was irresponsible, especially for someone in Jefferson's financial situation. Of course, Jefferson had no way of knowing that the nation would plunge into the financial abyss of 1819, taking Nicholas's money with it and ruining any fleeting hope of ending his life with settled debts. Mismanagement and bad luck were part of the story behind Jefferson's disastrous finances. Maybe the root of the problem, however, was his ironclad sense of what genteel honor obliged him to do. Whether it be to entertain guests, maintain his wine cellars, or assist an old friend, he simply kept spending.[35]

The Federalist satire by "Johannes Vonderpuff" had a point when it accused Jefferson of obscure academic interest in the Scriptures. Yet his fascination with the Bible was not casual. If it was largely academic, his studies of the Bible still bordered on an obsession. We might miss this fact because biblical studies was one of a number of topics in which he read voraciously. But over his long life, Jefferson could never get the Bible off his mind, as much as he dismissed the merits of speculative theology and "Platonism." He and Adams kept returning to dense doctrinal topics in their letters, and the Bible was pertinent to issues including Native Americans, linguistics, and education generally. We might recall that he created the first version of the Jefferson Bible "for the use of the Indians." Educated people needed to be familiar with the Bible. The most learned Americans ideally could read it in Greek. But at what point of a person's educational process should the Scriptures come into play? Jefferson thought the Bible was best left only to the most intellectually mature readers.

Jefferson's conflicted attitude toward the Bible was illustrated in a little-noted 1813 exchange of letters with Samuel Greenhow, treasurer of the Bible Society of Virginia. Greenhow was an Episcopal vestryman and successful merchant. Virginia's Bible Society was one of countless voluntary associations that sprang up during the Second Great Awakening. The Bible Society aimed to distribute free Bibles to poor people, the "ignorant and erring," and to the "Heathen." Jefferson would not seem like a promising donor for this venture, but Greenhow knew how to persuade him. The society was not sectarian, Greenhow insisted, and it drew support from across major Christian denominations. Distributing Bibles to families who could not afford one would improve literacy, ethics, and understanding of civil liberties. All these were worthy goals, regardless of "whether you or I receive this Book as a work of Inspiration." This was just the right way to frame the issue, and Jefferson sent Greenhow a donation of $50.[36]

He presumed that the Bible Society would not be "intermeddling" with the religions of other countries, for Jefferson could not abide missionaries trying to convert non-Christians in foreign lands. In a letter to John Adams, he called foreign missionaries in China "incendiaries . . . preparing to put the torch to the Asiatic regions." A visitor to Monticello likewise recorded Jefferson as saying that Christian missionaries were "not only impolitick, but unjust; for they carry misery & wretchedness into every country where they are introduced." What would Protestant Americans say if Catholics or Muslims came to America distributing copies of their holy books? "Shall we arrogate to ourselves that we are right & all the world beside are wrong?" Jefferson mused. He cautiously approved instructing intellectually advanced Native Americans in Christian principles, however. As for poor whites, Jefferson doubted that there were really many households in Virginia that did not already have a Bible, but if there were such households, it would be better for them to possess one. The main benefit in this, Jefferson told Greenhow, was that "there never was a more pure & sublime system of morality delivered to man than is to be found in the four evangelists." The Gospels were the core of biblical sublimity. The rest of the Bible was ethically mixed. Some portions were entirely worthless, such as Revelation, which he considered the "ravings of a maniac."[37]

This line of discussion clarifies what Jefferson was trying to accomplish in his second version of the Jefferson Bible. It had been a decade and a half since he produced "The Philosophy of Jesus of Nazareth," the text of which has been lost. The surviving "Life and Morals of Jesus of Nazareth" is what people usually mean by the Jefferson Bible. In both cases, he did not produce a whole Bible, only extracts from the four canonical Gospels. The second version was a fuller compilation. It included not just Jesus's teachings, but also accounts from his life and ministry. Jefferson literally cut out many of the miraculous claims of the Gospels, however, including the resurrection of Jesus. "Life and Morals" was a comparative polyglot with the verses in English, French, Greek, and Latin. He had ordered copies of the New Testament in these languages when he worked on "Philosophy of Jesus," but he did not use the non-English versions until his second Bible project.[38]

Jefferson's view of biblical authority was a regular discussion topic during his retirement. He still received correspondence from Trinitarian Christians who pled with him to put his faith fully in Christ and in God's revealed word. In 1814, Miles King, a ship captain and Methodist leader whom Jefferson had known professionally for many years, wrote Jefferson an exclamation-mark-laden evangelistic letter in which the essential message was "We must be born again or die forever!"[39]

Surprisingly, Jefferson responded to King's letter, reflecting on how one knows the truth about faith. King had intimated that God inspired him to write the letter to Jefferson, but Jefferson told King that reason was the only guide to divine verities. "Dispute as long as we will on religious tenets," he advised, "our reason at last must ultimately decide, as it is the only oracle which god has given us to determine between what really comes from him, & the phantasms of a disordered or deluded imagination." Jefferson implied that King suffered from a deluded imagination. When people believed they were operating under divine inspiration, Jefferson insisted that they were obligated to test that claim by reason. Reason was God's gift to humankind, the ultimate "umpire of truth."[40]

Jefferson also discussed his Gospel extracts with confidants in the mid-1810s. One of these friends was Charles Clay, his neighbor and a former pastor who had long ago resigned from the ministry after a salary dispute with his vestry. Clay got the impression that Jefferson planned to publish a version of his extracts, which Clay thought was a bad idea. He worried about Jefferson's beliefs, too, but Clay was even more worried that if Jefferson published the Gospel clippings, it would generate new attacks on his alleged infidelity. He wanted Jefferson to preserve his status as America's "Cedar of Libanus [Lebanon]," Clay wrote, referring to the stout tree mentioned dozens of times in the Bible. In contrast to Miles King, Clay wrote cautiously to Jefferson about the effects of yet another religious controversy. What if people began to see Jesus's teachings as sublime but *only* human ethics? "No System of morality however pure it might be," Clay warned, "yet without the Sanction of, divine authority stampt upon it, would have sufficient weight on Vulgar minds to ensure an Observance internal and external." He tentatively conceded that for refined minds like Jefferson's, religion as earthly morality alone might be effective. The "vulgar" needed more than human philosophy.[41]

Jefferson wrote back to his friend, who had performed the funeral for Jefferson's mother four decades earlier. Clay was right about the existence of the compilation, but he had gotten the wrong idea about it. Jefferson would never publish his extracts. Reforming American religion was hopeless, Jefferson had concluded. He was hesitant to even have conversations about faith except in "reasonable society," the members of which included John Adams and Clay himself. Jefferson figured that he had said more to Clay on the topic of religion than to anyone else. Clay had become Jefferson's neighbor and frequent conversation partner at isolated Poplar Forest. One wishes we knew more about the details of those conversations. Jefferson freely admitted to Clay that he reviled the priests of Jesus, "who have so much abused the pure and holy doctrines of their master. . . . While I have classed them with soothsayers and necromancers, I place him among the greatest of the reformers of morals, and scourges of priest-craft, that have ever existed." Jefferson never classed Clay among the clerical "necromancers," though. When Clay died in 1820, Jefferson lost his longest-term personal interlocutor on matters of faith.[42]

Jefferson also discussed plans for a new Bible compilation with another longtime friend, Charles Thomson. Thomson, the former secretary of the Continental Congress, was one of America's foremost biblical scholars. In

1808, Jefferson had corresponded with him about Thomson's English translation of the Septuagint. Now Jefferson sent him an admiring letter after Thomson forwarded him a copy of his 1815 *A Synopsis of the Four Evangelists*. Even though Jefferson had just sold the bulk of his library to Congress, he purchased a copy of Thomson's new book when he saw it advertised. He was even happier to obtain a personal copy from Thomson. Receiving it led Jefferson to tell Thomson about the "wee little book" he had also made from the Gospels, the "Philosophy of Jesus." He insisted that the first Jefferson Bible was "a document in proof that I am a *real Christian*, that is to say, a disciple of the doctrines of Jesus, very different from the Platonists, who call me infidel." "Platonists" was one of Jefferson's terms for Christians who maintained power via speculative metaphysics, such as notions about the Trinity, which he called "the mere Abracadabra" of the priests of Jesus. Jefferson told Adams that Plato himself had escaped obscurity by the "incorporation of his whimsies into the body of artificial Christianity." Jefferson noted that if he "had time I would add to my little book the Greek, Latin and French texts, in columns side by side." The concept of the second Jefferson Bible was crystallizing.[43]

Jefferson's letter to Thomson became the latest missive that got exposed to public view without his permission. A number of people in Philadelphia read it, and it triggered letters to him about the state of his beliefs, inquiring whether Jefferson had become a traditional Christian. Margaret Bayard Smith, a friend from his time as president, told him that the Thomson letter prompted rumors that he had "express'd opinions so highly favorable to the Christian religion, that they amount to a profession of faith." Thrilled by the prospect, she hoped that Jefferson might join the ranks of those promoting Sunday schools and Bible societies. "How glorious to the cause it would be, to see the name of one of the greatest of Statesmen & Philosophers enrol'd among that of Christians!" Smith exulted.[44]

Jefferson found himself in cleanup mode yet again. He promptly wrote back to Smith regarding his alleged conversion. The retired president assured her that, with regard to the Thomson letter, "no adherence to any particular mode of Christianity was there expressed; nor any change of opinions suggested." True religion was moral behavior. An individual was accountable to God alone. "It is in our lives, and not from our words, that our religion must be read. By the same test the world must judge me." To another inquirer, who wanted to include his ostensible conversion in a biographical sketch of Jefferson, the retired president admonished, "Say nothing of my religion. It is known to my god and myself alone."[45]

Thomson and Jefferson continued their discussion about the "real Christian" letter into 1817. Noting that a recent stroke had left him with memory loss, Thomson apologized to Jefferson for carelessly fueling rumors about Jefferson's conversion to Christian orthodoxy. Jefferson replied to Thomson (who was approaching ninety years old) that no explanation was necessary. The Virginian commonly redirected his anger over such episodes at Federalist critics, implying that he would do better than they would in the final judgment. "May they, with all their metaphysical riddles, appear before that tribunal with as clean hands and hearts as you and I shall. There, suspended in the scales of eternal justice, faith and works will shew their worth by their weight." At times, Jefferson not only asserted that there would be a divine reckoning after death, but that his own faith would be vindicated there. His enemies would be found wanting, exposed as hypocrites.[46]

The next step toward Jefferson's second compilation of the Gospels was an exchange with the Dutch émigré and Unitarian polymath Francis Adrian Van der Kemp. Van der Kemp was a friend of John Adams, Jefferson, and others in the Revolutionary generation. Adams had recently shown Van der Kemp his copy of Jefferson's "Syllabus" on Jesus's teachings. Van der Kemp requested a copy of the "Syllabus" from Jefferson for his own research, also asking for permission to reprint it anonymously in an English journal. Jefferson agreed. This illustrates how conflicted Jefferson was about publicizing his religious views. He told correspondents that he could not stand the thought of giving his enemies more ammunition regarding his beliefs. Yet he thought those beliefs were true, and that they would grow exponentially among rising generations of intelligent men. It was tempting to foster the spread of Unitarian ethics, even at the risk of more abuse from critics.[47]

Jefferson even offered to let Van der Kemp publish the "Philosophy of Jesus" as a companion to the "Syllabus." Employing his "diamonds in a dunghill" metaphor again, he told Van der Kemp how he had produced that first compilation twelve years earlier. Van der Kemp was thinking of writing a Unitarian-style biography of Jesus, a plan that Jefferson commended. If the "Syllabus," the "Philosophy of Jesus," and Van der Kemp's biography achieved wide circulation, Jefferson predicted, "the world will see, after the fogs shall be dispelled, in which for 14 centuries he has been enveloped by Jugglers to make money of him, when the genuine character shall be exhibited, which they have dressed up in the rags of an Impostor, the world, I say, will at length see the immortal merit of this first of human Sages." "Impostor" was a conventional epithet that Anglo-Americans used for Islam's Prophet Muhammad. Jefferson thought that priests and Platonist theologians had turned Jesus into an impostor as well. Building on the work of Priestley, Unitarians wished to return Jesus to his rightful place in the first rank of *human* sages. Jefferson did not realize that the disorganized Van der Kemp was never going to produce a biography of Jesus. Van der Kemp did publish Jefferson's "Syllabus" anonymously in London, although the editor indicated, to Jefferson's chagrin, that the author had been a leading figure in the American Revolution. (John Quincy Adams, in London at the time, correctly guessed that Jefferson was the author.) Van der Kemp's journal of choice had a limited circulation in England and much less in the United States, so the "Syllabus" did not generate much notice. Jefferson would have to wait longer for the world to hear the truth about the Unitarian Jesus.[48]

An exchange with William Short finally prompted Jefferson to produce a second version of his Bible. He and Short were comparing notes on their various illnesses, as old people sometimes do. Short made an offhand comment about his Epicurean principles inclining him to find pleasure in physical ease. Short identified Epicurus as the "wisest of all the ancient Philosophers." This led Jefferson to review his standard comparisons of the great teachers of antiquity. In the Gospels, he told Short, we possess "the outlines of a system of the most sublime morality which has ever fallen from the lips of man: outlines which it is lamentable he did not live to fill up. Epictetus & Epicurus give us laws for governing ourselves, Jesus a supplement of the duties & charities we owe to others." He mused on making another "Abstract from the Evangelists of whatever has the stamp of the eloquence and fine imagination of Jesus." He recalled how he had done the first such compilation at the President's House, but he admittedly did it "too hastily." It was time to compose another.[49]

11. "Dreams of the Future"

The Jefferson Bible was known only to a small circle of Jefferson's friends during his lifetime. Heeding their warnings, Jefferson never did publish "The Life and Morals of Jesus of Nazareth." Jefferson told a disappointed Mathew Carey, an enterprising Philadelphia publisher, that if he made "Life and Morals" public, "I should only add a unit to the number of Bedlamites." (Bedlam was a notorious mental hospital in London.) Jefferson saved the book for private use and as a basis for discussions with friends. Today, the cut-and-paste compilation has taken on a level of exposure that Jefferson would never have expected. At the Smithsonian's American History website, you can page through a high-resolution digital copy of the fragile book, which the museum acquired from a Jefferson descendant in 1895. The U.S. government published a facsimile of it in 1904. Then in 2011, the National Museum of American History restored the original volume, which allowed for the creation of a digital edition and a new, beautifully crafted facsimile.[1]

In "Life and Morals," Jefferson literally cut out Gospel passages from Greek, Latin, French, and English editions of the New Testament. He pasted them in parallel columns in a blank book, which he had bound with an expensive red leather cover. Thus it is not so much that Jefferson cut out the supernatural elements of the Gospels, but that he *left them behind* in gutted editions. This Jefferson Bible included more content than the "Philosophy" did, focusing on Jesus's life as well as his teachings. Jefferson took cues from Archbishop William Newcome's *A Harmony in Greek of the Gospels* (1778), a book that Jefferson owned after the sale of his library to Congress. (Jefferson's post-sale library still included dozens of sermons, tracts, and editions of the Bible.) Newcome had been an official in the Church of Ireland (Anglican) and an orthodox biblical scholar who argued against Joseph Priestley's novel interpretations of Christ's ministry.[2]

Scholars routinely note that Jefferson removed the miraculous content from the Gospels, and this was true in many cases. As historian Peter Manseau observes, Jefferson's approach has the curious effect of presenting the Gospel accounts of Jesus with "all set up and no pay off." Most important, the Jefferson Bible ends with Jesus's death and burial. The last verse he included was from Matthew 27, where the disciples "rolled a great stone to the door of the sepulchre, and departed." That's the last phrase in the book: there is no resurrection or ascension to heaven. It is easy to overstate how naturalistic Jefferson's extracts were, however. The eighty-four-page book includes passages dealing with the last days, the coming "great tribulation" for God's people, a fiery hell, the future resurrection of humankind, and the second coming of the "Son of Man." Jefferson's Jesus also has special foreknowledge of future events. Why Jefferson included this supernatural material in his compilation is not clear. Maybe he found those parts plausible. Perhaps he found it difficult to adhere strictly to naturalism, as the Gospels weave in many supernatural happenings along with Jesus's ethical teachings. Or maybe Jefferson just didn't think about the choices as much as we might expect.[3]

The opening page of clippings illustrates Jefferson's approach. He started with Luke 2, the narrative of Jesus's birth in Bethlehem. He skipped the angel Gabriel's announcement to the Virgin Mary that Jesus would be miraculously conceived by the Holy Spirit. He also excised Luke 2:8–20, regarding the angels' appearance to the shepherds announcing the birth of the Messiah and exclaiming, "Glory to God in the highest, and on earth peace, good will toward men." But Jefferson did not cut out all references to angels. For example, he included Jesus's teaching in Matthew 13:41–42 that "the Son of man shall send forth his angels, and they shall gather out of his kingdom all things that offend, and them which do iniquity; and shall cast them into a furnace of fire: there shall be wailing and gnashing of teeth." Presumably he included this passage because it was part of Jesus's explanation of a parable. Jefferson tended to include parables, even if they contained material he might consider objectionable or unreliable. He steered away from narratives in which supernatural beings were part of the action.[4]

The parables, the Sermon on the Mount, and similar passages were key because they demonstrated, Jefferson believed, the kind of moral behavior

God required for salvation. In contrast to the classic Protestant belief in salvation by grace alone, Jefferson believed that God would save people who behaved morally. This belief made Jefferson especially critical of the French reformer John Calvin. Jefferson had started making disparaging comments about John Calvin before he composed "The Life and Morals," apparently because of tracts he read about theological debates between Unitarians and traditional Congregationalists in New England. Increasingly Jefferson defined his religious views as anti-Calvinist. For example, he wrote about Calvinism to New Hampshire congressman Salma Hale, who had visited Monticello in 1818, discussed theology with Jefferson, and subsequently sent him pamphlets on the Unitarian controversy. Jefferson told Hale that "Calvinism has introduced into the Christian religion more new absurdities than its leader had purged it of old ones. Our saviour did not come into the world to save metaphysicians only. His doctrines are levelled to the simplest understanding: and it is only by banishing Hierophantic mysteries and Scholastic subtleties, which they have nick-named Christianity, and getting back to the plain and unsophisticated precepts of Christ, that we become real Christians." The followers of Calvin were not "real" Christians, or at least their faith was corrupt. He even told John Adams that Calvin was an "atheist" and that his religion was "daemonism." Here Jefferson turned tables on evangelical Christians, who conventionally asserted that "nominal" Christians were not real believers. The next year Jefferson wrote that he considered his religion to be "the reverse of Calvin's, that we are to be saved by our good works which are within our power, and not by our faith which is not within our power." Finally, he told Pastor Ezra Stiles Ely of Philadelphia that "you are a Calvinist. I am not. I am a sect by myself, as far as I know."[5]

Jefferson regarded himself as a sect by himself because he didn't agree with all of *Jesus's* teachings, even when reconstructed in their purity. He wrote to William Short in 1820, around the time he was finishing "The Life and Morals of Jesus of Nazareth." Jefferson said that he hoped to separate "the gold from the dross" in the Gospels, "restore to [Jesus] the former, & leave the latter to the stupidity of some, and roguery of others." Composing the Gospel extracts also gave Jefferson a fresh opportunity to assess what he accepted in Jesus's authentic teachings and what he did not. (Jefferson assumed that there must be *some* content in the Gospels that represented Jesus's actual philosophy. It was not all invented later by others.) Enclosing a copy of his "Syllabus of an Estimate of the Merit of the Doctrines of Jesus,

Compared with Those of Others" (1803), he told Short that "it is not to be understood that I am with him in all his doctrines." As we have seen, Jefferson considered himself a materialist, and he assumed that Jesus was a spiritualist. (In other words, Jesus believed that there was a nonmaterial realm of spirit.) Within months of explaining that contrast to Short, however, Jefferson speculated that maybe even Jesus was a materialist. Sure, he told John Adams, Jesus had said that God was a spirit in John 4:24, a verse he included in "Life and Morals." But Jesus didn't say that "spirit" wasn't material. Jefferson also noted that Jesus preached repentance for the forgiveness of sins, while Jefferson focused on good works as a "counterpoise" to sins. Still, he regarded Jesus's distillation of the greatest commandments "the sum of all relig[ion]." As taught by "its best preacher," those commandments were to "fear god and love thy neighbor." Such teachings involved "no mystery, need[ed] no explanation." They weren't Platonic enough for the priests of Jesus, though.[6]

As for Jesus's divinity, Jefferson told Short that he was convinced "that Jesus did not mean to impose himself on mankind as the son of god physically speaking." Any equivalence of Jesus with God was nonsense. But that Jesus "might conscientiously believe himself inspired from above, is very possible," Jefferson conceded. The idea that Jesus considered himself inspired by God was the belief of Unitarians such as Priestley. They rejected Trinitarianism, but they believed that Jesus was operating under divine sanction. Jefferson was not sure. Jesus "might readily mistake the coruscations [flashes] of his own fine genius for inspirations of a higher order. . . . How many of our wisest men still believe in the reality of these inspirations, while perfectly sane on all other subjects." For Jefferson, the Unitarians' belief that Jesus was divinely inspired was forgivable, but still nearly insane. In any case, Jefferson considered himself "authorized to conclude the purity and distinction of [Jesus's] character in opposition to the impostures which [the New Testament] authors would fix upon him."[7]

From childhood Thomas Jefferson had been tutored in rigorously Christian education, dating to his time at Rev. James Maury's Shadwell parish school. But he always felt that the conservative temperament of the church schools, and of the College of William and Mary, would obstruct the intellectual progress that Virginians needed. Through his career he tinkered with reforming Virginia education and politics on a progressive model, though he often struggled to turn his ideas into reality. One of his projects was organizing the state into "ward republics." The Anglican parish had been a primary unit of Virginia's social and educational organization since the colonial era. The parish vestries helped with poor relief, and what limited formal education there was for white boys was usually offered at the parish level. Jefferson figured he could make this system more coherent, comprehensive, and efficient if the state could take the smallest government units away from the churches. (He harbored similar concerns about the inefficiencies of county governments.) Jefferson did not exactly see his ward republics as anti-religious. He viewed poor relief and other forms of charity as Christian obligations that ward republics would perform better than parishes. But he certainly had no qualms about reducing the institutional power of churches, or separating their functions from the state. To that extent, the ward republics reflected an effort by Jefferson to further secularize state and local government.[8]

In 1810, Jefferson explained the concept of the ward republics, or "hundreds," to John Tyler, Sr., the governor of Virginia and father of the future president. Each hundred would have a school central enough that local children (presumably whites) could attend. Elected officials of each ward republic would "manage all its concerns" and "take care of its roads, its poor, & its police." Thus, the ward republic would take over civic functions once performed by priests and vestrymen. "These little republics would be the main strength of the great one," he assured the governor. He waxed biblical about the ward republic system: "Could I once see this I should consider it as the dawn of the salvation of the republic, & say with old Simeon 'nunc dimittas Domine.'" This last phrase, a common saying of Jefferson's, was a reference to Simeon's words in the Gospel of Luke, chapter 2: "Lord, now lettest thou thy servant depart in peace." Even Jefferson's thoughts on state secularization could come framed in biblical rhetoric.[9]

In 1816, a year in which Virginia buzzed with talk of constitutional reform, Jefferson pushed for the ward republics system. He thought its localism would reflect the most beneficial aspects of federalism, or the division of government authority into ever-smaller units. In his system, all would feel they had a stake in the ward to which they belonged. "If the Almighty has not decreed that Man shall never be free (and it is blasphemy to believe it)," Jefferson wrote, "the secret will be found to be in the making himself the depository of the powers respecting himself, so far as he is competent to them." The nation should only exercise functions that local governments could not, such as defense against foreign armies. Jefferson prayed that God would give Virginia officials the wisdom "to fortify us against the degeneracy of our government, and the concentration of all its powers in the hands of the one, the few, the well-born or but the many." Although Jefferson's plan sought to enhance white male democracy and reduce the power of parishes, it also echoed a traditional republican theme: the fear of consolidated power.[10]

Jefferson championed regular state constitutional reform, believing that states remained the primary arenas of day-to-day governance and laboratories for progressive political improvement. He was allergic to traditions that bound Americans to dead predecessors' decisions. That sentiment was most famously expressed in his 1789 statement that "the earth belongs in usufruct to the living." He similarly recommended constant reworking of laws and constitutions to suit the current generation. Jefferson would not have subscribed to what we might call a "living constitution" theory. Legislators had to amend and replace constitutions rather than allow judges to reinterpret the existing ones according to current mores. But he saw no point in undue veneration for existing constitutions. "Some men look at Constitutions with sanctimonious reverence, & deem them, like the ark of the covenant, too sacred to be touched. They ascribe to the men of the preceding age [the Revolutionary generation] a wisdom more than human, and suppose what they did to be beyond amendment." The Patriot fathers deserved respect, but Jefferson also believed that political experience and changing times required routine constitutional refreshment. The Virginia constitution should mandate revision of itself every nineteen or twenty years, he thought, to prevent political morbidity.[11]

The ward republics and local schools were the heart of Jefferson's vision for progressive reform. The ward republics remained elusive, although a new Virginia constitution in 1830 extended white male suffrage in ways that Jefferson would have supported. He rarely commented on voting rights for anyone but white men. As we have seen, he contrasted American women favorably with their French counterparts, telling Anne Willing Bingham in 1788 that "our good ladies, I trust, have been too wise to wrinkle their foreheads with politics." The immediate, short-term referent for Jefferson's "all men" in the Declaration of Independence was *political* men. In Jefferson's Virginia, that meant white men, not women, and not humankind generally.[12]

"I like the dreams of the future better than the history of the past," Jefferson told Adams in 1816. One such dream was his university. Like his idea of the ward republics, Jefferson had been thinking about a new Virginia university for a long time. He told his spiritual advisor Joseph Priestley about the prospective college when they began corresponding in 1800. The College of William and Mary, Jefferson wrote, was "just well enough endowed to draw out the miserable existence to which a miserable constitution has doomed it. It is moreover eccentric in its position, exposed to bilious diseases as all the lower country is. . . . We wish to establish in the upper & healthier country, & more centrally for the state a University on a plan so broad & liberal & modern, as to be worth patronizing with the public support." He hoped that Priestley would help him plan the university, and perhaps become one of the professors. Priestley sent Jefferson works by Thomas Cooper, Priestley's fellow philosopher-scientist, who also struck Jefferson as an excellent faculty candidate. Jefferson would come to regard Cooper as "one of the ablest men in America," though Cooper's reputation for religious skepticism would cause serious problems for Jefferson's scheme.[13]

Priestley gave Jefferson extensive suggestions about how to structure a university, but he was reluctant to join the faculty. In any case, Jefferson would have to wait until well after Priestley's death in 1804 for the university to become a reality. Virginia politicians rarely found any schools "worth patronizing with the public support," so Jefferson would have to scramble to get the new school going. He latched on to an existing scheme for an "Albemarle Academy" that the legislature had incorporated but that had not opened as of 1814. Jefferson and his legislative allies partially funded the academy through the sale of Episcopal glebe lands, property that had come to the church via its established status prior to the Revolution. By 1799, there was a popular movement to sell these lands and use the proceeds for projects, including schools. Jefferson and the trustees of Albemarle Academy got the name of the school changed to Central College, paving the way for it to become a university. Governor Wilson Cary Nicholas (whose ill-fated loan would soon complete Jefferson's financial ruin) recruited a powerful Board of Visitors, including the successive presidents James Madison and James Monroe.[14]

Finally, the board purchased land for the college just west of Char-lottesville in 1817, using funds from the glebe sales. Board members and local supporters held a cornerstone-laying ceremony, with Scripture readings and rituals led by a Masonic grand master. Freemasonry was an Enlightenment religious and social movement in Europe and America. Its adherents claimed to be restoring pure biblical religion. Freemasons emphasized virtue and downplayed sectarian theology. Jefferson was not a Freemason, but he had "great respect" for them, and President James Monroe (who attended the event) and other influential state politicians were Masons. Thus Jefferson was eager to have the university "commence under the regular auspices of this antient fraternity."[15]

It is routinely said that Jefferson wanted the University of Virginia to be a "secular" institution. Certainly it was to be a state-run, nonsectarian school. "Secular" may be misleading, however, as that term implies "irreligious" today. The university reflected Jefferson's own religious commitments. Jefferson was willing to accommodate the religious sensibilities of supporters, as seen in the Masonic ceremony. The university would decenter churches, chapel, and clergy, and focus on modern science as well as Christian-themed subjects including ethics, history, and classical languages. Jefferson's brand of secularism in education and politics did not entail the absence of ethics and religion, but it did mean freedom from denominational control (as seen in the ward republics). If anything, it was Jefferson's political enemies who wished to portray the University of Virginia as secular. Associating a public school with irreligion was a major liability in antebellum political culture.[16]

Even the decentered layout of Jefferson's "academical village" had ethical purposes. Instead of having the university centered on one main hall, he wanted to avoid any "large & common den of noise, of filth, & of fetid air. It would afford that quiet retirement so friendly to study, and lessen the dangers of fire, infection & tumult." (Jefferson could not resist the construction of the Rotunda, modeled on the Roman Pantheon, as a central building. As predicted, it was a routine site of fire and tumult during the 1800s.) "Large and crowded buildings in which youths are pent up," he continued, "are equally unfriendly to health, to study, to manners, morals & order." Although Jefferson at times expressed distaste for formal instruction in ethics, his college was still designed for the moral formation of its students based on Christian principles of the type that made it into Jefferson's extracts from the Gospels.[17]

Jefferson and his allies still needed to confirm Charlottesville as the site of the new university. In 1818, they fought off alternative sites in a process culminating in a legislative meeting in Rockfish Gap, west of Charlottesville. (Rockfish Gap today stands at the southern entrance to the Skyline Drive of Shenandoah National Park.) In anticipation of the occasion, Jefferson

University of Virginia Rotunda, ca. 1890–1910. (Courtesy Library of Congress)

drafted the Rockfish Gap Report. He again emphasized his decentered layout for the school as "advantageous to morals, to order, and to uninterrupted study." He also conceded that "a building of somewhat more size in the middle of the grounds, may be called for in time," but he did not wish to say more about the (expensive) Rotunda at that moment. As with all of Jefferson's architectural projects, the original buildings at the University of Virginia depended on enslaved laborers to erect them, including bondspeople owned by university officials and bondspeople rented from local masters. For example, after Jefferson's death, the university's proctor purchased the skilled Monticello slave Thrimston Hern, who built the stone steps leading to the Rotunda.[18]

The slave-built university would train future Virginia statesmen. Clergy in training would presumably go elsewhere, like the Virginia Presbyterians' Hampden-Sydney College, founded in 1775. Of course, some prospective pastors would eventually study at the University of Virginia, too, including the Baptist luminary and Confederate Army chaplain John A.

Broadus. As a professor, Broadus taught Latin and Greek at his alma mater before joining the faculty at Southern Baptist Theological Seminary. Even for Jefferson's statesmen, however, the University of Virginia would seek to develop "the reasoning faculties of our youth, enlarge their minds, cultivate their morals, & instill into them the precepts of virtue and order." Morals, virtue, and order were inevitably (though not exclusively) rooted in Christian categories in Jefferson's world.[19]

Comparing moral formation to horticulture, Jefferson asserted that sound education "engrafts a new man on the native stock, & improves what in his nature was vicious and perverse into qualities of virtue & social value." The New Testament used the term *new man*, as Jefferson surely recalled, for a person regenerated in Christ. Jefferson focused on the transformative power of education, rather than the transformative work of God, as key to virtuous living. But Christian morals still defined what virtue generally meant. Jefferson even claimed that a lack of education was the primary reason Native Americans were inferior to whites. Comparing them to religious traditionalists who defended established denominations, Jefferson wrote that Native Americans' "barbarism and wretchedness" resulted from "a bigotted veneration for the supposed superlative wisdom of their fathers, and the preposterous idea that they are to look backward for better things, and not forward, longing, as it should seem, to return to the days of eating acorns and roots, rather than indulge in the degeneracies of civilization." This type of comparison explains why some observers think that Jefferson meant *both* Native Americans and Federalist Christians when he wrote that the first Jefferson Bible was intended for the use of the "Indians."[20]

How "secular" was the curriculum at the University of Virginia? The most obvious change from a conventional college model was that Jefferson would hire no "professor of divinity" or theology. This was a crucial departure that Jefferson indicated was in deference to Virginia's constitution and the state's lack of an established church. Religious topics would not be absent from the curriculum, but subjects such as "the proofs of the being of a god, the creator, preserver, and supreme ruler of the universe, the Author of all the relations of morality, and of the laws and obligations these infer, will be within the province of the Professor of Ethics; to which adding the developments of these general principles of morality of those in which all sects agree." Instruction by the ethics professor would include principles of morality and theistic philosophy.[21]

Given his fondness for the classics, it was no surprise that Jefferson also wanted the university's curriculum to include Greek and Latin. He called these languages "the foundation common to all the sciences." As we have seen, Jefferson could not read Hebrew, and he seems to have added that language to the curriculum later, after writing the original draft of the Rockfish Gap Report. He knew that traditionalist Christian critics would pounce upon any evidence that the university was a bastion of skepticism, so perhaps he included Hebrew reluctantly. Moreover, instruction in Latin and Greek did not necessarily require attention to biblical texts or ecclesiastical history per se. It is not a stretch to imagine that Jefferson had such curricular content in mind (or at least training students to be able to read such texts), given his own interactions with the Greek and Latin versions of the New Testament, his familiarity with the Septuagint, and the fact that he made "Ecclesiastical History" and editions of the Bible part of the University of Virginia library. By the 1830s, students were using Latin and Greek grammars in courses, reading an assortment of Latin and Greek classics, and studying the Hebrew text of the Old Testament. At evangelical-leaning Dartmouth College during the same period, students also worked with nonbiblical classical texts, partly because they were supposed to have *already read* the Greek New Testament before they arrived on campus. Dartmouth seniors also reviewed the Greek New Testament at the end of their studies. Certainly, in the hands of a later University of Virginia instructor like John Broadus, Greek and Latin instruction would have biblicist purposes.[22]

Despite poor health and advancing age, Jefferson gave hands-on attention to the fledgling school, including the composition of its library. (One friend, Peachy Gilmer, described the former president as "engaged in the University project tooth and nail, knee deep in plans, estimates, & conjectures.") The Rotunda would house the library, putting the book collection at the heart of the university. In 1814, Jefferson told Thomas Cooper that he wanted the state legislature to look at purchasing his personal library as well as the library and lab equipment of the late Joseph Priestley. Jefferson despaired of that actually happening, however, and went on to sell his library to Congress. He kept purchasing books from dealers in Paris, London, and Philadelphia after the sale, however, with the idea of building yet another library that he would donate to the university. He intended to donate the books in his will, but his creditors' claims superseded the donation. His final library was auctioned off in 1829.[23]

By 1824 Jefferson had compiled a list of books he hoped to procure for the university library. He told James Madison that the hardest part of the list to compile was the category of "divinity." He had less trouble deciding about titles in ethics, morality, and Bible editions, but Jefferson was "at a loss" when it came to metaphysics. This struggle suggests Jefferson's lack of reading in theology (as opposed to the Bible itself), and his perception that no one's theology, even that of Priestley, entirely suited him. He asked for Madison's help, recalling Madison's early studies of biblical languages and theology at Princeton. Madison complied, noting that "altho' Theology was not to be taught in the University, its Library ought to contain pretty full information for such as might voluntarily seek it in that branch of Learning." Madison's list included titles such as the Anglican scholar Brian Walton's nine-language polyglot Bible as well as works by the church fathers and collections of medieval, Reformation, and early American figures of church history, such as Aquinas, Luther, Calvin, and Jonathan Edwards. Jefferson imported Madison's suggestions into his master list, however grudgingly he might have included titles by Calvin and Edwards. Adding a full list of the works of Joseph Priestley, Jefferson also included some of his old favorites such as the sermons of Laurence Sterne. Not all of Jefferson's books were immediately acquired, due to limited funds and lack of availability. Prioritizing preservation of the collection, Jefferson also mandated that the university librarian strictly oversee students' access to the books. The university library was originally scheduled to be open a total of one hour a week, and students needed a faculty member's permission to check out a book.[24]

The public financing of the university guaranteed that Jefferson's vision for education would clash with that of Virginia evangelicals. Until the late 1810s, Jefferson's tirades against evangelicals and Calvinists had mostly been directed at New Englanders, partly because southern evangelicals often sided with Jefferson in the name of religious liberty. But the University of Virginia was *going* to have a religious bent. Educators in Jefferson's age did not do much posturing about supposedly neutral theological education. If left in Jefferson's hands alone, the school's proclivities would certainly be Unitarian, if not deistic. He was not going to hire evangelical or Calvinist professors if he could help it. To traditionalist educators, this sort of exclusion was unacceptable. If taxpayers funded the university, those educators reasoned, then the school should reflect a common Christian view shared by most Virginians, not that of a Unitarian elite. Presbyterians, led by the minister and teacher John Holt Rice, attacked Jefferson's plans for the new school as both snobbish and deistic. Rice lambasted the anticipated costs of the university, saying the tuition (due to expensive buildings) would price out everyone but the children of wealthy planters. Moreover, Rice warned that the university would become "either a fountain of living waters diffusing health and vigour, or a poisoned spring spreading disease and death." Rice and Jefferson took opposite views of learning and moral formation, as Rice noted that one could "explore every field of human science" and still be a "profligate."[25]

Rice and his evangelical allies knew that funding for the university was tenuous, so they offered their political support in exchange for influence, hoping to save the university from Unitarianism. For example, Presbyterian pastor Conrad Speece wanted to impose a test of faith on all faculty, a test that Jefferson certainly could not pass. Speece suggested that all teachers should affirm the doctrine of the Trinity, the whole Bible as the "infallible standard of faith and practice," and similar beliefs. Professors would be disqualified if they had ever said or written anything against such doctrines. Speece also wanted the university to observe morning and evening chapel services, while Jefferson wished the school to have no formal chapel building or mandatory services. Speece knew that "infidels" would sneer at his proposals and "repeat their traditionary cant about bigotry and fanaticism." He welcomed their sneers, he said.[26]

Jefferson generally ignored the growing concerns about the theological commitments of the university. He had already approached Thomas Cooper about joining the faculty in 1817, so perhaps he felt that he could not renege. Cooper had encountered opposition due to his unorthodox beliefs in faculty positions he held in Pennsylvania. Jefferson would not be on the faculty, but Cooper seemed to manifest all that was disturbing about Jefferson's beliefs, in the view of his Presbyterian rivals. Interminable delays in the school's funding (and Jefferson's characteristic overspending on construction) gave John Holt Rice time to build opposition to Cooper's appointment.[27]

Rice launched the most significant attack on Cooper and Jefferson with a review of Cooper's edition of Joseph Priestley's writings, a book originally published in London in 1806. Rice said that the people of Virginia deserved to know what sort of person was joining the faculty of the new university. He deplored Cooper's apparent materialism, anti-Trinitarianism, and blasé attitude about the effects of atheism. For Rice, putting such men in places of authority risked the same violent consequences as France endured in its anti-Christian revolution. "Let the faith of a nation be undermined," Rice wrote, "let the control of religion be removed, let the whole community be without the fear of God before their eyes, and then a storm is raised compared with which the uproar of the elements, the desolations of the tornado and the earthquake, are a mere 'civil game.'"[28]

Jefferson was outraged by Rice's "squib," and he tried to explain to Cooper how Rice's attack would be received in Virginia. He believed that among all the prominent Protestant groups, it was only Presbyterian pastors (not even their laity) who opposed Jefferson's vision for the university. The Presbyterians were "violent, ambitious of power, and intolerant in politics as in religion and want nothing but license from the laws to kindle again the fires of their leader John Knox, and to give us a 2d blast from his trumpet." (This was a reference to the Scottish reformer Knox and his most notorious tract, *The First Blast of the Trumpet against the Monstrous Regiment of Women,* which opposed women rulers, including Queen Elizabeth I.) Jefferson scoffed at Rice's outlet, the *Virginia Evangelical and Literary Magazine.* "A dozen or two fanatics or bigots of his sect in this state may read his Evangel- ical magazine: but he could not more effectually have hidden his diatribe than by consigning it to that deposit." He did not think Rice would succeed in derailing Cooper's appointment.[29]

Jefferson was wrong. He had to inform Cooper less than a month later that, after further investigation, it turned out that it was not just Presbyte- rians who opposed Cooper's role at the University of Virginia. "All have sounded the tocsin of alarm on your appointment, as bringing into the insti- tution principles subversive of the religion of the land, and threatening dangerous effect on the youth who may come to it. Assuming your religious creed, they denounce it as boldly as if they really knew it, they alarm parents, and produce, as I am told, more extensive effect than I had supposed possible." Jefferson and the board thought it best to release Cooper from the faculty position. Cooper took a job at South Carolina College instead. There Cooper tutored students in both anticlerical and proslavery convictions.[30]

Jefferson and the board, wary of enduring more such episodes, sought to ameliorate traditionalists' concerns about the university. Jefferson wrote that the board did not want to convey that religion was "precluded" at the school. "The relations which exist between man and his maker, and the duties resulting from those relations, are the most interesting and important to every human being," he explained. The board offered to allow denominations to build "religious schools on the confines of the University." Students at those schools could study at the University of Virginia as well as receive training in their denomination's specific beliefs. None of the denominations took up the offer, however.[31]

As seen in Jefferson's stingy book-loaning policies, he could be heavy-handed in the administration of the University of Virginia as founding rector. He figured a combination of toughness on bad behavior and incentives for good behavior was necessary for students' moral formation. But except for the satisfaction of its mere existence, the university brought a lot of disappointment and worry to Jefferson's remaining years. The discouragement came from episodes like the Cooper debacle and from the roguery of students. Jefferson and the Board of Visitors were aware that student mischief was a problem at virtually every college in Europe and America. Jefferson's idealism about human nature did not blind him to the reality that many college students—especially sons of planters—arrived on campus with a sense of entitlement. They planned to party, and they did not intend to follow strict rules. Learning was incidental to their anticipated student experience. Jefferson kept up an avid correspondence with Thomas Cooper after he departed for South Carolina. In 1822 (several years before the University of Virginia opened for classes) he told Cooper that, aside from funding, the school's greatest challenge would be "the spirit of insubordination and self will which seizes our youth so early in life as to defeat their education, and the too little controul exercised by indulgent parents." He regarded youthful licentiousness as a grave threat to the university and to the republic; it was a devilish version of the pursuit of happiness.[32]

Southern deficiencies in education were especially alarming in light of the conflict over Missouri and slavery in 1819–20, an episode that Jefferson likened to a "fire bell in the night." During the congressional debate, South Carolina senator William Smith chided Jefferson for his incautious statements about slavery's immorality in *Notes on the State of Virginia* (statements routinely cited by emancipationists). Yet the statesman happily noted that Jefferson's "riper years" had corrected his naïveté about freedom and slavery. Despite his warnings about God's judgment on slavery, Smith noted, the Virginian had remained a slaveholder. The Missouri crisis got Jefferson thinking more in sectional terms than he had since the late 1790s. He worried that the North was advancing beyond the South educationally. Power followed knowledge as a rule of nature. Citing a phrase from Joshua 9, Jefferson warned that "the ignorant will forever be hewers of wood and drawers of water to the wise." Like many southern leaders in the antebellum era, Jefferson feared a permanent political and economic subservience to the northern states. Maybe enlightened colleges such as the University of Virginia and South Carolina College could postpone cultural degradation. The problem of white southerners sending their sons to northern colleges was a "canker" that was "eating at the vitals of our existence," he wrote. This made legislative support for the University of Virginia more urgent. Passing on learning to Virginia's sons was a "holy charge" that deserved the state's best effort.[33]

Jefferson did implement some permissive policies regarding student governance and discipline at the University of Virginia, but students were still banned from possessing alcohol, tobacco, guns, or pets. Students had to allow university officials to inspect their dorm rooms on demand. The school still scrambled to recruit enough qualified students in 1825, not least because the university was enormously expensive for the time, $400 a year. There were no scholarships to assist students of modest means, and of course no people of color or women attended (full integration and coeducational instruction did not arrive at the University of Virginia until the 1960s and '70s). Jefferson touted the first students as respectful toward the faculty, but from the start there were reports of license and impiety at the college. On "grounds" and in town, critics charged, the students were constantly engaged in "all kind of rascality and mischief." Jefferson was not surprised at the boorish behavior, as it followed scripted cultural expectations for young southern males asserting their independence. Their shenanigans, often fueled by alcohol, were repeated at colleges across the South, including Hampden-Sydney, William and Mary, and Thomas Cooper's South Carolina.[34]

Sometimes shenanigans turned into vicious assaults, with victims ranging from professors to bondspeople. In 1826 some University of Virginia students savagely beat an enslaved woman whom they accused of giving them venereal disease. She apparently suffered a long-term disability due to the assault, and her owner received $10 in damages. University officials were more concerned about an 1825 nighttime riot in which more than a dozen disguised students protested on the college lawn against their foreign-born professors. Faculty who tried to break up the riot got pelted with various

projectiles, and one of them was physically assaulted. When university officials demanded that students identify the rioters (who had worn masks), the
students uniformly refused.[35]

The Board of Visitors, including Madison and a frail Jefferson,
confronted the students at the Rotunda in October 1825. Jefferson stood
before the assembly and declared that this was the "most painful event of his
life." It felt like the death of an enlightened dream, and the distraught former
president was so overcome that he could not continue speaking. Another
board member, a prominent lawyer, took over and challenged the students'
sense of honor. That challenge, in addition to Jefferson's choked words, did
the trick. The offending students confessed. The board expelled four of
them. Christian critics said that the riot proved that the University of Virginia
was nothing but a "school of infidelity." But it did not take long for Jefferson's optimism about the school and its students to revive. He wrote to soon-
to-be Virginia governor William Branch Giles at the end of 1825, claiming
that "a finer set of youths I never saw assembled for instruction. They
committed some irregularities at first, until they learned the lawful length of
their tether." Jefferson anticipated that within fifteen years most of Virginia's
"rulers" would be graduates of the university, seeding the state with the
"correct principles" learned there. "They will exhibit their country in a
degree of sound respectability it has never known either in our days, or those
of our forefathers. I cannot live to see it," Jefferson acknowledged. "My joy
must only be that of anticipation," he concluded. Fulfillment of Jefferson's
dreams of the future lay beyond his darkening horizon.[36]

Conclusion

"All That Has Passed"

Thomas Jefferson never talked much about heaven or the afterlife. However, he took up the subject in 1817 with Abigail Adams. She was arguably the woman he respected most in the world. Jefferson and Adams had become friends during the 1780s in Paris, and Jefferson's estrangement from the Adamses after the 1800 election did not efface his fondness for her. Abigail was one of the only women Jefferson regarded as embodying both female domesticity and intellectual acuity, the latter a trait he normally associated with men. Adams wrote how she wished she were twenty years younger so she could visit Jefferson at his home. "But I am so far down Hill," she mused, "that I must only think of those pleasures which are past, amongst which, and not the least is my early acquaintance with, and the continued Friendship of the phylosopher of Monticello."[1]

Jefferson was touched by her comment. It prompted reflection about their respective futures. They couldn't go back twenty years; there would be no visits to the Adamses' home in Quincy, Massachusetts, or to Charlottesville. "Our next meeting must then be in the country to which [deceased loved ones] have flown," he said. "A country, for us, not now very distant. For this journey," he wrote, quoting Matthew 10, "we shall need neither gold nor silver in our purse, nor scrip, nor coats, nor staves." Advancing age and its deprivations were God's way of preparing them for the next life. "Nothing proves more than this that the being who presides over the world is essentially benevolent. Stealing from us, one by one, the faculties of enjoyment." One eventually loses every desire of life, except the wish to know what was happening with one's family and home. Jefferson seemed to be speaking in earnest, as his next thought was simultaneously whimsical and tender. Perhaps, he told Abigail, "one of the elements of future felicity is to be a constant and unimpassioned view of what is passing here. If so, this may well supply the wish of occasional visits." He likewise told John Adams that he imagined "we shall only be lookers on, from the clouds above."[2]

Abigail died in 1818, and Jefferson assured the grieving John that "the term is not very distant at which we are to deposit . . . our sorrows and suffering bodies, and to ascend in essence to an ecstatic meeting with the friends we have loved & lost and whom we shall still love and never lose again."[3]

In Jefferson's extraordinary "fire bell in the night" letter about the 1820 Missouri Compromise, he speculated that agitation over the future of slavery might lead to disunion. Disunion would destroy the great experiment started in 1776. Yet his onetime protégé, President James Monroe, signed the Missouri Compromise bills into law. The disconsolate Jefferson still professed to loathe slavery, but did not know how to effect emancipation without expatriation of the former enslaved people. "As it is," he concluded, "we have the wolf by the ear, and we can neither hold him, nor safely let him go. Justice is in one scale, and self-preservation in the other." Jefferson still hoped that adding more slave territory like Missouri would "dilute the evil" of slavery and "facilitate the means of getting finally rid of it." Jefferson's longtime French friend and Revolutionary War hero, the Marquis de Lafayette, could hardly believe the brilliant Virginian was serious about his theory of diffusion and emancipation. Lafayette told him that expanding slavery would undoubtedly make a "final liberation" more difficult to achieve.[4]

The festering crisis of union made Jefferson fear that the Patriots' labors and sufferings had been for nothing. "I regret that I am now to die in the belief that the useless sacrifice of themselves, by the generation of '76 to acquire self-government and happiness to their country, is to be thrown away by the unwise and unworthy passions of their sons, and that my only consolation is to be that I live not to weep over it." This is the way old men talk sometimes: everything is falling apart because of a faithless younger generation. Since he was trying to get the University of Virginia funded at the same time, he may have had political motivations for making the Missouri crisis seem as dire as possible. Nevertheless, Jefferson dreaded a national reckoning over slavery.[5]

Little had changed, then, in his views about bondspeople and the future of slavery. Enslaved people would be freed one way or the other, either voluntarily by masters, or involuntarily through revolution such as the one in Haiti in the 1790s. This was "written in the book of fate," as he put it in his *Autobiography* (1821). Even if emancipation occurred peacefully, race war would still loom, for the two races "cannot live in the same government" as equals. Since their reconciliation, Adams and Jefferson had left the slavery issue alone, but Jefferson brought it up again in early 1821. "What does the Holy alliance, in and out of Congress, mean to do with us on the Missouri question?" This "Holy alliance" was the northern-led faction trying to bring Missouri into the union under a plan for gradual emancipation. "The real question, as seen in the states afflicted with this unfortunate population, is, are our slaves to be presented with freedom and a dagger?" Jefferson associated precipitous plans for emancipation with genocide in the South.[6]

Adams took this unexpected opportunity to gently address slavery with Jefferson. He mentioned the topic just after noting books he had read about the religious leaders Emanuel Swedenborg and John Wesley. "Slavery in this Country I have seen hanging over it like a black cloud for half a Century," Adams lamented. "If I were as drunk with enthusiasm as Swedenborg or Wesley I might probably say I had seen Armies of Negroes marching and countermarching in the air shining in Armour." Adams, like Jefferson, feared a massive uprising of the enslaved. He did not wish to lecture Jefferson, however, about what the slave masters should do. "I constantly said in former times to the Southern Gentleman, I cannot comprehend this object I must leave it to you, I will vote for forcing no measure against your judgements, what we are to see God knows." Adams was concerned about Jefferson's inaction on slavery, but he could push the issue only so far without jeopardizing their friendship again.[7]

Jefferson's direct communication with enslaved people about slavery was, as one would expect, exceedingly limited. One especially wishes to know about any exchanges, even if allusive and indirect, that he and Sally Hemings might have had about the topic. One of the only surviving examples of written interaction with one of his enslaved people was a brief 1818 letter from a Poplar Forest bondswoman named Hannah. Jefferson's poor health delayed his arrival at Poplar Forest that year. Seemingly referring to a fire at the house, Hannah assured Jefferson that "your house and furniture are all safe. . . . I was sorry to hear that you was so unwell you could not come it grieve me many time." Then Hannah, likely an evangelical Christian, urged Jefferson to recognize God's providence in his life. "I hope as you have been so blessed in this that you considered it was god that done it and no other one we all ought to be thankful for what he has done for us we ought to serve and obey his commandments." Paraphrasing I Corinthians 9:24, she hoped that he would "set to win the prize and after glory run." Though she formulaically called herself a "poor ignorunt creature," she implied that there was more to life, and more to faith, than Jefferson realized.[8]

If national affairs were troubling, Jefferson's familial and financial situations were becoming wretched. His family's status fell far short of the tranquil ideal he had envisioned for his old age. A number of the Jefferson-Randolph men were heavy drinkers. Charles Bankhead, husband of Jefferson's grand-daughter Ann Cary Randolph, was the worst. He terrorized Ann, and once got into a brawl with Thomas Mann Randolph, Jr. (an alcoholic himself) at Monticello. Bankhead apparently hit Jefferson's enslaved butler Burwell Colbert when Colbert refused to give Bankhead access to the liquor cabinet. Randolph intervened and struck Bankhead with a fireplace poker, peeling the skin off one side of Bankhead's face. Then, in 1819, Bankhead got into a fight with Jefferson's beloved grandson Jeff Randolph on a Charlottesville street, with Bankhead wielding a knife and Randolph a whip. The fracas originated with rude comments Bankhead made to Randolph's wife. Jefferson reportedly rode into Charlottesville when he learned of the brawl, and found Randolph grievously injured with stab wounds. Randolph survived and kept managing Jefferson's business affairs, however.[9]

Jefferson might have considered 1819 the worst year of his life. His health was terrible, with bouts of rheumatism and acute constipation. The nation faced the Missouri crisis and the economic depression of 1819, while Virginia politicians and pastors wrangled over Jefferson's proposed univer-sity. Then there was the huge loan that Jefferson co-signed for Wilson Cary Nicholas (Jeff Randolph's father-in-law). The news of Nicholas's pending default reached Jefferson as he was "under the severest attack of rheumatism I have ever experienced," he told Nicholas in a lugubrious letter. "My limbs all swelled, their strength prostrate, & pain constant. But [the news] fills me with affliction of another kind, very much on your account, and not small on my own." Jefferson expressed confidence that Nicholas would escape the disaster, but the financial conditions in Virginia in 1819 made that unlikely. Instead, Jefferson proposed that Richmond's branch of the Bank of the United States extend his loans by deeding lands to a new co-signer. The co-signer turned out to be Jeff Randolph, who had just been knifed nearly to death. Nicholas died the next year, transferring the debt to Jefferson. If Jefferson died without paying the debt, responsibility would pass to Randolph.[10]

The last decades of Jefferson's life were heavy with unrelenting gloom over his finances, his health, and the nation's future. Jefferson did occasionally show sparks of confidence about the coming decades, such as his affirmation that the enslaved people would one day be free, even if it meant race war. He also told a correspondent he still hoped that "the genuine doctrine of one only God is reviving, and I trust that there is not a young man now living in the US. who will not die an Unitarian." (This might have been his most inaccurate prediction ever.) Likewise, Jefferson averred that if nothing had been added later to the teachings that "flowed purely from [Jesus's] lips," the whole world would have already become Christian. He even mused over the possibility of Unitarian itinerants bringing "doctrines truly evangelical" to Virginia. Like the traveling evangelists of the Great Awakenings, Jefferson imagined that these Unitarian preachers might be excluded from the Trinitarian churches, but they would find "acres of hearers and thinkers" in the fields. That all seemed like a pleasant dream, however. Jefferson knew that evangelical and Calvinist Christianity remained strong, even in New England, where Unitarianism was catching on in some circles. He railed against Calvinist "Platonizers" who ostensibly taught that there were three gods at "tritheistical schools" such as Andover Seminary in Massachusetts. He conceded that until Unitarian preachers could persuade open-minded Christians in places such as Charlottesville, he would likely remain a "Unitarian by myself."[11]

Jefferson in retirement also worried about the federal government. John Quincy Adams broke Virginia's twenty-four-year lock on the presidency in the 1824 election. Jefferson found Adams's victory alarming, despite his closeness with John Quincy's father. Jefferson tried to remain politically aloof, but he made it clear that he preferred William Crawford of Georgia as James Monroe's successor. Crawford might well have won if an 1823 stroke had not taken him out of contention. Adams emerged triumphant, vanquishing contenders including Henry Clay, John C. Calhoun, and Andrew Jackson. Adams endorsed a federal program of internal improvements to bolster national education and to facilitate transportation on the burgeoning frontier. Jefferson and many old-school Republicans, however, considered federal spending on roads, canals, and programs such as a proposed national university to be unconstitutional.[12]

When President Adams submitted his plan for internal improvements to Congress in 1825, Jefferson responded by sending Madison a "solemn *Declaration and Protest of the commonwealth of Virginia on the principles of the Constitution of the US. of America & on the violations of them.*" Jefferson was never entirely consistent in his defenses of federalism and state sovereignty. Going back to the Kentucky Resolutions of 1798, however, he was capable of occasional pyrotechnics in defense of states' rights. Speaking on behalf of the Virginia legislature, Jefferson's *Declaration and Protest* declared that "the federal branch has, assumed in some cases and claimed in others, a right of enlarging its own powers by constructions, inferences, and indefinite deductions, from those directly given, which this assembly does declare to be usurpations of the powers retained to the independent branches." The Constitution, which the framers intended to limit the power of the national government, gave it no authority to build roads and canals or open schools. Jefferson did not wish for Virginians to precipitously pursue secession, for they "would indeed consider such a rupture as among the greatest calamities." He posited that a constitutional amendment authorizing internal improvements could be acceptable. But a ruptured union was not actually the worst calamity Virginians could face. "There is yet one greater: submission to a government of unlimited powers."[13]

Madison was disinclined to promote the provocative *Declaration and Protest*. Jefferson himself came to regard it as "premature," telling Madison that he wrote it when "all was gloom" on the political horizon. The manifesto became widely known among states' rights apologists, however. Among these was U.S. senator Robert Y. Hayne of South Carolina, who quoted it in a celebrated debate with Daniel Webster of Massachusetts in 1830. It is uncertain what Jefferson would have thought of John C. Calhoun's program of nullification, which culminated in South Carolina's showdown with the Jackson administration in 1832–33. More importantly, we shouldn't assume that Jefferson would have supported secession in 1860–61, as he had an abiding attachment to the American union. But the *Declaration and Protest* gave future nullifiers and Confederates a plausible case that Jefferson would have been on their side.[14]

As far as Jefferson's finances, the gloom would not lift. Even as Jefferson's life drew to an end, he cast about for ways to settle his massive debts. As his daughter Martha told the story, the solution came to Jefferson one evening in early 1826. "Lying awake one night from painful thoughts, the idea of the lottery came [to Jefferson] like an inspiration from the realms of bliss." Even though a lottery required legislative approval, Jefferson told Jeff Randolph that if it worked, the people of Virginia might finally liberate the family from debt. He could put up parts of his real estate (not including Monticello) as prizes. Jefferson claimed to have "made it a rule never to engage in a lottery or any other adventure of mere chance," but that rule did not seem to preclude running a lottery for himself. This inconsistency seems to have occurred to Jefferson as he drafted the "Thoughts on Lotteries" essay right after his nocturnal inspiration about the scheme. Everything in life was subject to fortune, he reasoned, so why not engage in games of chance too? Jefferson's fellow planter John Hartwell Cocke, who also complained about Jefferson keeping Sally Hemings as a "substitute for a wife," lamented Jefferson's lottery plan. Cocke feared that Jefferson would "prostrate the moral sentiment of the Country which stood between him & his object. Alas, what a commentary upon public life does this winding up of Mr. Jefferson's career afford?"[15]

Approval of the lottery was uncertain. As legislators wavered, Jefferson worried that even this scheme might not save him. "I see in the failure of this hope a deadly blast of all peace of mind during my remaining days," he told Jeff Randolph. Randolph used Jefferson's misery to good political effect. Once the issue was framed as an expression of gratitude to Jefferson, legislators grudgingly authorized the lottery. Jefferson's supporters had to sweeten the pot by adding Monticello as one of the prizes; however, they stipulated that the mansion would remain Jefferson's until he died. The effort legislators made toward approving the lottery drained momentum from Jefferson's other main project, the University of Virginia. Lawmakers refused to fund the completion of the Rotunda. In the end, the lottery failed due to a lack of ticket sales. The family kept spending money, though, ordering a pianoforte from Boston over Jeff Randolph's objections. Less than two weeks before he died, Jefferson wrote a letter about an expected shipment of wine from the south of France—when he died, the Monticello cellar contained about fifty cases of wine, with more on the way.[16]

The disposition of Jefferson's property began in earnest when he composed his last will and testament in 1826. He gave Poplar Forest to his grandson Francis Eppes, who had lived there for several years and who advised Jefferson that when it rained, the mansion's roof leaked bucketsful of water.

Aside from Poplar Forest, Jefferson wrote ominously, "I subject all my other property to the payment of my debts." Since Thomas Mann Randolph, his son-in-law, was insolvent and unstable, Jefferson gave Monticello and its associated properties to Martha Jefferson Randolph. He made Jeff Randolph the executor of the will and one of the trustees of Martha's inheritance. (As a married woman in antebellum America, Martha had virtually no property rights.) Jefferson also gifted certain valuable items to particular individuals, such as a "gold-mounted walking staff of animal horn" to James Madison. His remaining books would go to the University of Virginia library, and he stipulated that his grandchildren would each get a gold watch.[17]

Jefferson also settled obligations to several bondspeople he knew personally, or to whom he was related. Echoing a parable of Jesus in Matthew 25, Jefferson freed his "good, affectionate, and faithful servant" Burwell Colbert and gave him $300 to supply him as a tradesman. He also arranged for the freedom of carpenter John Hemings and of blacksmith Joe Fossett, but not until a year after Jefferson's death. Jefferson stipulated that Madison and Eston, children of Sally Hemings, would be freed when they turned twenty-one, and further requested that the legislature exempt them from the law requiring freed slaves to leave the state. Until they reached adulthood, their remaining years of service were entrusted to John Hemings. Freeing Madison and Eston apparently fulfilled the promise that Jefferson made years earlier in Paris: if Sally would come back to Virginia with him, he would emancipate any children they had together.[18]

Sally herself was not mentioned in his will. In itself, this was not unusual, as most of the enslaved people he owned were not listed by name. One hundred and thirty of them were sold in 1827 to help settle his debts, though Hemings was not one of them. As historian Annette Gordon-Reed has explained, writing her name in his will might have reopened the question of their relationship. This was the last thing Jefferson wanted to do to his white family. Virginia law made it even more complicated to emancipate bondspeople older than forty-five (Hemings was fifty-three). Fearing that masters would abandon their aging bondspeople, the Virginia legislature prohibited the freeing of older enslaved people unless the master made reasonable financial provision for them. Jefferson had done this for Burwell Colbert, but openly providing for the mother of his enslaved children would have been unbearable. Finally, he would have had to request that the legislature give her an exemption from the rule of leaving the state.[19]

Given the simmering frustration with Jefferson over the University of Virginia and his near-failure to get the lottery approved, it was no guarantee that the legislature would have approved a request to let him emancipate Sally Hemings and allow her to remain in the state. Members of the larger Hemings family did not attract too much attention, but "Dusky Sally" was a presence that white legislators knew about. Jefferson surely did not want to remind them about her. After Jefferson's death, however, Sally was informally freed. She went to live in Charlottesville, where the 1830 census listed her as a free white woman (reminding us of her reputedly light-skinned complexion). Martha Randolph gave Hemings her "time," functionally emancipating her, shortly before Hemings's death in 1835. Hemings was presumably buried somewhere in Charlottesville, but the location of her grave is unknown.[20]

Hemings almost certainly attended to Jefferson, as did Burwell Colbert, in the days leading up to his death. Everyone at Monticello could see in June 1826 that Jefferson was dying. Yet the fiftieth anniversary of the Declaration of Independence loomed. Would he live to see that day? He declined an invitation to go to Washington to celebrate the anniversary, citing his poor health. But the opportunity gave Jefferson one more chance to frame American independence as "the Signal of arousing men to burst the chains, under which Monkish ignorance and superstition had persuaded them to bind themselves. . . . The general spread of the light of science has already laid open to every view the palpable truth that the mass of mankind has not been born, with saddles on their backs, nor a favored few booted and spurred, ready to ride them legitimately, by the grace of god." Jefferson still identified priestcraft and the divine right of kings as the great enemies of Revolutionary thought. White men were not given to rule over other white men. But what about white men ruling over white women, or over men and women of other races? (To be fair, women's suffrage was hardly a live discussion in the United States in 1826.) He did not address those questions; they remained unresolved.[21]

Jefferson had been preparing his whole adult life for how he would be remembered after death. Earlier in 1826, he even implored Madison to "take care of me when dead." He left a poem for Martha Randolph that spoke of his pain at leaving her and his hope for the next life. In particular, he looked forward to reunion with his long-deceased wife Martha and his daughter Mary: "Two Seraphs await me, long shrouded in death: I will bear them your love on my last parting breath."[22]

The scenes at Jefferson's deathbed became publicly contested. Jefferson's eulogist William Wirt, a devout Christian who served as attorney general under both James Monroe and John Quincy Adams, claimed that on the Fourth of July, Jefferson repeatedly whispered, "Nunc Domine dimittis," or "Now, Lord, let thy servant depart in peace." This was a phrase Jefferson had regularly quoted before, taken from the Gospel of Luke and the Book of Common Prayer. In another eulogy, the Harvard professor, Unitarian pastor, and future congressman Edward Everett made the same assertion about him saying "nunc dimittis." A newspaper report of Jefferson's death called "nunc dimittis" his "favorite quotation." But Jefferson's personal doctor Robley Dunglison, learning of Wirt's claim, denied it. "No such expression was heard by me," Dunglison wrote. The doctor seems only to have wanted to get the facts straight, however, as he did not deny that Jefferson died a man of faith. He described Jefferson's beliefs as "harmonizing more closely with that of the Unitarians than of any other denomination." Dunglison quoted Jefferson's sentiments, expressed late in life in two letters to children, as representative of those beliefs: "Adore God. Reverence and cherish your parents. Love your neighbor as yourself; and your country more than life. Be just. Be true. Murmur not at the ways of Providence. And the life into which you have entered will be the passage to one of eternal and ineffable bliss," Jefferson wrote. The former president modulated his expressed beliefs depending upon his audience, and women and children may have received a more conventional message than did respected male friends. Still, at the end of his life Jefferson seems to have believed in providence, the Golden Rule, and an afterlife.[23]

In one of the most astounding coincidences in American history, Jefferson and John Adams both passed away on July 4, 1826. Each assumed that the other survived him. Many Americans, understandably, received this "double apotheosis" as a sign from God. As William Wirt asked, "Is there a heart that did not quail at this close manifestation of the hand of Heaven in our affairs?" But what exactly God was saying to America in the two Founders' deaths was more difficult to discern.[24]

Family friend and Episcopal minister Frederick Hatch performed the funeral for Jefferson. Jefferson liked the minister and had donated money in 1821 to help build Hatch a parsonage in Charlottesville. (Jefferson also gave money to erect meetinghouses for the Episcopal, Presbyterian, and Baptist churches in Charlottesville.) Jefferson was buried in a coffin built by John Hemings, carpenter and half brother of Sally. Although it took some years for his gravestone to be erected, he left instructions that it was to identify him as

> Author of the Declaration of American Independence
> of the Statute of Virginia for religious freedom
> & Father of the University of Virginia

The epitaph was Jefferson's final effort to manage the nation's memory of him. These accomplishments were good choices for his gravestone. The Statute for Establishing Religious Freedom and the University of Virginia were arguably the two most significant instances (one might add the Louisiana Purchase) in which Jefferson's theories bore the most practical consequences. The university was probably the most notable episode in which Jefferson went from framing an enlightened idea to implementing it politically in the face of major opposition. Madison was the one who secured the passage of the Statute for Establishing Religious Freedom, but the law's reverberations have had massive national and global consequences for good, especially in influencing the religion clauses of the First Amendment to the Constitution: "Congress shall make no law respecting an establishment of religion, or prohibiting the free exercise thereof." And whatever incoherence Jefferson may have deposited in the Declaration, legions have hailed its soaring justification of independence and evocation of equality by creation as "America's creed," as Martin Luther King, Jr., put it.[25]

Jefferson left other legacies, too. Most obviously there was the dilemma of his stated views and lived realities of slavery. This was a grinding contradiction built into the nation's founding documents, including the Declaration. Although he was not at the Constitutional Convention, the three-fifths clause in the Constitution helped ensure that whatever qualms Jefferson and other masters had about slavery, they would exercise outsized political influence into the 1860s—and they often used that influence to protect and expand slaveholding. Virginia itself controlled the presidency for most of the nation's first thirty-five years under the Constitution.

The legacy Jefferson left at Monticello was personal and financial. He died more than $100,000 in debt, a crippling sum of roughly $2.6 million in today's money. Someone was going to have to pay. Now many of the people who had labored for his happiness would be sold at auction. Jeff Randolph placed ads for an executor's sale in the Charlottesville newspaper starting in late 1826. The sale, scheduled for January 15, 1827, would liquidate the "residue of the personal estate of Thomas Jefferson." The highlight of the event, displayed in bold letters at the top of the ad, was "130 valuable negroes." These were "believed to be the most valuable for their number ever offered at one time" in Virginia. Randolph also promised to sell the contents of the mansion, including Jefferson's art collection. The family would reserve paintings and busts of Jefferson himself for a later sale in Boston, where they hoped to fetch higher prices. As it turned out, the Boston sale was unsuccessful, and they had to ship most of the images of Jefferson back to Charlottesville.[26]

The enslaved people sold well, including eleven-year-old Peter Fossett, who recalled decades later that the death of Jefferson meant sorrow for his bondspeople. Fossett claimed that as a boy he did not understand what it meant to be a slave until he was "put upon an auction block and sold to strangers." Israel Jefferson noted bluntly that while Jefferson freed a small number of the bondspeople whom he knew personally, "the rest of us were sold from the auction block." As the minister and former slave James W. C. Pennington explained, a slave auction was arguably the defining feature of American chattel slavery. Its specter always hovered over enslaved people, however stable their current status seemed otherwise. "The being of slavery," Pennington wrote, "its soul and body, lives and moves in the chattel principle, the property principle, the bill of sale principle." Most of Jefferson's bondspeople avoided being sold out of state, the most feared fate of all. Many of them were sold away from their families, however. Peter Fossett, for example, was separated from his mother Edith and father Joe, the blacksmith whom Jefferson freed in his will. Peter's new owner refused to sell him to Joe Fossett when Joe sought to reunite his dispersed family members. Peter Fossett went up for sale again in 1850, and Joe was finally able to purchase his freedom. Peter moved to be with his family in Ohio, where he became a Baptist pastor. Few bondspeople sold away from their families in the antebellum period had happy conclusions to their stories, however.[27]

Monticello, always challenging to maintain, began to deteriorate immediately after the former president's death. Jefferson's longtime friend Margaret Bayard Smith visited the "desolate mansion" in 1828. She was haunted by what she found. "No kind friend with his gracious countenance stood in the portico to welcome us, no train of domestics hastened with smiling alacrity to show us forward." The mansion, the terraces, and the outbuildings were all succumbing to waterlogged rot. When Smith knocked at the door, "a little negro girl poorly dressed" answered and led the visitors into empty rooms. Martha Randolph, who had been nearly as ill as her father when he died, finally appeared as a ghostly presence, "like the spirit of the place, that had survived its body." She asked Smith to "excuse all that is wanting. . . . You know all that has passed."[28]

When Smith visited Monticello, Jeff Randolph had already decided to sell it. The family mourned the loss of the home. But they still staggered under their inherited debts, which would never allow them to preserve the mansion in its intended glory. Francis Eppes sold Poplar Forest the same year and moved to Florida. But Randolph struggled to find a buyer for Monticello. It took Randolph three years, and even then he could get only $7,000 for the house and surrounding acreage. The Randolphs kept the family cemetery.

The year of the sale was 1831, a time of turmoil unlike any Virginia had faced, perhaps, since Jefferson's ill-fated term as governor a half century earlier. In August 1831, the Virginia slave preacher Nat Turner led followers in one of the most devastating rebellions in American history. Almost sixty whites died, and hundreds of African Americans perished in a murderous backlash. That year also saw the emergence of a new northern-based movement for the immediate abolition of slavery led by William Lloyd Garrison. Writing in the first issue of his newspaper the *Liberator*, Garrison said that as he assented "to the 'self-evident truth' maintained in the American Declaration of Independence, 'that all men are created equal, and endowed by their Creator with certain inalienable rights—among which are life, liberty and the pursuit of happiness,' I shall strenuously contend for the immediate enfranchisement of our slave population." The Declaration had taken on a life of its own, inspiring America's most radical visions of freedom for slaves.[29]

The nullification crisis likewise loomed in 1831, in which the South Carolina followers of John C. Calhoun touted the right of states to nullify federal laws they regarded as unconstitutional. White southern support for nullification outside of South Carolina was sparse. Many in Virginia, including James Madison, regarded nullification as a desperate last resort. But some pro-nullification militants believed that reluctant Virginians were not honoring the memory of Jefferson. One South Carolinian wrote that Jefferson was arguably the "greatest benefactor of his race that ever existed. He taught mankind their rights—but, more than this, he taught them how to secure and to maintain them. And these lessons . . . have sunk deep into the minds of his countrymen in South Carolina." White southerners still had the wolf by the ear. Ultimately they would not let it go, even to preserve the nation whose independence Jefferson had declared.[30]

Notes

Epigraphs: TJ to Chastellux, Sept. 2, 1785; editorial note on TJ to Samuel Smith, Aug. 22, 1798, both in James P. McClure and J. Jefferson Looney, eds., *The Papers of Thomas Jefferson*, digital ed. (Charlottesville, Va., 2008–21).

Introduction

1. Joseph J. Ellis, *American Sphinx: The Character of Thomas Jefferson* (New York, 1996), xvii; Richard A. Samuelson, "Consistent in Creation: Thomas Jefferson, Natural Aristocracy, and the Problem of Knowledge," in Robert M. S. McDonald, ed., *Light and Liberty: Thomas Jefferson and the Power of Knowledge* (Charlottesville, Va., 2012), 77.
2. Francis D. Cogliano, *Thomas Jefferson: Reputation and Legacy* (Charlottesville, Va., 2006), 140; Robert M. S. McDonald, *Confounding Father: Thomas Jefferson's Image in His Own Time* (Charlottesville, Va., 2016), 13–14; Pauline Maier, *American Scripture: Making the Declaration of Independence* (New York, 1998).
3. Cogliano, *Reputation and Legacy*, 170–71.
4. Franklin Kalinowski, review of *"I Tremble for My Country": Thomas Jefferson and the Virginia Gentry*, by Ronald L. Hatzenbuehler, *Journal of American History* 94, no. 3 (Dec. 2007): 917–18; John B. Boles, *Jefferson: Architect of American Liberty* (New York, 2017), 3–5.
5. Brian Steele, *Thomas Jefferson and American Nationhood* (New York, 2012), 180–81; Paul Finkelman, "Jefferson and Slavery: 'Treason against the Hopes of the World,'" in Peter S. Onuf, ed., *Jeffersonian Legacies* (Charlottesville, Va., 1993), 181; Adam Rothman, *Slave Country: American Expansion and the Origins of the Deep South* (Cambridge, Mass., 2005), 2. The "Enlightenment" was unidirectional on few issues, but as of the Revolution there were growing numbers of Enlightenment-influenced advocates of abolition, especially in the northern states. Paul J. Polgar, *Standard-Bearers of Equality: America's First Abolition Movement* (Chapel Hill, N.C., 2019), 173.

6. Robert E. Shalhope, "Thomas Jefferson's Republicanism and Antebellum Southern Thought," *Journal of Southern History* 42, no. 4 (Nov. 1976): 529–56; Andrew Burstein, "'Dexterity and Delicacy of Manipulation': Biographers Henry S. Randall and James Parton," in Robert M. S. McDonald, ed., *Thomas Jefferson's Lives: Biographers and the Battle for History* (Charlottesville, Va., 2019), 73; Craig Bruce Smith, *American Honor: The Creation of the Nation's Ideals during the Revolutionary Era* (Chapel Hill, N.C., 2018), 19–21; Darren Staloff, *Hamilton, Adams, Jefferson: The Politics of Enlightenment and the American Founding* (New York, 2005), 242. Staloff argues persuasively that by the 1780s Jefferson was transitioning to a Romantic view of politics, partly out of frustration with his inability to effect Enlightenment-style reforms in Virginia (247–49). Southern gentility is a much-discussed topic, but see Bertram Wyatt-Brown, *Southern Honor: Ethics and Behavior in the Old South* (New York, 1982), 88–114; and on Jefferson, see Maurizio Valsania, *Jefferson's Body: A Corporeal Biography* (Charlottesville, Va., 2017), 19.

7. Shalhope, "Jefferson's Republicanism," 535; Edmund S. Morgan, *The Meaning of Independence: John Adams, George Washington, and Thomas Jefferson* (Charlottesville, Va., 2004), 64.

1. *"If There Is Such a Thing as a Devil"*

1. TJ to John Page, Dec. 25, 1762, in James P. McClure and J. Jefferson Looney, eds., *The Papers of Thomas Jefferson*, digital ed. (Charlottesville, Va., 2008–21), hereafter cited as *PTJ;* Jon Kukla, *Mr. Jefferson's Women* (New York, 2007), 19–20; Hannah Spahn, *Thomas Jefferson, Time, and History* (Charlottesville, Va., 2011), 76–77.

2. Susan Kern, *The Jeffersons at Shadwell* (New Haven, Conn., 2010), 16–17; John Ferling, *Jefferson and Hamilton: The Rivalry That Forged a Nation* (New York, 2013), 9–10.

3. Sarah N. Randolph, *The Domestic Life of Thomas Jefferson* (New York, 1871), 23; Lucia Stanton, *"Those Who Labor for My Happiness": Slavery at Thomas Jefferson's Monticello* (Charlottesville, Va., 2012), 104; Annette Gordon-Reed and Peter S. Onuf, *"Most Blessed of the Patriarchs": Thomas Jefferson and the Empire of the Imagination* (New York, 2016), 70.

4. The date of Jefferson's birth is in the "New Style" dating that Britain and its colonies switched to in 1752 when they moved from the Julian to the Gregorian calendar. In the "Old Style," Jefferson's birth date was April 2.

5. Henry Stephens Randall, *The Life of Thomas Jefferson* (New York, 1858), 1:17; [Thomas Anburey], *Travels through the Interior Parts of America* (London, 1789), 2:358–59; Julia Cherry Spruill, *Women's Life and Work in the Southern Colonies,* new ed. (New York, 1998), 33.

6. Kern, *Jeffersons at Shadwell,* 30–31; Eugene D. Genovese, *The Sweetness of Life: Southern Planters at Home,* ed. Douglas Ambrose (New York, 2017), 14; T. H. Breen, *The Marketplace of Revolution: How Consumer Politics Shaped American Independence* (New York, 2004), 171.

7. "Thomas Jefferson: Autobiography, 6 Jan.–29 July 1821, 6 January 1821," *Founders Online,* National Archives, https://founders.archives.gov /documents/Jefferson/98-01-02-1756; Kern, *Jeffersons at Shadwell,* 33.

8. William Mottolese, "'Almost an Englishman': Olaudah Equiano and the Colonial Gift of Language," in Greg Clingham, ed., *Questioning History: The Postmodern Turn to the Eighteenth Century* (Cranbury, N.J., 1998), 160.

9. Thomas Wilson, *The Knowledge and Practice of Christianity Made Easy* (London, 1741), x–xi; Randolph, *Domestic Life,* 34.

10. Sarah Rivett, *Unscripted America: Indigenous Languages and the Origins of a Literary Nation* (New York, 2017), 182–83; Gordon M. Sayre, "Jefferson and Native Americans: Policy and Archive," in Frank Shuffelton, ed., *The Cambridge Companion to Thomas Jefferson* (New York, 2008), 62–63; Robert L. Cord, "Mr. Jefferson's 'Nonabsolute' Wall of Separation between Church and State," in Garrett Ward Sheldon and Daniel L. Dreisbach, eds., *Religion and Political Culture in Jefferson's Virginia* (Lanham, Md., 2000), 174–75.

11. Edward L. Bond, ed., *Spreading the Gospel in Colonial Virginia: Sermons and Devotional Writings* (Lanham, Md., 2004), 2; Kern, *Jeffersons at Shadwell,* 164–65.

12. TJ to John Taylor, June 4, 1798, in *PTJ;* James A. Bear and Lucia C. Stanton, eds., *Jefferson's Memorandum Books* (Princeton, N.J., 1997), 1:22; Mary V. Thompson, *"In the Hands of a Good Providence": Religion in the Life of George Washington* (Charlottesville, Va., 2008), 40–41.

13. Kern, *Jeffersons at Shadwell,* 21, 146; Randolph, *Domestic Life,* 26; Kenneth A. Lockridge, *On the Sources of Patriarchal Rage: The Commonplace Books of William Byrd and Thomas Jefferson and the Gendering of Power in the Eighteenth Century* (New York, 1992), 70.

14. TJ to John Adams, Oct. 12, 1813, in *PTJ;* Kern, *Jeffersons at Shadwell,* 230–33; Richard Samuelson, "Jefferson and Religion: Private Belief, Public Policy," in Shuffelton, *The Cambridge Companion to Thomas Jefferson,* 148.

15. Henry Stephens Randall, *The Life of Thomas Jefferson* (New York, 1858), 1:41; TJ, Memorandum Books, 1771, in *PTJ;* Karl Lehmann, *Thomas Jefferson: American Humanist* (Charlottesville, Va., 1985), 53–54, 103.

16. Thomas S. Kidd, *Patrick Henry: First among Patriots* (New York, 2011), 75; Ralph Ketcham, *James Madison: A Biography* (Charlottesville, Va., 1990), 12.

17. TJ, *Notes on the State of Virginia,* in Merrill D. Peterson, ed., *Thomas Jefferson: Writings* (New York, 1984), 288; Eugene D. Genovese and Elizabeth Fox-Genovese, *Fatal Self-Deception: Slaveholding Paternalism in the Old South* (New York, 2011), 6–7; Steven C. Bullock, *Tea Sets and Tyranny: The Politics of Politeness in Early America* (Philadelphia, 2017), 221.

18. TJ, *Autobiography,* in Peterson, *Writings,* 4; Randolph, *Domestic Life,* 23; Randall, *Life,* 17.

19. TJ to Madame de Staël Holstein, Sept. 6, 1816, in *PTJ;* *Book of Common Prayer* (London, 1715), fol. 24; John K. Nelson, *A Blessed Company: Parishes, Parsons, and Parishioners in Anglican Virginia, 1690–1776* (Chapel Hill, N.C., 2001), 212, 224, 228–29; Kevin J. Hayes, *The Road to Monticello: The Life and Mind of Thomas Jefferson* (New York, 2008), 20; Kern, *Jeffersons at Shadwell,* 164–65. On the biblical texts of the funeral sermons, see William Douglas, *The Douglas Register,* ed. W. Mac. Jones (Richmond, Va., 1928), 334–46.

20. Hayes, *Road to Monticello,* 20–21; Douglas, *Douglas Register,* 355, 367.

21. TJ to William Duane, Aug. 12, 1810, *PTJ;* TJ to Mathew Carey, Nov. 22, 1818, in *PTJ;* TJ to John Cartwright, June 5, 1824, in H. A. Washington, ed., *The Writings of Thomas Jefferson* (Washington, D.C., 1854), 7: 355; Douglas L. Wilson, "Jefferson vs. Hume," *William and Mary Quarterly,* 3rd ser., 46, no. 1 (Jan. 1989): 49; Francis D. Cogliano, *Thomas Jefferson: Reputation and Legacy* (Charlottesville, Va., 2006), 24–25; Mark G. Spencer, *Hume's Reception in Early America,* rev. ed. (New York, 2017), 290.

22. TJ, *Autobiography,* 4.

23. TJ, *Autobiography,* 4; TJ to Joseph Priestley, Jan. 27, 1800, *Founders Online;* TJ to Jason Chamberlain, July 1, 1814, in *PTJ;* Peter S. Onuf, "Ancients, Moderns, and the Progress of Mankind: Thomas Jefferson's Classical World," in Peter S. Onuf and Nicholas P. Cole, eds., *Thomas Jefferson, the Classical World, and Early America* (Charlottesville, Va., 2011), 35–36.

24. TJ to John Brazer, Nov. 22, 1819, *Founders Online;* TJ to Rev. Matthew Maury, Jan. 8, 1790, *Founders Online.* See also Jefferson's subscription for Charles Thomson's translation of the Septuagint, TJ to Charles Thomson,

Jan. 11, 1808, and another edition he acquired from Frederick Winslow Hatch, Sept. 9, 1821, *Founders Online*. Charles B. Sanford, *Thomas Jefferson and His Library* (Hamden, Conn., 1977), 128–29; Wilson Jeremiah Moses, *Thomas Jefferson: A Modern Prometheus* (New York, 2019), 345; Lehmann, *American Humanist*, 58–59, 136; Andrew Burstein, *Jefferson's Secrets: Death and Desire at Monticello* (New York, 2005), 161; Onuf, "Jefferson's Classical World," 48. On Erasmus, see Ronald Hendel, *Steps to a New Edition of the Hebrew Bible* (Atlanta, 2016), 275.

25. TJ to Henry Remsen, Dec. 31, 1800, in *PTJ; American Citizen*, Nov. 1, 1800, 4; Carl J. Richard, *The Founders and the Bible* (Lanham, Md., 2016), 45. In February 1798 Jefferson also paid a subscription for a new hot press Bible, the first such Bible published in the United States. TJ, Memorandum Books, Feb. 26, 1798, in *PTJ*.

26. Hayes, *Road to Monticello*, 24–25.

27. Joan R. Gundersen, "Anthony Gavin's *A Master-Key to Popery:* A Virginia Parson's Best Seller," *Virginia Magazine of History and Biography* 82, no. 1 (Jan. 1974): 39–46.

28. Hayes, *Road to Monticello*, 24–25; Thomas S. Kidd, *George Whitefield: America's Spiritual Founding Father* (New Haven, Conn., 2014), 22; Catherine A. Brekus, *Sarah Osborn's World: The Rise of Evangelical Christianity in Early America* (New Haven, Conn., 2013), 81.

29. Hayes, *Road to Monticello*, 25; TJ to Thomas Jefferson Randolph, Nov. 24, 1808, in Edwin Morris Betts and James Adam Bear, Jr., eds., *The Family Letters of Thomas Jefferson* (Charlottesville, Va., 1986), 362–63.

30. TJ to Martha Jefferson, Mar. 19, 1784, in Betts and Bear, *Family Letters*, 25; Dumas Malone, *Jefferson the Virginian* (Boston, 1948), 40; Kern, *Jeffersons at Shadwell*, 165.

31. James Blair to the bishop of London, Feb. 19, 1742, in William Stevens Perry, ed., *Historical Collections relating to the American Colonial Church* (Hartford, Conn., 1870), 364; Hayes, *Road to Monticello*, 31–32.

32. Kidd, *Patrick Henry*, 27–28, 44–46.

33. TJ, *Jefferson's Literary Commonplace Book*, ed. Douglas L. Wilson (Princeton, N.J., 1989), 94, 174–75; Hayes, *Road to Monticello*, 41; George F. Sensabaugh, *Milton in Early America* (Princeton, N.J., 1964), 135–36. Maury wrote a long letter on his philosophy of classical education to Robert Jackson, July 17, 1762, in Edward L. Bond, ed., *Spreading the Gospel in Colonial Virginia: Sermons and Devotional Writings* (Lanham, Md., 2004), 347–68.

34. TJ to John Harvie, Jan. 14, 1760, in *PTJ*.

35. Mary R. M. Goodwin, *The College of William and Mary* (Williamsburg, Va., 1967), 4, https://research.history.org/DigitalLibrary/View/index.cfm?do c=ResearchReports%5CRR0210.xml.

36. TJ to John Harvie, Jan. 14, 1760, in *PTJ;* Stanton, *"Those Who Labor,"* 107–8.

37. TJ, *Autobiography,* 4; TJ to William Small, May 7, 1775, in *PTJ;* Garry Wills, *Inventing America: Jefferson's Declaration of Independence* (New York, 1978), 176–80; Craig Bruce Smith, *American Honor: The Creation of the Nation's Ideals during the Revolutionary Era* (Chapel Hill, N.C., 2018), 62–63. On Small's influence, see also TJ to Louis H. Girardin, Jan. 15, 1815, in *PTJ.*

38. TJ, "Notes for the Biography of George Wythe., ca. 31 Aug. 1820, 31 August 1820," *Founders Online;* TJ to Richard Price, Aug. 7, 1785, in *PTJ;* Smith, *American Honor,* 63–64; Paul Finkelman, "Thomas Jefferson and Anti-Slavery: The Myth Goes On," *Virginia Magazine of History and Biography* 102, no. 2 (Apr. 1994): 210–11; Joshua D. Rothman, *Notorious in the Neighbor-hood: Sex and Families across the Color Line in Virginia, 1787–1861* (Chapel Hill, N.C., 2003), 221–22.

39. TJ to John Page, Dec. 25, 1762, in *PTJ;* Jeff Broadwater, *Jefferson, Madison, and the Making of the Constitution* (Chapel Hill, N.C., 2019), 19–21.

40. TJ, "Whether Christianity Is Part of the Common Law?" [1764?], in Daniel L. Dreisbach and Mark David Hall, eds., *The Sacred Rights of Conscience* (Indianapolis, 2009), 541; TJ to Thomas Cooper, Feb. 10, 1814, in *PTJ;* Daniel L. Dreisbach, ed., *Religion and Politics in the Early Republic: Jasper Adams and the Church-State Debate* (Lexington, Ky., 1996), 12–14; Merrill D. Peterson, *The Jefferson Image in the American Mind,* new ed. (Charlottesville, Va., 1998), 95–96.

41. TJ to John Page, Jan. 23, 1764, TJ to William Fleming, Mar. 20, 1764, in *PTJ;* Kukla, *Mr. Jefferson's Women,* 21–26.

42. TJ to William Fleming, Mar. 20, 1764, in *PTJ;* Kukla, *Mr. Jefferson's Women,* 36–37; Darren Staloff, *Hamilton, Adams, Jefferson: The Politics of Enlighten-ment and the American Founding* (New York, 2005), 243.

43. TJ to William Fleming, Mar. 20, 1764, in *PTJ;* Denise A. Spellberg, *Thomas Jefferson's Qur'an: Islam and the Founders* (New York, 2013), 81–82.

44. Laurence Sterne, *The Sermons of Mr. Yorick* (London, 1760), 1:1, 7; TJ to Robert Skipwith, with a List of Books for a Private Library, Aug. 3, 1771, and TJ to John Minor, including an earlier letter to Bernard Moore, Aug. 30, 1814, in *PTJ;* Tim Parnell, "*The Sermons of Mr. Yorick:* The Commonplace

and the Rhetoric of the Heart," in Thomas Keymer, ed., *The Cambridge Companion to Laurence Sterne* (New York, 2009), 65–66; Andrew Burstein, *Letters from the Head and Heart: Writings of Thomas Jefferson* (Chapel Hill, N.C., 2002), 18–19; Paul Giles, *Transatlantic Insurrections: British Culture and the Formation of American Literature, 1730–1860* (Philadelphia, 2001), 100–101; Wills, *Inventing America*, 273; Kevin J. Hayes, *George Washington: A Life in Books* (New York, 2017), 214.

45. Marc Egnal, *A Mighty Empire: The Origins of the American Revolution*, new ed. (Ithaca, N.Y., 2010), 216; Bruce A. Ragsdale, *A Planters' Republic: The Search for Economic Independence in Revolutionary Virginia* (Madison, Wisc., 1996), 52.

46. Kidd, *Patrick Henry*, 51–52, 58–59.

47. TJ, *Autobiography*, 6.

2. *"I Speak the Sentiments of America"*

1. TJ, *Autobiography*, in Merrill D. Peterson, ed., *Thomas Jefferson: Writings* (New York, 1984), 8.

2. TJ, *Autobiography*, 8.

3. TJ, *Autobiography*, 8; Virginia House of Burgesses, *Tuesday, the 24th of May, 14 Geo. III, 1774* [Williamsburg, Va., 1774], broadside; Thomas E. Buckley, S.J., "Placing Thomas Jefferson and Religion in Context, Then and Now," in John B. Boles and Randal L. Hall, eds., *Seeing Jefferson Anew: In His Time and Ours* (Charlottesville, Va., 2010), 135; John Ragosta, *Religious Freedom: Jefferson's Legacy, America's Creed* (Charlottesville, Va., 2013), 8–9.

4. TJ to ——, July 26, 1764, in James P. McClure and J. Jefferson Looney, eds., *The Papers of Thomas Jefferson*, digital ed. (Charlottesville, Va., 2008–21), hereafter cited as *PTJ;* Douglas L. Wilson, ed., *Jefferson's Literary Commonplace Book* (Princeton, N.J., 1989), 23–24.

5. TJ to Isaac Story, Dec. 5, 1801, in *PTJ;* William D. Gould, "The Religious Opinions of Thomas Jefferson," *Mississippi Valley Historical Review* 20, no. 2 (Sept. 1933): 200; Jon Butler, *Becoming America: The Revolution Before 1776* (Cambridge, Mass., 2000), 310–11, n.45; Wilson Jeremiah Moses, *Thomas Jefferson: A Modern Prometheus* (New York, 2019), 349. Examples of Jefferson's continued interest in body-soul speculation include TJ to John Adams, Apr. 8, 1816, and TJ to Francis Adrian Van der Kemp, Feb. 9, 1818, in *PTJ.*

6. Frank L. Dewey, *Thomas Jefferson, Lawyer* (Charlottesville, Va., 1986), 10, 45.

7. Jon Kukla, *Mr. Jefferson's Women* (New York, 2007), 53, 191–192, 195; Gisela Tauber, "Thomas Jefferson: Relationships with Women," *American Imago* 45, no. 4 (Winter 1988): 434.

8. Thomas S. Kidd, *Benjamin Franklin: The Religious Life of a Founding Father* (New Haven, Conn., 2017), 82, 215; Peter R. Henriques, *Realistic Visionary: A Portrait of George Washington* (Charlottesville, Va., 2006), 67–68.

9. Kukla, *Mr. Jefferson's Women*, 55–56.

10. Barry Bergdoll, "Books, Buildings, and the Spaces of Democracy: Jefferson's Library from Paris to Washington," in Lloyd DeWitt and Corey Piper, eds., *Thomas Jefferson, Architect* (New Haven, Conn., 2019), 66; Annette Gordon-Reed, *The Hemingses of Monticello* (New York, 2008), 113; Jack McLaughlin, *Jefferson and Monticello: The Biography of a Builder* (New York, 1988), 154–55; TJ, Dec. 1770, Memorandum Books, in *PTJ*.

11. Gordon-Reed, *Hemingses*, 113; McLaughlin, *Jefferson and Monticello*, 156, 174–75; TJ, 1769, Memorandum Books.

12. Merrill D. Peterson, *Thomas Jefferson and the New Nation: A Biography* (New York, 1970), 23–24; "Scene or feeling" is from Charles A. Miller, *Jefferson and Nature: An Interpretation* (Baltimore, 1988), 102; Richard Slotkin, *Regeneration through Violence: The Mythology of the American Frontier, 1600–1860* (Middletown, Conn., 1973), 245–47; TJ to Maria Cosway, Oct. 12, 1786, *Founders Online;* TJ, *Notes on the State of Virginia*, in Peterson, *Writings*, 148; Darren Staloff, *Hamilton, Adams, Jefferson: The Politics of Enlightenment and the American Founding* (New York, 2005), 266–70; Peter S. Onuf, "Ancients, Moderns, and the Progress of Mankind: Thomas Jefferson's Classical World," in Peter S. Onuf and Nicholas P. Cole, eds., *Thomas Jefferson, the Classical World, and Early America* (Charlottesville, Va., 2011), 35; TJ to Joseph Priestley, Apr. 9, 1803, in *PTJ*.

13. TJ to Edward Coles, Aug. 25, 1814, *Founders Online;* David Ramsay to TJ, May 3, 1786, in *PTJ;* Hume, quoted in Isaac Kramnick, ed., *The Portable Enlightenment Reader* (New York, 1995), 629; Manisha Sinha, *The Slave's Cause: A History of Abolition* (New Haven, Conn., 2016), 87–90; Peter Kolchin, *American Slavery: 1619–1877* (New York, 2003), 88; Andrew Burstein, *Jefferson's Secrets: Death and Desire at Monticello* (New York, 2005), 120–21; Paul Finkelman, "Jefferson and Slavery: 'Treason against the Hopes of the World,'" in Peter S. Onuf, ed., *Jeffersonian Legacies* (Charlottesville, Va., 1993), 184–89; Bruce R. Dain, *A Hideous Monster of the Mind: American Race Theory in the Early Republic* (Cambridge, Mass., 2003), 30–31, 74–75; Frank Shuffelton, "Thomas Jefferson: Race, Culture, and the Failure of

Anthropological Method," in Frank Shuffelton, ed., *A Mixed Race: Ethnicity in Early America* (New York, 1993), 258; David Brion Davis, *The Problem of Slavery in the Age of Revolution, 1770–1823*, new ed. (New York, 1999), 195; Winthrop D. Jordan, *White over Black: American Attitudes toward the Negro, 1550–1812* (New York, 1977), 494–95.

14. TJ, "Advertisement for a Runaway Slave," Sept. 7, 1769, in *PTJ;* Finkelman, "Jefferson and Slavery," 190.

15. "Howell v. Netherland," in TJ, *Reports of Cases Determined in the General Court of Virginia* (Charlottesville, Va., 1829), 92; James L. Golden and Alan L. Golden, *Thomas Jefferson and the Rhetoric of Virtue* (Lanham, Md., 2002), 287–89; David Thomas Konig, "Jefferson and the Law," in Francis D. Cogliano, ed., *A Companion to Thomas Jefferson* (Malden, Mass., 2012), 355; Ari Helo, *Thomas Jefferson's Ethics and the Politics of Human Progress: The Morality of a Slaveholder* (New York, 2014), 251, n.98.

16. TJ to John Page, Feb. 21, 1770, in *PTJ.* Jefferson and his correspondents would occasionally speak of "gods," but he had little sympathy for polytheism. See, for instance, Maria Cosway to TJ, [Dec. 1, 1787?], in *PTJ.* He saw Trinitarian church teachings as "mere relapses into polytheism," TJ to Jared Sparks, Nov. 4, 1820, *Founders Online.*

17. George Wythe to TJ, Mar. 9, 1770, in *PTJ;* Douglas L. Wilson, "Jefferson's Library," in Merrill D. Peterson, ed., *Thomas Jefferson: A Reference Biography* (New York, 1986), 162–64.

18. Robert Skipwith to TJ, July 17, 1771, *Founders Online;* Wilson, "Jefferson's Library," 163; Frank Shuffelton, "Thomas Jefferson, Colporteur of the Enlightenment," in Robert M. S. McDonald, ed., *Light & Liberty: Thomas Jefferson and the Power of Knowledge* (Charlottesville, Va., 2012), 139–42.

19. TJ to Robert Skipwith, Aug. 3, 1771, in *PTJ;* Wilson, *Literary Commonplace Book,* 155–57; William Sherlock, *A Practical Discourse concerning a Future Judgment,* 6th ed. (London, 1704), 3; Golden and Golden, *The Rhetoric of Virtue,* xi; Charles B. Sanford, *The Religious Life of Thomas Jefferson* (Charlottesville, Va., 1984), 129; Eugene R. Sheridan, "Liberty and Virtue: Religion and Republicanism in Jeffersonian Thought," in James Gilreath, ed., *Thomas Jefferson and the Education of a Citizen* (Washington, D.C., 1999), 243–44; Peter Manseau, *The Jefferson Bible: A Biography* (Princeton, N.J., 2020), 20–23.

20. TJ to Robert Skipwith, Aug. 3, 1771, in *PTJ;* TJ to John Minor, including an earlier letter to Bernard Moore, Aug. 30, 1814, in *PTJ;* TJ to Peter Carr, Aug. 10, 1787, *Founders Online;* Kevin J. Hayes, *The Road to Monticello: The Life*

and Mind of Thomas Jefferson (New York, 2008), 127; Morris L. Cohen, "Thomas Jefferson Recommends a Course of Law Study," *University of Pennsylvania Law Review* 119, no. 5 (Apr. 1971): 823–44.

21. TJ, *Reports of Cases*, 96–97; Bernard Schwartz, ed., *Thomas Jefferson and Bolling v. Bolling* (San Marino, Calif., 1997), 64–66; Matthew Crow, *Thomas Jefferson, Legal History, and the Art of Recollection* (New York, 2017), 74–75; TJ to Thomas Adams, July 11, 1770, in *PTJ;* Buckley, "Jefferson and Religion," 134, 149, n.25.

22. TJ to James Ogilvie, Feb. 20, 1771, in *PTJ;* Kukla, *Mr. Jefferson's Women,* 68.

23. TJ to Thomas Adams, June 1, 1771, in *PTJ;* McLaughlin, *Jefferson and Monticello,* 364; Jennifer L. Anderson, *Mahogany: The Costs of Luxury in Early America* (Cambridge, Mass., 2012), 19.

24. TJ to Archibald Thweatt, May 29, 1810, in *PTJ;* Kukla, *Mr. Jefferson's Women,* 73–75; Henry Wiencek, *Master of the Mountain: Thomas Jefferson and His Slaves* (New York, 2012), 32.

25. Kukla, *Mr. Jefferson's Women,* 78–84.

26. Wilson, *Literary Commonplace Book,* 172, n.86; Hayes, *Road to Monticello,* 137–38.

27. TJ and John Walker to the Inhabitants of the Parish of St. Anne, [before July 23, 1774], in *PTJ;* Buckley, "Jefferson and Religion," 135.

28. "Subscription to Support a Clergyman in Charlottesville," [Feb. 1777], in *PTJ;* Charles Clay to TJ, Aug. 8, 1792, in *PTJ;* Mark Beliles, "The Christian Communities, Religious Revivals, and Political Culture of the Central Virginia Piedmont, 1737–1813," in Garrett Ward Sheldon and Daniel L. Dreisbach, eds., *Religion and Political Culture in Jefferson's Virginia* (Lanham, Md., 2000), 10–11; James H. Hutson, "Thomas Jefferson's Letter to the Danbury Baptists: A Controversy Rejoined," *William and Mary Quarterly* 56, no. 4 (Oct. 1999): 787; *The Plays of William Shakespeare* (London, 1768), 4:443.

29. Robert Carter to TJ, July 27, 1778, in *PTJ;* Edwin S. Gaustad, *Revival, Revolution, and Religion in Early Virginia* (Williamsburg, Va., 1994), 36–38; Andrew Levy, *The First Emancipator: Slavery, Religion, and the Quiet Revolution of Robert Carter* (New York, 2005), 90.

30. TJ to Nicholas Lewis, July 29, 1787, in *PTJ;* TJ to Thomas Adams, Feb. 20, 1771, in *PTJ;* William Cohen, "Thomas Jefferson and the Problem of Slavery," *Journal of American History* 56, no. 3 (Dec. 1969): 516–17; Kukla, *Mr. Jefferson's Women,* 68; Herbert E. Sloan, *Principle and Interest: Thomas Jefferson and the Problem of Debt* (New York, 1995), 14–21; T. H. Breen, *Tobacco Culture: The Mentality of the Great Tidewater Planters on the Eve of*

Revolution, new ed. (Princeton, N.J., 2001), 144–45; Bruce H. Mann, *Republic of Debtors: Bankruptcy in the Age of American Independence* (Cambridge, Mass., 2002), 139.

31. Lucia Stanton, *"Those Who Labor for My Happiness"*: Slavery at Thomas Jefferson's Monticello* (Charlottesville, Va., 2012), 106; Gordon-Reed, *Hemingses*, 110.

32. Stephen A. Conrad, "Putting Rights Talk in Its Place: The *Summary View* Revisited," in Onuf, *Jeffersonian Legacies*, 261.

33. TJ, "Draft of Instructions to the Virginia Delegates in the Continental Congress (MS Text of *A Summary View*, &c.)," in *PTJ*. The classic exploration of the Patriots' fear of conspiracy is Bernard Bailyn, *The Ideological Origins of the American Revolution*, rev. ed. (Cambridge, Mass., 1992), xiii.

34. Plain English, "To the Inhabitants of New-York," [New York, 1774], broadside; Joyce Appleby, *Liberalism and Republicanism in the Historical Imagination* (Cambridge, Mass., 1992), 155–58.

35. Lacy K. Ford, *Deliver Us from Evil: The Slavery Question in the Old South* (New York, 2009), 7–8; Edmund S. Morgan, *American Slavery, American Freedom: The Ordeal of Colonial Virginia* (New York, 1975), 376.

36. The drafts of *A Summary View* alternatively speak of "British corsairs," making clearer that Jefferson resented the preference for British shippers in the African slave trade. TJ, "Draft of Instructions," in *PTJ*; Peter S. Onuf, *Jefferson's Empire: The Language of American Nationhood* (Charlottesville, Va., 2000), 154–55; David Brion Davis, *The Problem of Slavery in the Age of Revolution, 1770–1823* (Ithaca, N.Y., 1975), 173; Pauline Maier, *American Scripture: Making the Declaration of Independence* (New York, 1997), 113; John Chester Miller, *The Wolf by the Ears: Thomas Jefferson and Slavery* (New York, 1977), 6–7.

37. Kenneth Morgan, *Slavery and the British Empire: From Africa to America* (New York, 2007), 85.

38. TJ, "Draft of Instructions," in *PTJ*; Peter S. Onuf, "Jefferson and American Democracy," in Cogliano, *Companion*, 403; Brian Steele, *Thomas Jefferson and American Nationhood* (New York, 2012), 22–23; Kevin J. Hayes, *George Washington: A Life in Books* (New York, 2017), 144; John Adams, [in Congress, May–July 1776], in *The Adams Papers*, digital ed., ed. Sara Martin (Charlottesville, Va., 2008–19).

39. Edmund Randolph, *History of Virginia*, ed. Arthur H. Shaffer (Charlottesville, Va., 1970), 213; Thomas S. Kidd, *Patrick Henry: First among Patriots* (New York, 2011), 97–99; Hayes, *Road to Monticello*, 162.

40. Hayes, *Road to Monticello*, 166–67; Richard Samuelson, "Thomas Jefferson and John Adams," in Cogliano, *Companion*, 318–32.

41. Leonard J. Sadosky, "Jefferson and International Relations," in Cogliano, *Companion*, 203; Hayes, *Road to Monticello*, 169; Robert G. Parkinson, *The Common Cause: Creating Race and Nation in the American Revolution* (Chapel Hill, N.C., 2016), 123.

42. TJ and John Dickinson, *Declaration of the Causes and Necessity of Taking Up Arms*, "IV. The Declaration as Adopted by Congress," [6 July 1775], in *PTJ*.

43. TJ, "Memorandum Books, 1775," in *PTJ*; G. S. Wilson, *Jefferson on Display: Attire, Etiquette, and the Art of Presentation* (Charlottesville, Va., 2018), 10–11; John Hailman, *Thomas Jefferson on Wine* (Jackson, Miss., 2006), 48.

44. TJ, "Memorandum Books, 1775."

45. TJ to John Randolph, Nov. 29, 1775, in *PTJ*.

46. TJ to John Randolph, Nov. 29, 1775, in *PTJ*; TJ to John Page, [ca. Dec. 10, 1775], in *PTJ*; James Simpson, *Burning to Read: English Fundamentalism and Its Reformation Opponents* (Cambridge, Mass., 2007), 153. "Kiss the rod" also appeared in Shakespeare, but Jefferson's wording is closer to Tyndale's.

47. TJ to Francis Eppes, Nov. 21, 1775, in *PTJ*; John Page to TJ, Nov. 24, 1775, in *PTJ*; Kolchin, *American Slavery*, 72; Parkinson, *Common Cause*, 153–63.

48. TJ, Memorandum Books, 1776, 1777, in *PTJ*; Thomas Nelson, Jr., to TJ, Feb. 4, 1776, in *PTJ*; Fawn M. Brodie, *Thomas Jefferson: An Intimate History* (New York, 1974), 112–13; Hailman, *Jefferson on Wine*, 51.

3. *"A Virginian Ought to Appear at the Head of This Business"*

1. John Adams to Timothy Pickering, Aug. 6, 1822, in Charles Francis Adams, ed., *The Works of John Adams* (Boston, 1850), 2:513–14; Pauline Maier, *American Scripture: Making the Declaration of Independence* (New York, 1997), 99–101.

2. TJ to Henry Lee, May 8, 1825, *Founders Online*.

3. TJ to Henry Lee, May 8, 1825, *Founders Online*; John Adams to TJ, Sept. 18, 1823, in Lester J. Cappon, ed., *The Adams-Jefferson Letters* (Chapel Hill, N.C., 1959), 598; Caroline Robbins, "Algernon Sidney's *Discourses concerning Government*: Textbook of Revolution," *William and Mary Quarterly*, 3rd ser., 4, no. 3 (July 1947): 270; Wilson Jeremiah Moses, *Thomas Jefferson: A Modern Prometheus* (New York, 2019), 148.

4. Algernon Sidney, *Discourses concerning Government* (London, 1751), 97; TJ to Robert Skipwith, Aug. 3, 1771, in James P. McClure and J. Jefferson Looney,

eds., *The Papers of Thomas Jefferson*, digital ed. (Charlottesville, Va., 2008–21), hereafter cited as *PTJ*; TJ to John Minor, including an earlier letter to Bernard Moore, Aug. 30, 1814, in *PTJ*; Alan Craig Houston, *Algernon Sidney and the Republican Heritage in England and America* (Princeton, N.J., 1991), 269; Nathan R. Perl-Rosenthal, "The 'Divine Right of Republics': Hebraic Republicanism and the Debate over Kingless Government in Revolutionary America," *William and Mary Quarterly*, 3rd ser., 66, no. 3 (July 2009): 539–41.

5. Sidney, *Discourses concerning Government*, 17, 270; George H. Smith, *The System of Liberty: Themes in the History of Classical Liberalism* (New York, 2013), 117. The extent to which Sidney's religion informed his politics is debated, but Michael Winship makes the case that Sidney's Calvinism was heartfelt and politically significant. Michael P. Winship, "Algernon Sidney's Calvinist Republicanism," *Journal of British Studies* 49, no. 4 (Oct. 2010): 755.

6. Mark David Hall, *Roger Sherman and the Creation of the American Republic* (New York, 2012), 59–60.

7. Hall, *Roger Sherman*, 60; Maier, *American Scripture*, 148.

8. Jefferson's "original Rough draught" of the Declaration of Independence, and the Declaration of Independence as Adopted by Congress, 1776, in *PTJ*; Thomas S. Kidd, *God of Liberty: A Religious History of the American Revolution* (New York, 2010), 142. On the meaning of "pursuit of happiness," see Carli N. Conklin, *The Pursuit of Happiness in the Founding Era: An Intellectual History* (Columbia, Mo., 2019), 3–8.

9. James Otis, *A Vindication of the Conduct of the House of Representatives* (Boston, 1762), 17–18; Kidd, *God of Liberty*, 138–39.

10. James Otis, *The Rights of the British Colonies Asserted and Proved* (Boston, 1764), 28–29.

11. Ruth Bogin, "'Liberty Further Extended': A 1776 Antislavery Manuscript by Lemuel Haynes," *William and Mary Quarterly*, 3rd ser., 40, no. 1 (Jan. 1983): 93–94; "'Natural and Inalienable Right to Freedom': Slaves' Petition for Freedom to the Massachusetts Legislature, 1777," *History Matters*, http://historymatters.gmu.edu/d/6237/; Rita Roberts, *Evangelicalism and the Politics of Reform in Northern Black Thought, 1776–1863* (Baton Rouge, La., 2010), 47–52.

12. TJ, *Notes on the State of Virginia*, in Merrill Peterson, ed., *Thomas Jefferson: Writings* (New York, 1984), 288–89; TJ to Jean Nicolas Démeunier, [June 26, 1786], in *PTJ*.

13. Analyses of Jefferson's statements on slavery, emancipation, and divine judgment are numerous, and often at odds. See, among others, Annette

Gordon-Reed and Peter S. Onuf, *"Most Blessed of the Patriarchs": Thomas Jefferson and the Empire of the Imagination* (New York, 2016), 92; Peter S. Onuf, *Jefferson's Empire: The Language of American Nationhood* (Charlottesville, Va., 2000), 147–51; Ari Helo, *Thomas Jefferson's Ethics and the Politics of Progress: The Morality of a Slaveholder* (New York, 2014), 178; Paul Finkelman, "Jefferson and Slavery: 'Treason against the Hopes of the World,'" in Peter S. Onuf, ed., *Jeffersonian Legacies* (Charlottesville, Va., 1993), 200–201; Caroline Winterer, *American Enlightenments: Pursuing Happiness in the Age of Reason* (New Haven, Conn., 2016), 155–57; Kevin R. C. Gutzman, *Thomas Jefferson, Revolutionary: A Radical's Struggle to Remake America* (New York, 2017), 127–28; Cara J. Rogers, "Jefferson's Sons: *Notes on the State of Virginia* and Virginian Antislavery, 1760–1832" (Ph.D. diss., Rice University, 2018), 117–18. On Jefferson's demurral, see Nicholas Guyatt, *Bind Us Apart: How Enlightened Americans Invented Racial Segregation* (New York, 2016), 251–57. Paul J. Polgar employs the term "first movement abolitionists" for abolitionists operating prior to the founding of the American Colonization Society in 1816. Polgar, *Standard-Bearers of Equality: America's First Abolition Movement* (Chapel Hill, N.C., 2019), 15, 217–19.

14. The Declaration of Independence, as adopted by Congress; Katherine Carté, *Religion and the American Revolution: An Imperial History* (Chapel Hill, N.C.: 2021), 209–18.

15. Jefferson's "original Rough draught" of the Declaration of Independence; the Declaration of Independence, as adopted by Congress; Robert G. Parkinson, "Friends and Enemies in the Declaration of Independence," in Joanne B. Freeman and Johann N. Neem, eds., *Jeffersonians in Power: The Rhetoric of Opposition Meets the Realities of Governing* (Charlottesville, Va., 2019), 16.

16. Jefferson's "original Rough draught" of the Declaration of Independence; Sidney Kaplan, "The 'Domestic Insurrections' of the Declaration of Independence," *Journal of Negro History* 61, no. 3 (July 1976): 243–47; John Chester Miller, *The Wolf by the Ears: Thomas Jefferson and Slavery* (New York, 1977), 6–11; Maier, *American Scripture*, 146–47; Robert G. Parkinson, *The Common Cause: Creating Race and Slavery in the American Revolution* (Chapel Hill, N.C., 2016), 253; Holly Brewer, "Slavery, Sovereignty, and 'Inheritable Blood': Reconsidering John Locke and the Origins of American Slavery," *American Historical Review* 122, no. 4 (Oct. 2017): 1076.

17. "Anecdotes of Benjamin Franklin," [ca. Dec. 4, 1818], in *PTJ*; Maier, *American Scripture*, 148–49; James P. Byrd, *Sacred Scripture, Sacred War: The Bible*

and the American Revolution (New York, 2013), 117–23; Conklin, *Pursuit of Happiness,* 54–55.

18. Jay Fliegelman, *Declaring Independence: Jefferson, Natural Language, and the Culture of Performance* (Stanford, Calif., 1993), 53.

19. TJ to Ellen Wayles Randolph Coolidge, Nov. 14, 1825, *Founders Online;* Susan R. Stein, *The Worlds of Thomas Jefferson at Monticello* (New York, 1993), 364–65.

20. TJ, Memorandum Books, 1776, in *PTJ;* Annette Gordon-Reed, *The Hemingses of Monticello: An American Family* (New York, 2008), 124–25.

21. "The Following Goods Are Sold by Nicholas Brooks," *Pennsylvania Ledger,* June 29, 1776, 1; TJ, Memorandum Books, 1776; TJ to Charles Willson Peale, July 18, 1824, *Founders Online;* Bill Pittman, "Thomas Jefferson's Toothbrush," *Colonial Williamsburg Teacher Gazette,* https://www.history.org/history/teaching/enewsletter/may03/iotm.cfm; Keith Thomson, *Jefferson's Shadow: The Story of His Science* (New Haven, Conn., 2012), 179.

22. John Adams to Abigail Adams, July 3, 1776, in *The Adams Papers,* digital ed., ed. Sara Martin (Charlottesville, Va., 2008–19).

23. TJ to Richard Henry Lee, July 8, 1776, in *PTJ;* John Page to TJ, July 20, 1776, in *PTJ;* TJ to Richard Henry Lee, July 29, 1776, in *PTJ.* Page's quote was from Joseph Addison, *The Campaign* (London, 1756), 12.

24. TJ to John Page, Aug. 5, 1776, in *PTJ;* Kevin J. Dellape, *America's First Chaplain: The Life and Times of the Reverend Jacob Duché* (Lanham, Md., 2013), 108.

25. John Adams to Abigail Adams, Aug. 14, 1776, in Martin, *Adams Papers;* Thomas S. Kidd, *Benjamin Franklin: The Religious Life of a Founding Father* (New Haven, Conn., 2017), 205; Dumas Malone, *Jefferson the Virginian* (Boston, 1948), 242; "Personal Seal," in *Thomas Jefferson Encyclopedia,* Monticello.org, https://www.monticello.org/site/research-and-collections/personal-seal; Daniel L. Dreisbach, *Reading the Bible with the Founding Fathers* (New York, 2017), 90.

26. "Report of the Committee," [Aug. 20, 1776], in *PTJ;* Dreisbach, *Reading the Bible,* 106–7.

27. TJ, Memorandum Books, 1776.

28. TJ, Memorandum Books, 1776; Andrew Burstein and Nancy Isenberg, *Madison and Jefferson* (New York, 2010), 47–48, 659, n.15.

29. Dreisbach, *Reading the Bible,* 57; Ralph Ketcham, *James Madison: A Biography* (Charlottesville, Va., 1990), 56–57; Jeff Broadwater, *James Madison: A Son of Virginia and a Founder of the Nation* (Chapel Hill, N.C., 2012), 3.

30. Madison to William Bradford, Jan. 24, 1774, *Founders Online*.

31. Gutzman, *Jefferson, Revolutionary*, 97; Kidd, *God of Liberty*, 53; Daniel L. Dreisbach, "Church-State Debate in the Virginia Legislature: From the Declaration of Rights to the Statute for Establishing Religious Freedom," in Garrett Ward Sheldon and Daniel L. Dreisbach, eds., *Religion and Political Culture in Jefferson's Virginia* (Lanham, Md., 2000), 138–40; Paul Douglas Newman, "James Madison's Journey to an 'Honorable and Useful Profession,' 1751–1780," in Stuart Leibiger, ed., *A Companion to James Madison and James Monroe* (Malden, Mass., 2012), 33.

32. TJ, *Autobiography*, in Merrill D. Peterson, ed., *Thomas Jefferson: Writings* (New York, 1984), 34. On North Carolina, see, for example, Mark D. McGarvie, "Disestablishing Religion and Protecting Religious Liberty in State Laws and Constitutions (1776–1833)," in T. Jeremy Gunn and John Witte, Jr., eds., *No Establishment of Religion: America's Original Contribution to Religious Liberty* (New York, 2012), 80.

33. "Jefferson's Outline of Argument in Support of His Resolutions," [Nov. 1776?], in *PTJ*; John Todd to TJ, Aug. 16, 1779, in *PTJ*; Garry Wills, *Under God: Religion and American Politics* (New York, 1990), 368; Carl J. Richard, *The Founders and the Bible* (Lanham, Md., 2016), 296.

34. "Declaration of the Virginia Association of Baptists," Dec. 25, 1776, in *PTJ*; Dreisbach, "Church-State Debate in the Virginia Legislature," 143–44.

35. TJ to Edmund Pendleton, Aug. 26, 1776, in *PTJ*; Miller, *Wolf by the Ears*, 20–21; Finkelman, "Jefferson and Slavery," 194–95; David Thomas Konig, "Jefferson and the Law," in Francis D. Cogliano, ed., *A Companion to Thomas Jefferson* (Malden, Mass., 2011), 361.

36. TJ, *Autobiography*, 44; TJ, *Notes on the State of Virginia*, 264; Finkelman, "Jefferson and Slavery," 196–97; John E. Selby, *The Revolution in Virginia, 1775–1783* (Charlottesville, Va., 1988), 158; Merrill D. Peterson, *Thomas Jefferson and the New Nation* (New York, 1970), 152; Francis D. Cogliano, *Thomas Jefferson: Reputation and Legacy* (Charlottesville, Va., 2006), 201.

37. TJ, *Autobiography*, 44; TJ, *Notes on the State of Virginia*, 264; Onuf, *Jefferson's Empire*, 151.

38. Jon Kukla, *Mr. Jefferson's Women* (New York, 2007), 79–80. Adding to the potential confusion about his daughters' names, Mary started to be called "Maria" beginning in 1789: "Maria Jefferson Eppes," in *Thomas Jefferson Encyclopedia*, Monticello.org, https://www.monticello.org/site/research-and-collections/maria-jefferson-eppes.

39. TJ, Memorandum Books, 1778; John Harvie to TJ, Sept. 15, 1778, in *PTJ*; "To the County Lieutenants," Mar. 26, 1781, in *PTJ*; Jack McLaughlin,

Jefferson and Monticello: The Biography of a Builder (New York, 1988), 166–67.

40. TJ to Isaac Zane, Feb. 26, 1778, in *PTJ;* McLaughlin, *Jefferson and Monticello,* 154, 243–44.

41. TJ to Richard Henry Lee, June 17, 1779, in *PTJ;* Alf J. Mapp, Jr., *Thomas Jefferson: America's Paradoxical Patriot* (Lanham, Md., 1987), 133–34.

42. TJ, *Autobiography,* 45; "A Bill for Amending the Constitution of the College of William and Mary," in *PTJ;* Peterson, *Jefferson and the New Nation,* 149; George Thomas, *The Founders and the Idea of a National University: Constituting the American Mind* (New York, 2015), 114.

43. Selby, *The Revolution in Virginia,* 204–8; Michael A. McDonnell, *The Politics of War: Race, Class, and Conflict in Revolutionary Virginia* (Chapel Hill, N.C., 2007), 343–44.

44. Proclamation Appointing a Day of Thanksgiving and Prayer, Nov. 11, 1779, in *PTJ;* Daniel L. Dreisbach, *Thomas Jefferson and the Wall of Separation between Church and State* (New York, 2002), 58–59.

45. TJ to William Preston, June 15, 1780, in *PTJ.*

46. Johann Ludwig de Unger to TJ, Nov. 13, 1780, in *PTJ;* TJ to James Wood, Nov. 7, 1780, in *PTJ;* Kevin J. Hayes, *The Road to Monticello: The Life and Mind of Thomas Jefferson* (New York, 2008), 221–22.

47. TJ to William Short, Apr. 13, 1820, in Dickinson W. Adams, ed., *Jefferson's Extracts from the Gospels* (Princeton, N.J., 1983), 391; TJ to John Adams, Aug. 15, 1820, in Cappon, *Adams-Jefferson Letters,* 568; Charles B. Sanford, *The Religious Life of Thomas Jefferson* (Charlottesville, Va., 1984), 148–49; Helo, *Jefferson's Ethics,* 80; Richard Samuelson, "Thomas Jefferson and John Adams," in Cogliano, *Companion,* 329–30. Other references to Origen include a purchase of two volumes by him, in "Lackington's Catalogue for 1792," in *PTJ;* TJ to Francis Adrian Van der Kemp, Feb. 9, 1818, in *PTJ;* and TJ to Thomas Cooper, Aug. 14, 1820, in *PTJ.*

48. TJ to Abner Nash, Jan. 16, 1781, in *PTJ;* McDonnell, *Politics of War,* 399–400.

49. Lucia Stanton, *"Those Who Labor for My Happiness": Slavery at Thomas Jefferson's Monticello* (Charlottesville, Va., 2012), 119.

4. *"It Is Not in My Power to Do Anything More"*

1. TJ to David Jameson, Apr. 16, 1781, in James P. McClure and J. Jefferson Looney, eds., *The Papers of Thomas Jefferson,* digital ed. (Charlottesville, Va., 2008–21), hereafter cited as *PTJ;* TJ to the Marquis de Lafayette, May 14,

1781, in *PTJ;* Michael Kranish, *Flight from Monticello: Thomas Jefferson at War* (New York, 2010), 238, 257.

2. TJ to George Washington, May 28, 1781, in *PTJ;* Kranish, *Flight from Monticello,* 265.

3. William Davies to TJ, Apr. 12, 1781, in *PTJ;* Kranish, *Flight from Monticello,* 271; Merrill Peterson, *Thomas Jefferson and the New Nation* (New York, 1970), 219.

4. Kranish, *Flight from Monticello,* 278.

5. "Diary of Arnold's Invasion and Notes on Subsequent Events in 1781," in *PTJ.*

6. "Diary of Arnold's Invasion and Notes on Subsequent Events in 1781"; James Callaway to TJ, June 4, 1781 (notes), in *PTJ;* John E. Selby, *The Revolution in Virginia, 1775–1783* (Williamsburg, Va., 1988), 282–83. Jefferson's "flight from Monticello" has continued to receive varied treatments from historians, some sympathetic, some not. Kranish's *Flight from Monticello,* the best single book on the episode, appreciates Jefferson's difficult situation but is still critical. For a more positive interpretation, see John B. Boles, *Jefferson: Architect of American Liberty* (New York, 2017), 99–102.

7. TJ to——, Nov. 29, 1821, in H. A. Washington, ed., *The Writings of Thomas Jefferson* (Washington, D.C., 1854), 7:228; Kranish, *Flight from Monticello,* 280.

8. Kranish, *Flight from Monticello,* 280–84.

9. Diary of John Adams, Mar. 15, 1776, *Founders Online;* James Callaway to TJ, June 4, 1781 (notes), in *PTJ; Letters of Joseph Jones of Virginia* (Washington, D.C., 1889), 82.

10. Richard Henry Lee to George Washington, June 12, 1781, in James Curtis Ballagh, ed., *The Letters of Richard Henry Lee* (New York, 1914), 2:233–35; Thomas S. Kidd, *Patrick Henry: First among Patriots* (New York, 2011), 158–59; Jon Kukla, *Patrick Henry: Champion of Liberty* (New York, 2017), 255–56.

11. Kukla, *Patrick Henry,* 256–57.

12. TJ to Isaac Zane, Dec. 24, 1781, in *PTJ;* TJ to James Madison, Dec. 8, 1784, in *PTJ;* Kidd, *Patrick Henry,* 159; Kukla, *Patrick Henry,* 258.

13. TJ, *Notes on the State of Virginia,* in Merrill Peterson, ed., *Thomas Jefferson: Writings* (New York, 1984), 216–17; TJ to William Gordon, July 16, 1788, in *PTJ;* Kranish, *Flight from Monticello,* 292–93, 298–99; Judith L. Van Buskirk, *Standing in Their Own Light: African American Patriots in the American Revolution* (Norman, Okla., 2017), 168.

14. TJ to Edmund Randolph, Sept. 16, 1781, in *PTJ; Journal of the House of Delegates of the Commonwealth of Virginia; Begun and Held in the Town of Richmond in the County of Henrico, on Monday, the First Day of October, in the Year of Our Lord One Thousand Seven Hundred and Eighty-One* (Richmond, Va., 1828), 36–38; Kranish, *Flight from Monticello*, 314.

15. Gordon S. Wood, *Friends Divided: John Adams and Thomas Jefferson* (New York, 2017), 146.

16. TJ to James Monroe, May 20, 1782, in *PTJ;* Richard K. Matthews, *The Radical Politics of Thomas Jefferson* (Lawrence, Kans., 1984), 91–92; Joyce Appleby, "What Is Still American in the Political Philosophy of Thomas Jefferson?" *William and Mary Quarterly,* 3rd ser., 39, no. 2 (Apr. 1982): 305; Richard A. Samuelson, "Consistent in Creation: Thomas Jefferson, Natural Aristocracy, and the Problem of Knowledge," in Robert M. S. McDonald, ed., *Light and Liberty: Thomas Jefferson and the Power of Knowledge* (Charlottesville, Va., 2012), 77.

17. Edmund Randolph to James Madison, June 1, 1782, cited in TJ to James Monroe, May 20, 1782, (editorial note), in *PTJ*.

18. TJ to James Monroe, May 20, 1782, in *PTJ;* James Monroe to TJ, June 28, 1782, in *PTJ*.

19. Lines Copied from Tristram Shandy by Martha and Thomas Jefferson [1782], in *PTJ;* Sarah N. Randolph, *The Domestic Life of Thomas Jefferson* (New York, 1871), 63; Jan Lewis, *The Pursuit of Happiness: Family and Values in Jefferson's Virginia* (New York, 1983), 69–70; Jon Kukla, *Mr. Jefferson's Women* (New York, 2007), 83–85.

20. TJ to the Marquis de Chastellux, Nov. 26, 1782, in *PTJ*.

21. TJ to the Marquis de Chastellux, Nov. 26, 1782, in *PTJ;* TJ, *Autobiography,* in Merrill D. Peterson, ed., *Thomas Jefferson: Writings* (New York, 1984), 46; TJ, Memorandum Books, 1783, in *PTJ;* Darren Staloff, *Hamilton, Adams, Jefferson: The Politics of Enlightenment and the American Founding* (New York, 2005), 350.

22. TJ to Martha Jefferson, Dec. 11, 1783, in *PTJ;* Cynthia A. Kierner, *Martha Jefferson Randolph: Her Life and Times* (Chapel Hill, N.C., 2012), 44.

23. TJ to James Madison, Apr. 25, 1784, *Founders Online;* TJ to George Washington, Mar. 15, 1784, in *PTJ;* James Morton Smith, ed., *The Republic of Letters: The Correspondence between Thomas Jefferson and James Madison, 1776–1826* (New York, 1995), 1:274–75.

24. TJ, *Notes on the State of Virginia,* 290; Roger G. Kennedy, *Mr. Jefferson's Lost Cause: Land, Farmers, Slavery, and the Louisiana Purchase* (New York, 2003),

81; Adam Rothman, *Slave Country: American Expansion and the Origins of the Deep South* (Cambridge, Mass., 2005), 24, 45; Christa Dierksheide, *Amelioration and Empire: Progress and Slavery in the Plantation Americas* (Charlottesville, Va., 2014), 45–46; Walter Johnson, *River of Dark Dreams: Slavery and Empire in the Cotton Kingdom* (Cambridge, Mass., 2013), 3–5, 24–25, 32; Christopher Michael Curtis, *Jefferson's Freeholders and the Politics of Ownership in the Old Dominion* (New York, 2012), 53–56. On Jefferson's and Madison's agrarian philosophy and virtue, see, among others, Douglass G. Adair, *The Intellectual Origins of Jeffersonian Democracy,* ed. Mark E. Yellin (Lanham, Md., 2000), 18.

25. "Jefferson's Observations on DéMeunier's Manuscript, 22 June 1786," in *PTJ;* William Cohen, "Thomas Jefferson and the Problem of Slavery," *Journal of American History* 56, no. 3 (Dec. 1969): 510; Robert F. Berkhofer, Jr., "Jefferson, the Ordinance of 1784, and the Origins of the American Territorial System," *William and Mary Quarterly,* 3rd ser., 29, no. 2 (Apr. 1972): 249; John Chester Miller, *The Wolf by the Ears: Thomas Jefferson and Slavery* (New York, 1977), 28–29; Paul Finkelman, "Jefferson and Slavery: 'Treason against the Hopes of the World,'" in Peter S. Onuf, ed., *Jeffersonian Legacies* (Charlottesville, Va., 1993), 199–200.

26. TJ to James Madison, Dec. 8, 1784, in *PTJ;* David N. Mayer, *The Constitutional Thought of Thomas Jefferson* (Charlottesville, Va., 1994), 159–63; Alan Taylor, *Thomas Jefferson's Education* (New York, 2019), 52.

27. Annette Gordon-Reed, *The Hemingses of Monticello: An American Family* (New York, 2008), 158–60.

28. Peterson, *Jefferson and the New Nation,* 303–5; Boles, *Architect of American Liberty,* 188.

29. Peter McPhee, *A Social History of France, 1780–1914,* 2nd ed. (New York, 2004), 11; Gordon-Reed, *Hemingses,* 172–76.

30. "Notes on Arranging Books at Monticello," [before Sept. 26, 1789], in *PTJ;* on Jefferson's records of French currency, see Memorandum Books, 1784, July 31, 1784, n. 65; TJ to James Monroe, Nov. 11, 1784, in *PTJ;* TJ to Abigail Adams, Sept. 4, 1785, in *PTJ;* Jack McLaughlin, *Jefferson and Monticello: The Biography of a Builder* (New York, 1988), 211–12; Peterson, *Jefferson and the New Nation,* 333; Kierner, *Martha Jefferson Randolph,* 51.

31. TJ, "Catalogue of Paintings," in *Thomas Jefferson Encyclopedia,* Monticello.org, https://www.monticello.org/site/research-and-collections/catalogue-paintings; TJ, Memorandum Books, 1785; "Jefferson's Hints to Americans Travelling in Europe," [1788], in *PTJ;* Susan R. Stein, *The Worlds of Thomas*

Jefferson at Monticello (New York, 1993), 146; Jon Meacham, *Thomas Jefferson: The Art of Power* (New York, 2012), 188.

32. William Howard Adams, *The Paris Years of Thomas Jefferson* (New Haven, Conn., 1997), 48; Andrew Burstein, *Jefferson's Secrets: Death and Desire at Monticello* (New York, 2005), 165; Christopher R. Altieri, *The Soul of a Nation: America as a Tradition of Inquiry and Nationhood* (Eugene, Ore., 2015), 73, n.27. "Plainest" quote is from Thomas Lee Shippen, in Peterson, *Jefferson and the New Nation*, 333.

33. TJ to James Monroe, June 17, 1785, in *PTJ;* Tom Cutterham, *Gentlemen Revolutionaries: Power and Justice in the New American Republic* (Princeton, N.J., 2017), 2.

34. TJ to John Page, May 4, 1786, in *PTJ;* Carl J. Richard, "The Classical Roots of the American Founding," in Daniel N. Robertson and Richard N. Williams, eds., *The American Founding: Its Intellectual and Moral Framework* (New York, 2012), 47; Jean M. Yarbrough, *American Virtues: Thomas Jefferson on the Character of a Free People* (Lawrence, Kans., 1998), 82.

35. TJ, Memorandum Books, 1784; TJ to Charles Bellini, Sept. 30, 1785, in *PTJ;* James B. Collins, *The State in Early Modern France* (New York, 1995), 182; John Hailman, *Thomas Jefferson on Wine* (Jackson, Miss., 2006), 75–79.

36. TJ to Ezra Stiles, July 17, 1785, in *PTJ;* TJ to Abigail Adams, June 21, 1785, in *PTJ;* TJ to James Maury, Dec. 24, 1786, in *PTJ;* Neven Leddy, "American Educations and Atlantic Circulations," in John A. Ragosta, Peter S. Onuf, and Andrew J. O'Shaughnessy, eds., *The Founding of Thomas Jefferson's University* (Charlottesville, Va., 2019), 45–46; Kierner, *Martha Jefferson Randolph*, 51–53, 64–65; editor's note on TJ to Elizabeth Wayles Eppes, Dec. 15, 1788, in *PTJ.*

37. Howard C. Rice, *Thomas Jefferson's Paris* (Princeton, N.J., 1976), 105–7; Timothy Trussell, "A Landscape for Mr. Jefferson's Retreat," in Barbara J. Heath and Jack Gary, eds., *Jefferson's Poplar Forest: Unearthing a Virginia Plantation* (Gainesville, Fla., 2012), 74–75.

38. TJ to John Banister, Jr., Oct. 15, 1785, in *PTJ;* Kierner, *Martha Jefferson Randolph*, 53; Catherine Kerrison, *Jefferson's Daughters: Three Sisters, White and Black, in a Young America* (New York, 2018), 39. Jefferson may have recalled the phrase "fidelity to the marriage bed" from David Hume. Hume, *An Enquiry concerning the Principles of Morals* (London, 1751), 66.

39. The literature on the Jefferson-Hemings affair is vast and contentious. Most academic historians, as well as the Thomas Jefferson Foundation, which operates Monticello, have accepted the idea that Jefferson fathered one or more of

Hemings's children. There remains a significant group of academic and popular dissenters from this view, however. I believe that the evidence is strong enough to assume that the relationship did occur. Some key books and articles in the debate include "Thomas Jefferson and Sally Hemings: A Brief Account," Monticello.org, https://www.monticello.org/thomas-jefferson/jefferson-slavery/thomas-jefferson-and-sally-hemings-a-brief-account/; "Minority Report," Monticello.org, https://www.monticello.org/thomas-jefferson/jefferson-slavery/thomas-jefferson-and-sally-hemings-a-brief-account/research-report-on-jefferson-and-hemings/minority-report-of-the-monticello-research-committee-on-thomas-jefferson-and-sally-hemings/; Annette Gordon-Reed, *Thomas Jefferson and Sally Hemings: An American Controversy* (Charlottesville, Va., 1998); "Forum: Thomas Jefferson and Sally Hemings Redux," *William and Mary Quarterly*, 3rd ser., 57, no. 1 (Jan. 2000): 121–210; Robert E. Turner, ed., *The Jefferson-Hemings Controversy* (Durham, N.C., 2001).

40. James Currie to TJ, Nov. 20, 1784, in *PTJ;* TJ to Francis Eppes, Aug. 30, 1785, in *PTJ;* Kukla, *Mr. Jefferson's Women,* 249, n.3.

41. TJ to Mary Jefferson, Sept. 20, 1785, in *PTJ;* TJ to Martha Jefferson, Dec. 22, 1783, in *PTJ;* Maurizio Valsania, *Jefferson's Body: A Corporeal Biography* (Charlottesville, Va., 2017), 181; Kathleen M. Brown, *Foul Bodies: Cleanliness in Early America* (New Haven, Conn., 2009), 143.

42. TJ to Francis Eppes, Aug. 30, 1785, in *PTJ;* Mary Jefferson to TJ, [ca. Sept. 13, 1785], in *PTJ.*

43. Francis Eppes to TJ, Apr. 14, 1787, in *PTJ;* Gordon-Reed, *Hemingses,* 191–92; Kukla, *Mr. Jefferson's Women,* 116–17.

5. *"I Am But a Son of Nature"*

1. TJ to Maria Cosway, Oct. 12, 1786, in James P. McClure and J. Jefferson Looney, eds., *The Papers of Thomas Jefferson,* digital ed. (Charlottesville, Va., 2008–21), hereafter cited as *PTJ;* William Howard Adams, *The Paris Years of Thomas Jefferson* (New Haven, Conn., 1997), 222–26.

2. Jon Kukla, *Mr. Jefferson's Women* (New York, 2007), 94–96; John P. Kaminski, ed., *Jefferson in Love: The Love Letters between Thomas Jefferson & Maria Cosway* (Madison, Wisc., 1999), 37–38.

3. TJ to Maria Cosway, Oct. 12, 1786, in Merrill D. Peterson, ed., *Thomas Jefferson: Writings* (New York, 1984), 867; Carl J. Richard, *The Battle for the American Mind: A Brief History of a Nation's Thought* (Lanham, Md., 2004), 101.

4. TJ to Maria Cosway, Oct. 12, 1786, in Peterson, *Writings*, 872; M. Andrew Holowchak, *Dutiful Correspondent: Philosophical Essays on Thomas Jefferson* (Lanham, Md., 2013), 82–90.

5. "Rose without its thorn" was a common proverb in English by the eighteenth century. TJ to Maria Cosway, Oct. 12, 1786, in Peterson, *Writings*, 874–76.

6. TJ to William Short, Mar. 27, 1787, in *PTJ.*

7. "Jefferson's Hints to Americans Travelling in Europe," [1788], in *PTJ.* On Jefferson's conflicted attitude about common farmers, see Nancy Isenberg, *White Trash: The 400-Year Untold History of Class in America* (New York, 2016), 87.

8. "Jefferson's Hints to Americans Travelling in Europe"; Elizabeth Cometti, "Mr. Jefferson Prepares an Itinerary," *Journal of Southern History* 12, no. 1 (Feb. 1946): 93; Adams, *Paris Years*, 112–14; Lloyd DeWitt, "What He Saw: Thomas Jefferson's Grand Tour," in Lloyd DeWitt and Corey Piper, eds., *Thomas Jefferson, Architect* (New Haven, Conn., 2019), 58.

9. Andrew Burstein and Nancy Isenberg, *Madison and Jefferson* (New York, 2010), 130, 168.

10. Garry Wills, *"Negro President": Jefferson and the Slave Power* (New York, 2003), 1–5; Sean Wilentz, *No Property in Man: Slavery and Antislavery at the Nation's Founding* (Cambridge, Mass., 2018), 10–11.

11. TJ to David Hartley, July 2, 1787, in *PTJ;* Allen Jayne, *Jefferson's Declaration of Independence: Origins, Philosophy, and Theology* (Lexington, Ky., 1998), 171.

12. Abigail Adams to TJ, Jan. 29, 1787, in *PTJ;* Burstein and Isenberg, *Madison and Jefferson*, 167–68.

13. TJ to Abigail Adams, Feb. 22, 1787, in *PTJ;* Brian Steele, *Thomas Jefferson and American Nationhood* (New York, 2012), 111–20.

14. TJ to William Stephens Smith, Nov. 13, 1787, in *PTJ;* Joyce Appleby, "What Is Still American in the Political Philosophy of Thomas Jefferson?" *William and Mary Quarterly*, 3rd ser., 39, no. 2 (Apr. 1982): 293.

15. TJ to William Stephens Smith, Nov. 13, 1787, in *PTJ;* TJ to Alexander Donald, Feb. 7, 1788, in *PTJ;* David N. Mayer, *The Constitutional Thought of Thomas Jefferson* (Charlottesville, Va., 1994), 96–97, 145–46; Michael J. Faber, *An Anti-Federalist Constitution: The Development of Dissent in the Ratification Debates* (Lawrence, Kans., 2019), 114, 316; Jeff Broadwater, *Jefferson, Madison, and the Making of the Constitution* (Chapel Hill, N.C., 2019), 211–13.

16. TJ to James Madison, Dec. 20, 1787, in *PTJ;* Joseph J. Ellis, *American Sphinx: The Character of Thomas Jefferson* (New York, 1996), 122; Burstein and Isenberg, *Madison and Jefferson*, 183–84.

17. TJ to Francis Hopkinson, Mar. 13, 1789, in *PTJ*; Broadwater, *Jefferson, Madison,* 232; Richard A. Samuelson, "Consistent in Creation: Thomas Jefferson, Natural Aristocracy, and the Problem of Knowledge," in Robert M. S. McDonald, ed., *Light and Liberty: Thomas Jefferson and the Power of Knowledge* (Charlottesville, Va., 2012), 77.

18. TJ to Peter Carr, Aug. 19, 1785, in *PTJ*; TJ, *Notes on the State of Virginia,* in Peterson, *Writings,* 273; Holowchak, *Dutiful Correspondent,* 159; Craig Bruce Smith, *American Honor: The Creation of the Nation's Ideals during the Revolutionary Era* (Chapel Hill, N.C., 2018), 177.

19. Peter Carr to TJ, Apr. 18, 1787, in *PTJ*; TJ to Peter Carr, Aug. 10, 1787, in *PTJ*; TJ to John Adams, Oct. 14, 1816, in *PTJ*. The literature on Scottish commonsense philosophy and the Enlightenment is vast. A recent assessment of Jefferson's place in the Enlightenment is Andrew Trees, "Apocalypse Now: Thomas Jefferson's Radical Enlightenment," in Joanne B. Freeman and Johann N. Neem, eds., *Jeffersonians in Power: The Rhetoric of Opposition Meets the Realities of Governing* (Charlottesville, Va., 2019), 200–202. On Jefferson's view of the moral sense, see Winthrop D. Jordan, *White over Black: American Attitudes toward the Negro, 1550–1812* (New York, 1977), 439; Lee Quinby, "Thomas Jefferson: The Virtue of Aesthetics and the Aesthetics of Virtue," *American Historical Review* 87, no. 2 (Apr. 1982): 343; James T. Kloppenberg, "The Virtues of Liberalism: Christianity, Republicanism, and Ethics in Early American Political Discourse," *Journal of American History* 74, no. 1 (June 1987): 22; Ari Helo, *Thomas Jefferson's Ethics and the Politics of Human Progress: The Morality of a Slaveholder* (New York, 2014), 61–64.

20. TJ to Peter Carr, Aug. 10, 1787, in *PTJ*.

21. TJ to Peter Carr, Aug. 10, 1787, in *PTJ*; TJ to Mary B. Briggs, Apr. 17, 1816, in *PTJ*; Karl Lehmann, *Thomas Jefferson: American Humanist* (Charlottesville, Va., 1985), 88–89; Charles B. Sanford, *The Religious Life of Thomas Jefferson* (Charlottesville, Va., 1984), 108–9; Hans W. Frei, *The Eclipse of Biblical Narrative: A Study of Eighteenth and Nineteenth Century Hermeneutics* (New Haven, Conn., 1974), 59.

22. TJ to Peter Carr, Aug. 10, 1787, in *PTJ*; Sanford, *Religious Life,* 83–85; Samuelson, "Consistent in Creation," 77. Arthur Scherr emphasizes Jefferson's "favorable opinion of atheism" in "Thomas Jefferson versus the Historians: Christianity, Atheistic Morality, and the Afterlife," *Church History* 83, no. 1 (Mar. 2014): 60–109. On France's virtuous atheists, see TJ to Thomas Law, June 13, 1814, in *PTJ*.

23. TJ to Peter Carr, Aug. 10, 1787, in *PTJ*.

24. "Notes on Heresy," [1776], in *PTJ*; TJ to J.P.P. Derieux, July 25, 1788, in *PTJ*; Richard Samuelson, "Jefferson and Religion: Private Belief, Public Policy," in Frank Shuffelton, ed., *The Cambridge Companion to Thomas Jefferson* (New York, 2009), 144; Dustin Gish and Daniel Klinghard, *Thomas Jefferson and the Science of Republican Government: A Political Biography of Notes on the State of Virginia* (New York, 2017), 130–32.

25. William Short to TJ, Mar. 9, 1788, in *PTJ*; Paul Frame, *Liberty's Apostle: Richard Price, His Life and Times* (Cardiff, Wales, 2015), 120–21, 172–73; Ruth Watts, *Gender, Power, and the Unitarians in England, 1760–1860* (New York, 2013), 60.

26. Richard Price to TJ, Oct. 26, 1788, in *PTJ*; TJ to Richard Price, Jan. 8, 1789, in *PTJ*.

27. TJ to Richard Price, July 12, 1789, in *PTJ*; Richard Price to TJ, Aug. 3, 1789, in *PTJ*; Nathaniel Lardner, *Two Schemes of a Trinity Considered* (London, 1784), 49; Michael J. McClymond and Gerald R. McDermott, *The Theology of Jonathan Edwards* (New York, 2012), 52; M. Andrew Holowchak, *Thomas Jefferson's Bible* (Boston, 2019), 10–11.

28. Abigail Adams to TJ, June 26, 1787, in *PTJ*; TJ to Abigail Adams, July 1, 1787, in *PTJ*; Abigail Adams to TJ, July 6, 1787, in *PTJ*.

29. Abigail Adams to TJ, June 26, 1787, in *PTJ*; Abigail Adams to TJ, June 27, 1787, in *PTJ*; Woody Holton, *Abigail Adams: A Life* (New York, 2009), 71; Annette Gordon-Reed, *The Hemingses of Monticello: An American Family* (New York, 2008), 198–200, 209.

30. E. A. Foster et al., "Jefferson Fathered Slave's Last Child," *Nature*, Nov. 5, 1998, 27–28; "An individual" quote from "Thomas Jefferson and Sally Hemings: A Brief Account," Monticello.org, https://www.monticello.org /thomas-jefferson/jefferson-slavery/thomas-jefferson-and-sally-hemings-a-brief-account/. For a review of the DNA findings and the case for the Jefferson-Hemings relationship, see Annette Gordon-Reed, *Thomas Jefferson and Sally Hemings: An American Controversy* (Charlottesville, Va., 1998), vii–xiii and passim. On the Madison Hemings letter, see, among others, Annette Gordon-Reed, "'Take Care of Me When Dead': Jefferson Legacies," *Journal of the Early Republic* 40, no. 1 (Spring 2020): 16. For a dissenting view on the DNA tests and the relationship, see Robert F. Turner, ed., *The Jefferson Hemings Controversy: Report of the Scholars' Commission* (Durham, N.C., 2001), 7–18.

31. "Memoirs of Madison Hemings," reprinted in Gordon-Reed, *Thomas Jefferson and Sally Hemings*, 246; TJ to Maria Cosway, Apr. 24, 1788, in *PTJ*;

Gordon-Reed, *Hemingses*, 282–83; George Green Shackelford, *Thomas Jefferson's Travels in Europe, 1784–1789* (Baltimore, Md., 1995), 141–42; Kaminski, *Jefferson in Love*, 23.

32. TJ to Edward Rutledge, Nov. 30, 1795, in *PTJ;* TJ to Angelica Schuyler Church, Nov. 27, 1793, in *PTJ;* Susan R. Stein, *The Worlds of Thomas Jefferson at Monticello* (New York, 1993), 37–38; John Wiltshire, *Samuel Johnson in the Medical World: The Doctor and the Patient* (New York, 1991), 234–35; Samuelson, "Consistent in Creation," 75. The letter to Church provides the framing anecdote for Annette Gordon-Reed and Peter S. Onuf's *"Most Blessed of the Patriarchs": Thomas Jefferson and the Empire of the Imagination* (New York, 2016), xiii–xiv.

33. Andrew Burstein, *Jefferson's Secrets: Death and Desire at Monticello* (New York, 2005), 186; Gordon-Reed and Onuf, *Most Blessed*, 129; Gordon-Reed, *Thomas Jefferson and Sally Hemings*, 119. The phrase "substitute for a wife" comes from the diary of Jefferson's planter associate John Hartwell Cocke, who also lamented "Mr. Jefferson's notorious example" in having children with an enslaved woman. Papers of John Hartwell Cocke, Small Special Collections Library, University of Virginia, https://small.library.virginia.edu/collections/featured/the-thomas-jefferson-papers/bibliography-of-sources-on-jefferson-and-the-hemings-family/papers-of-john-hartwell-cocke/.

34. Memorandum Books, 1787, in *PTJ;* Memorandum Books, 1788, in *PTJ;* Gordon-Reed, *Hemingses*, 236.

35. Memorandum Books, 1789; Adams, *Paris Years*, 274–75; Gordon-Reed, *Hemingses*, 298–99.

36. TJ to Madame de Bréhan, May 9, 1788, in *PTJ;* TJ to Anne Willing Bingham, May 11, 1788, in *PTJ;* Anne Willing Bingham to TJ, [June 1, 1787], in *PTJ;* Susan Branson, *These Fiery Frenchified Dames: Women and Political Culture in Early National Philadelphia* (Philadelphia, 2001), 139–40; Kukla, *Mr. Jefferson's Women*, 155–60; Fredrika J. Teute and David S. Shields, "Jefferson in Washington: Domesticating Manners in the Republican Court," *Journal of the Early Republic* 35, no. 2 (Summer 2015): 244–46.

37. TJ to Elizabeth Wayles Eppes, Dec. 15, 1788, in *PTJ*. Jefferson was mixing up statements about ravens and sparrows from the Gospel of Luke, chapter 12. TJ, Memorandum Books, 1788; Memorandum Books, 1789; TJ to John Jay, May 15, 1788, in *PTJ;* John Hailman, *Thomas Jefferson on Wine* (Jackson, Miss., 2006), 93, 135–36, 151, letter quoted on 135–36; Adams, *Paris Years*, 267; George M. Taber, *In Search of Bacchus: Wanderings in the Wonderful World of Wine Tourism* (New York, 2009), 16.

38. TJ to James Madison, Sept. 6, 1789, in *PTJ*; Edmund Burke, *The Works of Edmund Burke* (New York, 1860), 1:498; Herbert E. Sloan, *Principle and Interest: Thomas Jefferson and the Problem of Debt* (New York, 1995), 175–76; Herbert E. Sloan, "The Earth Belongs in Usufruct to the Living," in Peter S. Onuf, ed., *Jeffersonian Legacies* (Charlottesville, Va., 1993), 281–82; Roger G. Kennedy, *Mr. Jefferson's Lost Cause: Land, Farmers, Slavery, and the Louisiana Purchase* (New York, 2003), 253.

39. TJ to James Madison, Sept. 6, 1789, in *PTJ*; TJ to Martha Jefferson Randolph, Apr. 26, 1790, in *PTJ*. The best analysis of the "usufruct" letter is in Sloan, *Principle and Interest*, especially 50–55.

40. TJ to Maria Cosway, July 25, 1789, in *PTJ*; Sloan, *Principle and Interest*, 21; Gordon-Reed, *Hemingses*, 317; Philipp Ziesche, *Cosmopolitan Patriots: Americans in Paris in the Age of Revolutions* (Charlottesville, Va., 2010), 29–31. Some scholars of his finances believe that Jefferson's indebtedness was ultimately due to mismanagement rather than "profligacy." Jefferson, admittedly, did not engage in the kind of grotesque overspending that marked certain European royalty or aristocrats, but he struggled to make a connection between his spending and his inability to pay down debt. See Wilson Jeremiah Moses, *Thomas Jefferson: A Modern Prometheus* (New York, 2019), 416–17.

41. Gordon-Reed, *Hemingses*, 326–27. Some historians who affirm the Hemings-Jefferson relationship assign a later date to the beginning of their sexual connection (the mid-1790s). See Kukla, *Mr. Jefferson's Women*, 126–29.

42. Stein, *Worlds of Jefferson*, 24; Garry Wills, "The Aesthete," *New York Review of Books*, Aug. 12, 1993, https://www.nybooks.com/articles/1993/08/12/the-aesthete/; Dave DeWitt, *The Founding Foodies: How Washington, Jefferson, and Franklin Revolutionized American Cuisine* (Naperville, Ill., 2010), 121.

6. *"None of Us, No Not One, Is Perfect"*

1. Richard Price to TJ, May 4, 1789, in James P. McClure and J. Jefferson Looney, eds., *The Papers of Thomas Jefferson*, digital ed. (Charlottesville, Va., 2008–21), hereafter cited as *PTJ*.

2. TJ, "The Response," Feb. 12, 1790, in *PTJ*; TJ to Tench Coxe, June 1, 1795, in *PTJ*.

3. E. James Ferguson, *The Power of the Purse: A History of American Public Finance, 1776–1790* (Chapel Hill, N.C., 1961), 306–11; Madison, quoted in

Calvin H. Johnson, *Righteous Anger at the Wicked States: The Meaning of the Founders' Constitution* (New York, 2005), 241.

4. "Jefferson's Account of the Bargain on the Assumption and Residence Bills," [1792?], in *PTJ.*

5. "Jefferson's Account of the Bargain"; "Thomas Jefferson's Explanations of the Three Volumes Bound in Marbled Paper (the so-called "Anas")," *Founders Online;* Herbert E. Sloan, *Principle and Interest: Thomas Jefferson and the Problem of Debt* (New York, 1995), 150.

6. TJ to Martha Jefferson Randolph, July 17, 1790, in *PTJ;* David Williams, *Condorcet and Modernity* (New York, 2004), 92–94; Fawn M. Brodie, *Thomas Jefferson: An Intimate History,* rev. ed. (New York, 2010), 252; Cynthia A. Kierner, *Martha Jefferson Randolph, Daughter of Monticello: Her Life and Times* (Chapel Hill, N.C., 2012), 76–78.

7. TJ, "Opinion on the Constitutionality of a National Bank," Feb. 15, 1791, in Merrill D. Peterson, ed., *Thomas Jefferson: Writings* (New York, 1984), 416; TJ to Charles Yancey, Jan. 6, 1816, in *PTJ;* Stanley M. Elkins and Eric Mac-Kitrick, *The Age of Federalism* (New York, 1993), 232.

8. TJ to George Washington, May 8, 1791, in *PTJ;* TJ to Jean François Froullé, Oct. 10, 1792, in *PTJ;* "Notes on Heresy" [1776]; James Madison to TJ, July 13, 1791, *Founders Online;* Brian Steele, *Thomas Jefferson and American Nationhood* (New York, 2012), 203–4; Elkins and MacKitrick, *Age of Federalism,* 237; Richard A. Samuelson, "Consistent in Creation: Thomas Jefferson, Natural Aristocracy, and the Problem of Knowledge," in Robert M. S. McDonald, ed., *Light and Liberty: Thomas Jefferson and the Power of Knowledge* (Charlottesville, Va., 2012), 88; Jonathan I. Israel, *Democratic Enlightenment: Philosophy, Revolution, and Human Rights, 1750–1790* (New York, 2011), 138; Robert K. Faulkner, "Jefferson and the Enlightened Science of Liberty," in Gary L. McDowell and Sharon L. Noble, *Reason and Republicanism: Thomas Jefferson's Legacy of Liberty* (Lanham, Md., 1997), 49; Allen Jayne, *Jefferson's Declaration of Independence* (Lexington, Ky., 1998), 143–44; S. Gerald Sandler, "Lockean Ideas in Thomas Jefferson's Bill for Establishing Religious Freedom," *Journal of the History of Ideas* 21, no. 1 (Jan.–Mar. 1960): 116; Andrew Trees, "Apocalypse Now: Thomas Jefferson's Radical Enlightenment," in Joanne B. Freeman and Johann N. Neem, eds., *Jeffersonians in Power: The Rhetoric of Opposition Meets the Realities of Governing* (Charlottesville, Va., 2019), 212; Eugene R. Sheridan, "Liberty and Virtue: Religion and Republicanism in Jeffersonian Thought," in James Gilreath, ed., *Thomas Jefferson and the Education of a Citizen* (Washington, D.C., 1999), 247.

9. Alexander Hamilton to Edward Carrington, May 26, 1792, *Founders Online;* George Washington to TJ, Aug. 23, 1792, in *PTJ;* Robert M. S. McDonald, "The Hamiltonian Invention of Thomas Jefferson," in Douglas Ambrose and Robert W. T. Martin, eds., *The Many Faces of Alexander Hamilton: The Life and Legacy of America's Most Elusive Founding Father* (New York, 2006), 59–60.

10. TJ to Jonathan B. Smith, Apr. 26, 1791, in *PTJ;* TJ to James Madison, May 9, 1791, in *PTJ;* Elkins and MacKitrick, *Age of Federalism,* 237–39.

11. TJ to George Washington, May 8, 1791, in *PTJ;* John Adams to TJ, July 29, 1791, in *PTJ;* TJ to Thomas Paine, July 29, 1791, in *PTJ;* Jeffrey L. Pasley, *The First Presidential Contest: 1796 and the Founding of American Democracy* (Lawrence, Kans., 2013), 262–65.

12. John Adams to Abigail Adams, Dec. 28, 1792, *Founders Online;* John Adams to Abigail Adams, Feb. 3, 1793, *Founders Online;* Gordon S. Wood, *Friends Divided: John Adams and Thomas Jefferson* (New York, 2017), 267.

13. On the Haitian Revolution, see, among others, Laurent Dubois, *Avengers of the New World: The Story of the Haitian Revolution* (Cambridge, Mass., 2004).

14. TJ to James Monroe, July 14, 1793, in *PTJ;* TJ to William Moultrie, Dec. 23, 1793, in *PTJ;* TJ to St. George Tucker, Aug. 28, 1797, in *PTJ;* Tim Matthewson, "Jefferson and Haiti," *Journal of Southern History* 61, no. 2 (May 1995): 217; Ronald Angelo Johnson, *Diplomacy in Black and White: John Adams, Toussaint Louverture, and Their Atlantic World Alliance* (Athens, Ga., 2014), 173, 181–83.

15. TJ, *Notes on the State of Virginia,* in Peterson, *Writings,* 266–67; TJ to Thomas Cooper, Nov. 2, 1822, *Founders Online;* Arlette Frund, "Phillis Wheatley, a Public Intellectual," in Mia Bay et al. eds., *Toward an Intellectual History of Black Women* (Chapel Hill, N.C., 2015), 49; Bruce R. Dain, *A Hideous Monster of the Mind: American Race Theory in the Early Republic* (Cambridge, Mass., 2003), 1–6, 34.

16. William Andrews, "Benjamin Banneker's Revision of Thomas Jefferson: Conscience versus Science in the Early American Antislavery Debate," in Vincent Caretta and Philip Gould, eds., *Genius in Bondage: Literature of the Early Black Atlantic* (Lexington, Ky., 2001), 219.

17. Benjamin Banneker to TJ, Aug. 19, 1791, in *PTJ.*

18. Benjamin Banneker to TJ, Aug. 19, 1791, in *PTJ;* Andrews, "Banneker's Revision," 230–32.

19. TJ to Benjamin Banneker, Aug. 30, 1791, in *PTJ;* TJ to Condorcet, Aug. 30, 1791, in *PTJ;* Phocion, *Gazette of the United States,* Oct. 17, 1796; TJ to Joel

Barlow, Oct. 8, 1809, in *PTJ*; Andrews, "Banneker's Revision," 234–35; Winthrop D. Jordan, *White over Black: American Attitudes toward the Negro, 1550–1812* (New York, 1977), 452–53; Richard Newman, "'Good Communications Corrects Bad Manners': The Banneker-Jefferson Dialogue and the Project of White Uplift," in John Craig Hammond and Matthew Mason, eds., *Contesting Slavery: The Politics of Bondage and Freedom in the New American Nation* (Charlottesville, Va., 2011), 71; Wilson Jeremiah Moses, *Thomas Jefferson: A Modern Prometheus* (New York, 2019), 251–52.

20. TJ, *Notes on the State of Virginia*, 227; TJ to John Adams, June 11, 1812, in *PTJ*; Sarah Rivett, *Unscripted America: Indigenous Languages and the Origins of a Literary Nation* (New York, 2017), 214, 223; Lee Eldridge Huddleston, *Origins of the American Indians: European Concepts, 1492–1729* (Austin, Tex., 1967), 34–36; Bernard W. Sheehan, *Seeds of Extinction: Jeffersonian Philanthropy and the American Indian* (Chapel Hill, N.C., 1973), 59–65; Shalom Goldman, *God's Sacred Tongue: Hebrew in the American Imagination* (Chapel Hill, N.C., 2004), 1–2; Eran Shalev, *American Zion: The Old Testament as a Political Text from the Revolution to the Civil War* (New Haven, Conn., 2013), 121–25.

21. James Madison to TJ, Sept. 21, 1788, in *PTJ*; TJ to James Madison, Jan. 12, 1789, in *PTJ*; TJ to Benjamin Smith Barton, Apr. 3, 1814, in *PTJ*; TJ to Peter Wilson, Jan. 20, 1816, in *PTJ*; Rivett, *Unscripted America*, 182–83, 209.

22. William Linn to TJ, Feb. 8, 1798, in *PTJ*; TJ to William Linn, Apr. 2, 1798, in *PTJ*; Rivett, *Unscripted America*, 235–37; Anthony F. C. Wallace, *Jefferson and the Indians: The Tragic Fate of the First Americans* (Cambridge, Mass., 1999), 322–23.

23. TJ to William Short, Jan. 3, 1793, in *PTJ*; Darren Staloff, *Hamilton, Adams, Jefferson: The Politics of Enlightenment and the American Founding* (New York, 2005), 308; Peter S. Onuf, *The Mind of Thomas Jefferson* (Charlottesville, Va., 2007), 57; Trees, "Apocalypse Now," 207–8.

24. TJ to James Madison, July 7, 1793, *Founders Online*; Jeremy D. Bailey, *Thomas Jefferson and Executive Power* (New York, 2007), 90–92.

25. TJ to James Madison, July 7, 1793, *Founders Online*; James Roger Sharp, *American Politics in the Early Republic: The New Nation in Crisis* (New Haven, Conn., 1993), 80–81.

26. "A Peep into the Antifederal Club," 1793, John Carter Brown Library, https://jcb.lunaimaging.com/luna/servlet/detail/JCBMAPS~2~2~656~100498:A-Peep-into-the-Antifederal-Club; Albrecht Koschnik, "The Democratic Societies of Philadelphia and the Limits of the American Public Sphere, circa 1793–1795," *William and Mary Quarterly*, 3rd ser., 58, no. 3

(July 2001): 620; Jason Frank, *Constituent Moments: Enacting the People in Postrevolutionary America* (Durham, N.C., 2010), 147–51; David Waldstreicher, *In the Midst of Perpetual Fetes: The Making of American Nationalism, 1776–1820* (Chapel Hill, N.C., 1997), 231–32.

27. TJ to James Madison, June 9, 1793, in *PTJ;* Andrew Burstein and Nancy Isenberg, *Madison and Jefferson* (New York, 2010), 265–66.

28. TJ to Angelica Schuyler Church, Nov. 27, 1793, in *PTJ;* TJ to John Taylor, Dec. 29, 1794, *Founders Online;* M. Andrew Holowchak, *Dutiful Correspondent: Philosophical Essays on Thomas Jefferson* (Lanham, Md., 2013), 88–89; Annette Gordon-Reed and Peter S. Onuf, *"Most Blessed of the Patriarchs": Thomas Jefferson and the Empire of the Imagination* (New York, 2016), 47–48.

29. John Adams to John Quincy Adams, Jan. 3, 1794, *Founders Online;* John Adams to Abigail Adams, Jan. 6, 1794, *Founders Online.*

7. *"The Little Spice of Ambition"*

1. Jack McLaughlin, *Jefferson and Monticello: The Biography of a Builder* (New York, 1988), 261, 287. On the second Monticello's originality and traditionalism, see Camille Wells, *Material Witnesses: Domestic Architecture and Plantation Landscapes in Early Virginia* (Charlottesville, Va., 2018), 167–73.

2. Daniel Trump to TJ, May 6, 1801, in James P. McClure and J. Jefferson Looney, eds., *The Papers of Thomas Jefferson,* digital ed. (Charlottesville, Va., 2008–21), hereafter cited as *PTJ;* Maria Cosway to TJ, Dec. 4, 1795, in *PTJ.*

3. Eric Proebsting, "Seasons of Change: Community Life and Landscape at the Foot of the Blue Ridge Mountains, 1740–1860," in Barbara J. Heath and Jack Gary, eds., *Jefferson's Poplar Forest: Unearthing a Virginia Plantation* (Gainesville, Fla., 2012), 55–56; Ronald L. Hatzenbuehler, *"I Tremble for My Country": Thomas Jefferson and the Virginia Gentry* (Gainesville, Fla., 2006), 22.

4. TJ to Jean Nicolas Démeunier, Apr. 29, 1795, in *PTJ;* TJ to Thomas Mann Randolph, Jan. 23, 1801, in *PTJ;* Lucia Stanton, *"Those Who Labor for My Happiness": Slavery at Thomas Jefferson's Monticello* (Charlottesville, Va., 2012), 9–11, 77–79; Annette Gordon-Reed, *The Hemingses of Monticello: An American Family* (New York, 2008), 509; Joseph J. Ellis, *American Sphinx: The Character of Thomas Jefferson* (New York, 1996), 167–68; John M. Murrin, "The Great Inversion, or Court versus Country," in J.G.A. Pocock, ed., *Three British Revolutions: 1641, 1688, 1776* (Princeton, N.J., 1980), 417–18.

5. TJ to Thomas Mann Randolph, Dec. 4, 1801, in *PTJ;* Stanton, *"Those Who Labor,"* 186; Gordon-Reed, *Hemingses,* 551.

6. TJ to James Madison, Dec. 28, 1794, in *PTJ;* Thomas P. Slaughter, *The Whiskey Rebellion: Frontier Epilogue to the American Revolution* (New York, 1986), 191; Andrew Burstein and Nancy Isenberg, *Madison and Jefferson* (New York, 2010), 289–92; Brian Steele, "Thomas Jefferson, Coercion, and the Limits of Harmonious Union," *Journal of Southern History* 74, no. 4 (Nov. 2008): 845, n.87.

7. TJ to James Madison, Sept. 21, 1795, in *PTJ;* Todd Estes, "Jefferson as Party Leader," in Francis D. Cogliano, ed., *A Companion to Thomas Jefferson* (Malden, Mass., 2011), 137–38; Francis D. Cogliano, *Emperor of Liberty: Thomas Jefferson's Foreign Policy* (New Haven, Conn., 2014), 118–24. "Damn John Jay" from Jonathan J. Den Hartog, *Patriotism and Piety: Federalist Politics and Religious Struggle in the New American Nation* (Charlottesville, Va., 2015), 36.

8. TJ to James Madison, Apr. 27, 1795, in *PTJ.*

9. TJ to William Cocke, Oct. 21, 1796, in *PTJ.*

10. "From a Correspondent in Connecticut," *Minerva,* Sept. 3, 1796; Robert M. S. McDonald, "Was There a Religious Revolution of 1800?" in James Horn, Jan Ellen Lewis, and Peter S. Onuf, eds., *The Revolution of 1800: Democracy, Race, and the New Republic* (Charlottesville, Va., 2002), 178; *Gazette of the United States,* Oct. 27, 1796; Burstein and Isenberg, *Madison and Jefferson,* 315–16.

11. *Gazette of the United States,* Oct. 27, 1796; TJ, *Notes on the State of Virginia,* in Merrill Peterson, ed., *Thomas Jefferson: Writings* (New York, 1984), 285; Thomas E. Buckley, S.J., "Placing Thomas Jefferson and Religion in Context, Then and Now," in John B. Boles and Randal L. Hall, eds., *Seeing Jefferson Anew, in His Time and Ours* (Charlottesville, Va., 2010), 142; "Documents relating to the 1796 Campaign for Electors in Virginia," in *PTJ;* Jon Meacham, *Thomas Jefferson: The Art of Power* (New York, 2012), 300; TJ to James Madison, Jan. 1, 1797, in *PTJ.*

12. TJ to Edward Rutledge, Dec. 27, 1796, in *PTJ.*

13. John Adams, Inaugural Address, 1797, *The Avalon Project,* https://avalon .law.yale.edu/18th_century/adams.asp.

14. TJ to Philip Mazzei, Apr. 24, 1796, in *PTJ;* Douglas L. Wilson, ed., *Jefferson's Literary Commonplace Book* (Princeton, N.J., 1989), 20; Carl J. Richard, *The Founders and the Bible* (Lanham, Md., 2016), 91–92.

15. Editorial note, "Jefferson's Letter to Philip Mazzei," in *PTJ;* G. S. Wilson, *Jefferson on Display: Attire, Etiquette, and the Art of Presentation* (Charlottesville, Va., 2018), 112–14.

16. Edwin Morris Betts, ed., *Thomas Jefferson's Farm Book* (Charlottesville, Va., 1987), 57; TJ, Memorandum Books, 1797, in *PTJ;* Gordon-Reed, *Hemingses,* 530; TJ to John Beckley, Apr. 16, 1798, in *PTJ.*

17. TJ, *Notes on the State of Virginia,* 270; William Short to TJ, Feb. 27, 1798, in *PTJ;* Gordon-Reed, *Hemingses,* 536–37; Christa Dierksheide, "'The Great Improvement and Civilization of That Race': Jefferson and the 'Amelioration' of Slavery, ca. 1770–1826," *Early American Studies* 6, no. 1 (Spring 2008): 165–70; Mary V. Thompson, *"The Only Unavoidable Subject of Regret": George Washington, Slavery, and the Enslaved Community at Mount Vernon* (Charlottesville, Va., 2019), 301–3.

18. William Short to TJ, Feb. 27, 1798, in *PTJ;* TJ to William Short, Apr. 13, 1800, in *PTJ;* Gordon-Reed, *Hemingses,* 538–39; Herbert E. Sloan, *Principle and Interest: Thomas Jefferson and the Problem of Debt* (New York, 1995), 220; Cara J. Rogers, "The French Experiment: Thomas Jefferson and William Short Debate Slavery, 1785–1826," *American Political Thought* 10 (Summer 2021): 328, 354–55.

19. TJ to John Wise, Feb. 12, 1798, in *PTJ;* TJ to James Monroe, Mar. 21, 1798, in *PTJ;* James Madison to TJ, Apr. 2, 1798, *Founders Online;* James Roger Sharp, *American Politics in the Early Republic: The New Nation in Crisis* (New Haven, Conn., 1993), 171–76; Ronald L. Hatzenbuehler, *"I Tremble for My Country": Thomas Jefferson and the Virginia Gentry* (Gainesville, Fla., 2006), 100–101; Terri Diane Halperin, *The Alien and Sedition Acts of 1798* (Baltimore, 2016), 49; Cogliano, *Emperor of Liberty,* 116–17.

20. TJ to James Madison, Apr. 26, 1798, in *PTJ;* TJ to James Madison, May 3, 1798, in *PTJ;* TJ, "Course of Reading for Joseph C. Cabell," [Sept. 1800], in *PTJ;* Brian Steele, *Thomas Jefferson and American Nationhood* (New York, 2012), 242, n.21; Jonathan I. Israel, *The Enlightenment That Failed: Ideas, Revolution, and Democratic Defeat, 1748–1830* (New York, 2019), 683; Larry E. Tise, *The American Counterrevolution: A Retreat from Liberty, 1783–1800* (Mechanicsburg, Pa., 1998), 255–57; Robert E. Schofield, *The Enlightened Joseph Priestley: A Study of His Life and Work from 1773 to 1804* (University Park, Pa., 2004), 376–77; Caroline Winterer, *American Enlightenments: Pursuing Happiness in the Age of Reason* (New Haven, Conn., 2016), 185–87.

21. "An Act in Addition to the Act, Entitled 'An Act for the Punishment of Certain Crimes against the United States,'" 1798, https://www.ourdocuments.gov/doc.php?flash=false&doc=16&page=transcript.

22. Annette Gordon-Reed, *Thomas Jefferson and Sally Hemings: An American Controversy* (Charlottesville, Va., 1998), 59–60; Geoffrey R. Stone, *Perilous*

Times: Free Speech in Wartime from the Sedition Act of 1798 to the War on Terrorism (New York, 2004), 61–62.

23. TJ to John Taylor, June 4, 1798, in *PTJ;* Wilson Jeremiah Moses, *Thomas Jefferson: A Modern Prometheus* (New York, 2019), 272. On the Wandering Jew, see, for example, Frank Felsenstein, *Anti-Semitic Stereotypes: A Paradigm of Otherness in English Popular Culture, 1660–1830* (Baltimore, 1999), 60–66.

24. TJ to John Taylor, June 4, 1798, in *PTJ;* Cogliano, *Emperor of Liberty,* 136–38; Jeffrey L. Pasley, *"The Tyranny of Printers": Newspaper Politics in the Early American Republic* (Charlottesville, Va., 2001), 100.

25. The literature on the Kentucky and Virginia Resolutions is extensive, and sometimes contradictory. See, for example, Adrienne Koch and Harry Ammon, "The Virginia and Kentucky Resolutions: An Episode in Jefferson's and Madison's Defense of Civil Liberties," *William and Mary Quarterly* 3d ser., vol. 5, no. 2 (Apr. 1948): 145–76; K. R. Constantine Gutzman, "The Virginia and Kentucky Resolutions Reconsidered: 'An Appeal to the Real Laws of Our Country,'" *Journal of Southern History* 66, no. 3 (Aug. 2000): 473–96; David N. Mayer, *The Constitutional Thought of Thomas Jefferson* (Charlottesville, Va., 1994), 199–208; Steele, *American Nationhood,* 240–65; Kevin R. C. Gutzman, *Thomas Jefferson, Revolutionary: A Radical's Struggle to Remake America* (New York, 2017), 48–54.

26. "Jefferson's Fair Copy," [before Oct. 4, 1798], and "Resolutions Adopted by the Kentucky General Assembly," Nov. 10, 1798, in *PTJ;* "Resolutions in General Assembly," Dec. 3, 1799, *The Avalon Project,* https://avalon.law .yale.edu/18th_century/kenres.asp; Merrill D. Peterson, *Thomas Jefferson and the New Nation* (New York, 1970), 613–14; Steele, *American Nationhood,* 251–52; Sharp, *American Politics,* 200; Darren Staloff, *Hamilton, Adams, Jefferson: The Politics of Enlightenment and the American Founding* (New York, 2005), 328–30; Gutzman, *Jefferson, Revolutionary,* 54.

27. TJ to Elbridge Gerry, Jan. 26, 1799, in *PTJ;* Maurizio Valsania, *The Limits of Optimism: Thomas Jefferson's Dualistic Enlightenment* (Charlottesville, Va., 2011), 34; Edward J. Larson, *A Magnificent Catastrophe: The Tumultuous Election of 1800, America's First Presidential Campaign* (New York, 2007), 154–58.

28. TJ, "Course of Reading for William G. Munford," [Dec. 5, 1798], in *PTJ;* Kevin J. Hayes, *The Road to Monticello: The Life and Mind of Thomas Jefferson* (New York, 2008), 442–43.

29. TJ to William G. Munford, Feb. 27, 1799, in *PTJ;* Hayes, *Road to Monticello,* 443.

30. TJ to William G. Munford, June 18, 1799, in *PTJ;* Hayes, *Road to Monticello,* 443–44; Colleen A. Sheehan, *James Madison and the Spirit of Republican Self-Government* (New York, 2009), 145; M. Andrew Holowchak, *Thomas Jefferson: Moralist* (Jefferson, N.C., 2017), 111–15; William Howard Adams, *The Paris Years of Thomas Jefferson* (New Haven, Conn., 1997), 7; David Williams, *Condorcet and Modernity* (New York, 2004), 23–24.

31. TJ to Walter Jones, Jan. 2, 1814, in *PTJ;* Tench Coxe to TJ, June 21, 1799, in *PTJ;* Burstein and Isenberg, *Madison and Jefferson,* 346–48; Thomas S. Kidd, *Patrick Henry: First among Patriots* (New York, 2011), Peter S. Onuf, *Jefferson and the Virginians: Democracy, Constitutions, and Empire* (Baton Rouge, La., 2018), 73–74.

32. TJ to Charles Clay, Oct. 14, 1799, in *PTJ.*

33. TJ to Joseph Priestley, Jan. 18, 1800, in *PTJ;* "PRIESTLEY," *Gazette of the United States,* Dec. 7, 1799: 3; Jenny Graham, "Joseph Priestley in America," in Isabel Rivers and David L. Wykes, eds., *Joseph Priestley: Scientist, Philosopher, and Theologian* (New York, 2008), 224–28; Jenny Graham, *Revolutionary in Exile: The Emigration of Joseph Priestley to America, 1794–1804* (Philadelphia, 1995), 139–44; Peter Manseau, *The Jefferson Bible: A Biography* (Princeton, N.J., 2020), 31–34. On Jesus as a "private person," see J. T. Rutt, ed., *The Theological and Miscellaneous Works of Joseph Priestley* (London, 1820), 17:426. On Priestley's Socinianism, see J. D. Bowers, *Joseph Priestley and English Unitarianism in America* (University Park, Pa., 2007), 1–2 and passim. Jefferson and Bishop James Madison also exchanged letters expressing admiration for Priestley and discussing the Federalists' charges about the Illuminati conspiracy. TJ to Bishop James Madison, Jan. 31, 1800, and Bishop James Madison to TJ, Feb. 11, 1800, in *PTJ.*

34. On Franklin, see Thomas S. Kidd, *Benjamin Franklin: The Religious Life of a Founding Father* (New Haven, Conn., 2017), especially 207–8.

35. Larson, *Magnificent Catastrophe,* 141–42; Pasley, *"The Tyranny of Printers,"* 200–201. In America's Historical Newspapers database, a search on Jefferson (as of Dec. 17, 2019) in 1796 returned 129 hits, and in 1800 returned 2,003 hits.

36. *Gazette of the United States,* Sept. 11, 1800.

37. William Linn, *Serious Considerations on the Election of a President* (New York, 1800), in Daniel L. Dreisbach and Mark David Hall, eds., *The Sacred Rights of Conscience* (Indianapolis, 2009), 482–86; Alexander Hamilton to John Jay, May 7, 1800, *Founders Online;* McDonald, "Religious Revolution," 182–83; Dickinson W. Adams, ed., *Jefferson's Extracts from the Gospels* (Princeton, N.J., 1983), 10–12; Larson, *Magnificent Catastrophe,* 165–77; Den Hartog,

Patriotism and Piety, 60–61. Many others have discussed religion and the 1800 election, including Frank Lambert, "'God—and a Religious President . . . [or] Jefferson and No God': Campaigning for a Voter-Imposed Religious Test in 1800," *Journal of Church and State* 39, no. 4 (1997): 769–89; and Charles F. O'Brien, "The Religious Issue in the Presidential Campaign of 1800," *Essex Institute Historical Collections* 107, no. 1 (1971): 82–93.

38. [DeWitt Clinton], *A Vindication of Thomas Jefferson* (New York, 1800), in Dreisbach and Hall, *Sacred Rights of Conscience*, 494, 498, 509; "For the *Newport Mercury*," *Newport Mercury*, Sept. 30, 1800.

39. TJ to Jeremiah Moore, Aug. 14, 1800, in *PTJ*; Larson, *Magnificent Catastrophe*, 176; Forrest McDonald, *The Presidency of Thomas Jefferson* (Lawrence, Kans., 1976), 17; Thomas S. Kidd, *God of Liberty: A Religious History of the American Revolution* (New York, 2010), 240–42; James S. Kabala, *Church-State Relations in the Early American Republic* (Brookfield, Vt., 2013), 58; E. G. Swem, "The Disqualification of Ministers in State Constitutions," *William and Mary College Quarterly Historical Magazine* 26, no. 2 (Oct. 1917): 74–76. On the Federalist revivalists, see Den Hartog, *Patriotism and Piety*, 60, 66.

40. William Arthur to TJ, Jan. 8, 1801, in *PTJ*; TJ to James Monroe, May 26, 1800, in *PTJ*; Larson, *Magnificent Catastrophe*, 173; Constance B. Schulz, "'Of Bigotry in Politics and Religion': Jefferson's Religion, the Federalist Press, and the Syllabus," *Virginia Magazine of History and Biography* 91, no. 1 (Jan. 1983): 74–75; Fred C. Luebke, "The Origins of Thomas Jefferson's Anti-Clericalism," *Church History* 32, no. 3 (Sept. 1963): 347.

41. TJ to Richard Rush, May 13, 1813, in *PTJ*; Benjamin Rush to TJ, Aug. 22, 1800, in *PTJ*; Mark A. Noll, *America's God: From Jonathan Edwards to Abraham Lincoln* (New York, 2002), 64–65.

42. TJ to Benjamin Rush, Sept. 23, 1800, in *PTJ*; Edwin S. Gaustad, *Sworn on the Altar of God: A Religious Biography of Thomas Jefferson* (Grand Rapids, Mich., 1996), 181–86; John A. Ragosta, "The Virginia Statute for Establishing Religious Freedom," in Cogliano, *Companion*, 76–77.

43. Sharp, *American Politics*, 233–47; Larson, *Magnificent Catastrophe*, 243–54.

44. *Commercial Advertiser*, Oct. 1, 1800; Douglas R. Egerton, *Gabriel's Rebellion: The Virginia Slave Conspiracies of 1800 and 1802* (Chapel Hill, N.C., 1993), 7–9, 37, 114; William G. Merkel, "To See Oneself as a Target of a Justified Revolution: Thomas Jefferson and Gabriel's Uprising," *American Nineteenth Century History* 4, no. 2 (Summer 2003): 12–13; William W. Freehling, *The Road to Disunion: Secessionists at Bay, 1776–1854* (New York, 1991), 147.

45. Alexander Hamilton to James A. Bayard, Jan. 16, 1801, and Alexander Hamilton to Oliver Wolcott, Jr., [Dec. 1800], *Founders Online;* Sharp, *American Politics,* 250–60; Joanne B. Freeman, "A Qualified Revolution: The Presidential Election of 1800," in Cogliano, *Companion,* 148.

46. TJ to Spencer Roane, Sept. 6, 1819, *Founders Online;* TJ to Joseph Priestley, Mar. 21, 1801, in *PTJ;* TJ to Elbridge Gerry, Mar. 29, 1801, in *PTJ;* Sharp, *American Politics,* 271–72; Freeman, "Qualified Revolution," 146; Bruce Ackerman, *The Failure of the Founding Fathers: Jefferson, Marshall, and the Rise of Presidential Democracy* (Cambridge, Mass., 2005), 77–92; Richard Samuelson, "Jefferson, Adams, and the American Future," *Claremont Review of Books* (Winter 2010–Spring 2011): 69.

8. *"Diamonds in a Dunghill"*

1. TJ, "Summary of Public Service," [after Sept. 2, 1800], in James P. McClure and J. Jefferson Looney, eds., *The Papers of Thomas Jefferson,* digital ed. (Charlottesville, Va., 2008–21), hereafter cited as *PTJ;* Douglas Anderson, "Jefferson and the Democratic Future," in Frank Shuffelton, ed., *The Cambridge Companion to Thomas Jefferson* (New York, 2009), 196; Brian Steele, "Jefferson's Legacy: The Nation as Interpretive Community," in Francis Cogliano, ed., *A Companion to Thomas Jefferson* (Malden, Mass., 2012), 526; J. Jefferson Looney, "'Merely Personal or Private, with Which We Have Nothing to Do': Thomas Jefferson's Autobiographical Writings," in Robert M. S. McDonald, ed., *Thomas Jefferson's Lives: Biographers and the Battle for History* (Charlottesville, Va., 2019), 25–26.

2. Roger Griswold to Fanny Griswold, Jan. 12, [1801], William Griswold Lane Memorial Collection, Yale University Library, Manuscripts and Archives, New Haven, Conn. Thanks to Sam Young and Will Tarnasky for obtaining a copy of this letter. Jon Meacham, *Thomas Jefferson: The Art of Power* (New York, 2012), 333; James H. Hutson, "Thomas Jefferson's Letter to the Danbury Baptists: A Controversy Rejoined," *William and Mary Quarterly* 3d ser., 56, no. 4 (Oct. 1999): 786–87.

3. TJ to the House of Representatives, Feb. 20, 1801, in *PTJ;* The New Jerusalem Church of Baltimore to TJ, Mar. 4, 1801, in *PTJ.* The "God rides on the whirlwind" quote was an allusion to a Joseph Addison poem, which John Page also referenced in his famous letter to Jefferson of July 20, 1776.

4. TJ, First Inaugural Address, Mar. 4, 1801, in *PTJ;* Amanda Porterfield, *Conceived in Doubt: Religion and Politics in the New American Nation*

(Chicago, 2012), 157; Peter S. Onuf, *Jefferson's Empire: The Language of American Nationhood* (Charlottesville, Va., 2000), 106–8; Jean M. Yarbrough, *American Virtues: Thomas Jefferson on the Character of a Free People* (Lawrence, Kans., 1998), 190.

5. TJ, First Inaugural Address.

6. TJ, First Inaugural Address; Johann N. Neem, "A Republican Reformation: Thomas Jefferson's Civil Religion and the Separation of Church and State," in Cogliano, *Companion*, 92–94; Garrett Ward Sheldon, *The Political Philosophy of Thomas Jefferson* (Baltimore, 1991), 108; Robert A. Ferguson, *The American Enlightenment, 1750–1820* (Cambridge, Mass., 1997), 79.

7. From George III, King of Great Britain, Sept. 16, 1803, note on Anthony Merry, in *PTJ;* Joyce Appleby, *Thomas Jefferson* (New York, 2003), 47–49.

8. "Keeps a better" and "Epicurean delicacy" quotes in Lucia Stanton, *"Those Who Labor for My Happiness": Slavery at Thomas Jefferson's Monticello* (Charlottesville, Va., 2012), 41–42, also 45; John Edward Semmes, *John H. B. Latrobe and His Times, 1803–1891* (Baltimore, 1917), 12–13; Adams, quoted in Jack McLaughlin, *Jefferson and Monticello: The Biography of a Builder* (New York, 1988), 233.

9. Annette Gordon-Reed, *The Hemingses of Monticello: An American Family* (New York, 2008), 562–63; Stanton, *"Those Who Labor,"* 42–45. Freeman was owned by Dr. William Baker of Maryland, who initially hired him out as a servant to Jefferson. Callie Hopkins, "Slavery, Freedom, and the Struggle to Keep a Family Together," White House Historical Association, Jan. 31, 2019, https://www.whitehousehistory.org/slavery-freedom-and-the-struggle-to-keep-a-family-together.

10. TJ, Memorandum Books, 1803, in *PTJ;* John Hailman, *Thomas Jefferson on Wine* (Jackson, Miss., 2006), 256, 266; Stanton, *"Those Who Labor,"* 45.

11. TJ, Memorandum Books, 1804, in *PTJ;* Hailman, *Jefferson on Wine*, 270–74.

12. Jon Meacham, *Thomas Jefferson: The Art of Power* (New York, 2012), 354; James B. Conroy, *Jefferson's White House: Monticello on the Potomac* (Lanham, Md., 2019), 61–62.

13. Francis D. Cogliano, *Emperor of Liberty: Thomas Jefferson's Foreign Policy* (New Haven, Conn., 2014), 50–51, 149.

14. TJ to Andrew Sterett, Dec. 1, 1801, in *PTJ;* Cogliano, *Emperor of Liberty*, 154–55; Ann Thomson, *Barbary and Enlightenment: European Attitudes towards the Maghreb in the 18th Century* (Leiden, The Netherlands, 1987), 14.

15. "Extracts from the Letter of a Midshipman," Nov. 22, 1803, *New York Commercial Advertiser*, May 17, 1804. This letter was published in a wide

range of American newspapers in 1804. See also Patrick D. Bowen, *A History of Conversion to Islam in the United States*, vol. 1: *White American Muslims Before 1975* (Leiden, The Netherlands, 2015), 31–34; Cogliano, *Emperor of Liberty*, 159–71.

16. TJ, First Annual Message to Congress, Dec. 8, 1801, in *PTJ;* Daniel L. Dreisbach, *Thomas Jefferson and the Wall of Separation between Church and State* (New York, 2003), 57–58.

17. Delaware Baptist Association to TJ, June 26, 1801, in *PTJ;* TJ to Delaware Baptist Association, July 2, 1801, *PTJ;* Carl J. Richard, *The Founders and the Bible* (Lanham, Md., 2016), 307.

18. John Witte, Jr., and Joel A. Nichols, *Religion and the American Constitutional Experiment*, 4th ed. (New York, 2016), 113–15.

19. Danbury Baptist Association to TJ, Oct. 7, 1801, in *PTJ.*

20. Archibald Stuart to TJ, June 4, 1801, in *PTJ;* "S" to TJ, Apr. 20, 1802, in *PTJ;* Benjamin Vaughan to TJ, Mar. 15, 1801, in *PTJ;* TJ to Levi Lincoln, Aug. 26, 1801, in *PTJ.*

21. TJ to Samuel Miller, Jan. 23, 1808, *Founders Online;* Dreisbach, *Wall of Separation*, 58–59.

22. TJ to Levi Lincoln, Jan. 1, 1802, in *PTJ;* Draft Reply to the Danbury Baptist Association, [on or before Dec. 31, 1801], in *PTJ;* Levi Lincoln to TJ, Jan. 1, 1802, in *PTJ;* Dreisbach, *Wall of Separation*, 38–46; James H. Hutson, "Thomas Jefferson's Letter to the Danbury Baptists: A Controversy Rejoined," *William and Mary Quarterly*, 3rd ser., 56, no. 4 (Oct. 1999): 783–84; Neem, "Republican Reformation," 91–92.

23. TJ to the Danbury Baptist Association, Jan. 1, 1802, in *PTJ.*

24. TJ to the Danbury Baptist Association, Jan. 1, 1802, in *PTJ;* Dreisbach, *Wall of Separation*, 48–49.

25. Dreisbach, *Wall of Separation*, 76–82. On earlier uses of "wall of separation" based upon Ephesians 2, see, for example, Samuel Willard, *A Compleat Body of Divinity* (Boston, 1726), 650.

26. Dreisbach, *Wall of Separation*, 95–99; Donald L. Drakeman, *Church, State, and Original Intent* (New York, 2010), 21–22, 41–42.

27. L. H. Butterfield, "Elder John Leland, Jeffersonian Itinerant," *Proceedings of the American Antiquarian Society* 62 (1952): 219–20.

28. Butterfield, "John Leland," 188–89.

29. TJ to Thomas Mann Randolph, Jan. 1, 1802, in *PTJ;* Committee of Cheshire, Massachusetts, to TJ, Dec. 31, 1801, in *PTJ;* TJ to Committee of Cheshire, Massachusetts, Jan. 1, 1802, in *PTJ;* Butterfield, "John Leland," 222–23;

Jeffrey L. Pasley, "The Cheese and the Words: Popular Political Culture and Participatory Democracy in the Early American Republic," in Jeffrey L. Pasley, Andrew W. Robertson, and David Waldstreicher, eds., *Beyond the Founders: New Approaches to the Political History of the Early American Republic* (Chapel Hill, N.C., 2004), 35.

30. Manasseh Cutler to Joseph Torrey, Jan. 4, 1802, in William Parker Cutler and Julia Perkins Cutler, eds., *Life, Journals and Correspondence of Rev. Manasseh Cutler* (Cincinnati, 1888), 2:66–67; TJ, Memorandum Books, Mar. 29, 1802; "plenty wines" quoted in Manasseh Cutler journal, in footnote to TJ to Nathan Read, Feb. 4, 1802, in *PTJ;* Pasley, "Cheese and the Words," 35–36, 42; Dreisbach, *Wall of Separation,* 22–23.

31. Merrill D. Peterson, *Thomas Jefferson and the New Nation* (New York, 1970), 692–99.

32. Alexander Hamilton to Rufus King, 1802, *Founders Online;* Meacham, *Art of Power,* 369; Gordon S. Wood, *Empire of Liberty: A History of the Early Republic, 1789–1815* (New York, 2009), 383–85.

33. Leonard W. Levy, *Jefferson & Civil Liberties: The Darker Side* (Chicago, 1989), 56–58.

34. Annette Gordon-Reed, *Thomas Jefferson and Sally Hemings: An American Controversy* (Charlottesville, Va., 1998), 61; Joshua D. Rothman, "James Callender and Social Knowledge of Interracial Sex in Antebellum Virginia," in Jan Ellen Lewis and Peter S. Onuf, eds., *Sally Hemings & Thomas Jefferson: History, Memory, and Civic Culture* (Charlottesville, Va., 1999), 88–89.

35. TJ to Thomas McKean, Feb. 19, 1803, in *PTJ;* Harold Milton Ellis, *Joseph Dennie and His Circle* (Austin, Tex., 1915), 181–84; Levy, *Jefferson & Civil Liberties,* 58–59; Wendell Bird, *Criminal Dissent: Prosecutions under the Alien and Sedition Acts of 1798* (Cambridge, Mass., 2020), 364.

36. TJ to George Rogers Clark, Dec. 25, 1780, in *PTJ;* "A Treaty between the United States of America and the Kaskaskia Tribe of Indians," Aug. 13, 1803, in Richard Peters, ed., *The Public Statutes at Large* (Boston, 1846), 7:78–79; "James Madison's Remarks on the Draft," [Oct. 1, 1803], in *PTJ;* Robert L. Cord, "Mr. Jefferson's 'Nonabsolute' Wall of Separation between Church and State," in Garrett Ward Sheldon and Daniel L. Dreisbach, eds., *Religion and Political Culture in Jefferson's Virginia* (Lanham, Md., 2000), 174–75; John Ragosta, *Religious Freedom: Jefferson's Legacy, America's Creed* (Charlottesville, Va., 2013), 202–3.

37. TJ to Robert R. Livingston, Apr. 18, 1802, in *PTJ;* Cogliano, *Emperor of Liberty,* 190.

38. Cogliano, *Emperor of Liberty*, 192–94.

39. *Gazette of the United States*, July 11, 1803, 2; Dwight, quoted in Cogliano, *Emperor of Liberty*, 195, also see Cogliano, *Emperor of Liberty*, 174.

40. TJ to Joseph Priestley, Apr. 9, 1803, in *PTJ*.

41. Eugene R. Sheridan, introduction to Dickinson W. Adams, ed., *Jefferson's Extracts from the Gospels* (Princeton, N.J., 1983), 21–22; Constance B. Schulz, "'Of Bigotry in Politics and Religion': Jefferson's Religion, the Federalist Press, and the Syllabus," *Virginia Magazine of History and Biography* 91, no. 1 (Jan. 1983): 87–90; Paul K. Conkin, "The Religious Pilgrimage of Thomas Jefferson," in Peter S. Onuf, ed., *Jeffersonian Legacies* (Charlottesville, Va., 1993), 36–37.

42. Joseph Priestley, *Jesus and Socrates Compared* (Philadelphia, 1803), 36, 38–39; Sheridan, introduction, 15–16; TJ to Nicolas Gouin Dufief, May 5, 1803, in *PTJ*.

43. TJ to Joseph Priestley, Apr. 9, 1803, in *PTJ*; TJ to Edward Dowse, Apr. 19, 1803, in *PTJ*. On Jesus and deism, see also TJ to John Adams, May 5, 1817, in *PTJ*; Richard Samuelson, "Jefferson and Religion: Private Belief, Public Policy," in Shuffelton, *Cambridge Companion*, 143.

44. TJ to Benjamin Rush, Apr. 21, 1803, in *PTJ*.

45. TJ to Benjamin Rush, Apr. 21, 1803, in *PTJ*.

46. TJ, "Syllabus of an Estimate of the Merit of the Doctrines of Jesus," in TJ to Benjamin Rush, Apr. 21, 1803, in *PTJ*; Henry Dearborn to TJ, May 4, 1803, in *PTJ*.

47. TJ, "Syllabus"; TJ to Joseph Priestley, Apr. 24, 1803, in *PTJ*; TJ to William Baldwin, Jan. 19, 1810, in *PTJ*; Samuelson, "Jefferson and Religion," 146.

48. TJ to Francis Adrian Van der Kemp, Apr. 25, 1816, in *PTJ*. Jefferson also used the diamonds and dunghills analogy repeatedly in letters to Adams: TJ to John Adams, Oct. 12, 1813, in *PTJ*; TJ to John Adams, Jan. 24, 1814, in *PTJ*.

49. TJ to John Adams, Oct. 12, 1813, in *PTJ*; Sheridan, introduction, 27–28; Conkin, "Religious Pilgrimage," 39; Susan Bryan, "Reauthorizing the Text: Jefferson's Scissor Edit of the Gospels," *Early American Literature* 22, no. 1 (Spring 1987): 19–20; Charles B. Sanford, *The Religious Life of Thomas Jefferson* (Charlottesville, Va., 1984), 103.

50. TJ to Charles Thomson, Jan. 9, 1816, in *PTJ*; Forrest Church, "The Gospel According to Thomas Jefferson," in *The Jefferson Bible: The Life and Morals of Jesus of Nazareth* (Boston, 1989), 17–18.

9. *"Strange Inconsistant Man"*

1. TJ to John Page, June 25, 1804, in James P. McClure and J. Jefferson Looney, eds., *The Papers of Thomas Jefferson,* digital ed. (Charlottesville, Va., 2008–21), hereafter cited as *PTJ.*

2. TJ to John Page, June 25, 1804, in *PTJ.* TJ to Nicolas Gouin Dufief, May 5, 1803, in *PTJ,* acknowledges receipt of Pascal's *Pensées.* Alan Hájek, "Pascal's Wager," in Edward N. Zalta, ed., *The Stanford Encyclopedia of Philosophy* (Summer 2018), https://plato.stanford.edu/archives/sum2018/entries /pascal-wager/.

3. "The President's Respect for Religion," *New-York Herald,* Oct. 17, 1804; "For the *Pittsfield Sun,*" *Pittsfield Sun,* Apr. 23, 1804; *Republican Spy,* Apr. 30, 1804.

4. Elise Virginia Lemire, *"Miscegenation": Making Race in America* (Philadelphia, 2002), 16; G. S. Wilson, *Jefferson on Display: Attire, Etiquette, and the Art of Persuasion* (Charlottesville, Va., 2018), 155–56; Annette Gordon-Reed, *Thomas Jefferson and Sally Hemings: An American Controversy* (Charlottesville, Va., 1998), 72–73; "The Following We Believe to Be the Pithy Points of the Publication in Question," *Columbian Centinel,* Jan. 26, 1805; Fawn M. Brodie, *Thomas Jefferson: An Intimate History* (New York, 2010), 374; Robert M. S. McDonald, *Confounding Father: Thomas Jefferson's Image in His Own Time* (Charlottesville, Va., 2016), 146–47, 163; TJ, Second Inaugural Address, Mar. 4, 1805, *Founders Online.*

5. TJ to William Heath, Dec. 13, 1804, *Founders Online;* Merrill D. Peterson, *Thomas Jefferson and the New Nation* (New York, 1970), 799–800.

6. TJ, Second Inaugural Address, Mar. 4, 1805; Johann N. Neem, "A Republican Reformation: Thomas Jefferson's Civil Religion and the Separation of Church and State," in Francis D. Cogliano, ed., *A Companion to Thomas Jefferson* (Malden, Mass., 2011), 94; Thomas E. Buckley, S.J., "The Political Theology of Thomas Jefferson," in Merrill D. Peterson and Robert C. Vaughan, eds., *The Virginia Statute for Religious Freedom: Its Evolution and Consequences in American History* (New York, 1988), 95–96; Thomas E. Buckley, S.J., "Placing Thomas Jefferson and Religion in Context, Then and Now," in John B. Boles and Randal L. Hall, eds., *Seeing Jefferson Anew: In His Time and Ours* (Charlottesville, Va., 2010), 136–37; Robert N. Bellah, "Civil Religion in America," *Daedalus* 117, no. 3 (Summer 1988; orig. pub. Winter 1967): 104.

7. TJ to the Marquis de Lafayette, Jan. 20, 1811, in *PTJ;* TJ to Peter Carr, Aug. 10, 1787, in *PTJ;* Joseph Priestley, *Letters to the Philosophers and Politicians of France* (Boston, 1793), 4; TJ to George Ticknor, Nov. 25, 1817, in *PTJ.*

8. TJ to Thomas Cooper, July 9, 1807, *Founders Online;* Richard E. Ellis, *The Jeffersonian Crisis: Courts and Politics in the Young Republic* (New York, 1971), 234; Harry Y. Gamble, *God on the Grounds: A History of Religion at Thomas Jefferson's University* (Charlottesville, Va., 2020), 21.

9. David Johnson, *John Randolph of Roanoke* (Baton Rouge, La., 2012), 1–3; Annette Gordon-Reed and Peter S. Onuf, *"Most Blessed of the Patriarchs": Thomas Jefferson and the Empire of the Imagination* (New York, 2016), 238.

10. John Randolph to Caesar A. Rodney, Feb. 12, 1806, Caesar A. Rodney Papers, Library of Congress, Washington, D.C., cited in Johnson, *John Randolph,* 98, and in Noble E. Cunningham, Jr., "Who Were the Quids?" *Mississippi Valley Historical Review* 50, no. 2 (Sept. 1963): 256. Historians have often referred to Randolph's faction as the Quids, too, but that term was used for a number of local alliances before Randolph's split from Jefferson. Cunningham, "Quids," 254.

11. TJ to William Duval, June 14, 1806, *Founders Online;* TJ to Charles Clay, Jan. 11, 1807, *Founders Online.*

12. TJ to Charles Clay, Jan. 11, 1807, *Founders Online;* TJ to John Wayles Eppes, May 24, 1806, *Founders Online;* Jack McLaughlin, *Jefferson and Monticello: The Biography of a Builder* (New York, 1988), 264; Norman K. Risjord, *Thomas Jefferson* (Lanham, Md., 1994), 130.

13. Anonymous to TJ, Aug. 18, 1807, *Founders Online;* Francis D. Cogliano, *Emperor of Liberty: Thomas Jefferson's Foreign Policy* (New Haven, Conn., 2014), 231–33.

14. Cogliano, *Emperor of Liberty,* 237–38.

15. William Penn to TJ, Feb. 24, 1809, *Founders Online;* Anonymous to TJ, Aug. 25, 1808, *Founders Online;* Cogliano, *Emperor of Liberty,* 238–39.

16. Anonymous to TJ, Apr. 5, 1808, *Founders Online;* TJ to Samuel Miller, Jan. 23, 1808, *Founders Online;* Samuel Miller, *The Life of Samuel Miller* (Philadelphia, 1869), 132.

17. TJ to James Madison, May 22, 1809, in *PTJ;* TJ, "To the Inhabitants of Albemarle County," Apr. 3, 1809, in *PTJ;* Ronald L. Hatzenbuehler, *"I Tremble for My Country": Thomas Jefferson and the Virginia Gentry* (Gainesville, Fla., 2006), 129–30.

18. "Messrs Editors," *Public Advertiser,* Aug. 17, 1809; "Federalist Dictionary" clipping image and discussion in McDonald, *Confounding Father,* 150–52.

19. Gordon-Reed, *Thomas Jefferson and Sally Hemings,* 196; Joshua D. Rothman, *Notorious in the Neighborhood: Sex and Families across the Color Line in Virginia, 1787–1861* (Chapel Hill, N.C., 2003), 19.

20. "Elijah Fletcher's Account of a Visit to Monticello," May 8, 1811, in *PTJ;* Catherine Kerrison, *Jefferson's Daughters: Three Sisters, White and Black, in a Young America* (New York, 2018), 253; Alan Taylor, *Thomas Jefferson's Education* (New York, 2019), 173–74; Annette Gordon-Reed, *The Hemingses of Monticello: An American Family* (New York, 2008), 616–17.

21. TJ to Charles Thomson, Dec. 25, 1808, *Founders Online;* Charles B. Sanford, *Thomas Jefferson and His Library* (Hamden, Conn., 1977), 128–29; Kevin J. Hayes, *The Road to Monticello: The Life and Mind of Thomas Jefferson* (New York, 2008), 503–4.

22. Thomas Leiper to TJ, Jan. 15, 1809, *Founders Online;* TJ to Thomas Leiper, Jan. 21, 1809, *Founders Online;* Joseph Towers, *Illustrations of Prophecy* (London, 1796), title page; Joseph Priestley to T. Lindsey, Jan. 13, 1797, in John Towill Rutt, ed., *Life and Correspondence of Joseph Priestley* (London, 1832): 2:370; John Adams to TJ, Feb. 10, 1812, in *PTJ;* Robert Rix, *William Blake and the Cultures of Radical Christianity* (Burlington, Vt., 2007), 147.

23. Thomas Leiper to TJ, Dec. 9, 1813, in *PTJ;* TJ to Thomas Leiper, Jan. 1, 1814, in *PTJ.*

24. Goodwill to TJ, June 20, 1809, in *PTJ;* Goodwill to TJ, Aug. 24, 1812, in *PTJ.*

25. TJ to James Fishback (draft), Sept. 1809, in *PTJ;* James Fishback, *A New and Candid Investigation of the Question, Is Revelation True?* (Lexington, Ky., 1809), iv; M. Andrew Holowchak, *Thomas Jefferson: Moralist* (Jefferson, N.C., 2017), 163; Edwin S. Gaustad, *Sworn on the Altar of God: A Religious Biography of Thomas Jefferson* (Grand Rapids, Mich., 1996), 135–36; Arthur Scherr, "Thomas Jefferson versus the Historians: Christianity, Atheistic Morality, and the Afterlife," *Church History* 83, no. 1 (Mar. 2014): 82–83.

26. TJ to the Citizens of Washington, D.C., Mar. 4, 1809, in *PTJ.*

27. TJ to Joel Barlow, Dec. 31, 1809, in *PTJ;* TJ to Benjamin Smith Barton, Sept. 21, 1809, in *PTJ;* Sarah Rivett, *Unscripted America: Indigenous Languages and the Origins of a Literary Nation* (New York, 2017), 209–11.

28. TJ to John Barnes, Aug. 3, 1809, in *PTJ;* George Jefferson to TJ, Sept. 1, 1809, in *PTJ;* James Sidbury, "Thomas Jefferson in Gabriel's Virginia," in James Horn, Jan Ellen Lewis, and Peter S. Onuf, eds., *The Revolution of 1800: Democracy, Race, and the New Republic* (Charlottesville, Va., 2002), 213–14; Philip J. Schwarz, *Slave Laws in Virginia* (Athens, Ga., 2010), 47–48.

29. TJ, Memorandum Books, Jan. 9, 23, Feb. 6, 1809, in *PTJ.*

30. TJ to Thomas Mann Randolph, Jan. 17, 1809, *Founders Online;* TJ to James Madison, Apr. 19, 1809, in *PTJ;* Deed of John Freeman's Indenture to James

Madison, Apr. 19, 1809, in *PTJ;* Alan Pell Crawford, *Twilight at Monticello: The Final Years of Thomas Jefferson* (New York, 2008), 59–60; Lucia Stanton, *"Those Who Labor for My Happiness": Slavery at Thomas Jefferson's Monticello* (Charlottesville, Va., 2012), 53.

31. TJ to George Jefferson, May 1, 1809, in *PTJ;* TJ, Memorandum Books, Feb. 5, 1810.

32. Martha Jefferson Randolph to TJ, Mar. 2, 1809, *Founders Online;* TJ to Jonathan Shoemaker, Feb. 6, 1810, in *PTJ;* TJ to Jonathan Shoemaker, Apr. 22, 1810, in *PTJ;* John Barnes to TJ, Dec. 9, 1812, in *PTJ;* Edwin Morris Betts, ed., *Thomas Jefferson's Farm Book* (Charlottesville, Va., 1987), 369–75; TJ, Memorandum Books, 1812, n.4; T. H. Breen, *Tobacco Culture: The Mentality of the Great Tidewater Planters on the Eve of Revolution,* new ed. (Princeton, N.J., 2001), 94–95, 127–29.

33. Stanton, *"Those Who Labor,"* 188; Susan R. Stein, *The Worlds of Thomas Jefferson at Monticello* (New York, 1993), 146.

34. TJ, "Catalogue of Paintings," in *Thomas Jefferson Encyclopedia,* Monticello. org, https://www.monticello.org/site/research-and-collections/catalogue -paintings; Stein, *Worlds of Thomas Jefferson,* 145.

35. TJ, "Catalogue of Paintings"; Stein, *Worlds of Thomas Jefferson,* 146; Jon Meacham, *Thomas Jefferson: The Art of Power* (New York, 2012), 447.

36. John Hemings signed his name "Hemmings," and Jefferson sometimes spelled it that way too. TJ to Ellen Randolph Coolidge, Nov. 14, 1825, *Founders Online;* TJ, "Will and Codicil," Mar. 16–17, 1826, *Founders Online;* Stein, *Worlds of Thomas Jefferson,* 277, 282–83, 290; Gordon-Reed, *Hemingses of Monticello,* 648–49, 657–58; Kerrison, *Jefferson's Daughters,* 244.

37. TJ to Benjamin Rush, Dec. 5, 1811, in *PTJ;* Gordon S. Wood, *Friends Divided: John Adams and Thomas Jefferson* (New York, 2017), 360–63.

10. *"Coup de Grace"*

1. John Adams to TJ, Feb. 10, 1812, in James P. McClure and J. Jefferson Looney, eds., *The Papers of Thomas Jefferson,* digital ed. (Charlottesville, Va., 2008–21), hereafter cited as *PTJ;* David Holland, *Sacred Borders: Continuing Revelation and Canonical Restraint in Early America* (New York, 2011), 91–92, 95; Susan Juster, *Doomsayers: Anglo-American Prophecy in the Age of Revolution* (Philadelphia, 2003), 200–201.

2. John Adams to TJ, Feb. 10, 1812, in *PTJ.*

3. John Adams to TJ, Feb. 10, 1812, in *PTJ*. On Tenskwatawa, see, among others, R. David Edmunds, *The Shawnee Prophet* (Lincoln, Neb., 1983); Gregory Evans Dowd, *A Spirited Resistance: The North American Indian Struggle for Unity, 1745–1815* (Baltimore, 1992), especially ch. 6; and Adam Jortner, *The Gods of Prophetstown: The Battle of Tippecanoe and the Holy War for the American Frontier* (New York, 2012).

4. TJ to John Adams, Apr. 20, 1812, in *PTJ*; TJ to Peter Carr, Apr. 4, 1800, in *PTJ*; TJ to James Madison, Apr. 4, 1800, in *PTJ*; John Adams to TJ, May 3, 1812, in *PTJ*; Alan Taylor, *Thomas Jefferson's Education* (New York, 2019), 156–58; Holland, *Sacred Borders*, 92–93. On McPherson, see also Edmund Berkeley, Jr., "Prophet without Honor: Christopher McPherson, Free Person of Color," *Virginia Magazine of History and Biography* 77, no. 2 (Apr. 1969): 180–90.

5. TJ to John Adams, Apr. 20, 1812, in *PTJ*; Anthony F. C. Wallace, "'The Obtaining Lands': Thomas Jefferson and Native Americans," in James P. Ronda, ed., *Thomas Jefferson and the Changing West: From Conquest to Conservation* (Albuquerque, N.M., 1997), 37.

6. TJ to Gideon Granger, Sept. 20, 1810, in *PTJ*; TJ to John Adams, June 27, 1813, in *PTJ*; Alan Pell Crawford, *Twilight at Monticello: The Final Years of Thomas Jefferson* (New York, 2008), 70–74; Travis C. McDonald, Jr., "Constructing Optimism: Thomas Jefferson's Poplar Forest," *Perspectives in Vernacular Architecture* 8 (2000): 178, 191; Jessica Bowes and Heather Trigg, "Social Dimensions of Eighteenth- and Nineteenth-Century Slaves' Uses of Plants at Poplar Forest," in Barbara J. Heath and Jack Gary, eds., *Jefferson's Poplar Forest: Unearthing a Virginia Plantation* (Gainesville, Fla., 2012), 156; Caroline Winterer, "Thomas Jefferson and the Ancient World," in Francis Cogliano, ed., *A Companion to Thomas Jefferson* (Malden, Mass., 2011), 386; Annette Gordon-Reed and Peter S. Onuf, *"Most Blessed of the Patriarchs": Thomas Jefferson and the Empire of the Imagination* (New York, 2016), 264, 269. "Masterpiece" is from Howard Burns, "Thomas Jefferson, The Making of an Architect," in Lloyd DeWitt and Corey Piper, eds., *Thomas Jefferson, Architect* (New Haven, Conn., 2019), 30. Coolidge quoted in Ronald L. Hatzenbuehler, *"I Tremble for My Country": Thomas Jefferson and the Virginia Gentry* (Gainesville, Fla., 2006), 141.

7. McDonald, "Constructing Optimism," 188–90; Crawford, *Twilight at Monticello*, 74.

8. TJ to Reuben Perry, Apr. 16, 1812, in *PTJ*.

9. TJ, Sixth Annual Message to Congress, Dec. 2, 1806, *The Avalon Project*, https://avalon.law.yale.edu/19th_century/jeffmes6.asp; John Chester Miller, *The Wolf by the Ears: Thomas Jefferson and Slavery* (New York, 1977), 145; Adam Rothman, *Slave Country: American Expansion and the Origins of the Deep South* (Cambridge, Mass., 2005), 30.

10. John Lynch to TJ, Dec. 25, 1810, in *PTJ;* Kevin R. C. Gutzman, *Thomas Jefferson, Revolutionary: A Radical's Struggle to Remake America* (New York, 2017), 163–64; Ari Helo, *Thomas Jefferson's Ethics and the Politics of Human Progress: The Morality of a Slaveholder* (New York, 2014), 41–42; Peter S. Onuf, *The Mind of Thomas Jefferson* (Charlottesville, Va., 2007), 213–15.

11. TJ to John Lynch, Jan. 21, 1811, in *PTJ;* Gutzman, *Jefferson, Revolutionary,* 164; Andrew Burstein, "Jefferson in Retirement," in Cogliano, *Companion,* 223.

12. Edward Coles to TJ, July 31, 1814, in *PTJ;* Kurt E. Leichtle and Bruce G. Carveth, *Crusade against Slavery: Edward Coles, Pioneer of Freedom* (Carbondale, Ill., 2011), 14–15, 44–49; Gary B. Nash and Graham Russell Gao Hodges, *Friends of Liberty: Thomas Jefferson, Tadeusz Kosciuszko, and Agrippa Hull* (New York, 2008), 185–90; Nicholas Guyatt, *Bind Us Apart: How Enlightened Americans Invented Racial Segregation* (New York, 2016), 1–3.

13. TJ to Edward Coles, Aug. 25, 1814, in *PTJ;* TJ to William Short, Jan. 18, 1826, *Founders Online;* Annette Gordon-Reed, *Thomas Jefferson and Sally Hemings: An American Controversy* (Charlottesville, Va., 1998), 109, 134; Winthrop D. Jordan, *White over Black: American Attitudes toward the Negro, 1550–1812* (New York, 1977), 546–47.

14. TJ to Edward Coles, Aug. 25, 1814, in *PTJ.* On Jefferson's prayers during retirement, see Annette Gordon-Reed and Peter S. Onuf, *"Most Blessed of the Patriarchs": Thomas Jefferson and the Empire of the Imagination* (New York, 2016), 281.

15. Edward Coles to TJ, Sept. 26, 1814, in *PTJ.*

16. "Energetic and forcible" in Anonymous to TJ, May 26, 1816, in *PTJ;* David Barrow to TJ, Mar. 20, 1815, in *PTJ;* John B. Boles, *Jefferson: Architect of American Liberty* (New York, 2017), 476–77.

17. TJ to David Barrow, May 1, 1815, in *PTJ;* Miller, *The Wolf by the Ears,* 43; Hannah Spahn, *Thomas Jefferson, Time, and History* (Charlottesville, Va., 2011), 217–18.

18. TJ to John Adams, Aug. 22, 1813, in *PTJ;* John Adams to TJ, Sept. 14, 1813, in *PTJ;* Allen Jayne, *Jefferson's Declaration of Independence: Origins,*

Philosophy, and Theology (Lexington, Ky., 1998), 165–67; Charles B. Sanford, *The Religious Life of Thomas Jefferson* (Charlottesville, Va., 1984), 100–101.

19. TJ to John Adams, Aug. 22, 1813, in *PTJ;* Crawford, *Twilight at Monticello,* 184–85; M. Andrew Holowchak, *Thomas Jefferson's Bible* (Boston, 2019), 19. Jefferson also cited the Reverend Conyers Middleton, English skeptical writer and author of *A Free Inquiry into the Miraculous Powers, Which Are Supposed to Have Subsisted in the Christian Church* (1749), as a key theological influence. Holowchak, *Jefferson's Bible,* 138.

20. TJ to William Canby, Sept. 18, 1813, in *PTJ;* Sanford, *Religious Life,* 158. On Canby, see also footnote to William Canby to TJ, May 27, 1802, in *PTJ.* Canby apologized to Jefferson for the letter's publication, suggesting that someone may have stolen the letter from him and had it published, William Canby to TJ, May 13, 1816, in *PTJ.* For "Sage of Monticello," see, for example, *New Bedford Mercury,* Nov. 19, 1819. That moniker for Jefferson had begun to appear in print at least by the 1800 election debates.

21. Julian P. Boyd, "Subversive of What?" *Bulletin of the American Association of University Professors* 34, no. 3 (Autumn 1948): 527–28; Helo, *Jefferson's Ethics,* 170–71.

22. TJ to Nicolas Dufief, Apr. 19, 1814, in *PTJ.*

23. TJ to Thomas Law, Apr. 23, 1811, in *PTJ.*

24. TJ to Thomas Law, June 13, 1814, in *PTJ;* Helo, *Jefferson's Ethics,* 72.

25. TJ to Thomas Law, June 13, 1814, in *PTJ;* Lee Quinby, "Thomas Jefferson: The Virtue of Aesthetics and the Aesthetics of Virtue," *American Historical Review* 87, no. 2 (Apr. 1982): 343; Helo, *Jefferson's Ethics,* 64–68; Catherine A. Brekus, *Sarah Osborn's World: The Rise of Evangelical Christianity in Early America* (New Haven, Conn., 2013), 226. At the end of the letter to Law, Jefferson commended Lord Kames's *Essays on the Principles of Morality and Natural Religion* as one of the "ablest advocates" of the moral sense, though he said it had been fifty years since he read Kames.

26. TJ to Paul Clay, [ca. July 12, 1817], in *PTJ;* TJ to Charles Clay, July 12, 1817, in *PTJ;* Jean M. Yarbrough, *American Virtues: Thomas Jefferson on the Character of a Free People* (Lawrence, Kans., 1998), 158–59.

27. TJ to Joseph Priestley, Apr. 9, 1803, in *PTJ;* Thomas S. Kidd, *Benjamin Franklin: The Religious Life of a Founding Father* (New Haven, Conn., 2017), 159–61; Helo, *Jefferson's Ethics,* 68.

28. TJ to Thomas Law, Apr. 23, 1811, in *PTJ;* Dumas Malone, *Jefferson and His Time: The Sage of Monticello* (Boston, 1981), 169–84.

29. TJ to Samuel H. Smith, Sept. 21, 1814 (II), in *PTJ.*

30. TJ to Peter H. Wendover (draft), Mar. 13, 1815, in *PTJ;* TJ to Benjamin Waterhouse, Oct. 13, 1815, in *PTJ;* Sam Haselby, *The Origins of American Religious Nationalism* (New York, 2015), 115–16; Jonathan J. Den Hartog, *Patriotism and Piety: Federalist Politics and Religious Struggle in the New American Nation* (Charlottesville, Va., 2015), 88–89.

31. "To Thomas Jefferson, Esq.," *Federal Republican,* Oct. 18, 1814; Malone, *Sage of Monticello,* 176–77; Herbert E. Sloan, *Principle and Interest: Thomas Jefferson and the Problem of Debt* (New York, 1995), 218; Peter Manseau, *The Jefferson Bible: A Biography* (Princeton, N.J., 2020), 40–42.

32. TJ to John Wayles Eppes, June 30, 1820, *Founders Online;* Crawford, *Twilight at Monticello,* 157–59; Gordon-Reed and Onuf, *"Most Blessed of the Patriarchs,"* 54–56; William Cohen, "Thomas Jefferson and the Problem of Slavery," *Journal of American History* 56, no. 3 (Dec. 1969): 518–19.

33. TJ to Thomas Appleton, Jan. 14, 1816, in *PTJ;* TJ to Mathew Carey, Sept. 1, 1816, in *PTJ.*

34. TJ to Giovanni Carmignani, July 18, 1816, in *PTJ;* Crawford, *Twilight at Monticello,* 92–93; Sloan, *Principle and Interest,* 220.

35. TJ to James Madison, Feb. 17, 1826, *Founders Online;* Wilson Cary Nicholas, "Enclosure: Commission Appointing Central College's Board of Visitors," Oct. 18, 1816, in *PTJ;* Sloan, *Principle and Interest,* 219–20.

36. Samuel Greenhow to TJ, Nov. 11, 1813, in *PTJ;* TJ to John Adams, Nov. 25, 1816, in *PTJ;* TJ to Samuel Greenhow, Jan. 31, 1814, in *PTJ;* Sheila R. Phipps, *Genteel Rebel: The Life of Mary Greenhow Lee* (Baton Rouge, La., 2004), 21; Daniel L. Dreisbach, *Reading the Bible with the Founding Fathers* (New York, 2017), 253, n.46.

37. TJ to John Adams, Nov. 25, 1816, in *PTJ;* TJ to Samuel Greenhow, Jan. 31, 1814, in *PTJ;* "Josephus B. Stuart's Account of a Visit to Monticello," Dec. 24, 1816, in *PTJ;* TJ to Alexander Smyth, Jan. 17, 1825, *Founders Online.*

38. Dickinson W. Adams, ed., *Jefferson's Extracts from the Gospels* (Princeton, N.J., 1983), 30; Harry R. Rubenstein and Barbara Clark Smith, "History of the Jefferson Bible," in *The Jefferson Bible* (Washington, D.C., 2011), 27–30.

39. Miles King to TJ, Aug. 20, 1814, in *PTJ.*

40. TJ to Miles King, Sept. 26, 1814, in *PTJ.*

41. Charles Clay to TJ, Dec. 20, 1814, in *PTJ;* Charles Clay to TJ, Feb. 8, 1815, in *PTJ.* On Clay, see William Meade, *Old Churches, Ministers and Families of Virginia* (Philadelphia, 1857), 2:48–50.

42. TJ to Charles Clay, Jan. 29, 1815, in *PTJ;* S. Allen Chambers, Jr., *Poplar Forest and Thomas Jefferson* (Little Compton, R.I., 1993), 58.

43. TJ to John Adams, July 5, 1814, in Lester J. Cappon, ed., *The Adams-Jefferson Letters* (Chapel Hill, N.C., 1959), 433; Robert Patterson to TJ, Nov. 24, 1815, in *PTJ;* TJ to Charles Thomson, Jan. 9, 1816, in *PTJ;* TJ to Francis Van der Kemp, July 30, 1816, in *PTJ;* J. Ramsey Michaels, "Charles Thomson and the First American New Testament," *Harvard Theological Review* 104, no. 3 (July 2011): 349; Adams, *Jefferson's Extracts,* 32–33; Karl Lehmann, *Thomas Jefferson: American Humanist* (Charlottesville, Va., 1985), 84–86.

44. Margaret Bayard Smith to TJ, July 21, 1816, in *PTJ.*

45. TJ to Margaret Bayard Smith, Aug. 6, 1816, in *PTJ;* TJ to Joseph Delaplaine, Dec. 25, 1816, in *PTJ.*

46. Charles Thomson to TJ, Jan. 7, 1817, in *PTJ;* TJ to Charles Thomson, Jan. 29, 1817, in *PTJ.*

47. Francis Adrian Van der Kemp to TJ, Mar. 24, 1816, in *PTJ;* TJ to Francis Adrian Van der Kemp, Apr. 25, 1816, in *PTJ.*

48. TJ to Francis Adrian Van der Kemp, Apr. 25, 1816, in *PTJ;* TJ to Francis Adrian Van der Kemp, Mar. 16, 1817, in *PTJ;* Thomas S. Kidd, *American Christians and Islam: Evangelical Culture and Muslims from the Colonial Period to the Age of Terrorism* (Princeton, N.J., 2009), 9; Adams, *Jefferson's Extracts,* 34–36; Harry F. Jackson, *Scholar in the Wilderness: Francis Adrian Van der Kemp* (Syracuse, N.Y., 1963), 246–52.

49. William Short to TJ, Oct. 21, 1819, *Founders Online;* TJ to William Short, Oct. 31, 1819, *Founders Online;* Adams, *Jefferson's Extracts,* 37.

11. *"Dreams of the Future"*

1. TJ to Mathew Carey, Nov. 11, 1816, in James P. McClure and J. Jefferson Looney, eds., *The Papers of Thomas Jefferson,* digital ed. (Charlottesville, Va., 2008–21), hereafter cited as *PTJ;* "Thomas Jefferson's Bible," Smithsonian National Museum of American History, https://americanhistory.si.edu /JeffersonBible/; *The Jefferson Bible* (Washington, D.C., 2011).

2. Eugene R. Sheridan, introduction to Dickinson W. Adams, ed., *Jefferson's Extracts from the Gospels* (Princeton, N.J., 1983), 37; Nathaniel P. Poor, *Catalogue: President Jefferson's Library* (Washington, D.C., 1829), 9–10; Lynn Zastoupil, "'Notorious and Convicted Mutilators': Rammohun Roy, Thomas Jefferson, and the Bible," *Journal of World History* 20, no. 3 (Sept. 2009): 410.

3. For examples of supernatural content, see *Jefferson Bible,* 19, 25, 31, 55, 59, 63 [Jefferson's handwritten page numbers]; Peter Manseau, *The Jefferson Bible: A Biography* (Princeton, N.J., 2020), 70–72.

4. *Jefferson Bible*, I, 25; M. Andrew Holowchak, *Thomas Jefferson's Bible* (Boston, 2019), 110–18.

5. Benjamin Waterhouse to TJ, Sept. 1, 1815, in *PTJ;* TJ to Salma Hale, July 26, 1818, in *PTJ;* TJ to Thomas B. Parker, May 15, 1819, in *PTJ;* TJ to Ezra Stiles Ely, June 25, 1819, in *PTJ;* TJ to John Adams, Apr. 11, 1823, *Founders Online.*

6. TJ to William Short, Apr. 13, 1820, *Founders Online;* TJ to John Adams, Aug. 15, 1820, in Lester J. Cappon, ed., *The Adams-Jefferson Letters* (Chapel Hill, N.C., 1959), 568; TJ to George Logan, Nov. 12, 1816, in *PTJ;* Richard Samuelson, "Jefferson and Religion: Private Belief, Public Policy," in Frank Shuffelton, ed., *The Cambridge Companion to Thomas Jefferson* (New York, 2009), 147.

7. TJ to William Short, Aug. 4, 1820, *Founders Online;* Ari Helo, *Thomas Jefferson's Ethics and the Politics of Human Progress: The Morality of a Slaveholder* (New York, 2014), 82; Jean M. Yarbrough, *American Virtues: Thomas Jefferson on the Character of a Free People* (Lawrence, Kans., 1998), 184–85.

8. Helo, *Jefferson's Ethics,* 165.

9. TJ to John Tyler, May 26, 1810, in *PTJ;* Garrett Ward Sheldon, "Liberalism, Classicism, and Christianity in Jefferson's Political Thought," in Garrett Ward Sheldon and Daniel L. Dreisbach, eds., *Religion and Political Culture in Jefferson's Virginia* (Lanham, Md., 2000), 96; Richard K. Matthews, *The Radical Politics of Thomas Jefferson: A Revisionist View* (Lawrence, Kans., 1984), 81–88; Jennings L. Wagoner, Jr., *Jefferson and Education* (Charlottesville, Va., 2004), 37, 72.

10. TJ to Joseph C. Cabell, Feb. 2, 1816, in *PTJ;* Carl Edward Skeen, *1816: America Rising* (Lexington, Ky., 2003), 166–67; Maurizio Valsania, "Beyond Particularism: Thomas Jefferson's Republican Community," in Peter Nicolaisen and Hannah Spahn, eds., *Cosmopolitanism and Nationhood in the Age of Jefferson* (Heidelberg, Germany, 2013), 95–96; Kevin R. C. Gutzman, *Thomas Jefferson, Revolutionary: A Radical's Struggle to Remake America* (New York, 2017), 64–65; Matthew Crow, *Thomas Jefferson, Legal History, and the Art of Recollection* (New York, 2017), 235–37.

11. Thomas Jefferson to "Henry Tompkinson" (Samuel Kercheval), July 12, 1816, in *PTJ.*

12. TJ to Anne Willing Bingham, May 11, 1788, in *PTJ;* Brian Steele, *Thomas Jefferson and American Nationhood* (New York, 2012), 66–70; Jan Lewis, "'The Blessings of Domestic Society': Thomas Jefferson's Family and the Transformation of American Politics," in Peter S. Onuf, ed., *Jeffersonian Legacies* (Charlottesville, Va., 1993), 136–38.

13. TJ to John Adams, Aug. 1, 1816, in Cappon, *Adams-Jefferson Letters,* 485; TJ to Joseph Priestley, Jan. 18, 1800, in *PTJ;* TJ to Joseph Cabell, June 27, 1810, in *PTJ.*

14. TJ, Draft Bill to Create Central College and Amend the 1796 Public Schools Act [ca. Nov. 18, 1814], in *PTJ;* Thomas E. Buckley, *Establishing Religious Freedom: Jefferson's Statute in Virginia* (Charlottesville, Va., 2013), 99.

15. TJ to Alexander Garrett and Valentine W. Southall, Sept. 23, 1817, in *PTJ;* Alan Taylor, *Thomas Jefferson's Education* (New York, 2019), 195; Garry Wills, *Mr. Jefferson's University* (Washington, D.C., 2002), 21–22; Thomas S. Kidd, *Benjamin Franklin: The Religious Life of a Founding Father* (New Haven, Conn., 2017), 76–78; J. Jefferson Looney, "From Academy to College to University: The Prehistory of the University of Virginia," in John A. Ragosta, Peter S. Onuf, and Andrew J. O'Shaughnessy, eds., *The Founding of Thomas Jefferson's University* (Charlottesville, Va., 2019), 15–16. Jefferson has frequently been identified as a Freemason, but there is no definitive evidence to suggest that he was one. "Fraternal Organizations," in *Thomas Jefferson Encyclopedia,* Monticello.org, https://www.monticello.org/site/research-and-collections/fraternal-organizations.

16. Daniel Walker Howe, "Religion and Education in the Young Republic," in Wilfred M. McClay, ed., *Figures in the Carpet: Finding the Human Person in the American Past* (Grand Rapids, Mich., 2007), 404.

17. TJ, "To the Trustees of the Lottery for East Tennessee College," May 6, 1810, in *PTJ;* TJ to Nathaniel Bowditch, Oct. 26, 1818, in *PTJ;* M. Andrew Holowchak, *Thomas Jefferson's Philosophy of Education: A Utopian Dream* (New York, 2014), 69; Julie A. Reuben, "The Changing Contours of Moral Education in American Colleges and Universities," in Elizabeth Kiss and J. Peter Euben, eds., *Debating Moral Education: Rethinking the Role of the Modern University* (Durham, N.C., 2010), 30.

18. "Jefferson's Draft of the Rockfish Gap Report of the University of Virginia Commissioners," [ca. June 28, 1818], in *PTJ;* Lucia Stanton, *"Those Who Labor for My Happiness": Slavery at Thomas Jefferson's Monticello* (Charlottesville, Va., 2012), 140; Louis P. Nelson, "The Architecture of Democracy in a Landscape of Slavery: Design and Construction at Jefferson's University," in Lloyd DeWitt and Corey Piper, eds., *Thomas Jefferson, Architect* (New Haven, Conn., 2019), 110.

19. "Jefferson's Draft of the Rockfish Gap Report"; University of Virginia, *Alumni Bulletin* 10, nos. 4–5 (Aug.–Oct. 1917): 339; Harry Y. Gamble, *God on*

the Grounds: A History of Religion at Thomas Jefferson's University (Charlottesville, Va., 2020), 89–90.

20. "Jefferson's Draft of the Rockfish Gap Report"; Matthew Crow, *Thomas Jefferson, Legal History, and the Art of Recollection* (New York, 2017), 268; Paul H. Mattingly, *American Academic Cultures: A History of Higher Education* (Chicago, 2017), 47; Adams, *Jefferson's Extracts,* 28.

21. "Jefferson's Draft of the Rockfish Gap Report"; Wilson Jeremiah Moses, *Thomas Jefferson: A Modern Prometheus* (New York, 2019), 326.

22. "Jefferson's Draft of the Rockfish Gap Report"; *Catalogue of the Officers and Students of the University of Virginia, Session of 1832–1833* (Charlottesville, Va., 1833); "Jefferson's University . . . The Early Life," University of Virginia Library, http://juel.iath.virginia.edu/resources#_ftn6; Endrina Tay, "Forming the Body of a Library Based on the 'Illimitable Freedom of the Human Mind,'" in Ragosta, Onuf, and O'Shaughnessy, *Jefferson's University,* 212–13; Wagoner, *Jefferson and Education,* 140. On Dartmouth, see Dartmouth College, *Catalogue* (Boston, 1824), 16–18. Thanks to Benjamin Leavitt for this reference and information on Dartmouth's curriculum.

23. TJ to Thomas Cooper, Jan. 16, 1814, in *PTJ;* Gilmer, quoted in Taylor, *Jefferson's Education,* 196; Tay, "Body of a Library," 209–10, 219, n.16.

24. TJ to James Madison, Aug. 8, 1824, in *Papers of James Madison,* digital ed., ed. J.C.A. Stagg (Charlottesville, Va., 2010–21); James Madison to TJ, Sept. 10, 1824, in *Papers of James Madison;* TJ, Catalog of Books for the University of Virginia Library [manuscript], June 3, 1825, Special Collections Library, University of Virginia, https://search.lib.virginia.edu/catalog/u2741760#?c=0&m=0&s=0&cv=51&xywh=-172%2C1860%2C2453%2C3030; TJ to Francis Adrian Van der Kemp, Feb. 9, 1818, in *PTJ;* Tay, "Body of a Library," 215, 217.

25. John Holt Rice to Archibald Alexander, Sept. 3, 1818, in William Maxwell, *A Memoir of the Rev. John H. Rice, D.D.* (Philadelphia, 1835), 150; Cameron Addis, "The Jefferson Gospel: A Religious Education of Peace, Reason, and Morality," in Robert M. S. McDonald, ed., *Light and Liberty: Thomas Jefferson and the Power of Knowledge* (Charlottesville, Va., 2012), 111–12; Taylor, *Jefferson's Education,* 224.

26. Conrad Speece, "On the University of Virginia," *Mountaineer,* May 30, 1816, 189–91; Taylor, *Jefferson's Education,* 225.

27. Cameron Addis, "Jefferson and Education," in Francis D. Cogliano, ed., *A Companion to Thomas Jefferson* (Malden, Mass., 2011), 465–66; Wagoner, *Jefferson and Education,* 126.

28. John Holt Rice, "Review," *Virginia Evangelical and Literary Magazine* 3 (Feb. 1820): 74; Taylor, *Jefferson's Education*, 226.

29. TJ to Thomas Cooper, Mar. 13, 1820, *Founders Online*.

30. TJ to Thomas Cooper, Apr. 8, 1820, *Founders Online;* Robert P. Forbes, "Slavery and the Evangelical Enlightenment," in John R. McKivigan and Mitchell Snay, eds., *Religion and the Antebellum Debate over Slavery* (Athens, Ga., 1998), 87–93.

31. Minutes of the Board of Visitors of the University of Virginia, Oct. 7, 1822, *Founders Online;* Sheldon, "Jefferson's Political Thought," 100. Harry Gamble suggests that the denominational schools were not Jefferson's idea and that he only grudgingly accepted the proposal. Gamble, *God on the Grounds,* 42.

32. TJ to Thomas Cooper, Mar. 9, 1822, *Founders Online;* Taylor, *Jefferson's Education*, 258–59.

33. TJ to Thomas Cooper, Mar. 9, 1822, *Founders Online;* TJ to James Breckenridge, Feb. 15, 1821, *Founders Online;* Edward B. Rugemer, *Slave Law and the Politics of Resistance in the Early Atlantic World* (Cambridge, Mass., 2018), 254; Addis, "Jefferson and Education," 466–67; Darren Staloff, "The Politics of Pedagogy: Thomas Jefferson and the Education of a Democratic Citizenry," in Frank Shuffelton, ed., *The Cambridge Companion to Thomas Jefferson* (New York, 2009), 137. Stuart Leiberger has argued that some of Jefferson's more shrill comments about Missouri and the possibility of disunion were penned for specific political reasons, including funding for the University of Virginia, and did not necessarily reflect sustained conviction. Leiberger, "Thomas Jefferson and the Missouri Crisis: An Alternative Interpretation," *Journal of the Early Republic* 17, no. 1 (Spring 1997): 124, 127–28.

34. Taylor, *Jefferson's Education*, 262–64; Lorri Glover, *Southern Sons: Becoming Men in the New Nation* (Baltimore, 2007), 63, 73.

35. Taylor, *Jefferson's Education*, 270; Maurie D. McInnis, "Violence," in Maurie D. McInnis and Louis P. Nelson, eds., *Educated in Tyranny: Slavery at Thomas Jefferson's University* (Charlottesville, Va., 2019), 109–10.

36. Henry Tutweiler, *Early Years of the University of Virginia* (Charlottesville, Va., 1882), 11; TJ to William Branch Giles, Dec. 26, 1825, *Founders Online;* Taylor, *Jefferson's Education*, 272, "school of infidelity" quoted at 274; Rex Bowman and Carlos Santos, *Rot, Riot, and Rebellion: Mr. Jefferson's Struggle to Save the University That Changed America* (Charlottesville, Va., 2013), 33–43.

Conclusion: *"All That Has Passed"*

1. Abigail Adams to TJ, Dec. 15, 1816, in James P. McClure and J. Jefferson Looney, eds., *The Papers of Thomas Jefferson*, digital ed. (Charlottesville, Va., 2008–21), hereafter cited as *PTJ*.

2. TJ to Abigail Adams, Jan. 11, 1817, in *PTJ;* TJ to John Adams, May 17, 1818, in *PTJ*.

3. TJ to John Adams, Nov. 13, 1818, in *PTJ;* Annette Gordon-Reed and Peter S. Onuf, *"Most Blessed of the Patriarchs": Thomas Jefferson and the Empire of the Imagination* (New York, 2016), 310.

4. TJ to John Holmes, Apr. 22, 1820, *Founders Online;* TJ to Marquis de Lafayette, Dec. 26, 1820, *Founders Online;* Lafayette to TJ, July 1, 1821, quoted in Nicholas Guyatt, *Bind Us Apart: How Enlightened Americans Invented Racial Segregation* (New York, 2016), 165; Andrew Burstein, "Jefferson in Retirement," in Francis D. Cogliano, ed., *A Companion to Thomas Jefferson* (Malden, Mass., 2011), 228–29; Francis D. Cogliano, *Thomas Jefferson: Reputation and Legacy* (Charlottesville, Va., 2006), 204; Kevin R. C. Gutzman, "Thomas Jefferson's Virginian Revolution," in Joanne B. Freeman and Johann N. Neem, eds., *Jeffersonians in Power: The Rhetoric of Opposition Meets the Realities of Governing* (Charlottesville, Va., 2019), 122.

5. TJ to John Holmes, Apr. 22, 1820, *Founders Online*.

6. TJ, *Autobiography,* in Merrill D. Peterson, ed., *Thomas Jefferson: Writings* (New York, 1984), 44; TJ to John Adams, Jan. 22, 1821, *Founders Online;* Robert E. Shalhope, "Thomas Jefferson's Republicanism and Antebellum Southern Thought," *Journal of Southern History* 42, no. 4 (Nov. 1976): 552.

7. John Adams to TJ, Feb. 3, 1821, *Founders Online;* Peter S. Onuf, "Founding Friendship: John Adams, Thomas Jefferson, and the American Experiment in Republican Government, 1812–1826," in Celeste-Marie Bernier, Judie Newman, and Matthew Pethers, eds., *The Edinburgh Companion to Nineteenth-Century American Letters and Letter-Writing* (Edinburgh, Scotland, 2016), 306; Gordon S. Wood, *Friends Divided: John Adams and Thomas Jefferson* (New York, 2017), 418.

8. Hannah to TJ, Nov. 15, 1818, in *PTJ;* Jack McLaughlin, *Jefferson and Monticello: The Biography of a Builder* (New York, 1988), 120–21; Alan Taylor, *Thomas Jefferson's Education* (New York, 2019), 156.

9. Lucia Stanton, *"Those Who Labor For My Happiness": Slavery at Thomas Jefferson's Monticello* (Charlottesville, Va., 2012), 182; Alan Pell Crawford, *Twilight at Monticello: The Final Years of Thomas Jefferson* (New York, 2008), 164–67.

10. TJ to Wilson Cary Nicholas, Aug. 11, 1819, *Founders Online;* Crawford, *Twilight at Monticello,* 178–79, 198–99.

11. TJ to Timothy Pickering, Feb. 27, 1821, *Founders Online;* TJ to Benjamin Waterhouse, June 26, 1822, *Founders Online;* TJ to Benjamin Waterhouse, July 19, 1822, *Founders Online;* TJ to Benjamin Waterhouse, Jan. 8, 1825, *Founders Online;* Shalhope, "Jefferson's Republicanism," 540–41.

12. Merrill D. Peterson, *Thomas Jefferson and the New Nation* (New York, 1970), 1002–3; John Lauritz Larson, *Internal Improvement: National Public Works and the Promise of Popular Government in the Early United States* (Chapel Hill, N.C., 2001), 161.

13. TJ, *Declaration and Protest of the Commonwealth of Virginia* (1825), *Founders Online;* Kevin R. C. Gutzman, "Thomas Jefferson's Virginian Revolution," in Freeman and Neem, *Jeffersonians in Power,* 122–23.

14. TJ to James Madison, Jan. 2, 1826, *Founders Online;* "Debate in the Senate," *Niles' Weekly Register,* Feb. 27, 1830, 24; Brian Steele, *Thomas Jefferson and American Nationhood* (New York, 2012), 262; Crawford, *Twilight at Monticello,* 216–20.

15. Martha Jefferson Randolph to Ellen W. Randolph Coolidge, Apr. 5, 1826, in "Jefferson Quotes and Family Letters," Monticello.org, http://tjrs.monticello.org/letter/1035; TJ to the Trustees of the Lottery for East Tennessee College, May 6, 1810, in *PTJ;* TJ, "Thoughts on Lotteries," ca. Jan. 20, 1826, *Founders Online;* John Hartwell Cocke to Joseph C. Cabell, Feb. 15, 1826, quoted in Taylor, *Jefferson's Education,* 278.

16. TJ to Jeff Randolph, Feb. 8, 1826, *Founders Online;* TJ to George Stevenson, June 26, 1826, *Founders Online;* Taylor, *Jefferson's Education,* 278–80; Crawford, *Twilight at Monticello,* 233; John Hailman, *Thomas Jefferson on Wine* (Jackson, Miss., 2006), 370.

17. TJ, "Will and Codicil," Mar. 16–17, 1826, *Founders Online;* Crawford, *Twilight at Monticello,* 234–35.

18. TJ, "Will and Codicil"; Annette Gordon-Reed, *The Hemingses of Monticello: An American Family* (New York, 2008), 648.

19. Gordon-Reed, *Hemingses of Monticello,* 657–59.

20. Gordon-Reed, *Hemingses of Monticello,* 659–66.

21. TJ to Roger Chew Weightman, June 24, 1826, *Founders Online;* Michael P. Zuckert, *Natural Rights and the New Republicanism* (Princeton, N.J., 1998), 30.

22. TJ to James Madison, Feb. 17, 1826, *Founders Online;* Andrew Burstein, *Letters from the Head and Heart: Writings of Thomas Jefferson* (Charlottesville,

Va., 2002), 87; Cynthia A. Kierner, *Martha Jefferson Randolph, Daughter of Monticello: Her Life and Times* (Chapel Hill, N.C., 2012), 203.

23. *A Selection of Eulogies Pronounced in the Several States in Honor of Those Illustrious Patriots and Statesmen, John Adams and Thomas Jefferson* (Hartford, Conn., 1826), 424–25; Edward Everett, *An Address Delivered at Charlestown* (Boston, 1826), 34; Samuel X. Radbill, ed., "The Autobiographical Ana of Robley Dunglison, M.D.," *Transactions of the American Philosophical Society* 53, no. 8 (1963): 32–33; TJ to Thomas Jefferson Grotjan, Jan. 10, 1824, *Founders Online.*

24. Wirt, in *Selection of Eulogies,* 425; Andrew Burstein, *Jefferson's Secrets: Death and Desire at Monticello* (New York, 2005), 277–78.

25. TJ to Frederick Hatch, Dec. 8, 1821, *Founders Online;* TJ, Memorandum Books, 1824, *Founders Online;* Cogliano, *Reputation and Legacy,* 137–38.

26. "Executor's Sale," *Central Gazette* (Charlottesville), Jan. 13, 1827, reproduced in Lucia Stanton, *Free Some Day: The African-American Families of Monticello* (Charlottesville, Va., 2000), 141; Crawford, *Twilight at Monticello,* 249.

27. James W. C. Pennington, *The Fugitive Blacksmith* (London, 1819), iv; Stanton, *Free Some Day,* 142–43; Walter Johnson, *Soul by Soul: Life inside the Antebellum Slave Market* (Cambridge, Mass., 1999), 19; "Peter Fossett," in *Thomas Jefferson Encyclopedia,* Monticello.org, https://www.monticello.org/site/research-and-collections/peter-fossett.

28. Margaret Bayard Smith, *The First Forty Years of Washington Society,* ed. Gaillard Hunt (New York, 1906), 230–31; Crawford, *Twilight at Monticello,* 252.

29. David F. Ericson, *The Debate over Slavery: Antislavery and Proslavery Liberalism in Antebellum America* (New York, 2000), 18.

30. "South Carolina in Reply to Virginia," *Richmond Enquirer,* Aug. 14, 1832; Shalhope, "Jefferson's Republicanism," 555–56; Jeff Broadwater, *James Madison: A Son of Virginia and a Founder of the Nation* (Chapel Hill, N.C., 2012), 204.

Acknowledgments

Of the making of books about Jefferson there is no end, and I trust that the scholarly community of Jeffersonians will forgive this intrusion. Like all works on Jefferson, my book is profoundly indebted to *The Papers of Thomas Jefferson* project, the digitization of which has made it possible to locate previously obscure references in his vast body of writings and correspondence. I am also grateful to Founders Online, which has provided transcriptions of documents not yet included in *The Papers of Jefferson* project.

I am also thankful for the monumental work of past and present Jefferson scholars. I try to give adequate credit to that deep heritage of Jefferson scholarship in the endnotes. These scholars' books and articles have taught me much about Jefferson, race, the Hemings family, Monticello, and the world of Revolutionary and early national Virginia. I doubt that these historians would agree with everything I say here, but I hope they will not doubt that I am building on their foundation.

I am grateful to Baylor Ph.D. students Paul Gutacker, Matt Millsap, and Sam Young for their research assistance on this book, and especially to my doctoral student Kristina Benham for compiling and annotating numerous references for me in Jefferson's vast body of writings. As always, I appreciate the unfailing support of Barry Hankins, Byron Johnson, and many other friends and colleagues at Baylor. Thanks to my friend and Baylor colleague Ronald Johnson for reading and commenting on the manuscript, and to the anonymous readers for Yale University Press. I am also grateful for friends and colleagues at Midwestern Baptist Theological Seminary, where I serve as a distinguished visiting professor of church history. Thanks to my friend and literary agent Giles Anderson, and to the wonderful team at Yale University Press, including my editor Jennifer Banks.

As always, I am most grateful for Ruby, Jonathan, and Josh.

Index